ॐ The Rhythm of Eternity ॐ

# MAKING SENSE OF HISTORY
*Studies in Historical Cultures*
General Editor: Stefan Berger
Founding Editor: Jörn Rüsen

Bridging the gap between historical theory and the study of historical memory, this series crosses the boundaries between both academic disciplines and cultural, social, political and historical contexts. In an age of rapid globalization, which tends to manifest itself on an economic and political level, locating the cultural practices involved in generating its underlying historical sense is an increasingly urgent task.

Volume 1
*Western Historical Thinking: An Intercultural Debate*
    Edited by Jörn Rüsen

Volume 2
*Identities: Time, Difference, and Boundaries*
    Edited by Heidrun Friese

Volume 3
*Narration, Identity, and Historical Consciousness*
    Edited by Jürgen Straub

Volume 4
*Thinking Utopia: Steps into Other Worlds*
    Edited by Jörn Rüsen, Michael Fehr, and Thomas W. Rieger

Volume 5
*History: Narration, Interpretation, Orientation*
    Jörn Rüsen

Volume 6
*The Dynamics of German Industry: Germany's Path toward the New Economy and the American Challenge*
    Werner Abelshauser

Volume 7
*Meaning and Representation in History*
    Edited by Jörn Rüsen

Volume 8
*Remapping Knowledge: Intercultural Studies for a Global Age*
    Mihai Spariosu

Volume 9
*Cultures of Technology and the Quest for Innovation*
    Edited by Helga Nowotny

Volume 10
*Time and History: The Variety of Cultures*
    Edited by Jörn Rüsen

Volume 11
*Narrating the Nation: Representations in History, Media and the Arts*
    Edited by Stefan Berger, Linas Eriksonas, and Andrew Mycock

Volume 12
*Historical Memory in Africa: Dealing with the Past, Reaching for the Future in an Intercultural Context*
    Edited by Mamadou Diawara, Bernard Lategan, and Jörn Rüsen

Volume 13
*New Dangerous Liaisons: Discourses on Europe and Love in the Twentieth Century*
    Edited by Luisa Passerini, Lilianna Ellena, and Alexander C.T. Geppert

Volume 14
*Dark Traces of the Past: Psychoanalysis and Historical Thinking*
    Edited by Jürgen Straub and Jörn Rüsen

Volume 15
*A Lover's Quarrel with the Past: Romance, Representation, Reading*
    Ranjan Ghosh

Volume 16
*The Holocaust and Historical Methodology*
    Edited by Dan Stone

Volume 17
*What is History For? Johann Gustav Droysen and the Functions of Historiography*
    Arthur Alfaix Assis

Volume 18
*Vanished History: The Holocaust in Czech and Slovak Historical Culture*
    Tomas Sniegon

Volume 19
*Jewish Histories of the Holocaust: New Transnational Approaches*
    Edited by Norman J.W. Goda

Volume 20
*Helmut Kohl's Quest for Normality: His Representation of the German Nation and Himself*
    Christian Wicke

Volume 21
*Marking Evil: Holocaust Memory in the Global Age*
    Edited by Amos Goldberg and Haim Hazan

Volume 22
*The Rhythm of Eternity: The German Youth Movement and the Experience of the Past, 1900–1933*
    Robbert-Jan Adriaansen

# THE RHYTHM OF ETERNITY

## The German Youth Movement and the Experience of the Past, 1900–1933

Robbert-Jan Adriaansen

berghahn
NEW YORK · OXFORD
www.berghahnbooks.com

First published in 2015 by
Berghahn Books
www.berghahnbooks.com

©2015, 2020 Robbert-Jan Adriaansen
First paperback edition published in 2020

All rights reserved. Except for the quotation of short passages for the purposes of criticism and review, no part of this book may be reproduced in any form or by any means, electronic or mechanical, including photocopying, recording, or any information storage and retrieval system now known or to be invented, without written permission of the publisher.

**Library of Congress Cataloging-in-Publication Data**
Adriaansen, Robert-Jan.
 The rhythm of eternity: the German youth movement and the experience of the past, 1900-1933 / Robbert-Jan Adriaansen.
   pages cm. --  (Making sense of history; volume 22)
 Includes index.
 ISBN 978-1-78238-768-8 (hardback: alk. paper) -- ISBN 978-1-78238-769-5 (ebook)
 1. Youth movements--Germany--History--20th century. 2. Youth--Germany--History--20th century. 3. Germany--Civilization--20th century. I. Title.
 HQ799.G3A37 2015
 305.235094309'04--dc23

2015002047

**British Library Cataloguing in Publication Data**
A catalogue record for this book is available from the British Library

ISBN: 978-1-78238-768-8 (hardback)
ISBN: 978-1-78920-850-4 (paperback)
ISBN: 978-1-78238-769-5 (ebook)

# Contents

List of Illustrations — vi

Preface — vii

**Introduction:** The German Youth Movement and the Problem of History — 1

**Chapter 1:** Wandervogel, Freideutsche Jugend and the Spirit of 1813 — 27

**Chapter 2:** The Experience of the Past — 56

**Chapter 3:** The Postwar Crisis of Experience and the Religious Turn — 89

**Chapter 4:** Immanent Eschatology and Medieval Forms — 119

**Chapter 5:** In Search of the Spiritual Motherland — 158

Conclusion — 187

Sources and Literature — 197

Index — 213

# Illustrations

**Figures**

**Figure 1.1**  The Monument to the Battle of the Nations in Leipzig. Postcard, around 1913.   29

**Figure 2.1**  *Gemeinschaft*. Photo by Julius Groß, Archiv der deutschen Jugendbewegung, around 1922.   62

**Figure 3.1**  Ferdinand Hodler, *Der Auszug deutscher Studenten in den Freiheitskrieg von 1813*, 1908–09. Wikimedia Commons.   107

**Figure 4.1**  The Neue Schar in Eisenach. Photo by Julius Groß, Archiv der deutschen Jugendbewegung, 1920.   124

**Tables**

**Table 5.1**  Summer hikes to the border regions and abroad by groups of the Deutsche Freischar.   166

# Preface

In 2008, when I started my research, I was a total stranger to the history of the German youth movement. At least I did know that there had been (and still is) a youth movement in Germany, that it had significant cultural influence and that it left behind a great variety of primary sources. When an earlier topic for my research proved to be untenable due to a lack of sources, the youth movement came to me as – one might say – destiny. A first visit to Ludwigstein Castle in Hesse, where the youth movement's archives are housed, provided an immediate introduction to youth movement culture as I sat beside the campfire singing German folk songs with youth movement 'seniors'. The experience was heartwarming and alienating at the same time, as I felt welcomed as a foreign guest, but also felt like an intruder, impeding the rites and customs of old friends reuniting. After explaining the next day to Jürgen Reulecke what my intended research would focus on, he started elaborating on his own childhood experiences in the youth movement, concluding that I should not forget 'experience' (*Erlebnis*). Puzzled if he meant his own childhood experiences or my experiences that weekend, I only realized later that it must have been experience per se. Experience would become a key concept in my analysis, and had I not been grasped by my own experience of hospitality and intrusion I would possibly have missed the importance of pre-rational experience and its consequences for historical thought.

Yet, the completion of this study is not only the result of experience. It is the result of tiresome labour, of reading and re-reading sources and literature, of mastering the meaning of the specific idiom of a foreign youth culture, of tracing unavailable books and articles, of writing and re-writing notes and chapters, and of very few moments of enlightenment. As solitary as the work of a historian may seem, he cannot do without a supportive environment. Therefore, I would like to thank my wife Maaike, my family and friends. A few good laughs with them kept me living in the present.

My venture was financed by the Erasmus School of History, Culture and Communication, and supported intellectually by my colleagues at the Center for Historical Culture at Erasmus University Rotterdam. Our research group meetings have stimulated the reflection on my work – not only because they provided a critical dissection of the first drafts of some of my chapters, but also because papers of colleagues engaged in other fields of study showed me what historiography could and should be like. I would also like to thank the research group on the philosophy of history at Radboud University in Nijmegen for the opportunity to present a draft paper on my thesis in the informal setting of one of their meetings. I am grateful to Rüdiger Ahrens and Malte Lorenzen for bringing together young academics from various disciplines who study various aspects of the German youth movement. Exchanging ideas with this group at Ludwigstein Castle affirmed my experience of hospitality, and certainly diminished the feeling of intrusion. I would like to thank Stefan Berger and Adam Capitanio for their patience and support when finalizing the manuscript, and the anonymous reviewers for their constructive criticism. I would especially like to thank Thomas Kohut, who twice read the manuscript and provided me with numerous useful suggestions for improvement.

Foremost, I am grateful for the support of the director of the Center for Historical Culture, Maria Grever. Her enthusiasm, as well as her inspiration and encouragement in our discussions, have been indispensable for the completion of this project.

INTRODUCTION

# The German Youth Movement and the Problem of History

> Instead of the old myths of death and resurrection, of victory and twilight of the gods, which the Enlightenment removed from people's consciousness, the nineteenth century has justified the barren idea that life moves like some sort of transportation on a straight road, and that one can increase speed or change direction. However, life never advances one-dimensionally, neither forwards nor backwards; neither upwards nor downwards – it rather breathes in space.
>
> – Georg Götsch, 'Die Jugendbewegung als Volksgewissen'[1]

Georg Götsch, quoted above, was one of the most prominent leaders of the German youth movement in the 1920s. According to him, in the course of three decades the youth movement had developed a collective mentality that was broader than that of children revolting against the demands of the parental generation. The children indeed refused to follow the road signs on the street of life. But rather than plotting their own route, they rejected the entire concept of life as a one-dimensional path forward, as well as the idea that the individual has the full autonomy and capability to choose his own route.

Modern ideas of the autonomy of the subject and the unilinearity of time, as symbolized in the image of the one-dimensional road, were fundamental premises for the modern conception of history. This conception saw history as the domain of the conscious and progressive self-realization of mankind – a conception that Götsch attributed to the nineteenth century, to positivism and to the parental generation. The youth movement's alternative was a 'vital conception of history', which spurred an engagement with 'spiritual ancestors' who are still 'immediately alive'.² Using vitalist language to explain this understanding of history, Götsch resorted to the metaphor of the heart. Implying that the rejection of tradition in the modern, progressive worldview would in the end result in the death of a nation, the youth movement tried to clean the 'old blood vessels' to the 'heart of the nationhood'.³ Götsch warned that this operation of 'revitalizing' the nation by tapping the vital source of tradition should not be done away with as mere 'Romanticism'. In his view this conception of history was not a 'reaction', and nor did it refer to forward or backward orientations: 'It does not matter that something is happening, but that it is done in conjunction with the eternal law. This is the meaning of history'.⁴

On a phenomenological level, 'summer and winter' and 'past and future' are not values to which man relates himself, but eternal rhythms that revolve around him, and present themselves as destiny. The magic of the youth movement was that it enabled youth to concretely experience such rhythms in their main activities in an age which longed for a new metaphysics. In hiking through the pastures of the German countryside, in singing folk songs around a comforting old fireplace, in the bonds of comradeship forged on a journey through the Bohemian Forest, or in the spell of an old mystery play, traces of the eternal were spurred.

Götsch's ideas on history may appear rather opaque today – if not incomprehensible. His vitalist vocabulary and focus on mythical time make it all too easy to cast judgment on these ideas or to interpret them as escapist attempts to 'flee' into a mythical past in reaction to whatever identity problems the 'reality' of post-Versailles Germany caused. Such objections are as easy a score today as they were in 1928. Götsch however knew that he was operating on the brink of two worldviews and two different conceptions of history, and went to great lengths to convince his readers. The youth movement attested to a different 'reality' than the 'materialized' world, he argued. Besides materialism the movement also rejected idealism to the extent that both 'no longer have a connection to the dormant reality of the centre of the world – a centre which does not revolve, so that everything can revolve around it'.⁵ These young wanderers focused on 'form' rather than on ideas, on images rather than concepts; body and spirit were not posed in an oppositional scheme.

Today, it is common scholarly knowledge that in modernity, individuals, social entities and also social movements like the youth movement use historical memory and historical consciousness to provide themselves with a sense of identity by temporally distinguishing or associating themselves with what came before, and by projecting an expectation of coming achievements into the future.⁶ This procedure is explained clearly by Jörn Rüsen when he states that 'identity is located at the threshold between origin and future, a passage that cannot be left alone to the natural chain of events but has to be intellectually comprehended and achieved'.⁷ Identity has to be actively constructed by recalling past events, through which individuals or collectives can 'fixate' themselves in time by emphasizing historical continuities or discontinuities. Götsch's 'vital conception of history' is difficult to explain in reference to contemporary theories of memory and historical consciousness. It was an engagement with tradition, but did not refer to linear time. Rather than – like Rüsen – situating the 'origin' in the historical past, Götsch understood it in spatial terms as a 'centre' or 'heart'. The German youth movement did not just remember differently but expressed views and ideas based on a specific conception of history that cannot be equated with what we usually call 'modern historical consciousness' – which, in the words of Hans-Georg Gadamer, means the 'full awareness of the historicity of everything present' and the temporal structure of tradition, constituted by a process that is articulated in developmental and evolutionary terms.[8]

Why would the interwar German youth movement go beyond defining its own identity – or the generational identity of its members – in relation to the past, and challenge the predominant mode of historical thought itself? And what can identity be based upon when one rejects history as its main source? In order to answer these questions, I will explore the conceptions of history and time in the German youth movement between the moment the 'free' German youth movement – the umbrella term for those youth associations that were led and organized by youth itself with as little adult interference as possible – was established around 1900, and the rise of Nazism, after which the 'free' youth movement was soon dissolved. Hence, I limit my study to the Wilhelmine era (1871–1918) and the Weimar period (1918–1933) of German history. Examining what was left of the youth movement in Nazi Germany would also require an in-depth analysis of the specific historical culture of Nazi Germany, which is far beyond the scope of this study, because the ideological historical culture of Nazi Germany strove towards a discontinuation with earlier Wilhelmine and Weimarian historical cultures on almost all fronts.[9]

In this chapter I will present the guiding question of my research. Three theoretical notions will provide an interpretive framework in order to explain the significance of my question: experience, representation and presence. After presenting my research question, I will discuss two important historiographical debates to contextualize my research, namely the German youth movement and the historiographical discussion on the 'Conservative Revolution'. I will end the chapter with an explanation about sources and methods, and give the outline of the study.

## Aims and Research Question

This study focuses on the development of various conceptions of history in the German youth movement in the first decades of the twentieth century. The youth movement was an educative environment in which young people grew up together, shared the same 'space of experience', and phrased ideas on past, present and future on the basis of these shared experiences.[10] My aim, however, is not just to write a history of the youth movement's historical development. The case of the youth movement opens up the larger philosophical question on the possibilities and impossibilities of thinking 'beyond' modernity by revising the premises of modern historical thought. Is this 'beyond' necessarily a future beyond – something to be achieved through human action over the course of time – or can it be thought of as something that already was, and ever will be? These are not just abstract philosophical questions, but problems rooted and expressed in culture. Studying the *practical* ways in which the youth movement attempted to overcome a modern, 'historical' worldview next to its *ideas* about it can shine light on the possibilities and impossibilities of trying to surpass the epistemic boundaries of one's culture.

In order to achieve these aims, this study will answer the following research question: *Which dominant conceptions of history and time circulated in the German youth movement between 1900 and 1933, and how did these relate to historical representations and historical experience?*

This question requires elaboration on two points: we first need to know what history meant in modernity in order to be able to understand which notion of history the youth movement challenged. To understand the various arguments put forward against the modern conception of history we will also have to establish a basic understanding of the central function of reason and language in this notion of history. But as today's theory of history is still very much indebted to the presumptions of modern historical consciousness, we secondly need to establish a theoretical and methodological framework that does not treat both positions as incommensurable.

First, the term 'conception of history' does not refer to the past as such, but to ideas on what history is and how past, present and future relate to each other. This requires a meta-perspective on the idea of history. Thus, the question is not whether one looks at history from the perspective of a social historian, a political policymaker or a traumatized war victim, but what the premises are of a specific conception of history. Reinhart Koselleck's well-known thesis on the rise of modern historical consciousness tells us that between approximately 1750 and 1850 a radical change took place in the Western conception of history. He bases his thesis on a semantic study of the concept of 'history' which reveals that, in this period in the German-speaking countries, 'history' (*Geschichte*) started to be used as a collective singular. Instead of referring to a multiplicity of narratives, the term 'history' was increasingly used to denote one historical process of which all different narratives were a part. Besides now referring to unilinear development, the function of history changed due to a second development: the term 'history' (*Geschichte*) also became synonymous with what was previously known in

German as *Historie* – the 'study' of man's deeds. Because in modern German (like in English) history came to mean both the course of events and the conscious apprehension of these events, the concept could be interpreted as a Kantian transcendental category; so history that depended on human action and human consciousness no longer required God or nature as its source.[11] Koselleck calls this the 'makeability of history' – the idea that history no longer simply took place with and through man, but was at the disposal of man to be forged.[12] Whereas the multiple histories of previous times functioned as templates of practical knowledge on human or state affairs, the unilinear conception of history developed in modernity granted no such possibilities, because history now referred to a process of development. The idea that man is subdued to cosmic cycles and repetitive patterns, made way for the idea that man could determine his own fate and that it was even man's moral goal to overcome his natural impulses in a rational and progressive self-manifestation. History now reflected the process of this development. It was this modern conception of history that the youth movement reacted against. The meta-historical question therefore is: on which premises did they try to overcome modern historical consciousness?

Second, because the youth movement's critique of the modern idea of history also contained a critique on the primacy of reason, a mere analysis of the intellectual history of the youth movement will not suffice. I will counter the intellectual development of the critique of historical thought in the youth movement with an analysis of the practical ways in which they alternatively apprehended the past. Most notably, their apprehension of the past included a turn away from cognition towards *Erlebnis* (lived or direct experience). In the general sense we will see that direct experience refers to the experience of *Gemeinschaft* (community), and more concretely to what the German historian Hermann Mau once defined rather opaquely as 'the direct experience of the revitalization of all relations of life through finding back the archetypical forms of human association'.[13]

Through lived experience, the youth movement tried to tap into the pre-rational sources and primal origins of life (a quest that August Wiedmann defines as 'the tendency to penetrate to the presumed primal layers of existence'), be it primal social relations in community, or relations to nature, history, life or the cosmos.[14] Experience was defined as something non-rational, something that eludes cognitive comprehension and is as such intuitively given to those who are receptive to it. Therefore, exactly lived experience could point into a direction beyond what is rationally comprehensible. Modern rationalism, after all, has been regarded as a central cause of the loss of authentic being ever since the eighteenth century. Analysing a movement that defied rationalism and emphasized the value of lived experience poses a problem of understanding: one can look at the preconditions and effects of experience, one can rethink experience, but one can neither relive an experience nor rationally analyse the contents of experience without turning it into an 'object' of cognition.[15] How then, are we to write a history of such intangibilities?

The common escape out of this aporia is to historicize the discourse of the youth movement. Dietmar Schenk, for example, argued that although the group-bound *Erlebnis* of the youth movement was intangible, the *discourse* in which the youth movement articulated their experience was far from isolated. Therefore, not experience itself 'but the discourse of "*Erlebnis*" as an expression of a particular timely consciousness' should be subject of historical analysis.[16] Today, this approach is the rule rather than the exception. In the humanities the theory that reality is a discursive construction is broadly accepted, as is the idea that to analyse 'reality' we have to dissect the way meaning is constructed.[17] This applies to history and memory as well. Hayden White cast the definite blow to 'naive' historical realism by arguing in *Metahistory* that the historical text does not entail a referential to a historical 'reality', but is historically constructivist in the sense that it constitutes meaning only in the *mise en scène* of the historian.[18] Rather than speaking of describing or interpreting the past, speaking of the historian representing the past eludes the realist assumption that the past itself has meaning, for representation points at the narrative activity of the historian as being constitutive for all historical meaning.[19] In a similar way, memory studies state that remembering – both individually and collectively – is a narrative praxis, aimed at the establishment of a sense of identity by narratively bridging the 'gap' between present and past, and establishing a sense of historical meaning and continuity.[20]

The gains of representationalism – the idea that in absence, the past can be permeated only through signs, the most prominent of which is descriptive language – notwithstanding, recent literature has increasingly emphasized the flaws and shortcomings of this approach. Frank Ankersmit – once a prime contributor to the discourse on historical representation – notes that representationalism has consistently forgotten the author who writes the historical text. Although the historical narrative is no mimetic reduction of a past reality, this does not imply that the author cannot be enthused, or even enthralled, by a pre-reflexive experience of the past.[21] Yet, Ankersmit's theory of historical experience keeps revolving around the idea that the past is something absent and at distance. According to Ankersmit, (sublime) historical experience is an alternative and more immediate mode of permeating an absent past, as in the moment of experience the boundaries of subject and object fade away and the past is suddenly present. Yet, the sublimity of such a moment is dictated by the experience that once the magic disappears, one is left with a trauma – the trauma that the past has gone and will never return. Ankersmit's philosophy of historical experience thus presumes that in modernity, historical distance is a natural state of affairs, and that the presence of the past can be established momentarily, but cannot be overcome.

More fundamental insights in the limits of historical thought, which take the problems of modern metaphysics into account, can be derived from Hans-Ulrich Gumbrecht's theory of presence. For Gumbrecht, both representation and memory fall under the heading of 'meaning culture', which denotes the specific modern mode of making sense of the world through meaning. Gumbrecht analyses the prime emphasis on meaning and interpretation as an effect of modern Western metaphysics, which – since Descartes – rests on the dichotomy between subject and object. In this dichotomy, practically everything – even the body – can be objectified and discerned from the observer. Next to 'meaning cultures', Gumbrecht situates 'presence cultures', which – such as classical Aristotelian philosophy and medieval Scholasticism – do not discern between subject and object, are not based on a progressive conception of time, and emphasize spatiality over temporality. It is important to emphasize that the distinction between 'presence' and 'meaning' cultures is ideal typical in the Weberian sense, as Gumbrecht consistently emphasizes that all cultures and cultural expressions are based on a specific configuration of both meaning and presence effects. It is, however, the self-descriptions of cultures that tend to opt for one or the other.

Gumbrecht exemplifies his distinction by adding a number of other distinctions to it. For meaning cultures the mind or consciousness is the locus of self-reference, while in presence cultures the body – not Foucault's objectified 'Body', but the existential body – has this function. Meaning cultures route man's relation to the world through subjectivity, while presence cultures see the body as embedded in a cosmology. In meaning cultures, the material signifier has a purely spiritual meaning, while in presence cultures substance and form take hold in the sign. In meaning cultures, man's vocation is the transformation of the world, while in presence cultures man aims to inscribe oneself into cosmological rhythms. And – besides a number of other distinctions – meaning cultures have time as their primordial dimension and associate consciousness with time, while presence cultures emphasize the spatial dimension in which humans relate to the things of the world.

The great value of the distinction between meaning culture and presence culture is that it can help us to clarify the extent to which and the ways in which the youth movement tried to alter modern, progressive thought. Although Gumbrecht acknowledges that this distinction only makes sense when used in a meaning culture – of which contemporary scholarly thought is still part – it is sophisticated enough not to take all presuppositions of meaning culture as the normative basis of proper thought. This study will benefit from these insights in three ways.

A first advantage is that meaning and presence cultures are not found to be mutually exclusive: '*all* cultures and cultural objects', Gumbrecht states, 'can be analysed as configurations of both meaning effects and presence effects, although their different semantics of self-description often accentuate exclusively one or the other side'.[22] There is therefore no need to adapt an entirely new vocabulary to denote what could not be grasped in modern concepts – as for example Martin Heidegger found himself obliged to do by recasting German concepts and neologisms with pre-Socratic meaning in order to disclose the domain of 'Being' on an existential level, rather than on the representational level of modern thought. Although Gumbrecht and theorists of history such as Eelco Runia have started a search to find figures of speech in which presence can be 'stored', my primary concern is not to somewhat disclose the presence of the youth movement to the contemporary reader, but to analyse the ways in which the youth movement tried to overcome a set of values that Gumbrecht attributes to 'meaning cultures', such as rationalism, subjectivism and individualism, by resorting to 'presence effects'.[23] For me, Gumbrecht's concepts primarily have heuristic value.

A second advantage follows from the first. When we regard 'meaning' and 'presence' cultures not to be mutually exclusive, we can move beyond that often challenged, but still predominant, modern predicament, namely the idea that there is no way 'back' to a 'state' of 'presence'. Since the late 1700s, 'presence cultures' have been exoticized and historicized, for example in the image of the 'noble savage', which situated the 'natural' man whose nobility rested on the fact that he was not corrupted by the immoral side effects of modernity either in the distant past (e.g. the Tacitan German) or in an earlier state of historical 'development' (e.g. the native American). To return to this 'natural' state of being was impossible, because modern man – to put it in a Hegelian way – had become conscious of the inner workings of history as a process of the conceptual self-realization of spirit. And as one cannot 'undo' consciousness, modern man is bound to live in the void between past and future. The dominance of modern historical consciousness also temporalized attempts to overcome its own predicaments as escapes into an idealized past or flights forwards into an ever unattainable utopian future.

Third, Gumbrecht's framework is especially beneficial when it comes to historical time. Because presence effects challenge the dominance of the linear conception of time, they do not necessarily have to appear as 'nostalgic', 'unrealistic' or 'escapist' in this analytical framework. However, in the historiography of the youth movement the 'meaning' bias has been so overwhelming that – as we have seen – the youth movement's attitude to history and society has too often been judged 'Romantic' and 'escapist', thereby setting aside the possibility that they tried to overcome modernity not by changing the course of history, but by challenging the premises of modern temporality itself. The use of the concepts 'meaning culture' and 'presence culture' enables me to show the ways in which the youth movement tried to challenge and to overcome this dominance by altering the configuration of presence and meaning effects, without having to judge these by the standards of modern meaning cultures.

In this study, I will grasp the interplay between 'meaning' and 'presence' in the apprehension of the past by combining an analysis of the discursive constitution of historical, eschatological and mythical *theories* and *ideas* in the youth movement with an analysis of the *practices* and *experiences* of the youth movement. In this way, my analysis will show how in modernity, presence was not absent, but a very real and culturally expressed mode of apprehending the world beyond cognition or consciousness. After all, the movement was – in the words of Thomas Nipperdey – primarily about 'mood, about horizon, about implicit valuations, rather than about a consistent framework of thought or attitudes'.[24] Moreover, taking both 'meaning' and 'presence' into account enables me to show how these notions are intertwined, and how they only oppose each other in an ideal typical way, rather than being two mutually exclusive and incommensurable paradigms.

## The German Youth Movement in Historiography

The German youth movement was a broad phenomenon. It developed out of the Wandervogel, an association that was established in 1901 to promote hiking among secondary schoolboys. After a few years, the initial Wandervogel-Ausschuß für Schülerfahrten e.V. (1901–1904), split up into various new branches, which then spread across Germany; all of them supported hiking among the generally higher educated boys and (since 1906) girls from middle-class families.[25] In 1913 most of these branches were again reunited. In the same year, the Freideutsche Jugend was established as an umbrella organization for a variety of academic student associations that were affiliated with the Wandervogel, or at least had similar ideas on social and educational reform. When these organizations dissolved in the economic and political turmoil of the young Weimar Republic, the youth movement was continued in a large number of local wandering groups and associations until a new elan sprang from the scouting movement, which led to the rise of the so-called Bündische Jugend. The Bündische Jugend was an umbrella concept that was used to refer to the various Wandervogel, scouting and – depending on the level of independence from adult influence – confessional youth associations that were developing new styles and new ideologies in the 1920s and early 1930s. Although these organizations had a less coherent organizational structure than the Wandervogel, from 1926 onwards, a significant number of *Bünde* merged in the Deutsche Freischar.[26] The saying goes that where three Germans gather, they establish an association – true indeed for the youth movement, but an impossibility for the historian.[27]

We can discern three modes of emplotment in the historiography of the youth movement, which correspond to different interpretations of the movement's 'Romanticism'. The first is the narrative of the social emancipation of youth. This is perhaps the oldest narrative emplotment in youth movement historiography, for it was already present in the first history of the Wandervogel, published by former member Hans Blüher in 1912. Blüher's *Wandervogel* has been subjected to fierce criticism ever since its publication. Numerous factual incongruities have made the history questionable in the first place.[28] His idolatry of Wandervogel-founder Karl Fischer, his Freudianism, his anti-Semitism, his struggle with female involvement, and his early argument that homoeroticism was the prime cohesive factor of the movement have all added to the controversial status of his work. However, what remained influential is the basic plotline of his Wandervogel history: the idea that the German youth movement initiated a Romantic revolt of German youth against the petrified petty bourgeois culture of Wilhelmine Germany. In Blüher's view, Romanticism was deployed as a vehicle for emancipation. This idea has been especially popular in the field of the (history of) pedagogy. Educationalists and historians of education have interpreted the youth movement as an actor favouring the emancipation of youth – a fourth emancipatory movement after the emancipation of the bourgeoisie, the emancipation of the proletariat and the emancipation of women.[29] Although more recent literature has challenged this interpretation by emphasizing the involvement of adults and the continuation of bourgeois values within the movement, the basic assumption that the youth movement was a collective social entity that developed a new set of social values in opposition to bourgeois, Wilhelmine society remains unchallenged.[30]

Second, there is the narrative of anti-modernism. Hans-Ulrich Wehler sums it up when he calls the Wandervogel 'anti-liberal and anti-democratic, anti-urban and anti-industrial', and recognizes an apparently cultivated 'jingoistic-Germanic social romanticism' to be an escape from bourgeois society.[31] In this narrative, the 'Romanticism' of the youth movement was a reactionary, rather than an emancipatory force. The most widely read history of the youth movement in the English language – Walter Laqueur's *Young Germany* – also adheres to such a *Sonderweg*-interpretation of the history of the youth movement. In Laqueur's view, the Wandervogel had two options in their 'revolt' against the alienation of modern bourgeois society: they could either have adopted a progressive ideology of social revolution that would take society *beyond* bourgeois modernity, or a reactionary stance *against* bourgeois modernity. As Social Democracy was no option for the middle-class youths who made up the Wandervogel, what was left was a Romantic idolization and 'glorification of the past fraught with misgivings for the future'.[32] Their Romanticism became apparent in their wanderings, in the songs they sang and in the tales they told. 'Their return to nature was romantic, as were their attempts to get away from a materialistic civilization, their stress on the simple life, their rediscovery of old folk songs and folklore, their adoption of medieval names and customs.'[33] Their veneration of the Middle Ages and exaltation of peasant life were plain reactionism for Laqueur, just as in his eyes Romanticism in general was a simple reaction to the Enlightenment. Although the youth movement remained immature and rather naive, it did not adequately prepare youth for the challenges ahead and made them unfit for democracy, freedom and humanism.³⁴ Although many Wandervögel opposed National Socialism, Laqueur argues that they did contribute to the general *völkisch* Romantic atmosphere and to the apolitical attitudes that in turn facilitated the rise of Nazism.³⁵

Third, in the first decades after the Second World War, some authors connected the youth movement's 'anti-modernism' even more explicitly to the rise of Nazism.³⁶ The youth movement was criticized because the movement was intellectually inspired by the same *völkisch* and otherwise right-wing authors as the Nazis, and it was argued that the youth movement paved the way for National Socialism on the basis of the fact that the Hitler Youth copied the style of the Bündische Jugend to a large extent. Such arguments, however, are good examples of fallacious historical reasoning and have been debunked many times.³⁷ Yet, the apparent lack of sufficient English literature on the topic means that the interpretation of the youth movement as a proto-fascist movement still resonates today.³⁸ Literature that dismisses this thesis often does so in line with Laqueur, who argued that the situation was too complex to identify a singular causal connection between the youth movement and National Socialism.³⁹ Rejecting this thesis along with Laqueur can, however, imply following him in his *Sonderweg*-argumentation.⁴⁰

Recently the dominance of Laqueur's interpretation has been challenged. In *Turning to Nature in Germany* (2007), John Alexander Williams criticized earlier historiography for exaggerating the right-wing aspects of 'back-to-nature' movements in Germany – including the Wandervogel – on the basis of the fraught dichotomy of an irrational Romantic reaction to a rational Enlightenment. This critique is valid, because this fraught interpretation still echoed the caricature nineteenth-century liberalism made of Romanticism by unjustly equating it with the Restoration. Williams convincingly argues that the nationalism of the Wandervogel had little to do with the social Darwinist and racialist nationalism that gained ground across Europe in the early 1900s, and that they dropped 'such jingoism in favour of an older, more humanistic and Romantic version of cultural nationalism'.⁴¹ Unfortunately, Williams trades the confusing concept of Romanticism for an even more confusing notion of 'nature'. Undefined, 'nature' still appears in his book as the Rousseauist antipode of modern, urban society.

Several recent publications have shifted attention to the individual and collective biographies of the members of the youth movement. In 2013, Barbara Stambolis edited a huge volume gathering biographies of sixty-one prominent members of the youth movement, tracing the influence of the youth movement on their individual life courses and through them the influence of the youth movement on society. The project showed the complexity and contradictions of relating individual actions later in the life course to adolescent experiences in the youth movement.⁴² This does not mean that there was no coherence in the memories and self-narratives of members of various *Bünde*, as Thomas Kohut showed in his analysis of the memories of the members of the Freideutsche

Kreis, an association established in 1947 by former members of the Bündische Jugend. Collective recollection, sharing memories and stories have generated a striking narrative coherence in the oral history interviews of the members of the Freideutsche Kreis that Kohut analysed.[43]

The fact that after the Second World War members of the youth movement flocked together and developed a memory culture has provided German historiography of the youth movement with an additional problem to deal with. A significant part of youth movement historiography has been written by former members or sympathisers of the Wandervogel and Bündische Jugend. This accounts especially for historiography until the 1980s, when members of this specific generation were still productive authors.[44] Although many of their writings possess significant scholarly qualities, overall problems include the requirement of prerequisite knowledge by the reader, as many authors wrote from personal experience, and an apologetic stance when it comes down to the problem of Nazism. This resulted in a literature that, as Peter Stachura put it, 'when not downright polemical or propagandistic is of fragmentary and of limited value'.[45] More recently, Christian Niemeyer has shown that even Werner Kindt's landmark youth movement sourcebooks were edited in a way that expressed a 'reflexive denial' of those elements that could be connected to the rise of Nazi ideology.[46]

Niemeyer goes even further on his quest to remind his readers of the 'dark side of the bright moon of the youth movement' by arguing that German historians still have a positive bias today.[47] By treating the pre-war Wandervogel movement as the 'actual' youth movement and denouncing the often politically radicalized Bündische Jugend to be 'unactual', the purported myth of political innocence was maintained.[48] In this way a discontinuity is constructed in which the Wandervogel and Freideutsche Jugend are dissociated from fascism and can be remembered as politically innocent. Although Niemeyer's critique of the selective bias of the editors of Kindt's sourcebook is valid, his attempt to reveal the 'positive' bias of the general youth movement historiography seems to be fuelled by a bias itself: the bias of guilt which also haunts German historiography. Both positions are rooted in the belief that the youth movement is part of, and an actor in, the course of causally related events which we usually call 'history'.

I would pose the question differently. Instead of treating the youth movement as a social force which played a role in the historical development of Wilhelmine and Weimar Germany, I will study the movement as an educative realm in which young people could orient themselves on their lives, the world, the past, the present and the future. Then, the question is not to what extent the youth movement codetermined German history, but to what extent the movement provided a milieu in which conceptions of past, present and future were negotiated. Hermann Mau warned as early as 1948 that interpreting the movement in line with the general developments of German history bears the danger of projecting the modern idea of history onto the youth movement:

> This is obviously a fault of historical thought. We cannot categorize the youth movement by the concept of development which we are familiar with in historical observation, for the youth movement is not developing. The moving force springs from a consistent direct experience, which is not subjected to conversion.[49]

More recently Kathleen Canning argued with regard to the Weimar Republic that 'Weimar actors scarcely experienced time in the linear form that characterizes most narrative emplotments of the republic's history'.[50] In order to be able to analyse the ways in which time was experienced, I will analyse the youth movement as a social realm in which the world was experienced and comprehended, rather than as a cohesive force in Germany's historical development.

## The 'Conservative Revolution' and the Limits of Historical Thought

In Wilhelmine and Weimar Germany, the youth movement obviously did not stand alone in its experiments with different conceptions of history. In the historiography of Weimar Germany, the Bündische Jugend, with the Wandervogel as its precursor, is often regarded as a part of Germany's 'Conservative Revolution' – the denominator for a broad cultural movement in which analogous conceptions of history were developed. According to Armin Mohler, the 'Conservative Revolution' is an umbrella concept comprising a great variety of movements and individuals which together make up 'that spiritual movement of regeneration that tried to clear away the ruins of the nineteenth century and tried to create a new order of life'.[51] In his well-known dissertation *Die Konservative Revolution in Deutschland 1918–1932* (1950), Mohler presents a taxonomy of this rather heterogeneous 'movement'. He discerned *völkisch* authors, Young Conservatives such as Oswald Spengler and Arthur Moeller van den Bruck, National Revolutionaries such as the Jünger brothers, and also two more organized movements: the Landvolkbewegung and the Bündische Jugend. What this broad spectrum of conservative movements and individuals shared was a common attitude towards life, society and politics, rather than a concrete political programme or a well-defined ideology. 'Conservative Revolutionaries' agreed in their rejection of Enlightenment ethics, rationalism and liberalism – they basically agreed in the rejection of the entire mentality which had come to define modernity in the course of the nineteenth century. Rejecting early nineteenth-century conservatism as being merely driven by a reactionary attempt to restore the *ancien régime*, the 'Conservative Revolution' strove for a new synthesis in what was understood as a disintegrated and individualistic modern society. For many, the main source of inspiration for such a synthesis was the conceptually opaque, but intuitively 'clear' factor: 'life'.

Because terms such as 'life' were understood in the Nietzschean sense as referring to a pre-rational domain beyond metaphysics, and because such thought was based on the conviction that the world could not be grasped rationally and conceptual language was not adequate enough to capture life in its fullness, scholarly analysis of the 'Conservative Revolution' has been severely hampered. This is a great aporia of the 'Conservative Revolution': any analysis of this intellectual movement is necessarily incomplete, inadequate and reductionist, because the 'Conservative Revolution' defies the premises of analytic thought itself.

Mohler was well aware of this problem. He knew that dealing with the 'Conservative Revolution' meant dealing with an 'intellectual anti-intellectualism' that had produced a 'literature of the unliterary': this literature was convinced that the world extends far beyond what concepts and meaning can convey, and that the poetic word – the image – is better fit to disclose lived reality.[52] Grasping together authors as diverse as Thomas Mann, Hugo von Hofmannsthal, Stefan George, Houston Stewart Chamberlain, Arthur Moeller van den Bruck and a broad array of political, social, economic and cultural thinkers of the German right, Mohler contends that it is useless to try to understand their mentality through the endless list of ideological '-isms' they themselves and their opponents produced. Instead of attempting to analyse an incoherent discourse as a discourse, Mohler focused on *Leitbilder* or 'guiding images', such as *Große Mittag* ('Great Afternoon') or *Wiedergeburten* ('reincarnations'). He thus actually studied the 'Conservative Revolution' on conservative terms, which does not surprise, given the fact that he had been a sympathizer with the German Right ever since he had defected from the Swiss army in 1942 in an attempt to join the Waffen SS. In the Bundesrepublik, Mohler was a well-known proponent of political conservatism and an early critic of Germany's *Vergangenheitsbewältigung* – preluding Ernst Nolte's position in the *Historikerstreit* of 1986.[53]

In the 1990s, the concept 'Conservative Revolution' received strong criticism from Stefan Breuer, who emphasized that the use of the concept as a denominator for the broad German right between National Conservatism and National Socialism was an invention of postwar intellectual history. The concept presupposed a non-existing coherent conservative discourse in the interwar period, which was sometimes also at odds with the self-image of its protagonists.[54] Nonetheless, Breuer too seems to recognize some coherence in the variety of conservatives in the Weimar Republic, as he proposes to replace the ambiguous term 'Conservative Revolution' with the term 'new nationalism'. After all, these conservatives were generally nationalists, albeit in an irrational and holistic way compared to the 'old' liberal nationalism of the *Kaiserreich*.[55] The fact that Breuer gives way for a reinstatement of the simplified opposition between 'nationalist' conservatism and 'internationalist' communism is not the only problem with such a deconstruction. When he states that 'no distinctive identity can be discerned' and that therefore the 'Conservative Revolution' should be 'erased from the list of political currents of the twentieth century', Breuer apparently regards the German Right solely as a political movement striving for social and political change, rather than a worldview or collective mentality striving for a reorientation of the premises of modern thought. In my view Breuer disregards the utopian element of the 'Conservative Revolution' as his definition of conservatism remains in binary opposition to liberalism.[56]

Nonetheless over the last two decades, broader historiography on Weimar Germany has increasingly recognized that the future horizon of the era was fundamentally open and that it was basically a 'playground' for formulating and living new conceptions of time and history. In his landmark review essay 'Did Weimar Fail?' (1996), Peter Fritzsche noted that it was time to put the dominant historiographical inquiry into the reasons of the failure of the Weimar Republic behind us, and, rather than thinking back from a dramatic ending, start focusing on the possibilities the era prompted. In this historiographical shift, Weimar was increasingly interpreted as a 'postwar workshop in which ... more or less fierce versions of the future were constructed', rather than an era that saw the birth and collapse of a democratic political system.[57] On a grass-roots level, the political divisions between left and right were not as clear-cut throughout the Weimar era as the street battles between the political left and right suggest. Political and cultural thought and action did not thrive as much on closed ideologies and systems of thought as earlier historiography contended – Weimar rather was an age of new ideas and social experiments in the light of an indeterminate future. The traditional 'split' in Weimar historiography between those who saw the era in reference to a German *Sonderweg* as a prelude to Nazism, and those who emphasized sudden discontinuity in the Nazi rise to power, seemed to have been overcome. It led Fritzsche to state that 'perhaps the long awaited "new paradigm" for German history has arrived in the form of the disavowal of the master narrative of the Republic in the name of the eclectic experimentalism of Weimar'.[58] The rise of Nazism could now be interpreted as the radical outcome of this contingency, rather than the necessary result of Germany's historical development – or its discontinuous antipode. In constructivist phraseology, Weimar became an era in which new social and political identities were (re-)constructed, and in which the nation was reinvented and reimagined.

Of vital importance for this interpretation of Weimar history was the publication of Detlev Peukert's *Die Weimarer Republik. Krisenjahre der klassischen Moderne* (1987). Peukert tried to think beyond the *Sonderweg* and reinterpreted Weimar history as a 'crisis of classical modernity'. 'Classical modernity' was the period in (German) history stretching from the 1890s to 1933 in which the great advantages – but also the disadvantages – of technological and industrial 'progress' became palpable in Germany. On the one hand there was exhilaration for, for example, Germany's colonial ambitions and the Zeppelin, while on the other hand the traditionally humanist educated class was challenged by the rise of technicians and engineers. Nature preservation and the *völkisch* idealization of a bucolic Germany can be seen as reactionary attempts to cope with the increasing pace of social, economic and technological change.

But while for Peukert the term 'crisis' still referred to a factual condition, recent literature attempts to overcome such substantialism by analysing the 'crisis' in Weimar Germany as a narrative construct.[59] The narrative of crisis in Weimar Germany was, as Benjamin Ziemann puts it, a 'cultural form which could be used to imagine and reflect upon possible scenarios for a renewal of society', rather than a reflection of a measurable process of cultural demise.[60] Yet such conclusions hint at the same interpretation: Weimar Germany as an era with a fundamentally open horizon of expectation. Rüdiger Graf stressed that 'crisis' should be understood in its original meaning as a time of decision. According to him, historians have too often adopted the narrative of the critics of irrationalism, of the moderate rationalist republicans of the 1920s, which generally stated that a turn to irrational sentiments was a reflex caused by the socio-economic and cultural uncertainty in postwar Germany. From this perspective, Graf argues, 'crises destroyed formerly secure expectations of the future, thereby creating insecurity and pessimistic sentiments among the people. Intellectuals allegedly overcompensated for this loss of security, producing apocalyptic fears or utopias and visions of stable orders, and thereby futurizing political, social and economic discourses'.[61] By understanding crisis in its original Greek meaning, Graf disposes of the modern dichotomy between objective reality and subjective meaning – in which the latter represents the first. Speaking of crisis is not just the representation of, or reaction against, a crisis in (social) reality, but an existential moment of decision in which the situation itself is rendered in the light of future possibilities. His solution was to study the use of the term 'crisis' as a narrative strategy to cope with a (not necessarily or inherently negative) situation, rather than using crisis as an objective cause for uncertainty and impending doom.

Following Graf's valid critique of the 'naive' conception of crisis in historiography, we can see that there is more at stake than a difference in the way 'naive' historians and Weimar intellectuals used the concept of 'crisis' to construct historical meaning in the emplotment of their narratives. Their conceptions of history and time also differ. We have already noted this problem with respect to the 'Conservative Revolution'. In reference to the broader history of Germany, the problem of historical time becomes best visible in Jeffrey Herf's well-known book *Reactionary Modernism* (1984).

Questioning the way in which a strong opposition against Enlightenment and democratic values was combined with an enthusiasm for technology in Nazi Germany, Herf analyses the question of technology in the work of a number of 'Conservative Revolutionaries' such as Oswald Spengler, Ernst Jünger, Carl Schmitt, Werner Sombart and Hans Freyer. However, when we acknowledge that these authors tried to overcome modern historical thought, it is valid to question the paradox of the 'reconciliation' between anti-modernist, illiberal, romantic and irrational German nationalisms and highly rationalistic technology that Herf observes. Herf's analysis basically relies on the classical antithesis between progression and regression: technology represents progress, and conservative anti-modernism represents a backward-looking longing for times past. Both orientations thus presuppose a linear understanding of time as progression. This is exactly what makes reconciliation between conservatism and technology paradoxical.

When we bear in mind that this linear understanding of time was exactly what the 'Conservative Revolution' strove to overcome, we can ask ourselves whether an analysis that is itself based on a linear understanding of time contributes to the understanding of the 'Conservative Revolution'. The question Herf should have answered is not why 'illiberalism' and 'anti-modernism' reconciled with technology in Weimar Germany, but why for interwar conservative thinkers, illiberalism and technology could not account as antithetic. The answer has already been given by Mohler: those who make up the 'Conservative Revolution' are those who 'attack the foundations of the century of progress and still do not wish to restore any kind of *ancien régime*'.[62] Despite the fact that contemporary historiography increasingly emphasizes the open 'horizon of expectation' in the Weimar Republic, the contemporary critique of the 'Conservative Revolution' as an analytical concept tends to overlook this temporal dimension: the shared attempt to overcome the progressive and linear conception of history.

## Sources, Method and Outline of the Study

One of the advantages of the youth movement for the historian is that it has produced a great variety of sources that make it possible to counter an analysis of its historical thought with a study of actual experiences and practices. For my selection of the sources, this means that I will analyse the discourse of the main journals of the youth movement, of its main protagonists, leaders and intellectual teachers, and will juxtapose these thoughts with more personal testimonies in (local) journals, autobiographies and diaries.[63] Although I have translated quotations from these German sources into English, the specific use and meaning of notions such as *Erlebnis* compel me to keep using these concepts in the German language.

I will not solely rely on the traditional sources of youth movement historiography, which comprise the innumerable programmatic essays in which the youth movement's leadership or other stakeholders tried to define the meaning of the youth movement for themselves, for others or for German society in general. I will treat the movement as a milieu in which young people grew up, educated themselves, made friends, tried to get hold of the world and 'lived'. Therefore, I will counter these programmatic self-definitions with a focus on experience. When focusing on experience, a problem with the sources arises that Theodor Wilhelm – member of the Deutsche Freischar until 1933 and professor in pedagogy at the University of Kiel – noted in 1963: 'literature – what has been written and printed – is an inadequate source when one tries to capture the reality of the lived existence of a part of German youth. One ought to take this life itself into account'.[64]

Hans-Joachim Schoeps noted as well that the youth movement was a deep, intuitive experience: 'Who was actually moved by it, could never let it go, and who has not experienced the youth movement himself, but only heard of it or is only acquainted with it through literature – for them the inner essence remained hidden'.[65] Ironically, this is how historiography had acquainted the youth movement: through a reading of its literature, which is a reading of the literature of the movement's leadership. In 1979 Ulrich Aufmuth still emphasized that almost the entire body of secondary literature on the youth movement 'equals its symbolic, ideological, and programmatic expressions often in a culpable manner with reality'.[66] These sources do express the ideas and ideologies of the leadership of the movement and of others who tried to mobilize the movement for their own agendas, and often express what the youth movement 'actually was', or ought to be. Little do these sources reflect the lived experience of those involved in the youth movement. This problem was already noted in 1923 by the cultural philosopher Viktor Engelhardt, who stressed that the common practice of interpreting the movement by the words of its leadership leads to serious misconceptions, because in such analysis one only encounters the 'leading spirits, who before the public perhaps never emphasize their inner being [*Wesen*] in full exposure. Also, the real life of the youth is certainly not mentioned in its literature – yes, this true life cannot at all be put into words'.[67]

Whereas my analysis of the main discourse on history and time is indeed based on the writings of the main protagonists and leaders of the youth movement that were published in main journals, books, founding documents and other documents such as circulars, the experience of time and history will be grasped through an analysis of *Fahrtenberichte*, which are testimonies of the many hikes the associations undertook. There are two types of *Fahrtenberichte*. First, local chapters kept track of their hikes in *Fahrtenbücher*, books in which an account of the hike was written down after arrival. Second, *Fahrtenberichte* were published in journals. Contrary to the accounts in *Fahrtenbücher*, these are individual testimonies, often well written, as they were liable to be published. Whereas the *Fahrtenbuch* was a collective diary, often a literal account of the hike, *Fahrtenberichte* soon became a genre of its own. In 1932, Karl Will noted that 'the *Fahrtenbericht* can currently be seen as the most common literary manifestation of youth'.[68] By then, it had become a genre with its own idiom and narrative structure.[69]

The publication of *Fahrtenberichte* reached a peak in the years before the war. Many *Gaublätter* – journals of regional branches of the youth movement – were established after 1911 and published numerous hiking reports. While the selection of the main journals I analyse equals the size and influence of the associations and *Bünde* that published them, the selection of local Gaublätter for the analysis of experiences is random to the extent that I do not intend to analyse or compare the *representation* of experience in these different journals. Rather than comparing the representation of experience between the 'Protestant North' and the 'Catholic South', or the 'West-oriented Rhineland' and 'East-oriented Silesia' – which would require a representative selection of sources from various German regions – my main question focuses on the tensions between ideology and experience. The *Erlebnisberichte*, which provide the content for this analysis, have been selected on the basis of the metareflections on experience itself by their authors. Thus, authors who simply depict what factually happened on a hike have less relevance than authors who reflect on their own emotions, intuitions, feelings and thoughts during a hike.

In the early 1920s, the number of published *Erlebnisberichte* dwindled. This was not only due to the organizational disintegration of the youth movement, but also to the economic crisis and hyperinflation, which severely hampered publication. In the second half of the 1920s, when the economy started to recover and the youth movement was reorganized under the aegis of the Bündische Jugend, the number of *Erlebnisberichte* rose again. Moreover, the radius of the hikes expanded enormously in the 1920s, reaching into other countries and even other continents. Not only did this result in an upsurge of travelogues, in some cases it would also lead to a professionalization of travel writing. The Nerother Wandervogel, for example, travelled the world on the revenues of the books and films they made of earlier trips. Although these sources will give us insight in the practical experience of the youth movement, we must recall that Engelhardt uttered that in general the essence of the Wandervogel can never be grasped in words; and it would indeed be rather naive to believe that it would be possible to reconstruct inner experience through the reading of a representation. But again, my aim is not to reconstruct the impossible, but to see how experiences and social practices such as travelling, dancing, singing and performing plays functioned as 'presence effects'.

I will commence this study by recounting, in the first chapter, the history, up to 1914, of the Wandervogel – the youth movement with which the 'free' German youth movement commenced – and the Freideutsche Jugend, an umbrella organization of youth organizations that targeted students rather than secondary school pupils. But in parallel with this history of a young movement defining itself, I analyse how it related to the historical culture of Wilhelmine Germany. I focus particularly on two domains, namely school history and national remembrance. It was in opposition to these two factors that the youth movement defined itself and started to search for alternative interpretations of the past. This chapter, however, mainly discusses the way in which the movement's leadership interpreted things.

The second chapter has a grassroots approach. It focuses on direct experience as an alternative mode of apprehending the past within the Wandervogel, and covers the period between 1910 and 1918. This chapter is meant to counter the first chapter, which still follows the discourse of the youth movement's leadership, and shows how, on the level of everyday activities such as hiking, the Wandervogel approached heritage – the material and immaterial traces of the past – empathically rather than cognitively.[70] This chapter is based on travel reports, out of which two recurrent concepts are distilled: direct experience (*Erlebnis*) and attunement (*Stimmung*). These will be guiding concepts in exploring how the past was experienced in hikes.

The third chapter takes us into the war, and traces how historical memory gained a different meaning, function and foundation as the result of an upsurge of religiosity in the movement. At the same time a generational conflict occurred, in which the pre-war youth movement was accused of an escapist Romanticism and individualism. Experience was still of vital importance, but rather than strengthening individual development, it was now put in service of an eschatological expectation that prophesized the coming of a new era, a new German *Volksgemeinschaft* and a new mode of being. The development of these eschatological beliefs is explained by tracing the development of a new religiosity that had taken hold of the movement in the course of the First World War.

The fourth chapter discusses the period after the downfall of the Wandervogel movement in the early 1920s. Under the influence of rogue Boy Scout organizations, the Bündische Jugend arose from the Wandervogel's ashes, and incorporated the new eschatological beliefs in its goals and practices. This chapter mainly focuses on the position of the Middle Ages within these beliefs – not only because there was a revival of medievalism in the movement, but also because the focus on medievalism can clarify the changed function and position of a historic era in a cosmological worldview.

Finally, the fifth chapter focuses on the period from around 1926 to 1933 – a period in which the Bündische Jugend increasingly looked and travelled abroad. A number of foreign travel destinations will be analysed in which the main question is how 'the abroad' fuelled the utopian expectation of the youth movement. Rather than interpreting the utopian in the conventional way, as an ideal society to be realized in the future through human agency, I ask the question: how was the youth movement's eschatology spatialized in these foreign journeys?

In the concluding chapter, I will summarize the findings of my research and provide a synthesis of the development of conceptions of history and time in the German youth movement.

# Notes

1. Georg Götsch, 'Die Jugendbewegung als Volksgewissen', *Deutsche Freischar* 3 (1928) 117–19: 117.
2. Ibid., 118.
3. Ibid., 118.
4. Ibid., 118.
5. Ibid., 119.
6. In the last two decades, the body of literature on memory and identity has expanded rapidly. Knowing that any enumeration of literature would be incomplete, I would like to refer to these handbooks as entries into the field of 'memory studies': Astrid Erll, *Kollektives Gedächtnis und Erinnerungskulturen* (Stuttgart: Metzler, 2005); Astrid Erll and Ansgar Nünning, *Cultural Memory Studies: An International and Interdisciplinary Handbook* (Berlin: Walter de Gruyter, 2008). On the topic of the youth movement, memory and identity, see: Sabine Autsch, *Erinnerung – Biographie – Fotografie. Formen der Ästhetisierung einer jugendbewegten Generation im 20. Jahrhundert* (Potsdam: Verlag Berlin-Brandenburg, 2000); Hans Ulrich Thamer, 'Der Meißner-Tag: Probleme einer jugendbündischen Erinnerungskultur', in Botho Brachmann et al. (eds), *Die Kunst des Vernetzens. Festschrift für Wolfgang Hempel* (Berlin: Verlag für Berlin-Brandenburg, 2006), 399–409.
7. Jörn Rüsen, 'Introduction: Historical Thinking as Intercultural Discourse', in Jörn Rüsen (ed.), *Western Historical Thinking: An Intercultural Debate* (New York: Berghahn Books, 2002), 1–11: 1.
8. Hans-Georg Gadamer, 'The Problem of Historical Consciousness', in Paul Rabinow and William M. Sullivan (eds), *Interpretive Social Science: A Second Look* (Berkeley: University of California Press, 1987), 82–140: 110; Maria Grever, 'Nationale identiteit en historisch besef. De risico's van een canon in de postmoderne samenleving', *Tijdschrift voor Geschiedenis* 119(2) (2006), 160–77; Jörn Rüsen, 'Historical Consciousness: Narrative Structure, Moral Function, and Ontogenetic Development', in Peter Seixas (ed.), *Theorizing Historical Consciousness* (Toronto: University of Toronto Press, 2004), 63–85.
9. Wolfgang Hardtwig, *Hochkultur des bürgerlichen Zeitalters* (Göttingen: Vandenhoeck & Ruprecht, 2005), 101. See also: Detlev J.K. Peukert, *The Weimar Republic: The Crisis of Classical Modernity* (London: Penguin, 1991), 3–18, 275–81. For the concept 'historical culture', see: Maria Grever, 'Fear of Plurality: Historical Culture and Historiographical Canonization in Western Europe', in Angelika Epple and Angelika Schaser (eds), *Multiple Histories? Changing Perspectives on Modern History* (Frankfurt and New York: Campus Verlag, 2009), 45–62: 54–55; Jörn Rüsen, 'Was ist Geschichtskultur? Überlegungen zu einer neuen Art, über Geschichte nachzudenken', in Jörn Rüsen (ed.), *Historische Orientierung: über die Arbeit des Geschichtsbewußtseins, sich in der Zeit zurechtzufinden* (Cologne: Böhlau, 1994), 3–26; Bernd Schönemann, 'Geschichtskultur als Forschungskonzept der Geschichtsdidaktik', *Zeitschrift für Geschichtsdidaktik* 1(200) (2002), 78–86.
10. For the concept 'space of experience', see: Reinhart Koselleck, '"Space of Experience" and "Horizon of Expectation": Two Historical Categories', *Futures Past: On the Semantics of Historical Time* (Cambridge: MIT Press, 1985), 267–324.
11. Reinhart Koselleck, 'On the Disposability of History', in Reinhart Koselleck (ed.), *Futures Past: On the Semantics of Historical Time* (New York: Columbia University Press, 2004), 192–204: 196.
12. Ibid., 199.
13. Hermann Mau, 'Die deutsche Jugendbewegung, Rückblick und Ausblick', *Zeitschrift für Religions- und Geistesgeschichte* 2(7) (1948), 135–49: 136.
14. August K. Wiedmann, *The German Quest for Primal Origins in Art, Culture, and Politics 1900–1933: die "Flucht in Urzustände"* (Lewiston, NY: E. Mellen Press, 1995), 4.
15. Robert George Collingwood, 'History as Re-enactment of Past Experience', in Robert George Collingwood (ed.), *The Idea of History* (Oxford: Oxford University Press, 1946), 282–302.
16. Dietmar Schenk, *Die Freideutsche Jugend, 1913–1919/20: Eine Jugendbewegung in Krieg, Revolution und Krise* (Münster: LIT-Verlag, 1991), 4.

17. The classical formulation of this social constructivism can be found in: Peter L. Berger and Thomas Luckmann, *The Social Construction of Reality: A Treatise in the Sociology of Knowledge* (Garden City, NY: Anchor, 1967). On the relationship between social constructivism and the 'linguistic' and 'cultural' turns in the humanities, see: Georg G. Iggers, *Geschichtswissenschaft im 20. Jahrhundert* (Göttingen: Vandenhoeck & Ruprecht, 2007), 124ff; Alun Munslow, 'Constructionist History', in Alun Munslow (ed.), *The Routledge Companion to Historical Studies. Second Edition* (London: Routledge, 2006), 66–67.

18. Hayden White, *Metahistory: The Historical Imagination in Nineteenth-Century Europe* (Baltimore, MD: Johns Hopkins University Press, 1973).

19. Frank Ankersmit, 'Historical Representation', *History and Theory* 27(3) (1988), 205–28: 209–11.

20. Astrid Erll, 'Cultural Memory Studies: An Introduction', in Astrid Erll and Ansgar Nünning (eds), *Cultural Memory Studies: An International and Interdisciplinary Handbook* (Berlin: Walter de Gruyter, 2008), 1–15: 2.

21. Frank Ankersmit, *De sublieme historische ervaring* (Groningen: Historische Uitgeverij, 2007), 12.

22. Hans Ulrich Gumbrecht, *Production of Presence: What Meaning Cannot Convey* (Stanford: Stanford University Press, 2004), 19.

23. Hans Ulrich Gumbrecht, 'Presence Achieved in Language (With Special Attention Given to the Presence of the Past)', *History and Theory* 45(3) (2006), 317–27; Eelco Runia, 'Presence', *History and Theory* 45, no. 1 (2006) 1–29.

24. Thomas Nipperdey, 'Jugend und Politik um 1900', in Walter Rüegg (ed.), *Kulturkritik und Jugendkult* (Frankfurt am Main: Vittorio Klostermann, 1974), 96.

25. For a study of the social background of the *Wandervögel*, see: Ulrich Aufmuth, *Die deutsche Wandervogelbewegung unter soziologischem Aspekt* (Göttingen: Vandenhoeck & Ruprecht, 1979), 106ff.; Walter Jantzen, 'Die soziologische Herkunft der Führungsschicht der deutschen Jugendbewegung 1900–1933', in *Führungsschicht und Eliteproblem. Jahrbuch III der Ranke-Gesellschaft* (Frankfurt am Main: Moritz Diesterweg, 1957), 127–35.

26. Clear estimations on the numerical size of the youth movement cannot be given. General estimations of the membership of the Wandervogel and Freideutsche Jugend range from 50,000 to 60,000 in 1914; the Bündische Jugend is estimated at 60,000 in 1925. The sphere of influence of the youth movement was, however, far greater than its numerical size, as style, practices and ideas were increasingly appropriated by adult-led youth organizations. According to Jakob Müller, the 'aura' of the youth movement was reaching some five million youths until 1933. On these estimations and calculations, see: Jakob Müller, *Die Jugendbewegung als deutsche Hauptrichtung neukonservativer Reform* (Zurich: Europa Verlag, 1971), 389–90.

27. For this saying, see: Hermann Bausinger, *Typisch deutsch: wie deutsch sind die Deutschen?* (Munich: Beck, 2000), 66–72. For the vast array of youth organizations in the Weimar Republic, see: Günter Ehrenthal, *Die deutschen Jugendbünde. Ein Handbuch ihrer Organisation und ihrer Bestrebungen* (Berlin: Zentral-Verlag, 1929); Rudolf Kneip, *Jugend der Weimarer Zeit: Handbuch der Jugendverbände 1919–1938* (Frankfurt a/M: Dipa-Verlag, 1974).

28. Cf. Walther Gerber, *Zur Entstehungsgeschichte der deutschen Wandervogelbewegung. Ein kritischer Beitrag* (Bielefeld: Gieseking, 1957), 62 ff., 72 ff., 96 ff.; Georg Korth, *Wandervogel 1896–1906: quellenmässige Darstellung nach Karl Fischers Tagebuchaufzeichnungen von 1900 und vielen anderen dokumentarischen Belegen* (Frankfurt a/M: Dipa-Verlag, 1967), 27–28, 70 ff., 89–90.

29. Eduard Spranger, 'Fünf Jugendgenerationen 1900–1949', in Eduard Spranger (ed.), *Pädagosische Perspektiven. Beiträge zu Erziehungsfragen der Gegenwart* (Heidelberg: Quelle & Meyer, 1955), 25–57: 30. In generational theory, the youth movement was also regarded as an expression of the emancipatory dialectics of history: Karl Mannheim, 'The Problem of Generations', *Essays on the Sociology of Knowledge* (New York: Routledge & Kegan Paul, 1952), 276–320: 288, 309. On the problems of this type of generational thinking, see: Robbert-Jan Adriaansen, 'Generaties, herinnering en historiciteit', *Tijdschrift voor Geschiedenis* 124(2) (2011), 221–37.

30. Research on the development of value orientations in the youth movement include: Aufmuth, *Die deutsche Wandervogelbewegung unter soziologischem Aspekt*, Otto Neuloh and Wilhelm Zilius, *Die Wandervögel. Eine empirisch-soziologische Untersuchung der frühen deutschen Jugendbewegung* (Göttingen: Vandenhoeck und Ruprecht, 1982).

31. Hans-Ulrich Wehler, *Das Deutsche Kaiserreich* (Göttingen: Vandenhoeck & Ruprecht, 1973), 127.

32. Walter Laqueur, *Young Germany: A History of the German Youth Movement* (New Brunswick: Transaction Publishers, 1984), 6.

33. Ibid., 6.

34. Ibid., 236–37.

35. When using the term 'Wandervogel', I refer to the totality of youth associations which referred to themselves as such – i.e. Der Ausschuß für Schülerfahrten e.V. (1901–1904), the Wandervogel – eingetragener Verein zu Steglitz (1904–1912), the Alt-Wandervogel e. V. (1904–1926), the Wandervogel, Deutscher Bund für Jugendwanderungen (1907–1911/13), the Jung-Wandervogel (1910–1916), the Wandervogel e.V. (1913-1922), and the various associations which continued the Wandervogel-legacyc in the 1920s and 1930s. But when I use the term 'Wandervögel', I refer to the *members* of these associations.

36. Howard Becker, *German Youth: Bond or Free* (New York: Oxford University Press, 1946); George L. Mosse, *The Crisis of German Ideology: Intellectual Origins of the Third Reich* (New York: Grosset and Dunlap, 1964); Harry E. Pross, *Jugend Eros Politik. Die Geschichte der deutschen Jugendverbände* (Frankfurt a/M: Büchergilde Gutenberg, 1965); Fritz R. Stern, *The Politics of Cultural Despair: A Study in the Rise of the Germanic Ideology* (Berkeley: University of California Press, 1961).

37. For the literature against the continuity thesis between the German youth movement and the Hitler Youth, see: Arno Klönne, *Jugend im Dritten Reich: die Hitler-Jugend und ihre Gegner* (Cologne: PapyRossa, 2003); Jürgen Reulecke, 'Hat die Jugendbewegung den Nationalsozialismus vorbereitet? Zum Umgang mit einer falschen Frage', in Wolfgang R. Krabbe (ed.), *Politische Jugend in der Weimarer Republik* (Bochum: Universitätsverlag Dr. N. Brockmeyer, 1993), 222–43.

38. See, for example: Keith Hetherington, *Expressions of Identity: Space, Performance, Politics* (London: SAGE, 1998), 86–87.

39. Laqueur, *Young Germany*, viii.

40. See, for example: Peter D. Stachura, *The German Youth Movement 1900–1945: An Interpretative and Documentary History* (London: Macmillan, 1981).

41. John Alexander Williams, *Turning to Nature in Germany: Hiking, Nudism, and Conservation, 1900–1940* (Stanford, CA: Stanford University Press, 2007), 260.

42. Barbara Stambolis, 'Einleitung', in Barbara Stambolis (ed.), *Jugendbewegt geprägt. Essays zu autobiographischen Texten von Werner Heisenberg, Robert Jungk und vielen anderen* (Göttingen: V&R unipress, 2013), 13–42: 24.

43. Thomas A. Kohut, *A German Generation: An Experiential History of the Twentieth Century* (New Haven, CT: Yale University Press, 2012).

44. Cf. W. Gerber, *Zur Entstehungsgeschichte der deutschen Wandervogelbewegung. Ein kritischer Beitrag* (Bielefeld: Gieseking, 1957); Werner Kindt, *Grundschriften der deutschen Jugendbewegung, Dokumentation der Jugendbewegung I* (Düsseldorf: Diederichs, 1963); Rudolf Kneip, *Wandervogel – Bündische Jugend 1909–1943. Der Weg der sächsischen Jungenschaft zum großen Bund* (Frankfurt am Main: Dipa-Verlag, 1967); Karl O. Paetel, *Jugend in der Entscheidung 1913 – 1933 – 1945* (Bad Godesberg: Voggenreiter, 1963); Karl Seidelmann, *Bund und Gruppe als Lebensformen deutscher Jugend: Versuch einer Erscheinungskunde des deutschen Jugendlebens in der ersten Hälfte des XX. Jahrhunderts* (Munich: Wiking Verlag, 1955); Gerhard Ziemer and Hans Wolf, *Wandervogel und freideutsche Jugend* (Bad Godesberg: Voggenreiter, 1961).

45. P. Stachura, *The German Youth Movement 1900–1945: An Interpretative and Documentary History* (London: Macmillan, 1981), 5.

46. Christian Niemeyer, 'Jugendbewegung und Nationalsozialismus', *Zeitschrift für Religions- und Geistesgeschichte* 57(4) (2005), 337–65: 337; Christian Niemeyer, 'Werner Kindt und die

"Dokumentation der Jugendbewegung". Text- und quellenkritische Beobachtungen', *Historische Jugendforschung. Jahrbuch des Archivs der deutschen Jugendbewegung* 2 (2005), 230–49; Christian Niemeyer, *Die dunklen Seiten der Jugendbewegung. Vom Wandervogel zur Hitlerjugend* (Tübingen: A. Francke Verlag, 2013), 19–63. Kindt published his sourcebook in three volumes: Kindt, *Grundschriften der deutschen Jugendbewegung*; Werner Kindt, *Die Wandervogelzeit. Quellenschriften zur deutschen Jugendbewegung 1896–1919* (Düsseldorf: Diederichs, 1968); Werner Kindt, *Dokumentation der Jugendbewegung. Band III: Die deutsche Jugendbewegung 1920 bis 1933. Die Bündische Zeit* (Düsseldorf: Diederichs, 1974).

47. Christian Niemeyer, 'Sozialpädagogik und Jugendbewegung', in Christian Niemeyer (ed.), *Sozialpädagogik als Wissenschaft und Profession* (Weinheim: Juventa Verlag, 2003), 110–22: 107.

48. Ibid., 107; Niemeyer, 'Jugendbewegung und Nationalsozialismus', 117–18.

49. Mau, 'Die deutsche Jugendbewegung, Rückblick und Ausblick', 136.

50. Kathleen Canning, 'The Politics of Symbols, Semantics, and Sentiments in the Weimar Republic', *Central European History* 43 (2010), 567–80: 572.

51. Because of incoherence, Mohler consequently puts the concept of the 'Conservative Revolution' in quotation marks. Armin Mohler, *Die konservative Revolution in Deutschland 1918–1932. Ein Handbuch* (Darmstadt: Wissenschaftliche Buchgesellschaft, 1972), xxviii. English translation cited from: Keith Bullivant, 'The Conservative Revolution', in Anthony Phelan (ed.), *The Weimar Dilemma: Intellectuals in the Weimar Republic* (Manchester: Manchester University Press, 1985), 47.

52. Mohler, *Die konservative Revolution*, 19.

53. Claus Leggewie, *Der Geist steht rechts: Ausflüge in die Denkfabriken der Wende* (Berlin: Rotbuch, 1987), 187–211.

54. Stefan Breuer, *Anatomie der konservativen Revolution* (Darmstadt: Wissenschaftliche Buchgesellschaft, 1993), 1.

55. Ibid., 186–87.

56. Ibid., 181.

57. Peter Fritzsche, 'Review: Did Weimar Fail?', *The Journal of Modern History* 30(3) (1996), 629–56: 656.

58. Ibid., 631.

59. Cf. Moritz Föllmer and Rüdiger Graf, *Die 'Krise' der Weimarer Republik: Zur Kritik eines Deutungsmusters* (Frankfurt am Main: Campus Verlag, 2005), 19; Rüdiger Graf, *Die Zukunft der Weimarer Republik: Krisen und Zukunftsaneignungen in Deutschland 1918–1933* (Munich: Oldenbourg Wissenschaftsverlag, 2008).

60. Benjamin Ziemann, 'Weimar was Weimar: Politics, Culture and the Emplotment of the German Republic', *German History* 28(4) (2010), 542–71: 553.

61. Rüdiger Graf, 'Either–Or: The Narrative of "Crisis" in Weimar Germany and in Historiography', *Central European History* 43 (2010), 592–615: 598. See also: Graf, *Die Zukunft der Weimarer Republik*.

62. Mohler, *Die konservative Revolution*, 11.

63. For a review of the youth movement's journals, see: Herbert Schierer, *Das Zeitschriftenwesen der Jugendbewegung : ein Beitrag zur Geschichte der Jugendzeitschrift* (Berlin: Lorentz, 1938).

64. Theodor Wilhelm, 'Der geschichtliche Ort der deutschen Jugendbewegung', in Werner Kindt (ed.), *Grundschriften der Deutschen Jugendbewegung* (Düsseldorf: Eugen Diederichs Verlag, 1963), 7–29.

65. Hans-Joachim Schoeps, *Die letzten dreissig Jahre. Rückblicke* (Stuttgart: Klett, 1956), 32.

66. Aufmuth, *Die deutsche Wandervogelbewegung*, 31.

67. Viktor Engelhardt, *Die deutsche Jugendbewegung als kulturhistorisches Phänomen* (Berlin: 1923), 119. Walter Sauer argues the same: Walter Sauer, 'Die deutsche Jugendbewegung – Schwierigkeiten einer Ortsbestimmung', in Walter Sauer (ed.), *Rückblicke und Ausblicke die deutsche Jugendbewegung im Urteil nach 1945* (Heidenheim: Südmarkverl. Fritsch, 1978), 9–41: 20.

68. Carl Will, *Das deutsche Jugendwandern* (Hilchenbach: Reichsverband für Deutsche Jugendherbergen, 1932), 11.

69. Cf. Helmut Henne, 'Zur Sprache der Jugend im Wandervogel. Ein unbekanntes Kapitel deutscher Sprachgeschichte', *Zeitschrift für germanistische Linguistik* 9 (1981), 20–33; Gerhard Schrank and Richard Schuch, *Wandervögel im Hunsrück: das Fahrtenbuch der Birkenfelder Wandervögel von 1914 bis 1933* (Nijmegen: Schank, 2001), 104–25; Erich Strassner, 'Zur Sprache der Wandervogel 1890 bis 1923', *Neuphilologische Mitteilungen* 108(2) (2007), 399–422.

70. For this definition of heritage, see: Maria Grever, Pieter de Bruijn and Carla van Boxtel, 'Negotiating Historical Distance: Or, How to Deal with the Past as a Foreign Country in Heritage Education', *Paedagogica Historica* 48(6) (2012), 873–87: 880.

CHAPTER 1

# Wandervogel, Freideutsche Jugend and the Spirit of 1813

The year 1913 contained the most important commemorative events that Wilhelmine Germany would witness. These were in addition to the three annual non-religious national holidays that celebrated the establishment of the German Empire and the house of Hohenzollern: on 18 January, the establishment of the German Empire was commemorated, followed by the emperor's birthday (*Kaisergeburtstag*) on 27 January; the annual festive calendar was then usually closed with Sedan Day (*Sedantag*), which commemorated 2 September 1870 when Prussian forces decisively defeated the French army near Sedan in Lorraine, leading to the French defeat and eventually to the foundation of the German Empire.[1] However, this year, the national commemorative liturgy was marked by two special events: the 25-year reign of Emperor Wilhelm II and the centennial of the Battle of the Nations, the *Völkerschlacht* near Leipzig, where in October 1813 the Prussian-led Sixth Coalition decisively defeated Napoleon. This special commemorative year forced those involved in the youth movement to take position in relation to the 'official' German historical culture, which prompted reflections on the nature of history, on the state of the historical education of youth and on the tasks of the youth movement in general. It called for metareflection on both German historical culture and the ways the youth movement itself had hitherto dealt with the past.

This chapter focuses on how the youth movement's position to German historical culture evolved, as well as the negotiation of this position, which went hand in hand with the rise of the youth movement in Wilhelmine Germany. I will start by outlining the historical culture of the Wilhelmine Kaiserreich in relation to which the youth movement had to position itself, after which I will trace the organizational development of the youth movement since its rise in the late 1890s. I will analyse how the hikes they organized prompted a 'discovery' of German folk culture, and study the process of making the revival of folklore meaningful among their ranks by means of appropriating ideas from various critics of modernity as well. At the end of this chapter, I will return to 1913 and draw conclusions on the question of the extent to which the German youth movement negotiated its own space for dealing with the past, apart from 'official' historical culture.

## The Historical Culture of the Kaiserreich

The commemorative year 1913 was the apex in a battle for German memory, which had been shimmering for several decades. It was strife between the statist and dynastical conception of German history of Wilhelm II on the one hand, and the national conservatism of the bourgeoisie on the other. Often captured in the rather opaque term 'Wilhelminism', the official historical culture of the Kaiserreich was based on the masculine and martial public image of the monarch and the Hohenzollern dynasty. It was the dynasty that functioned as the historicized binding element of the German nation. At the same time this image ignored the rupture with the Holy Roman Empire: its final destruction after more than eight hundred years by Napoleon and the French in 1806. As the dynasty was a Prussian dynasty, the history of Germany was often equated with the history of Prussia. Heinrich von Treitschke's interpretation of the German unification as the product of the Prussian mission to realize the potential of the German nation served as an intellectual legitimization for this type of political Prussianism.[2] It was this 'official' historical culture that filled most of the festivities of 1913 with military parades, torchlight processions, patriotic speeches and historical re-enactments. There was, however, one event that the Kaiser could not appropriate: the centennial of the Battle of the Nations in October 1813.

The centennial became a display of the bourgeoisie's dedication to the nation. Since the 1890s, nationalist pressure groups such as the Pan-German League, the H.T.K. Society and the Navy League had gained ground by mobilizing the masses. This was an extra-parliamentary movement that phrased a nationalist ideology in opposition to the apolitical conception of the nation to which national liberalism still adhered. The liberal conception of the nation was found to be increasingly untenable in a society where Catholics and Socialists claimed their part.[3] For nationalist bourgeois pressure groups, the centennial posed an opportunity for the construction of a national memory that could unify the German people in a national or cultural consciousness that surpassed both the emperor's Prussianism as well as liberal nationalism.[4] Although bourgeois pressure groups had often proven to be a convenient means for the

**Figure 1.1** The Monument to the Battle of the Nations in Leipzig. Postcard, around 1913.

government to stir mass support, the centennial confirmed where the Kaiser and the bourgeois right diverged: not on the industrial, colonial or imperial tasks ahead, but on the interpretation of history and nation in the name of which these challenges could be accomplished. The colossal 91-metre-tall landmark Monument to the Battle of Nations (Figure 1.1), which was erected in Leipzig in 1913 and inaugurated by the emperor, did not refer to the Hohenzollern. It was a sacral temple of the German nation, bearing allegories to German virtues like loyalty, sacrifice and faith.

A few days before the German nation commemorated the 'birthday of the German people' with the consecration of the monument, thirteen youth groups gathered at the Hohe Meißner, a hill in the Hessian mountain massif. It was an attempt to celebrate rather than commemorate the same event. A motley crew of free university student associations, Wandervögel, reform schools and life reform associations gathered in explicit opposition to both the emperor's Prussianism and the nationalism of the bourgeois pressure groups. They vowed against the 'cheap patriotism, which appropriates the heroic deeds of the ancestors in grand terms, without feeling obliged to act on one's own behalf; which exhausts national sentiments in the compliance to certain political formulas, in the manifestation of the desire for the external expansion of power and in the rupture of the nation by political sedition'.[5]

These groups sensed that the spirit in which the official commemorations were held was greatly at odds with the 'spirit of 1813'. They believed the 1813 revolt against French repression was characterized by a sense of national regeneration expressing the will to shape a new destiny for the German nation, free of oppression and foreign intrusion. Official commemorative events opened no such future visions. Patriotism only focused backwards, aimed at arousing deep nostalgic feelings often at the expense of historical truth, without opening up new prospects. The lack of future perspectives had turned history into an arena of politics, resulting in a disintegration of the nation into classes, corporations and individuals, rather than unifying the nation.[6] These youth groups celebrated 1813 explicitly in the spirit of the earliest commemorations of the Battle of the Nations: the national celebrations of 1814, the Wartburg Festival of 1817 and the Hambach Festival of 1832.[7] The pending mass events in Leipzig were countered with small-scale festivities, including sport games, singing folk songs, folk dancing, and a performance of Goethe's *Iphigenie*. But the open renunciation of German historical culture by a small, but increasingly audible part of youth was hard to grasp for contemporary commentators. These activities were hard to place in the political spectrum of Wilhelmine Germany.[8]

What appears as a renunciation of German historical culture was not, in fact, as radical as it seems. The gathering of thirteen youth groups at the Hohe Meißner did not renounce patriotism or nationalism per se, but the kind of patriotism that applauded the achievements of the past, without providing any sense of responsibility towards the future. It was, as one member of the Jung-Wandervogel called it, 'patriotism of the act' rather than 'patriotism of the word' that they proclaimed.[9] The Meißner hill counts as one of the prime *lieux de mémoire* of the German youth movement.[10] The physical location became a site where old and new generations commemorated the origin of their movement, and where they also strove to find self-assurance, new tasks and new identities when confronting new times and new problems in 1923, 1933, 1946, 1963 and 1988.[11] But the Meißner was also a symbolic site of memory, recollecting the spirit of awakening and commencement with which German youth cast off the strains of bourgeois society. The Meißner became the focal point of the narrative of generational revolt with which the movement started fashioning itself, despite having already been in existence for more than a decade. The spirit of revolt and self-determination was captured in what became known as the 'Meißner formula', which read: 'The Freideutsche Jugend is determined to fashion its life on its own initiative, on its own responsibility and in inner sincerity'.[12]

## The Birth of the Wandervogel

The early history of the German youth movement is well known to the extent that it has often been levitated to mythical proportions. It all started with the Wandervogel, a hiking organization for schoolboys that developed in the last decade of the nineteenth century out of the stenography class of the young teacher Hermann Hoffmann. Teaching the Stolze-Schrey shorthand – a stenographic method – at the humanistic gymnasium (grammar school) of the suburban village of Berlin-Steglitz (15,000 residents), Hoffmann often spoke about his holiday hikes to the Harz Mountains, to the Fichtelgebirge in Bavaria and to Venice. Enthusing his pupils, he organized several hikes at their request, from spring 1896 onwards. With extraordinary consent of the parents and the principal – who sent his own son along – Hoffmann and his pupils would undertake several single-day hikes on Sundays, and in the holidays longer expeditions to the Harz (1897), the Rhine (1898) and the Bohemian Forest (1899) were organized.[13]

Hoffmann fashioned these hikes in the style of his own wanderings: 'strenuous hikes, a basic lifestyle on low expenses, cooking on improvised spirit stoves ..., sleeping in village inns, barns, sectional tents, sometimes in middle-class accommodations; sedulous singing (folk songs, *Wanderlieder* and student songs)'.[14] It is important to notice that hiking in a group with pupils of various ages and of different social backgrounds, as Hoffmann did, created a type of comradeship unique in Wilhelmine Germany, where the class and age differences were virtually unbridgeable at school and where social relationships between students were formal and impersonal. Hoffmann's personality and humorous style turned what he jokingly called his 'horde' into a close-knit group of friends during the hike, who nonetheless respected Hoffmann's position as a teacher.[15]

The collective experience was so enthusing that when Hoffmann was appointed to the consulate in Constantinople in 1900, his former student Karl Fischer took up the organization of the hikes, devoted to Hoffmann's request to 'promote this type of youth wandering among German youth beyond the borders of Steglitz'.[16] After Fischer took his final exams, he safeguarded the continuation of the wanderings of the Steglitz stenography students by establishing the *Ausschuß für Schülerfahrten e. V.* in November 1901. This 'Committee for the Organization of School Excursions' consisted of a number of notable Steglitz citizens, including writers and physicians, as well as recent gymnasium graduates Karl Fischer, Bruno Thiede, Siegfried Copalle and Wolf Meyen. The actual body of wanderers now became known as Wandervögel. The name 'Wandervogel' ('migratory bird') was either derived from a popular song based on a poem by Otto Roquette, or found in a poem written on a tombstone that Wolfgang Meyen – the youngest of the early Wandervögel – had stumbled upon on a walk to Berlin-Dahlem.[17] When, after 1904, the committee was rebranded 'Parents and Friends Advisory Council' (*'Eufrat'*), a mere formal status of adult supervision within the Wandervogel was endorsed: the practical leadership was in the hands of the young students or older secondary school pupils who led the hikes. This organizational structure would largely remain the same among the various brands of Wandervogel that developed after the founding of the *Ausschuß für Schülerfahrten* in the Steglitz Town Hall cellar on 4 November 1901.

The early years of the Wandervogel were characterized by the search for a form of hiking. The initial premises for a proper hike had been set by Hoffmann: the young wanderer had to seek an 'independence from the inns' and other institutions of modern travel in order to be able to travel on a low budget.[18] In these early years, the self-fashioning of the Wandervogel was primarily a case of defining oneself in opposition to other travellers. The modern tourist was despised – not yet for being petty bourgeois, but for having traded the Romanticism of the journey for leisure and luxury. The Steglitz schoolboys rather found models in the peddlers and wandering artisans whom they met on the country roads. Ironically the practice of the wandering artisan flourished again in the last decades of the nineteenth century, as journeymen extended their traditional 'three years and a day' *Wanderschaft*, because the fierce competition with factory-produced commodities caused a decrease in available job positions.[19] Wolfgang Meyen, in particular, 'loved every bloke that has gone half mad by the burning sun and moved with tottering knees, covered with fleabites'. He chatted with them on the roads, loved their adventures and wisdoms, and took over their idiom. For Meyen, 'the real romantic Wandervogel is a mixture between a German student, a peddler and a wandering scholar from the Middle Ages'.[20]

This latter source of inspiration had profound influence on the organization of the Wandervogel. Karl Fischer found in the medieval wandering scholars (*Vaganten*; Lat.: vagans/vagus) a model that stood far from modern issues of consumer tourism. Fischer subsequently divided his troop of Wandervögel hierarchically in *Bachanten* (this phonetic transmutation was probably used to avoid association of *Vagant* with the word vagabond – *Vagabund*), *Burschen* and *Scholaren*.[21] The inspiration for framing the Wandervogel as a group of wandering scholars was largely based on the reading of Romantic literature. Clemens Brentano's *Chronika eines fahrenden Schülers* (1818) was passed on among the Wandervogel, and the other German writer and poet, Johann Gottfried Seume, had somewhat become a 'patron saint'.[22] His *Spaziergang nach Syrakus* (1803) was part of the Wandervogel canon. However, older sources such as the memoirs of the humanist scholar Thomas Platter (1499 –1582), Hans Sachs' *Der fahrende Schüler im Paradies* (1550) and Grimmelshausen's *Simplicissimus* (1668) made up a significant part of the Wandervogel corpus. In his student digs, Fischer – now a law and sinology student – told many stories of bygone adventures of wandering scholars to the young Wandervogel. Wolfgang Meyen and Hans Breuer sang many songs, accompanied by the guitar – an instrument that had been forgotten since the Biedermeier era. They sang and relived the words of a well-known student song, originally written by Austrian poet Ottokar Kernstock: 'Sumus de vagantium ordine laudando. Petimus viaticum porro properando'.[23]

At the turn of the century, Steglitz was a town on the outskirts of Berlin, not yet engulfed by the rapidly expanding city, and it was as such a refuge for the educated middle classes who were escaping the city's damp conditions. It was a typical suburb, which housed university professors, pensioned army officers and civil servants who endorsed the Prussianism and historical culture of Wilhelmine society. Heinrich Becker, one of the first Wandervögel, recalled that:

Order and faithfulness were the values that they served: faithfulness to God, king and country. God was the God about whom ministers appointed by the state preached every Sunday ..., the militant God of Luther who in times of need 'made iron grow'. The king was the supreme commander, who was also called 'Emperor of Peace' whenever it better fitted in a celebratory speech. The fatherland was primarily Prussia and its 'shining armour' on land and at sea. That there was also a German Empire was seen as clear proof that God especially loved the Prussian state and that Bismarck – the forger of the empire – was an instrument of God as well as the finisher of Prussian history.[24]

Yet, not everyone in Steglitz was as ardent an advocate of nationalism as the higher echelons of the educated bourgeoisie. There was for example a Catholic minority, as well as a Pentecostal movement, which opposed the rationalism of the Evangelical Church. For the intellectual and ideological development of the Wandervogel, the presence of a number of *völkisch*-oriented authors and artists in Steglitz was important. For the Wandervogel, fuel for criticism of this type of nationalism was also provided by a Classics teacher at the Steglitz gymnasium: Ludwig Gurlitt.

Gurlitt was a noted scholar of Cicero, and also a reform pedagogue who wrote a number of books that were highly critical of both the pedagogical and the nationalistic aspects of German, and especially Prussian, education. The general argument in his work was that the Prussian school overburdened the pupil, and that *Bildung* – the founding principle of German academic and grammar school education – had been forsaken. Instead, education pursued an inferior *Halbbildung* – by which Gurlitt meant the mere absorption of educational material by the pupil without understanding and without appropriation. The general education of the gymnasium only supported mediocrity and disregarded the development of individual traits of character, as it required pupils to subordinate to preconceived ideas on German citizenship. Gurlitt took a stand against almost all bourgeois securities of the Wilhelmine Empire: against the monopolization of faith by the state and against the Prussian-monarchist sense of patriotism that the government required the schools to instil in their pupils. Gurlitt however, was not anti-national, but tried to redefine the national in what he believed to be a less artificial way. He contended that a nation could not be forged through war, propaganda or indoctrination; rather, it 'had to be the task of the coming century to let the political unity be followed by a purely spiritual unity'.[25] This spiritual unity could not be brought about when the genesis of the German nation was presented as a historical necessity, nurtured by the many state-sponsored commemorations of the Wilhelmine Empire: '[T]rue love for the fatherland cannot be generated through official boisterous Sedan Days and other commemorative festivals, through vainglorious national monuments, through a history education fuelled by patriotism'.[26]

His answer to these shortcomings was an education for personality, in which 'personality' comprises the given qualities and character traits of the individual. Personality should not be oppressed by demanding that a child fit into a pattern of expectation, but should be nurtured by teachers who are able to use their own personality to inspire pupils to bring those inborn qualities to fruition. Such pleas for the child's self-education were often heard in reform-pedagogical literature of the time. Nonetheless, Gurlitt caused quite a stir with these views at the German Congress of Philologists and Educators in 1905, as a majority of his colleagues took offence to the idea that children (like women) had a personality in the first place. Preferring 'consciousness' – a more traditional concept in German philosophies of *Bildung* – over 'personality', some critics held on to their belief in the naivety of the child, and argued that education was a moral 'development' of becoming conscious. In that case 'personality' might be the final stage of education. It was, however, unthinkable that a child could be *born* with a personality and could therefore be 'morally neutral'.[27] Pious critics held the opinion that a child is born in sin, and that becoming a devout Christian was the goal of education.[28]

Karl Fischer had a more *völkisch*-nationalist political orientation.[29] The *Oberbachant* Fischer was well informed in the national-conservative literature that the educated middle class of Steglitz read, as were his *Bachanten*. According to Wandervogel Siegfried Copalle, 'all national and *völkisch* authors and poets were known to us: Lagarde, Langbehn, Chamberlain, Gobineau, Bartels, Ammon, Sohnrey, Lienhard and many, many more'.[30] Furthermore, the leadership in the early Wandervogel was influenced by the *völkisch*-national Heimatschutz and Heimatkunst movements, and by the Dürerbund.[31] They read the journals *Der Kunstwart* and *Die Heimat*, and authors from various reform movements such as Ferdinand Avenarius, Paul Schultze-Naumburg and Adolf Damaschke.[32] The word *völkisch* actually entered the Wandervogel in these years as somebody noticed the term in Friedrich Lange's *Deutsche Zeitung*, an ultra-national newspaper that promoted the pan-German cause.[33] Thus, the political outlook of the leadership of the early Wandervogel was to a large extent the same as their parents.[34] In 1962, Walter Laqueur summarized their position: 'The Wandervogel, consciously or unconsciously, was part of the general stream of right-wing nationalism, which in Germany is really a pleonasm; in contrast to other European countries, nationalism there has always been monopolized by the right wing'.[35]

On a *Fahrt*, Fischer would recite from the work of Paul de Lagarde and Julius Langbehn, and he was thoroughly aware of the problematic situation of the German *Volkstum*, which at the time expressed itself most vividly in Austria-Hungary, where tensions between the German and Czech populations were omnipresent.[36] At the age of only thirteen Fischer had stated that, 'all Germans on the earth should create a loyal, conspired community, for the glory and honour of the fatherland'.[37] The 1897 'Badeni crisis' – the Austrian parliamentary crisis about the concessions of Prime Minister Kazimierz Badeni to the use of Czech language in Bohemia and Moravia – had made him aware of the pan-German cause. It was therefore no coincidence that the summer hike of 1903 led to the Bohemian Forest, an Austro-Hungarian region where the language and culture conflict between the Germans and Slavs had reached boiling point. Here, the Wandervogel showed special interest in the work of the Settlement Committee (*Ansiedlungskommision*), which aimed at increasing 'German' land ownership at the expense of the Czech population.[38] The greeting 'Heil' – that would become common in the Wandervogel movement – was borrowed from the Austrian *deutschvölkisch* students who had introduced it in the 1890s.[39] Through a Wandervogel-schoolmate whose father – Paul Förster – had an influential position in the Pan-German League, the Wandervögel were invited to attend their solstice celebration at the Müggelberge in 1902 and 1903.[40] The solstice celebration, which was an expression of Germanic nationalism and anti-Semitism, would eventually become a prime event in the Wandervogel calendar, albeit in a less political way. Nonetheless, Karl Fischer's early Wandervogel was, in its search for a proper model, clearly influenced by the national and *völkisch* thinking of their parents, many of whom – including Förster – would be involved in the movement as members of the *Eurfrat*.[41]

In 1904, a cultural difference between upper-middle class and lower-middle class members, as well as an aversion to Fischer's rather authoritarian leadership, led to the first of many breaks within the Wandervogel. Fischer's opponents continued in the *Wandervogel, Eingetragener Verein zu Steglitz* (Steglitzer e.V.) under the leadership of Siegfried Copalle. The *Alt-Wandervogel* (AWV) proceeded under the leadership of Karl Fischer.[42] The difference between the AWV and the Steglitzer e.V. was a matter of style and art of wandering. While the AWV aimed at the continuation of the established tradition of Romantic *Bachantentum*, the Steglitzer e.V. was a matter of a more intellectual and aesthetic wandering.[43] They abolished the 'Romantic' idiom in favour of more neutral terms: *Bachant* simply became *Führer* (leader), the term *Fahrt* was changed in favour of the terms *Reise* (journey) and *Ausflüge* (trip). The Steglitzer e.V. did not strive for a more 'touristic' approach to wandering, but noted that '"Fahrt" had something artificial for us as if we were not speaking of us as the living, but of miniature knights'.[44]

Karl Fischer founded the Alt-Wandervogel in autumn 1904. The feeling of being betrayed by the Steglitzer e.V. was omnipresent and he accused the Steglitzer e.V. of accepting too many teachers in its ranks. Because the e.V. was chaired by Ludwig Gurlitt, they were said to have attracted too many 'pedagogical freethinkers' who disacknowledged the value of wandering. The association was also accused of forsaking the tradition of harshness and boldness in favour of intellectualism.[45] But whereas the Steglitzer e.V. reached out into the world of science and culture to find meaning for hiking, the AWV turned inwards and strengthened the bond with its leader Karl Fischer in an atmosphere of masculine loyalty, resembling the ideal of the *Männerbund*, which would become a widespread doctrine in the broader youth movement after the First World War.[46]

One member of the Alt-Wandervogel – Hanz Atzrott – later recalled how Karl Fischer 'spoke to us about German spirit and German loyalty. We felt connected to him in real masculine loyalty [*Mannentreue*]'.[47] From this perspective, it may not surprise that when in 1906 the Jena-chapter of the AWV proposed the introduction of girls into the association, this proposal was rejected. Only from 1911 onwards were girls accepted in the AWV, and then only in distinct 'girls-only' chapters. Wandering together, which was not uncommon in the Steglitzer e.V., would never be accepted in the AWV. The AWV would remain the most conservative of all Wandervogel associations and would carry on both the ideals of vagrancy and the legacy of Karl Fischer, long after he was dispatched as a soldier to the German colony of Qingdao in China in 1906.

## Modes of Wandering

The quest for intellectual renewal in the Steglitzer e.V. had not yet resulted in the construction of a distinct group identity, which would only become prominent around 1910. Yet, the Steglitzer e.V. contributed significantly to the reflection on the means and purposes of hiking, beyond the level of schoolboy adventure. Primarily, they wanted 'to refine and deepen wanderings through fostering transmitted cultural property'.[48] The fact that almost the entire leadership of the Steglitzer e.V. consisted of university students contributed to the more intellectual scope of the association. A first result of the more reflective focus was the cultivation of singing. In 1905 a Wandervogel songbook was printed as an attempt to gather a corpus of songs which expressed the 'spirit' of the Wandervogel. The *Wandervogel-Liederbuch* was composed of songs which had proven to resonate within the movement: predominantly songs derived from songbooks of student and gymnastics associations, with a few older folk songs from the published collection of musicologist Max Friedlaender.[49] It was through the music teacher at the Steglitz gymnasium, Max Pohl – who tended to sing old folk songs that he discovered in the books of Friedlaender and other collectors like Hans Magnus Böhme and Rochus von Liliencron – that the folk song entered the Wandervogel.[50]

The hiking practice of the Steglitzer e.V. differed significantly from the old days. Siegfried Copalle criticized Fischer's strenuous hikes for their unreflective attitude and their inability to pay proper attention to the surroundings: 'Leaning forward, even without a backpack, the eyes on the ground, vigorously paddling with the arms, they trotted along like they were facing an enemy'.[51] Lighthearted wandering, exposing receptivity towards the landscape, and displaying an affirmative attitude towards life in general would fit the Wandervögel better if they wanted to wander in a 'meaningful' way.[52] In practice, the Steglitzer e.V. still tended to hike in large groups of sometimes forty or fifty people; wandering in small groups of six to eight people was a later innovation. War games were played in the open, and every wanderer cooked his own meal along the way. Pupils of different ages wandered together, and at this moment, personal relationships still bore the formality of public life. It was, however, not the 'outer forms of the hiking technique' which the Steglitzer e.V. sought to change – instead, most important for the Wandervogel was an 'inner, intellectual content, a real art of wandering'.[53] Without denouncing the value of strenuous long-distance hikes, which was already under scrutiny by 1905, Copalle explored the possibilities of a 'Kritik des reinen Gehens'.[54] It was a plea for a wandering deprived from the gaudy sentimentalism of medieval vagrancy. Simply light hearted being on the road, on the tedious country roads of Brandenburg, was for Copalle a goal in itself. It may not surprise that his AWV opponents recognized a return to modern tourism in pleas like this.

More influential in the construction of a collective Wandervogel identity, in reflecting on the purposes of hiking and in introducing a coherent social criticism in the movement, was Frank Fischer (not related to Karl Fischer), a student in Germanic philology and co-founder of the Steglitzer e.V. Fischer too grew up in a family with strong nationalist orientations: he read the *Deutsche Zeitung* and had a reserved attitude towards Jews. These orientations and tendencies would, however, dwindle during his study and during his time in the Wandervogel.[55] Although acknowledging that he was not really into questions of ideology and worldview, he admitted in 1906 that he had once pondered about the question of the free will. In so far as it concerned the then often discussed 'battle of *Weltanschauung*', Fischer discerned between the 'national, militaristic and vocational understanding' represented by the publisher of the *völkisch*-nationalist *Deutsche Zeitung*, Friedrich Lange, and the 'youthful individualistic mindset' of his friends of the Wandervogel.[56]

As national thinking especially urged the middle-class citizen to vocationally support the national cause, the identity of the individual was often equal to his profession. In Wilhelmine Germany, public and private life overlapped to such an extent that one did not hold a post as teacher, minister, jurist or government official, but one *lived* the life of, for example, a teacher. Although these typical *Bildungsbürgerliche* professions held a high social esteem – not least as compensation for the lack of political representation – the prospect of entering such a profession had a stifling effect on those young Wandervögel who were on the brink of making career choices. Frank Fischer at least concluded that 'man is not his profession, but more'.[57] In this light, it may not surprise that he was a strong proponent of engaging one another in the Wandervogel with the cordial 'du' instead of the formal 'Sie'. This could have been the start of engaging the other as a fellow human, instead of a social type.

The impact of the deformalization of social relations in the Wandervogel must not be underestimated. It was a first step in the acknowledgement that the typified world of the educated middle classes reduced the individual to being subject to social values, to the state, to the nation – in sum: to history. The youth movement's answer was, however, not just to reclaim the autonomy of the subject, but to declare the entire idea of typification, and therewith the entire idea of typified thinking, to be a mere effect of modern adulthood. The world of adulthood was 'objective' in the twofold meaning of the word: both a realm of objectified social relationships and an unavoidable goal in life. After all, was not the ultimate goal of youth to incorporate into society? By claiming youth to be a phase of life not yet 'corrupted' by adult mores, the Wandervogel would frame themselves as standing closer to life than adults who depended on social expectation and conformation. In Frank Fischer's years with the Steglitzer e.V., he would not endorse these arguments – this rhetoric would rise in the early 1910s – but he did make a similar distinction between the motif of the wanderer and that of the 'tourist'.

Drawing inspiration from a broad range of authors, including Wilhelm Heinrich Riehl, Gottfried Keller, Friedrich Nietzsche,[58] and most of all from the young author Hermann Hesse, Frank Fischer acknowledged that wandering was neither a physical exercise, nor a light-hearted, playful activity. Wandering was acquisition. Meaningful wandering required a conscientious effort. It was all too easy to conform to the conventional gaze with which the Baedecker travel guide prompts one to look at one's environment. However, Fischer argued, if you call a site beautiful just because it lives up to the expectations created by the travel guide, the site itself has no real value and becomes interchangeable. Here he introduced the notion of *Erlebnis* (direct or immediate experience) as a means to appropriate a site without the mediation of the interpretive templates of travel guides:

> Travel should always mean immediate experience, and one can only experience something valuable in environments to which one is connected emotionally. An occasional jolly outing, a merry evening in some beer garden, or a boat trip on a random lake are in themselves not experiences; [they provide] no enrichment of our lives, no increasingly strengthening impulses.[59]

For Frank Fischer, wandering meant having a deeper connection with the area you visit – an understanding of the way in which a city or landscape has evolved historically – not as a coincidence, but as a necessity. In a region one visits, nothing is isolated from its surroundings. It is the wanderer's duty to understand whatever he encounters as being an integral and causal part of the environment. Such an understanding requires as well a thorough preparation and knowledge of the region as an adaptation to it. According to Fischer's source, Hermann Hesse, one can wish the 'Venetians to be more spirited, the Neapolitans to be quieter, the Bernese to be more polite, the chianti to be sweeter and the coastal lagoons to be steeper', but a true understanding of the visited region only comes with the unprejudiced ability to be sincerely surprised about whatever will cross your path.[60] When one is able to have such an understanding, people, landscapes, customs and cuisines are not judged by the standards of the purportedly civilized, but on their own merits.

The moral and intellectual superiority of the bourgeois tourist had no place in Hesse's art of travel; it was the ability to see the characteristics of a region and the unprejudiced openness to experiencing these elements that made travel in general and wandering in particular worthwhile. These abilities did not require a specific object of interest, such as purportedly beautiful scenery or a Baedecker-featured historical landmark, but might provide a meaningful experience of every environment the wanderer encounters. Getting away from the beaten track may often open up unexpected environments. For Hesse, the art of wandering was in the end an art of life:

> A strong nostalgia for the sources of life, and a desire to feel cordial and unified with all living, creating, growing things, is their key to the mysteries of the world, which they happily and eagerly pursue not only in foreign travels, but in the rhythm of daily life and experience as well.[61]

Wandering as a 'free and intellectual vital activity', as Frank Fischer put it, strongly opposed the AWV's 'nature-boy romanticism, which imitated alleged wandering scholarship'.[62] In fact, the 'tendency towards the *Altdeutsche*', which can be directed back to Karl Fischer, works 'unintentionally comical' on the beholder. In its continuation of this Romantic tradition, the AWV was blamed for having created a new conventionalism itself, founded on the basis of an intimate group culture with its own slang and customs. The historical 'masquerade' thus reinvented the problematic disposition of bourgeois wandering it initially opposed: the tendency to interpret the world in pre-established frames of reference.[63]

Although the construction of a specific Wandervogel identity had only just begun, between 1905 and 1907 the movement quickly expanded beyond the Berlin area. While the Steglitzer e.V. never really surpassed the level of a local Brandenburgian association, the AWV would go nationwide with large departments in, for example, Hamburg, Leipzig and Frankfurt. In 1907, the AWV counted approximately 1,600 members and the e.V. 639.[64] Members who moved to another city with their parents or who went to university founded new chapters – a development that made the Wandervogel a nationwide phenomenon within a decade.

## Self-definition and Cultural Criticism

When, in 1907, chapters from Jena and Delmenhorst split from the Alt-Wandervogel over the issue of girls, not only was a new Wandervogel-association born but a new phase in the history of the movement commenced. The new Wandervogel, Deutscher Bund für Jugendwanderungen (DB) would take a leading role and contribute decisively to the self-understanding of the various Wandervogel associations. Not only did the DB encourage wandering among girls, but also among classes other than the *Bildungsbürgertum*. The majority of the members of the DB were students at an *Oberrealschule* or a *Realgymnasium* – schools in which the teaching of science had prevalence over the classical languages. Even pupils from the common *Volksschule* were accepted; as a consequence the DB generally represented the left-liberalism of the new urban middle classes, rather than the conservatism of the higher and educated middle classes.[65]

The consumption of alcohol – another issue of conflict in the AWV – was forbidden (later nicotine would follow), and local chapters were given a larger autonomy than in the AWV. The fact that the DB quickly gained popularity was partly due to its abstinence. The DB leader, Ferdinand Vetter, was a convinced follower of the *Lebensreform* movement, and was an active member of the Deutsche Bund abstinenter Studenten (DBaSt). The initial success of the DB was a result of the constructive cooperation of his friends from the DBaSt as Wandervogel leaders, and of the participation of members of Germania, Abstinentenbund an deutschen Schulen as Wandervögel.

The focus on abstinence would, however, not drastically alter their practice of hiking, for alcohol consumption had never really been a serious problem within the movement. The most significant change can be found in the revitalization of wandering as an art, and the construction of a Wandervogel identity and self-awareness on this very basis. Despite the fact that the DB came from the ranks of the AWV, the continuity with the 'meaningful wandering' of the Steglitzer e.V. was greater. The DB too renounced the cult of wandering scholarship as a false Romanticism, and aimed at a reorientation of wandering as an art in the light of German authors and poets Ernst Moritz Arndt, Friedrich Ludwig Jahn and Riehl. To them, wandering was neither a vehicle for 'playing' a medieval scholar or a vagabond after reading, for example, a play by Hans Sachs, nor was it a more developed form of playing cowboys and Indians after reading the novels of Karl May. No – wandering was a moral activity. This revitalization was mainly the merit of the friends and DB leaders Hans Breuer and Hans Lißner, whose Wandervogel academic circle from Heidelberg, the Pachantey, would become the carrier of the construction of a distinct 'Wandervogel culture'.[66]

The life of Hans Breuer represents the development of the self-conception of the Wandervogel. As the son of a glass manufacturer, he moved to Berlin-Friedenau as a 16-year-old, entered the gymnasium at Steglitz, and by 1899 he had participated in the hike with Hoffmann to the Bohemian Forest. Here, the otherwise reserved boy blossomed and 'discovered another world and developed another character'.[67] In the years that followed, it was Breuer who, together with Wolf Meyen, imitated the manners and idiom of journeymen and vagabonds, including the comradely interaction, the singing of beer songs and the revolutionary songs of 1848, and who supported a loose clothing style and equally loose personal hygiene. Breuer followed Karl Fischer in the AWV and kept wandering in Fischer's 'harsh' style while studying medicine in Marburg, Tübingen and Munich. When he changed to study in Heidelberg, he joined the Wandervogel DB with his Heidelberger Pachantey. As the name indicated, the Heidelberger Pachantey was also founded in line with the cult of the wandering scholar. However, the involvement in the DB, which led to the supervision of a group of Wandervogel girls with whom a harsh wandering would not have resonated, would eventually make him to abandon the harsh and wild Romanticism in favour of a more cultivated and ideological Wandervogel-style. When, in 1910, Breuer became leader of the entire DB and his friend Hans Lißner became editor of their journal, the influence of the Heidelberger Pachantey on the broader movement reached its peak.[68]

Within the AWV, the criticism of the cult of the wandering scholar and the imitation of journeymen and drifters had grown stronger as well, and they too looked to the DB for answers. In this way, the DB in general and the Heidelberger Pachantey in particular became sources of inspiration for the entire Wandervogel movement. Questions on wandering with girls and *Volksschüler*, on abstinence, on the acquisition of *Landheime*, on sleeping accommodation, and eventually on the unification of the broader Wandervogel movement were widely discussed and, under the auspices of the DB, the Wandervogel gained its well known outer appearance. The days of wandering in a school uniform were gone. The loden suit which had already been propagated by the Steglitzer e.V. became common, and shorts were introduced as well. Most characteristic was the introduction of the Schiller collar, which replaced the standing collar. The adaptation of a distinct clothing style thus became one of their first explicit attempts to distance themselves from bourgeois society. Especially for the girls this may be called revolutionary, for wearing a 'dirndl gown' and pigtails made quite a difference.[69] The distinct clothing style not only testified to the influence of the life reform movement, but to a new interest as well: an interest in peasantry and folk culture.[70]

With Breuer, the voice of cultural criticism became more audible in the Wandervogel, as his attempts to give meaning to the practice of wandering were directly oriented against the problematic aspects of modern society. The most innovative contribution to the construction of a Wandervogel culture was the discovery of the folk song. In 1909, Breuer published a songbook called the *Zupfgeigenhansl*, which became an instant hit. It contained a selection of historical songs, religious songs and folk songs, part of which he and his friends had collected themselves during their hikes in the countryside. The goal was to provide the youth movement with a collection of songs to sing in gatherings and during hikes. This would stimulate group life better than the student drinking songs that were still often sung. The discovery of old songs hidden in the waning traditional folklore of Germany's rural areas instilled the Wandervögel with the sense of awakening. Wandervogel Otto Bojarzin compared this discovery to the awakening of Grimm's Sleeping Beauty after years of sleep.[71]

In 1910, Breuer and Lißner initiated a merger of the different Wandervogel associations. It took, however, until 1912 for a common agreement to be established, and the Wandervogel DB, the Steglitzer e.V., and a large part of the Alt-Wandervogel merged in the 'Wandervogel e.V., Bund für deutsches Jugendwandern' (short: Wandervogel e.V.). Although the Alt-Wandervogel continued to exist, two-thirds of its local chapters went over to the Wandervogel e.V. The Jung-Wandervogel – a group with radical views on the autonomy of youth, which split from the AWV in 1910 – also refused the merger. When the Freideutsche Jugend was established in 1913, the involvement of other reform-oriented youth groups and associations provided the critique of German historical culture with new arguments.

## Gustav Wyneken, *Der Anfang* and the Critique of Historical Education

Although criticism of the school system had been aired in the Wandervogel, it did not play a significant part in its self-definition as a youth movement. Perhaps the most ardent criticism of the school system appeared in *Der Anfang*, a journal of grammar school students edited by the reform pedagogue Gustav Wyneken, which was published monthly in 1913 and 1914.[72] The journal became one of the most audible propagators of the autonomy of youth before the war. The articles were a call to consciousness of youth as a social force that was solely responsible for shaping its own life, and were primarily directed against the philistinism of the German and Austrian educational tradition. In the first edition, in an article published under the pseudonym 'Ardor', the young Walter Benjamin – a former pupil of Wyneken – argued for the return of judgement in history and German courses. Literary history had been the history of literary styles, and literary classics were read as such – with emphasis on grammar, syntax and the skills of translation – but with no interest in the meaning or depth of its contents.[73] The next edition saw another rant against the philistinism and the 'false Romanticism' of the school by Benjamin.[74] This criticism of the educational system was validated by the Berlin schoolboy Richard Werner, who testified out of personal experience that the educational system systematically failed to connect history to the present. Rather than learning to critically understand the genesis of the contemporary social order: 'we learn by heart which army corps stood at Gravelotte; we burden our heads with endless columns of figures, and in class we repeat back the words of the history teacher by uttering dates mixed with meaningless phrases'. He concluded that apparently Germany did not want 'a thinking and acting population, but a mindless one that only parrots dogmas'.[75]

To a large extent, the critique of historical culture aired in *Der Anfang* was inspired by what Gustav Wyneken had published in his 1913 book *Schule und Jugendkultur*.[76] Wyneken had developed and promoted the idea that youth had to create its own culture, rather than adapting uncritically to the cultural mainstream. He had been a teacher at the reform boarding school in Haubinda for almost a decade, and since 1906 he was the leader of his own well-known reform school in Wickersdorf. His pedagogical and philosophical thoughts were a mixture of an idealism of spirit and a Nietzschean vitalism, of which the latter was of crucial importance.

In 1874, Friedrich Nietzsche had published the second part of his *Unzeitgemäße Betrachtungen: Vom Nutzen und Nachteil der Historie für das Leben*, in which he criticized the belief that man is the product of history and objected to the way history was treated in education: as an end in itself. The deep conviction that the essence of man could be found in his historicity meant that history in itself became the focal point of education and that the culturally educated German understood himself as someone with a special knowledge about the cultural and historical achievements of the German nation. None of this, Nietzsche contended, contributed to the continuous creative process of life. The 'historical education of modern man' placed a heavy burden on the future-oriented, creative aspects of life; and the philistine conception of culture forgot that culture is not a set of fixed assets to boast about, but something to be shaped continuously.[77] In the midst of these pessimistic ruminations, Nietzsche put his hopes on youth, 'for youth still possesses that instinct of nature which remains intact until artificially and forcibly shattered by this education'.[78] And with this 'instinct of nature', Nietzsche meant the vital impulses to actively shape one's own life and the future of one's own nation. But first, youth had to free life itself from the 'malady of history'. Because 'excess of history has attacked life's plastic powers; it no longer knows how to employ the past as a nourishing food'.[79]

This critique of the 'historical education' of modern man served as an inspiration for Wyneken's ideas on *Jugendkultur*. Wyneken stated that throughout the course of history, youth had always been deprived of cultural participation and took no part in the spiritual life of a people. The school still 'confined' youth. In the parental home, youth was expected to imitate adults in behaviour and opinion.[80] Now was the time for youth to actively participate in the cultural process and to shape culture by itself. With 'youth culture', he meant culture per se, as shaped by youth. Although refusing to give a final definition, Wyneken defined culture in Nietzschean terms as 'a unity, a uniform feeling, a style, a common instinct, which expresses itself creatively'.[81] But for a theory of youth culture, Wyneken surprisingly resorted to idealist, mainly Hegelian, phraseology. Drawing a clear distinction between a materialist bourgeois philistinism and the spiritual character of youth, Wyneken argued that it was youth that clung to absolute values that it sought to realize. Therefore youth was the dialectic antithesis of the material adult world.[82]

Wyneken's Hegelianism was also the basis of his critique of history education. He discerned three stages in the education of history. The first is the stage of naivety: historical facts and events function merely as benchmarks for personal interest. Its antithesis is found in a 'critical-objective' education that teaches that historical events are not isolated occurrences, but necessities of natural law, and tries to understand it objectively without prejudice. The third stage, which Wyneken believed was imminent, was the synthesis of both earlier stages. In this stage, man is still aware of the forces that have shaped history and humanity – but now he believes that 'humanity has outgrown its hitherto passive role, that it stands before the awakening that a teleological view of history is increasingly valid, namely in the sense that mankind will determine its own objectives'.[83] In the light of these three stages, history education had a moral task: to teach that the world into which one is born is not just the result of the development of an objective spirit that governs over man through the state, through institutions and tradition, but that this world is liable for change and that man has the autonomy to achieve this. A passive conception of history had to make way for an active one, which had to clarify how the course of history testifies to the struggle of spirit for autonomy.

But in order to enable schools to contribute to a *Jugendkultur*, school reforms were necessary. Contributing to school reform was what Wyneken wanted to be the prime challenge of the Freideutsche Jugend. It was a call not easily accepted by everyone involved in the project of the Freideutsche Jugend – many regarded Wyneken's involvement as an attempt to hijack the young movement for his own programme. Wyneken's relationship with the Wandervogel was equally problematic, as he had been critical of the Wandervogel, who in his eyes had a too Romantic orientation to the past, which was unproductive and could not bring new spiritual-intellectual culture about.[84] The problematic relationship between Wyneken and the broader youth movement became clear in 1913.

## The Spirit of 1813

The commemoration of the Battle of Leipzig offered a first public opportunity for the youth movement to posit an alternative way of approaching the past. The first announcement issued by the organizational committee stated: 'Above all we hate the fruitless patriotism, which only debauches in words and feelings, which delightedly orients itself backwards – often at the expense of historical truth – without setting itself new goals'.[85] The Freideutsche Jugendtag was thus not meant to be a display against patriotism per se, but a display against a certain form of patriotism, namely the kind that takes the nation for granted and lavishes itself on the great accomplishments and monumental actions of one's forebears, without contemplating on one's own responsibility with regard to the nation. Such a use of history also made the public vulnerable to abuse by political parties and currents to rally the public for their particular aim.[86]

This position was widely shared in the youth movement. The Jung-Wandervogel stressed the value of 'patriotism of the deed' over 'patriotism of the word', and regretted that 'thousands will let these days pass, without generating the courage for new actions, for fresh, active patriotism'.[87] A Silesian Wandervogel criticized the public commemorations of the Battle of Leipzig and the Napoleonic wars for remaining without any moral obligation. For the vast majority of Germans the commemoration was a temporary uproar of patriotic frenzy, after which life would settle as before. He argued that in a couple of years the Leipzig monument, as well as the many other memorial stones and columns, would be passed by with the same indifference with which one passes by the war memorials of the Wars of German Unification.[88]

The Thurinigian Wandervogel Karl Balser attacked contemporary memory culture for endorsing a blind national pride at the expense of a naive interpretation of the foreign. He supported the 'more silent' voices in Germany, who based their patriotism on their 'strong feeling for the cohesion of the people' and on 'their proud consciousness of the true virtues of the German past'.[89] The youth movement was one of these more silent voices. 'True' German virtues were something different from an 'appropriation' or 'construction' of a national identity through historical narrative or through an aesthetic reception of German landscape.

Balser's comment was more than a critique of German patriotism as a lamentable form of nationalism. It also contained a refutation of the epistemological premises of German nationalism, which – since liberalism had resorted to positivism in the mid nineteenth century – had seen history as the domain of man's intentional action and could thus establish a direct causal connection between the events of 1813 and the rise of the German Empire. For the youth movement this was morally unjustifiable, because what it meant to be German was defined by history and not by oneself, and what one ought to do in life was equated to what had been done previously. Instead, a different interpretation of nationalism that was morally justifiable was found in the forgotten tradition of German idealism. Balser quite easily summarized the youth movement's nationalism by connecting idealism to the Wandervogel's very practical engagement with folk culture:

> Because we trace German character in many of its primordial expressions – e.g. the folk song – and in the monuments of real German culture (and not just the past) and learn to respect it, but also recognize the errors of our own – in short, because we let spirit step in besides the purely exterior elements of patriotism – which is:

the understanding of and the respect for the will, the aspiration and the longing of the German people throughout the centuries up until our own days.[90]

On 11 October 1913, more than two thousand members and representatives of various youth associations gathered at the Meißner hill in Hesse. Many of these associations were student associations in which former Wandervögel had found an academic home, such as the Deutsche Akademische Freischar, the romantically inclined Serakreis from Jena, and the Akademische Vereinigung in Marburg and in Jena. Other associations present included Wyneken's Freie Schulgemeinde from Wickersdorf, and *Lebensreform* associations such as the Deutscher Bund abstinenter Studenten, Germania and the Bund abstinenter Schüler. Although the Jungwandervogel was present, as well as the Bund deutscher Wanderer from Hamburg, the Alt-Wandervogel and Wandervogel e.V. were not officially represented. While dance, songs and plays represented the social life of the various youth organizations, the speeches of leaders and invited speakers such as the theologian Gottfried Traub, the poet Ferdinand Avenarius, and Gustav Wyneken conveyed the meaning of the gathering.

In his opening speech on the evening before the celebration festivities, Bruno Lemke – Wandervogel, member of the Akademische Vereinigung Marburg and co-organizer – immediately drew the implications of the youth movement's critique of German historical culture. Rather than seeing the events of 1813 as founding events of the German state, he shifted attention from these accomplishments to the spirit, attitude, hope and strife of the younger generation of a hundred years ago. In comparison, present-day youth lacked the unity derived from a shared goal, fragmented as it was as a result of the political and confessional disputes of the previous decades. The youth of 1813 stood unified by adhering to a common idea – the idea of a German Empire. Whether or not this idea could actually be accomplished was irrelevant to the way in which it had replenished German culture and to the way it provided a focal point for constitutive and creative action for an entire generation. In a similar way, contemporary youth should define a leading idea to overcome both its own fragmentation and to become carriers of a creative culture. To become a 'carrier of culture' meant for Lemke not simply appropriating what has been transmitted, but meant an 'inner co-creation, from which one's own vitality grows and invigorates – for youth should not merely appropriate culture, but should someday also carry it forth'.[91]

By defining the task of youth this way, Lemke implied that the problem of Wilhelmine Germany was that it fostered a petrified understanding of culture, in which culture comprised a set of historically given facts and values to be internalized by the younger generation. By praising the 'spirit' of 1813 rather than the historical events, he put his own understanding of culture into practice. Lemke thus put the past in the service of the future, as he encouraged his own generation to act creatively.

## The Self-Education of Youth as a Revival of German Idealism

The adage of creative action was mainly derived from Johann Gottlieb Fichte's *Addresses to the German Nation* – a series of speeches delivered in Berlin in 1807 and 1808, in which the philosopher called for the national education of the politically inexistent German nation in opposition to French domination. It was a plea for a national regeneration on Germany's own account, free from foreign templates. The arguments that Fichte put forward were used by the youth movement to answer the question of education, of how to relate to the demands of a state and society alien to youth.

In his speech on the Meißner, Gottfried Traub nonetheless emphasized that the Freideutsche Jugend's commemoration of 1813 was not dominated by the spirit of Fichte, but by 'cheers and band music'.[92] What did this mean? Fichte was not commemorated as the fierce proponent for a virulent nationalism that still resonates in historiography today.[93] Rather, Fichte was valued for the more subtle logic that framed his thoughts on the nation as the goal of moral education. The main idea, which was derived from Fichte's *Addresses*, was, as the philosopher Eugen Kühnemann summarized it to the Freideutsche Jugend: 'the world – that is just you'.[94] The task was to be an 'I' ('*Ich*') and therefore to be the world. This meant that at such a moment the world is imperative to the 'I' – nature is imperative thought, morality is imperative will, and God is imperative faith. 'The complete man would in this sense be a piece of living knowledge, morality, beauty and religion at once. To him the world was a single imperative of his spirit, a single spiritual act of the I.'[95] In this logic it makes no sense to regard the world as something external to the I, something that does not require commitment, for this would render life meaningless and would denounce the I existence and freedom. This would be the case if one takes transmitted ideas on truth, morality or aesthetics for granted. It was therefore Kühnemann's call to the youth movement to 'think, work, create, believe, as if nothing from the past binds and constrains you'.[96] However, this was not meant as a rejection of old ideas. The I could not simply be established in binary opposition to what came before, because this implies remaining bound to it. Rather, it was the task to carry personal responsibility for the world in which and with whom one lives.

The revival of idealism in the youth movement had one significant consequence for the conception of time implicit in this idealism. The old Neokantian philosopher Paul Natorp – the academic 'mentor' of the Akademische Vereinigung Marburg – remarked that the term 'Freideutsch' referred to little less than what Fichte meant with 'free' ('*frei*') and 'German' ('*Deutsch*'). In his seventh address, Fichte explained that 'free' appeared to be the outstanding feature of Germanness: the already mentioned ability to educate oneself in spiritual independence of external influences. The prime lesson Natorp drew from Fichte for the youth movement was that such an education required freedom and responsibility, but that education could never be oriented towards the particular, towards what was manifest and realized in time:

> Exactly from him we should have learned that freedom is an idea, the existence of which is granted as little as the idea of community. The existent community does not need to educate the community that already is, but has to educate the eternally becoming community to the eternally becoming. Neither does a Self that already is have to educate this Self (this makes no sense), but the becoming Self the becoming.[97]

Identity is defined as never finished, as something continuously becoming, and as such as a perennial task of every individual and collective anew. And as all identities are continuously becoming, identity cannot be established in binary opposition to an Other, for the Other is in flux as well.

At the Meißner, these insights were expressed in the creation of what became known as the 'Meißner formula', the programmatic maxim that I have quoted earlier, on which all the associations present could agree: 'The Freideutsche Jugend is determined to fashion its life on its own initiative, on its own responsibility and in inner sincerity'.[98] Nonetheless, this call for moral autonomy in the constitution of identity would not remain undisputed. Soon after the establishment of the Freideutsche Jugend, fears rose that the new movement was being used by *Lebensreformer* and by educational reformers such as Wyneken to promote their own agendas.

The conflict came to a head at a meeting in Marburg in 1914, where Paul Natorp and Ferdinand Avenarius, the editor of the journal *Der Kunstwart*, took sides with a fraction of former Wandervogel against the more radical *Anfang* circle around Gustav Wyneken. The discussion focused on the issue of the extent to which the quest for the autonomy of world constitution necessarily implied a rejection of existing culture. Opposing Wyneken by claiming that youth was part of a larger process of cultural development, Natorp stressed that self-cultivation is a process unfolding in stages, which does not commence with emancipation from all traditional bonds and social constraints, but merely results in it. Self-cultivation in self-chosen communities was something better suited to those who were at the age of the university student, rather than the schoolboys who made up the editorial team of *Der Anfang*.[99]

The conclusion at Marburg was that the Freideutsche Jugend was to be an addendum to traditional educational institutions like the school and the family, rather than a surrogate.[100] The outcome was a revised formula, that read:

> The Freideutsche Jugend is a community of youth organizations, whose common ground is to be created and sustained by youth, and whose common goal is to complement values gained and transmitted by the older generation through a development of its own strengths, on its own responsibility, with inner sincerity. Every alignment with economical, religious, or political affiliations is rejected.[101]

Wyneken's radical quest for historical discontinuity had been replaced by the task of the continuing appropriation and adaptation of transmitted values to the requirements of the age.

## Conclusion

The German youth movement commenced with the Wandervogel, which gained popularity in the early 1900s as a hiking association. As the Wandervogel expanded, so did its self-conception. As a bourgeois association with mainly higher-educated members, the Wandervogel initially resorted to the kind of *völkisch* ideology which was at hand in the parental home. Later, partly under influence of the *Lebensreformbewegung*, the Wandervogel got increasingly acquainted with the discourse of cultural criticism in the German Empire and set itself moral goals. The movement understood itself as an educational sphere next to the parental home and the school, in which the self-education of 'personality' was the prime goal. Subsequently, in defining its own style, the Wandervogel discovered folk culture in which it found replenishment for the problems associated with modernity.

As the Wandervogel grew older and a greater number of its members flocked to university, various academic equivalents of the Wandervogel were established. In the Freideutsche Jugend the question of history was discussed in a more intellectual and less practical way. With regard to historical culture, criticism boiled down to two focal points: historical education and public commemoration. The recurrent argument was that German history was presented as a fait accompli, which in school was the result of a positivist scientific emphasis on facts and events rather than ideas, and in public commemoration the result of the attempt to legitimize the social and political structures of the Wilhelmine Empire by historicizing them. Answers to these problems were found in establishing the youth movement as a movement for the self-education of the individual and the community. This idea of self-education was thematized in a Fichtean phraseology as an autonomous operation in which history had no educational value of its own. History only had meaning and value to the extent that it was part of the free process in which the 'I' constitutes the world.

This supports David James's thesis that Fichte's *Addresses* 'anticipated' the argument that the study of history has no value on its own, but that it should be put in service of life, as Friedrich Nietzsche put forward in his essay *On the Use and Abuse of History for Life*.[102] That is to say, in the youth movement Fichte was attributed the function Nietzsche could have had as the intellectual source from which arguments against the historical culture of Wilhelmine Germany were drawn. As Christian Niemeyer has argued, Nietzsche was only rarely read in the youth movement before the war, arguably because schools and parents saw a danger in Nietzsche's 'immoral' ideas and in his destructive critique of

German nationalism. Fichte posed no such threat, but provided likewise arguments for an education not burdened by inherited dogmas imposed on the younger generation.[103]

Traditional points of interest for the youth movement fitted in these goals of moral education, as it was argued that folk culture, rather than modern culture, was an expression of authenticity. It was the disappearing – but still existing – proof that an original culture was still within grasp. And although the danger of becoming 'salon farmers' by naively imitating folk culture and turning it into masquerades was omnipresent, the educational aim that the youth movement's leadership advocated was directed at valuing folklore for its authenticity.[104] When Hans Breuer asked how new culture could be established in the 'unredeemed age of technology, industry and science', his answer was 'to become German again' through a 'natural education' of wandering over 'old Frankish streets', and passing by grand 'gothic cathedral towers'.[105] By rooting these educational goals in the forgotten tradition of German idealism – notably in the philosophy of Fichte – the youth movement constructed an educational programme which depended on the self-constitution of identity.

Yet, the revival of German idealism did not entail a revival of the classical theories of *Bildung*. Although the critique of the German educational system included the critique that the proper ideals of *Bildung* had been forgotten, the idea of self-formation entailed the belief that youth had the power, authority and possibility to educate itself. This reduced the authority of the classical humanist canon and of teachers as educators. Self-education relied not on what had historically been established as proper moral educational goals, but on the possibility to educate oneself on one's own behalf. Therefore, instead of looking for historical templates, fellow Wandervögel who had developed a 'personality' and the ability to explore the world on their own behalf were regarded as the best educators. They could, after all, function as inspiring examples for young Wandervögel. In a similar way, landscapes, old monuments, folk culture and general German history could function as sources for the replenishment of Germanness. These achievements of German history were not valuable because they were historical or because they represented German greatness, but because they existed for the fleeting 'now' as sources for an ever-replenishing Germanness.

In the next chapter, I will analyse the actual engagement of the youth movement with such material and immaterial sites of heritage. We will see how the break with traditional educational ideas and with traditional views on historical distance urged for a different mode of appropriating the past.

# Notes

1. Barbara Hanke, *Geschichtskultur an höheren Schulen von der Wilhelminischen Ära bis zum Zweiten Weltkrieg. Das Beispiel Westfalen* (Münster: LIT Verlag, 2010).

2. Wolfgang Hardtwig, *Deutsche Geschichtskultur im 19. und 20. Jahrhundert* (Munich: Oldenbourg, 2013), 74ff.; Brent Orlyn Peterson, *History, Fiction, and Germany: Writing the Nineteenth-century Nation* (Detroit: Wayne State University Press, 2005), 139ff. On the role of historians in the process of nation-building, see: Stefan Berger, Mark Donovan and Kevin Passmore, *Writing National Histories: Western Europe Since 1800* (London: Routledge, 2002); Stefan Berger and Chris Lorenz, *Nationalizing the Past: Historians as Nation Builders in Modern Europe* (New York: Palgrave Macmillan, 2010).

3. Cf. David Blackbourn and Geoffrey Eley, *The Peculiarities of German History: Bourgeois Society and Politics in Nineteenth-century Germany* (Oxford: Oxford University Press, 1984), 263–64; Geoff Eley, *Reshaping the German Right: Radical Nationalism and Political Change after Bismarck* (New Haven, CT: Yale University Press, 1980).

4. Rudi Koshar, *Germany's Transient Pasts: Preservation and National Memory in the Twentieth Century* (Chapel Hill, NC: University of North Carolina Press, 1998).

5. Arthur Kracke, *Freideutsche Jugend: zur Jahrhundertfeier auf dem Hohen Meißner 1913* (Jena: Diederichs, 1913), 4.

6. Cf. Ersnt Lissauer, '1813 und Wir', *Die Tat. Sozialreligiöse Monatsschrift für deutsche Kultur* 5 (1913), 90–98.

7. Barbara Stambolis, 'Wallfahrtsstätten der Religion, der Nation und der Jugend. Zur Bedeutung heiliger Orte in der Jugendbewegung', *Jahrbuch des Archivs der deutschen Jugendbewegung* 20 (2002), 148–58: 150–51.

8. Gustav Mittelstraß, *Freideutscher Jugendtag* (Hamburg: Adolf Saal, 1919), 7. For the press coverage of the event, see: Winfried Mogge and Jürgen Reulecke, *Hoher Meißner 1913: der Erste Freideutsche Jugendtag in Dokumenten, Deutungen und Bildern* (Cologne: Verlag Wissenschaft und Politik, 1988), 307–45.

9. 'Oktober 1913', *Jung-Wandervogel. Zeitschrift des Bundes für Jugendwandern "Jung-Wandervogel"* 3(6) (1913), 87.

10. For the well-known concept *lieu de mémoire*, see: Pierre Nora, 'Between Memory and History: Les Lieux de Mémoire', *Representations* 26 (1989), 7–24.

11. Hans Ulrich Thamer, 'Das Meißner-Fest der Freideutschen Jugend 1913 als Erinnerungsort der deutschen Jugendbewegung', *Jahrbuch des Archivs der deutschen Jugendbewegung* NF5 (2008), 169–90; Thamer, 'Der Meißner-Tag', 400–401.

12. Mittelstraß, *Freideutscher Jugendtag*, 12–13. English translation cited from: Fritz Borinski and Werner Milch, *Jugendbewegung: The Story of German Youth* (London: Clarke & Co., 1945), 13.

13. Ziemer and Wolf, *Wandervogel und freideutsche Jugend*, 32.

14. Siegfried Copalle, *Chronik der Deutschen Jugendbewegung* (Bad Godesberg: Voggenreiter Verlag, 1954), 11.

15. Fritz Hellmuth, 'Mit Spirituskocher und Regenschirm', in Gerhard Ziemer and Hans Wolf (ed.), *Wandervogel und Freideutsche Jugend* (Bad Godesberg: Voggenreiter, 1961), 43–44; Georg Korth, *Wandervogel 1896–1906: quellenmässige Darstellung nach Karl Fischers Tagebuchaufzeichnungen von 1900 und vielen anderen dokumentarischen Belegen* (Frankfurt am Main: dipa-Verlag, 1967), 44–46.

16. Hermann Hoffmann, 'Die Fichtenberg-Abrede', in Werner Kindt (ed.), *Die Wandervogelzeit. Quellenschriften zur deutschen Jugendbewegung 1896–1919* (Düsseldorf: Eugen Diederichs Verlag, 1968), 39.

17. For a discussion of the controversialities on the origins of this name, see: Winfried Mogge, *"Ihr Wandervögel in der Luft ...": Fundstücke zur Wanderung eines romantischen Bildes und zur Selbstinszenierung einer Jugendbewegung* (Würzburg: Königshausen & Neumann, 2009), 27–52.

18. Hoffmann, 'Hoch das Wandern!', in Werner Kindt (ed.), *Die Wandervogelzeit. Quellenschriften zur deutschen Jugendbewegung 1896–1919* (Düsseldorf: Eugen Diederichs Verlag, 1968), 31.

19. John R. Gillis, *Youth and History* (New York: Academic Press, 1974), 52ff.

20. Hans Blüher, *Wandervogel 1–3. Geschichte einer Jugendbewegung*, Part I (Frankfurt am Main: Dipa-Verlag, 1976), 120.

21. In constructing a hierarchy, Fischer followed an earlier initiative of Hoffmann, who had used a similar hierarchy without consistent historical reference since the hike to the Bohemian forest in 1899. Cf. Henne, 'Zur Sprache der Jugend im Wandervogel', 22–27. Korth also refers to the Böhmerwaldfahrt as the moment when Fischer gathered a circle of trustees who supported his quest for Vagantentum. Cf. Korth, *Wandervogel 1896–1906*, 51. Furthermore, it must be noted that in Southern Germany the Wandervogel used the term *Pachanten* instead of *Bachanten*. Cf. Werner Helwig, *Die Blaue Blume des Wandervogels: Vom Aufstieg, Glanz und Sinn einer Jugendbewegung. Überarbeitete Neuausgabe* (Baunach: Deutscher Spurbuchverlag, 1998), 32f.

22. Blüher, *Wandervogel 1–3*, part I, 135.

23. 'We are of the roaming order of travelling scholars, and ask for provisions to hasten forward'; Gerber, *Zur Entstehungsgeschichte der deutschen Wandervogelbewegung*, 46; Ziemer and Wolf, *Wandervogel und freideutsche Jugend*, 48.

24. Heinrich Becker, *Zwischen Wahn und Wahrheit: Autobiographie* (Berlin: Verlag der Nation, 1972), 31–33. The passage on the growing iron – a reference to the raising of arms – was quoted from Ernst Moritz Arndt's *Vaterlandslied* (1813). On *fin-de-siècle* Steglitz, see also: Günter Köhler, 'Steglitz zur Jahrhundertwende. Preußens größtes Dorf, ein zentraler Ort des Bildungsbürgertums', in Gerhard Ille and Günter Köhler (eds), *Der Wandervogel. Es begann in Steglitz* (Berlin: Stapp Verlag, 1987), 9–29.

25. Ludwig Gurlitt, *Der Deutsche und sein Vaterland. Politisch-pädagogische Betrachtungen eines Modernen* (Berlin: Verlag von Wiegandt & Grieboy, 1902), 23.

26. Ibid., 104.

27. K. Dissel and R. Rosenhagen, *Verhandlungen der achtundvierzigsten Versammlung deutscher Philologen und Schulmänner in Hamburg vom 3. bis 6. Oktober 1905* (Leipzig: Teubner, 1906), 69–70.

28. Ludwig Gurlitt, *Pflege und Entwicklung der Persönlichkeit* (Leipzig: R. Voigtländer, 1905), 51.

29. Uwe Puschner defines the *völkisch* movement as 'an over-arching collecting point for, in particular, those who aspired to reform culture and lifestyles, for anti-ultramontanists, anti-Semites, eugenicists, and many more. The lowest common denominator was the shared political goal of a "rebirth of the German *Volkstum*" defined in terms of race and religion'. Uwe Puschner, '"One People, One Reich, One God". The Völkische Weltanschauung and Movement', *Bulletin (German Historical Institute)* 24(1) (2002), 5–28: 9. Other seminal works on the *völkisch* movement include: Stefan Breuer, *Die Völkischen in Deutschland: Kaiserreich und Weimarer Republik* (Darmstadt: Wissenschaftliche Buchgesellschaft, 2008); Jost Hermand, *Old Dreams of a New Reich: Volkish Utopias and National Socialism* (Bloomington: Indiana University Press, 1992); Mosse, *The Crisis of German Ideology*; Uwe Puschner, *Die völkische Bewegung im wilhelminischen Kaiserreich: Sprache, Rasse, Religion* (Darmstadt: Wissenschaftliche Buchgesellschaft, 2001); Stern, *The Politics of Cultural Despair*.

30. Friedrich Copalle, cited in: Gerber, *Zur Entstehungsgeschichte der deutschen Wandervogelbewegung*, 83.

31. On the Heimat movement, as well as on the concept of *Heimat*, see: Celia Applegate, *A Nation of Provincials: The German Idea of Heimat* (Berkeley: University of California Press, 1990).

32. Mogge, *"Ihr Wandervögel in der Luft ..."*, 100–101.

33. *Neue Bund* 1922 15. 2, 344. Vgl. Helmut Wangelin, 'Der Wandervogel und das Völkische', *Jahrbuch des Archivs der deutschen Jugendbewegung* (1970), 43–77: 45.

34. Gerber, *Zur Entstehungsgeschichte*, 84.

35. Laqueur, *Young Germany*, 75.

36. Richard Hinton Thomas, *Nietzsche in German Politics and Society, 1890–1918* (Manchester: Manchester University Press, 1983), 99.

37. Fischer made this remark in an entry submitted to the youth magazine *Der Gute Kamerad*; cited from Gerber, *Zur Entstehungsgeschichte*, 85. In 1922, Fischer endorsed this in: Karl Fischer, 'Randbemerkung', *Der Neue Bund* 1(22) (1922), 343–46.

38. Luise Fick, *Die deutsche Jugendbewegung* (Jena: Diederichs, 1940), 39.

39. Copalle, *Chronik der Deutschen Jugendbewegung*, 12.

40. Ibid., 15. Already in Hoffmann's era, they had themselves held a solstice celebration in the Bavarian Forest (1899). Cf.: Hoffmann, 'Aus der Frühzeit des Wandervogels', 38.

41. Mogge, "*Ihr Wandervögel in der Luft ...*", 99–103.

42. The Steglitzer e.V. was also referred to as 'Steglitzer Wandervogel', or simply 'EV'. It must not be confused with the Wandervogel e.V., which was the name of the unified Wandervogel after 1912.

43. Korth attributes this distinction to Blüher and speaks of a 'terrible simplification'. Bruno Thiede, for example, was more a romantic than an aesthetic type, while he did support Copalle's case. Korth is right that the distinction between aesthetic and romantic wandering was not the primary cause of the disruption within the Ausschuss für Schülerfahrten; it was, however, an effect which grew stronger when the two opposing fractions profiled themselves. Korth, *Wandervogel 1896–1906*, 84.

44. Frank Fischer, 'Der Steglitzer Wandervogel 1905 und 1906', in Werner Kindt (ed.), *Die Wandervogelzeit. Quellenschriften zur deutschen Jugendbewegung 1896–1919* (Düsseldorf: Eugen Diederichs Verlag, 1968), 82–88: 83.

45. Blüher, *Wandervogel 1–3*, Bd. 2: 17.

46. Claudia Bruns, *Politik des Eros: der Männerbund in Wissenschaft, Politik und Jugendkultur (1880–1934)* (Cologne: Böhlau, 2008); Jürgen Reulecke, 'Männerbund versus Familie. Bürgerliche Jugendbewegung und Familie in Deutschland im ersten Drittel des 20. Jahrhunderts', in Thomas Koebner (ed.), *Mit uns zieht die Zeit: der Mythos Jugend* (Frankfurt am Main: Suhrkamp, 1985), 199–223.

47. Hanz Atzrott, cited in: Gerber, *Zur Entstehungsgeschichte*, 81.

48. Ernst Schottky, 'Der Steglitzer Wandervogel 1907 und 1908', in Werner Kindt (ed.), *Die Wandervogelzeit. Quellenschriften zur deutschen Jugendbewegung 1896–1919* (Düsseldorf: Eugen Diederichs Verlag, 1968), 88–93: 89.

49. Siegfried Copalle, 'Des Wandervogels Liederbuch; Vorwort', in Werner Kindt (ed.), *Die Wandervogelzeit. Quellenschriften zur deutschen Jugendbewegung 1896–1919* (Düsseldorf: Eugen Diederichs Verlag, 1968), 81–82: 81. Cf. 'Wandervogel'; Eingetragener Verein zu Steglitz, *Des Wandervogels Liederbuch* (Berlin and Osterwieck: A.W. Zickfeldt, 1905).

50. Andrea Neuhaus, *Das geistliche Lied in der Jugendbewegung: zur literarischen Sakralität um 1900* (Tübingen: Francke, 2005), 86.

51. Sigfried Copalle in a letter to Heinrich Ahrens (1942), cited in: Gerber, *Zur Entstehungsgeschichte*, 59.

52. Copalle, 'Des Wandervogels Liederbuch; Vorwort'.

53. Frank Fischer, Friedrich Brauns and W. Liebenow, *Wandern und Schauen. Gesammelte Ausätze* (Hartenstein: Greifenverlag, 1921), 6.

54. Siegfried Copalle, 'Lob der Landstraße. Erinnerungen an die Berlin-Wittenberger Chaussee', in Gerhard Ziemer and Hans Wolf (ed.), *Wandervogel und Freideutsche Jugend* (Bad Godesberg: Voggenreiter, [1905] 1961), 99–103: 102.

55. Helmut Wangelin, *Der Wandervogel in Tagebüchern Frank Fischers und anderen Selbstzeugnissen* (Tübingen: Selbstverlag, 1982), 92–96.

56. Diary entry by Frank Fischer, 4 April 1906, ibid., 30.

57. Ibid., 31.

58. Before his engagement in the Steglitzer Wandervogel, Fischer had established the student association 'Frohliche Wissenschaft' in Göttingen, a name which alludes explicitly to Nietzsche.

59. Hermann Hesse, cited in: Frank Fischer, 'Oratio pro domo', in Frank Fischer (ed.), *Wandern und Schauen. Gesammelte Aufsätze von Frank Fischer* (Hartenstein: Greifenverlag, 1921), 11–16: 12.; Cf. Hermann Hesse, *Wandern und Reisen, Dürerbund 14. Flugschrift zur ästhetischen Kultur* (Munich: Callwey, 1906), 2.

60. Hesse, *Wandern und Reisen*, 3.

61. Ibid., 8.

62. Frank Fischer, 'Unser Wandern', in Werner Kindt (ed.), *Grundschriften der deutschen Jugendbewegung* (Düsseldorf: Eugen Diederichs Verlag, 1963), 79–82: 80.

63. Ibid., 81.
64. Walter Köhler, 'Der Steglitzer Wandervogel E.V. von 1908 bis Anfang 1912', in Kindt, *Die Wandervogelzeit*, 98–102: 98; Ziemer and Wolf, *Wandervogel und freideutsche Jugend*, 144.
65. Wilfried Breyvogel, *Eine Einführung in Jugendkulturen: Veganismus und Tattoos* (Wiesbaden: VS Verlag, 2005), 13.
66. Kindt, *Die Wandervogelzeit*, 143.
67. Gerhard Ille, 'Steglitzer Wandervogelführer. Lebenswege und Lebensziele', in Gerhard Ille and Günter Köhler (eds), *Der Wandervogel. Es begann in Steglitz* (Berlin: Stapp Verlag, 1987), 99–127: 110.
68. On Hans Breuer, see: Hans Breuer, *Erinnerung und Vermächtnis: ein Gedenkbüchlein um Hans Breuer* (Hartenstein: Matthes, 1932); Heinz Speiser, *Hans Breuer, Wirken und Wirkungen: eine Monographie* (Witzenhausen: Stiftung Jugendburg Ludwigstein, 1977).
69. Marion Grob, *Das Kleidungsverhalten jugendlicher Protestgruppen in Deutschland im 20. Jahrhundert: am Beispiel des Wandervogels und der Studentenbewegung* (Münster: Coppenrath, 1985), 168–71.
70. For the influence of the Reform movement on the pre-war Wandervogel, see: Sabine Weißler, *Fokus Wandervogel: der Wandervogel in seinen Beziehungen zu den Reformbewegungen vor dem Ersten Weltkrieg* (Marburg: Jonas Verlag, 2001).
71. Otto Bojarzin and Ludwig Tschuncky, *Vom Wandervogel und vom bunten Rock. Skizzen und Erzählungen* (Wolfenbüttel: Zwissler, 1916), 57.
72. Although becoming a public journal in 1913, *Der Anfang* was the continuation of a student journal that had been published in hectograph between 1908 and 1910, and that had seen some irregular publications in 1911.
73. Walter Benjamin, 'Unterricht und Wertung', *Der Anfang* 1(1) (1913), 6–10.
74. Walter Benjamin, 'Romantik', *Der Anfang* 1(2) (1913), 38–42.
75. Richard Werner, 'Was wir nicht lernen', *Der Anfang* 1(4) (1913), 108–10: 109.
76. Gustav Wyneken, *Schule und Jugendkultur* (Jena: Eugen Diederichs Verlag, 1919).
77. Friedrich Nietzsche, 'On the Uses and Disadvantages of History for Life', in Friedrich Nietzsche (ed.), *Untimely Meditations* (Cambridge: Cambridge University Press, 1997). 57–124: 116.
78. Ibid., 117.
79. Ibid., 120.
80. Gustav Wyneken, *Was ist "Jugendkultur"? Öffentlicher Vortrag gehalten am 30. Oktober 1913 in der Pädagogischen Abteilung der Münchner Freien Studentenschaft* (Munich: Steinicke, 1919), 5.
81. Ibid., 15. Cf. Peter Dudek, *Fetisch Jugend: Walter Benjamin und Siegfried Bernfeld – Jugendprotest am Vorabend des Ersten Weltkrieges* (Bad Heilbrunn/Obb.: Klinkhardt, 2002), 20–21.
82. Philip Lee Utley, 'Radical Youth: Generational Conflict in the Anfang Movement, 1912 – January 1914', *History of Education Quarterly* 19(2) (1979), 207–28: 211–12. See also: Richard W. Dougherty, *Eros, Youth Culture and Geist: The Ideology of Gustav Wyneken and its Influence upon the German Youth Movement* (Madison: University of Wisconsin, 1978).
83. Gustav Wyneken, 'Die Idee des Geschichtsunterrichts', in Gustav Wyneken (ed.), *Der Kampf für die Jugend: Gesammelte Aufsätze* (Jena: Eugen Diederichs, 1919), 41–54: 46.
84. Wyneken, *Was ist "Jugendkultur"?*, 6–7.
85. Kracke, *Freideutsche Jugend*, 3.
86. Ibid., 4.
87. 'Oktober 1913'.
88. Steinberg, 'Dem Vaterlande!', *Wandervogel. Gaublatt für Schlesien*, April (1913), 25–26.
89. Karl Balser, 'Und wir?', *Fahrtenblatt des Wandervogels Nordthuringgau* 5(10) (1913), 19–21: 19.
90. Ibid.
91. Bruno Lemke, *Einleitungsworte bei der Aussprache des ersten Freideutschen Jugendtages am 10. Oktober 1913, auf dem "Hanstein"*, ed. Gustav Mittelstraß, *Freideutscher Jugendtag 1913* (Hamburg: Adolf Saal, 1919), 17.

92. Gottfried Traub, *Ansprache auf dem "Hohen Meißner" am Abend des 11. Oktobers*, ed. Gustav Mittelstraß, *Freideutscher Jugendtag 1913* (Hamburg: Adolf Saal, 1919), 22.

93. In the introduction to their recent edition of the *Addresses*, Bela Kapossy, Isaac Nakhimovsky and Keith Tribe state that the interpretation of Fichte as a proponent for a 'moral alternative' to German nationalism has mainly survived in French historiography and is still 'largely unfamiliar to readers of English today'. Cf. Johann Goetlieb Fichte, *Addresses to the German Nation* (Indianapolis: Hackett Publishing Company, Inc., 2013), x.

94. Eugen Kühnemann, 'Der deutsche Idealismus und die Jugend', in Kracke, *Freideutsche Jugend*, 116.

95. Ibid.

96. Ibid., 117.

97. Paul Natorp, *Hoffnungen und Gefahren unserer Jugendbewegung* (Jena: Eugen Diederichs, 1920), 16.

98. Mittelstraß, *Freideutscher Jugendtag*, 12–13. English translation cited from: Borinski and Milch, *Jugendbewegung: The Story of German Youth*, 13.

99. Franz-Michael Konrad, '"… Unsere einzige, unsere letzte Hoffnung". Die Jugendbewegung als Thema und Herausforderung der Pädagogik Paul Natorps', *Pädagogische Rundschau* 55(5) (2001), 523–42: 529–30.

100. *Die Marburger Tagung der Freideutschen Jugend* (Hamburg: A. Saal, 1914), 23.

101. Ibid., 28.

102. David James, 'Fichte on the Vocation of the Scholar and the (Mis)use of History', *The Review of Metaphysics* 63(3) (2010), 539–66: 560.

103. Much has been written about the youth movement's appropriation of Nietzsche. This literature is basically concerned with the question of to what extent Nietzsche was a 'prophet' of the youth movement, as a 1929 article contended: Oscar Schütz, 'Friedrich Nietzsche als Prophet der deutschen Jugendbewegung', *Neue Jahrbücher für Wissenschaft und Jugendbildung* 5 (1929), 64–80. Christian Niemeyer has argued that Nietzsche was hardly read in the Wandervogel before the war, as it was prohibited by parents, but these conclusions are obviously not applicable to the *Anfang* circle: Christian Niemeyer, '"Plündernde Soldaten". Die pädagogische Nietzsche-Rezeption im Ersten Weltkrieg', *Zeitschrift für Pädagogik* 45(2) (1999), 209–29; Christian Niemeyer, 'Nietzsche als "Prophet der Jugendbewegung" – ein Mißverständnis?', in Renate Reschke (ed.), *Zeitenwende – Wertewende: Internationaler Kongreß der Nietzsche-Gesellschaft zum 100. Todestag Friedrich Nietzsches vom 24.–27. August 2000 in Naumburg* (Berlin: 2001), 181–87: 186–87. See also: Justus H. Ulbricht, 'Nietzsche als "Prophet der Jugendbewegung"? Befunde und Überlegungen zu einem Rezeptionsproblem', in Ulrich Herrmann (ed.), *'Mit uns zieht die neue Zeit …' Der Wandervogel in der deutschen Jugendbewegung* (Weinheim: Juventa, 2006), 80–114.

104. Walter Fischer, 'Salonbauern', *Wandervogel* 8(3) (1913), 87–88.

105. Hans Breuer, 'Herbstschau 1913: Plus ultra', *Wandervogel* 8(10) (1913), 282–85: 283.

CHAPTER 2

# The Experience of the Past

'It had to be in the year 1912, on December 23,' the novelist Manfred Hausmann wrote, 'when we – a dozen boys of the Alt-Wandervogel – took the train from Göttingen to Eichenberg, and waded cross-country through the high snow towards the castle ruin Hanstein.'[1] In those days, wandering still had an air of novelty and discovery – especially for the fourteen-year-old Hausmann, who had only joined the Wandervogel several weeks before. The Alt-Wandervogel's Christmas celebration under the beamed ceiling of Hanstein became a lasting experience for Hausmann.

> For the first time, I saw a Christmas tree, which had no other decoration than a few candles and appeared so woodish, so pristine with its widely branched, very fragrant foliage. For the first time, I heard the nativity story in the grand, masculine language of the poet of the Heliand. For the first time the inconceivably sweet melody of 'Susani, Susani' – acclaimed by fiddles and flutes – exalted my innermost. For the first time, I experienced community. For the first time, I was no longer alone.[2]

Of all these experiences, one in particular stuck out. Before they went to sleep, Hausmann groped his way up the stairs of one of the castle's towers. With the starry skies above him, the snowy valley of the river Werra at his feet, and the silhouette of the castle with the candle-lit Knight's Hall behind him, the young Wandervogel experienced a moment of epiphanic intensity:

> Suddenly a very deep happiness came over me. How dreamily appeared the soft silver mountain country with its shades, how mysterious appeared the boundless

Notes for this section begin on page 83

night with its sparkling constellations! How abysmal was the silence! How I loved it all! How I loved the world!'³

However, this excessive bliss did not bring his soul to peace – rather, Hausmann became sad and restless, for he knew that he was never to experience a moment of such intense felicity again. A longing, a *Sehnsucht* got hold of him:

> A hunch came over me that nothing, which a person experiences on earth, is capable of quenching the restlessness in him. Even in its finest beauty was the world not perfect, not salvation, not comforting in the end. There was something in me, in my quivering boy's heart, which yearned for a beatitude and beauty and truth beyond the shimmering splendour of the world, beyond every piece of earthly bliss, which should be without the whiff of melancholy, without brokenness, without insufficiency. That night on the tower of Hanstein Castle I learnt for the first time, and only in a vague and boyish manner, what it is, when a person is overwhelmed by the desire for God.⁴

Accounts such as these make up a significant part of the content of the youth movement's journals and provide another entry into the movement's understanding of history and time apart from the programmatic essays written by its leadership. Hiking reports were written with great pathos and with the intention to disclose an unarticulated world of moonlight, dewdrops, colours, rain, anxiety and exhilaration. Concepts such as *Erlebnis* (lived experience), *Stimmung* (attunement), *unmittelbar* (immediate) and *das Ganze* (totality) were used to denote a pre-rational experience of which it was argued time and again that it could not be conveyed in language, and that one ought to have experienced it oneself to be able to comprehend its full grasp.⁵

In this chapter, I will analyse how the youth movement sought answers to the problems it recognized in German historical culture which we have analysed in the previous chapter. First, I will explain the historical background and the use of the concept of *Erlebnis* in the youth movement in relation to the idea of history. Then I will discuss how lived experience functioned as a way to bridge historical distance, and how experience opened the way to conceive history as a process of sedimentation of living tradition. Finally, I will discuss how experience was given cultural meaning. Because in experience history and community were immediately present, many ideas formulated in the youth movement took experience as the basis for a nation or society beyond the 'cold', 'distanced' and 'impersonal' rationale of modernity. I will analyse this transition from experience to meaning by focusing on two cases. First, I will analyse the way in which encountering Jewish heritage by the Jewish youth movement Blau-Weiß was related to their ideas on Jewishness. Second, I will show how the encounter with Flemish heritage by Wandervogel soldiers during the Great War resulted in notions of a postwar regeneration of Germany.

## History and Lived Experience

According to Hans-Georg Gadamer, *Erlebnis* was an 'almost sacred clarion call' for the youth movement. The concept disclosed the possibility to grasp life as an undividable unity, and connects life to totality and infinity. *Erlebnis* contrasts the 'abstractness of understanding and the particularity of perception or representation'.[6] Although the concept is a neologism which became prominent only in the 1870s, *Erlebnis* has a similar pantheistic undertone as concepts from the vocabulary of German idealism. *Erlebnis* too referred to the temporal experience of totality – of the eternal, so to speak. Yet, while idealism situated the nexus between the temporal and the eternal in the spiritual domain, *Erlebnis* referred to the actual mental and physical experience of the world as given.

With respect to history, Reinhart Koselleck clarifies the position of experience by stating that in early modern times, the old German denominator for experience – *Erfahrung* – started to lose its meaning of inquiry, of actively acquiring knowledge. In premodern times, this inquiry conflated with history (*Historie*) to the extent that history referred to the study of human action and not yet to the past. In the early modern era, *Erfahrung* lost the dimension of inquiry: 'the "methodological" pathway of trial was weeded out and lost'.[7] Two dimensions which were present in the 'old' concept of experience were now separated: the cognitive or mental activity of acquiring knowledge and the direct experience of lived reality. Whereas the cognitive dimension of inquiry was no longer referred to as experience, the term was now only used to denote that which appears as a given, be it moral truth which is clear in the *Erfahrung* of the Enlightenment's moral philosophy, or lived reality which is at hand in the *Erlebnis* of Wilhelm Dilthey's late nineteenth-century philosophy of life, as well as in the language of reform groups such as the youth movement. Experience thus became the opposite of thought or conscious reflection, and the problematic relationship between the study of history (*historia rerum gestarum*) and the experience of the past (of the *res gestae*) was born. Yet, the modern concept of history (*Geschichte*) did contain what the old concept of experience now lacked – the unity of cognition and experience, which referred to both the *historia rerum gestarum* and the *res gestae*. The 'experienceable' past and the knowledge of, or narrative about, the past are both contained in the dual meaning of the modern concept of history, but the dissolution of the old unity of the concept of experience now made it possible to discern between method and substance with regard to history.

The problem with history, as it was articulated in the pre-war youth movement, primarily had to do with the relationship between cognition and experience. The critique on Wilhelmine political historical culture was that it imposed a cognitively constructed interpretation of history onto youth which lacked any experienceable substance. The criticism of history education was a variety of the same logic, as the school was accused of providing an overly scientific history education in which the past appeared as 'dead' book knowledge. The alienation of history was perceived to be the result of history no longer being the recording of human experience. The answer to which the youth movement was more or less intuitively drawn was that experience itself could disclose the past; that whereas cognition was method without substance, direct experience (*Erlebnis*) contained both. Thus, the turn towards 'lived experience' was rooted in the same unease which had drawn philosophers such as Wilhelm Dilthey and Edmund Husserl to the concept, namely: 'the new, distanced attitude that historical consciousness takes to tradition'.[8] Whereas for philosophers such as Dilthey and Husserl, *Erlebnis* provided a tool for an epistemology of the humanities beyond positivism, the youth movement used the concepts *Erleben* and *Erlebnis* in a more intuitive way to denote the same movement of eluding the distance to nature, history and the world in general, which was generated by a culture of rational objectification.

According to the German philosopher Konrad Cramer, the concept of *Erlebnis* has a twofold meaning, which is reflected in the ways the concept was used.[9] First, *Erlebnis* refers to the immediacy, pre-reflexivity and pre-conceptuality of experience. Through *Erlebnis* one could apprehend the world on one's own terms, apart from any conceptual mediation – a connotation derived from the original meaning of the concept as 'being alive when something happens'.[10] This aspect of *Erlebnis* is best explained by referring to the way in which Wilhelm Dilthey attributes lived experience to the phenomenological domain in which man is pre-reflexively related to the world of which he himself is part. Dilthey exemplifies Cramer's distinction by discerning *Erlebnis* from *Erkenntnis* (conceptual cognition or cognitive judgement) and argues that – contrary to what positivism wants us to believe – the manifold manifestations in which the world appears to us should not solely be understood as objects of cognition. Conceptual cognition is in fact an ideal abstraction of the phenomenal context or nexus of life – the total body of *Erlebnisse* – which precedes it.[11] The popular use of the concept of *Erlebnis* in the youth movement shows striking similarities to Dilthey's interpretation of this concept. Although Dilthey was not widely read – especially not among the Wandervögel – and although the youth movement had 'not produced a Wilhelm Dilthey', a theorist of *Erlebnis*, the concept of *Erlebnis* did entail the same connotation of pre-cognitive world-appropriation and direct engagement with the world.[12] Already the Wandervogel DB used the concept in this way when it phrased its main goal to be 'promoting wandering among youth of the German tongue, to awaken the senses to the beauty of nature, to awaken sympathy for all living things and creatures, and to give youth the opportunity to get to know and love their German homeland and its people in its original, particularity through personal experience [*Erlebnis*]'.[13]

*Erlebnis* was often defined as a mode of grasping the world in a radically different and more original and 'vivacious' way than through what was called 'deceased' book knowledge. For example: after visiting a cathedral one Wandervogel noted in reference to this monument: 'dead I saw you lying in the coffins of the dead books – alive you rise before me under God's vivacious sun out of your vivacious works'.[14] The rejection of the *Baedecker* which we have discussed in the previous chapter is also part of the attempt to replace mere cognitive understanding by an *Erlebnis* which drew from the full context of the site, including smells, sounds, the weather, the presence of friends – in fact all elements which codetermine the way the site is present to the observer before objectification. Hjalmar Kutzleb – since 1910 a leader figure in the Jung-Wandervogel – recalled that 'who wandered in our style did not perceive landscape through the filter of a travel guide, but eye to eye'.[15] The Wandervogel, he stated, even disposed of the criteria 'beautiful, ugly, Romantic and picturesque', and took the world as it was present, and therefore also as something strange, as something that could surprise you.[16] Wandervogel artist Max Heilmann articulated this view as follows:

> The Wandervogel does not want to enjoy the pleasures of travelling like the individual songs of a variety show – he wants to experience [*Erleben*]. I do not say: to experience *something* – this would mean as much as craving for sensation – no, everything that he encounters must become experience [*Erlebnis*] to him. Landscape character, mood, natural events, encounters and the exchange of ideas with local inhabitants, the sounds of songs and strings – everything merges into great images in which he himself lives as a figurine. In this empathic appropriation, in this deepening of perception and in the receptiveness that has grown through constant training, he comes close to being an artist; yes, he even becomes one as far as 'life' is concerned. He distinguishes himself eventually from the practising artist only through the fact that he does not reproduce; or better, through the fact that he moulds experience [*Erlebnis*] into lasting values.[17]

Furthermore, it was important for the youth movement that *Erlebnis* did not depend on concepts and meaning as a key to understanding. *Erlebnis* was non-rational and was as such available to anybody with the right sensitivity – not only to the learned.

Second, according to Cramer, *Erlebnis* also denotes the *content* of what is experienced.[18] Something can be *an* immediate experience. Yet, an *Erlebnis* was irrelevant when isolated from its context and from the meaningful totality – from what Wilhelm Dilthey called the life nexus. We find a similar use of *Erlebnis* as the content of experience in a more rudimentary form in the vocabulary of the youth movement. In, for example, Hausmann's epiphanic *Erlebnis* at Hanstein Castle, the hermeneutics of *Erlebnis* becomes clear at two levels. The first level points at the momentary experience at the castle itself. The occurrences of hearing the nativity story and singing Christmas songs became an *Erlebnis* only as they were embedded in the totality of the situation: the setting of the castle, the winter night and the heat of the fire. The sensory perception of melody or the cognitive perception of the story appeared to Hausmann as part of a meaningful totality, and out of this totality, individual elements like the nativity story and the song derived their meaning. Without this totality – which Hausmann ultimately called God – the occurrences of the night would not have been an *Erlebnis*. The second level encompasses the totality of life experience. Hausmann embeds the *Erlebnis* of Hanstein Castle in the totality of his personal life experience, as he retrospectively gives the experience meaning as a formative experience in his life narrative. Out of the total plot of this narrative, the experience becomes formative; but being formative for life is not in itself a quality of the experience.

However, as the totality of meaning in which the experience is embedded is not a finite totality (as experience unfolds itself in reference to continuously evolving life and history), an experience can never be reduced to a certain rationally comprehendable and definable content. Therefore, non-rational immediacy remains the most significant quality of *Erlebnis*, as the experience itself refuses to be absorbed into a definable context.[19] Every representation of *Erlebnis* therefore necessarily reduces the full context of experience to a few definable aspects. This problem of representation was subject to continuous debate within the youth movement. Writing about experiences was regarded valuable, because reworking experiences afterwards meant incorporating them into one's own life, turning them into lasting experiences that could help to shape personality. Special booklets were published in which hiking experiences could be written down, and it was urged that these were treated like diaries, but were only meant to capture the experience when one was still in its spell.[20] Only the essentials had to be written down in these booklets – no technical details, but 'instantaneous pictures' lacking romantic pathos and sentimentalities.[21] The quality of a certain atmosphere would reveal itself again when remembering the experience; obfuscating a mood by trying to grasp the irrepresentable in words would undo this memory effect. It was often rejected when an author of a hiking report explicitly intended to recreate the 'experienced mood' for the reader, and tried to compensate his artistic shortcomings with bombastic language.[22] The words had to come from within, and should not be written down with the intent to fill a magazine.

While Hausmann defined the referential totality of experience as 'God', usually the totality in which *Erlebnis* was believed to be embedded was called *Gemeinschaft* (community).[23] Until the war this referential community was primarily the group of fellow Wandervogel with whom one went on a hike. In 1922, Alfred Heidenreich mused on the following scene from his pre-war Wandervogel days:

> We are lying together on a hill by night. In front of us a valley. On the far edge a fir forest has been planted. As we laid there we are immersed in its beauty. We are not bothered by its size, not by its value, not by its scientific meaning. We only see beauty. The towering trunks, the melancholic clouds immersed in the dark branches. We feel all that silently grows yearning for the night. We sense the rough pliability, the swaying strength of the wood. The evening wind may caress its

forehead. When we laid there immersed in the gaze and 'dreamt' – what did we then actually do? We diverted our attention to the external world, but we grasped more than the senses could provide. We sensed through feeling also the intrinsic value of the things around us. We gasped the non-sensuous, the supra-sensuous, the 'Spiritual'. Something very significant befell us when we sank away in the gaze together: in these moments we were conscious of the most intimate community. Exactly this is important, because out of this I permitted myself to conclude what will initially appear very bold: we grasped the supernatural 'objectively'. Perhaps everyone expressed it differently, but everyone spoke to the other out of the depths of the soul. There were no discussions, for everyone experienced the most inner community.[24]

Experiencing together endorsed the belief that *Erlebnis* was not subjective. At the same time it could also provide a way of understanding each other on a level that went deeper than the formal social conventions of Wilhelmine society. The relationship between direct experience and community was actually rather straightforward: because direct experience was holistic by nature, the bond with the fellows with whom one shared the experience, or who were part of the experience, was also regarded to be holistic. Thus, experience-based community could be considered to be more authentic than society, in the sense that community emanated from experience, whereas society lacked such an inner content and was mere outer form.

## The Dissolution of Historical Distance

In the youth movement's critique of Wilhelmine historical culture, the problem that history was dissociated from individual life and lacked moral implications was particularly a problem of historical distance. *Erlebnis* provided an alternative to the idea that history was a radically distant and qualitatively different

**Figure 2.1** *Gemeinschaft*. Photo by Julius Groß, Archiv der deutschen Jugendbewegung, around 1922.

past. Through the direct experience of heritage and the hermeneutic operation of embedding this experience in life, history could be understood as a continuous stream of living and reviving tradition. *Erlebnis* thus became a vital element in overcoming the issue of historical distance. The notion of living tradition was especially relevant in relation to the experience of what was called the *Volk* – which before the war denoted primarily the rural population of Germany, without the ideological undertone it would later receive.

In an article on 'German History', published prior to the centennial of the Battle of the Nations, Frank Fischer asked himself whether or not 'in our wanderings, in our work and in our goal a natural relationship with the history of the *Volk* has grown'.[25] For the Wandervögel, hiking took place in the tension between city and countryside, in which the city represented bourgeois modernity – a time out of joint – and a rural Germany which represented the opposite: tradition, certainty and unity with nature. For Fischer, it was clear that the acceleration of history had had its effect on youth: the rush forward had made society less historical and more rootless.[26] This was problematic for youth, as goals in life changed as rapidly as the times. As a consequence, plans remained unfinished. However, the Wandervogel did not aim to change the times themselves, but, Fischer argued, the movement provided a frame of orientation for youth in these anxious times. For those for whom the Wandervogel was not mere leisure, but an 'affiliation to the innermost existence', the movement offered a space of 'quiet growth'.[27] By seeking new ways of living and new expressions in dance and song, the Wandervogel opted for a path of steady growth, rather than taking a giant leap forward like Wyneken's *Anfang* circle promoted. The Wandervogel's relationship to the past was therefore different from that of Wyneken, and was more in line with Natorp: they did abandon the learned patriotism and militarism as artificial constructs, and found in wandering a possibility to connect to the past in a vivacious way.

For Fischer, this connection was not a one-way process of appropriation of history as an 'object' of inquiry by a contemporary 'subject'. Rather, Fischer used the metaphor of dialogue to indicate that the 'presence' of heritage alone bears relevance:

> What is form out there, like nature; what is shaped by man and still remains; what still lets man's moulding hand be recognized in its gestures – this speaks to all who learn to listen. Not only churches and castles speak like this, also towns, streets and roads; stretches of land, settlements and cultivated areas; forests and even streams. But it is slow speech, which starts on a small and the smallest scale – not with deep wisdom. It is nonetheless clear that whoever sees historically possesses this rich and vivid image, rather than that dryer image turned away from reality.[28]

Fischer envisaged history as a continuous stream in which human action, thought and feeling is sedimented in the heritage that man leaves behind. This conception of history solved what he believed to be the main problem of history education: the dissociation between the present and the past as an effect of rational objectification. In his view the past was not something at distance, closed off from the present and accessible only through reason, but the past was virtually present in the lifeworld, and it defined human life in a more immediate way. Thus Fischer could speak of a past that approaches the present, instead of a present that appropriates the past. This palpable past was immediately present in hiking, in which one encounters historical layers in the landscape as part of the lifeworld, rather than as book knowledge in the confines of the classroom. But knowledge and experience were not perceived as being mutually exclusive. Rather, the past was immediately given in experience, but needed cognitive expression to be comprehendible. At the same time, factual knowledge was required for the Wandervogel to be receptive to experience in the first place.

To facilitate a meaningful, experience-based hiking rather than rambling around, book lists were published in the journals to read about the areas they were about to visit. Although secondary literature was regarded as informative, primary sources were preferred because they aired the 'spirit' in which certain relics had been manufactured. The massive historical sourcebook project *Voigtländers Quellenbücher*, for example, which by 1912 saw its fortieth volume published, was recommended among Wandervögel because the primary sources available there were more 'original' than historical narratives. The idea of the 'originality' of the sources was based on the belief that sources could elude the objectification of history in historical narrative, as the sources presented history not as a matter of fact that ought to have a meaning in itself, but showed how the experiences of historical figures were shaping their lives and indirectly shaping history. The sources did not show history as a closed and distant past, but history as a process of continuous formation: 'thus we obtain insights in the vivacious formation of history; we are no longer content with the ready facts that school education provides for us'.[29] The letters of Albrecht Dürer, Martin Luther and Count Blücher, the diary of Thomas Platter, and also very recent eye-witness accounts of the rebellion of the Nama in German South-West Africa, all provided direct entry into history as the domain of the formation of human life.

Knowledge was not required to affirm the truth of the perception of heritage as an object, but to enable the experience of this object of a specific historical form – as an expression of the spiritual-cultural life of a historical age. Therefore testimonies of the experiences of others were also relevant. Fischer, for example, advised to read Goethe's article 'Von deutscher Baukunst' (1772) when visiting the Strasbourg Cathedral, for it could enable the Wandervogel to 'experience the ensoulment and exaltation of the stone in all nerves and helps to understand the force of medieval forms of society, cities and church masons' guilds'.[30] These words make clear that Fischer's understanding of history was deeply morphological. For him, the ecclesial architecture of the Middle Ages is 'the deepest expression of the still unlayered and unrefined inner life to be found. Saint Michael's Church in Hildesheim, Hersfeld Abbey, Mainz Cathedral, and Strasbourg Cathedral express their age with unifying force, while today the stones lack speech. Every historical era still accumulated in words and tones, she spoke for eternity in stone. Therefore the shortest path to the soul of an age leads through its buildings'.[31]

In 1918, this interpretation of the experience of the past was endorsed when Wandervogel Hellmut Mebes emphasized that the movement was all but a 'literary club', but nonetheless needed knowledge as a prerequisite for the 'historical experience of a landscape'.[32] Yet, to be able to turn scientific knowledge into experience during a hike was a matter of practice. Everyone could read Goethe and understand the striking ways he experienced history, but: 'not everyone is a Goethe, not everyone experiences history spontaneously when he stands before the ruin, or the monument'.[33] The receptivity for *Erlebnis* was the product of education. This is where the value of leadership comes in. Leadership was not demonstrated by transmitting knowledge as if knowledge had value in itself. For the Wandervogel, knowledge only had value when it could be related to experience – therefore the task of the leader on a hike was to enable experience by passing knowledge, by making knowledge palpable in experience. Frank Fischer compared this concept of learning to the medieval university, where the transmission of values, narratives, beliefs and insights still had a significant role besides learning.[34] In a similar way, Mebes emphasized that the leader had an educative role to generate an atmosphere and to transmit that knowledge, which would enable his group to experience the past. 'Only at the right moment, at sunset below a castle, by moonlight overlooking a town, a well-told story about local history instead of a fairy tale – then the entire band "experiences" "history". Or at the standing Tetzel-stone near Elm, or at Regenstein Castle in the Harz Mountains, a raid by knights and servants with different historical roles: then the entire band experiences history.'[35] The question 'why?' was not difficult to answer for Mebes: 'One values the Heimat when one is rooted, therefore one must know how it came to be. One understands the present only when one knows its historical development. And above all, one does not just tramp around aimlessly'.[36]

In the many travelogues and *Erlebnisberichte* that the Wandervogel wrote, historical distance was breeched because in experience, time presented itself as a continuous flow, as *durée*, in which the past, present and future were immediately related to each other. Today, this temporality is usually referred to as 'historicity' (*Geschichtlichkeit*), which – when understood in reference to Martin Heidegger's thought – denotes the original situation in which being (*Dasein*) finds itself in time, a situation in which man finds himself prior to rational contemplation, and in which he is immediately related to the past and the future.[37] This situation does not mean that we understand our lives to take place at some point in historical time – as a point in history – but that history is in 'us', because it defines the situation in which we find ourselves; it determines language, customs and traditions which we cannot but use or relate to, and it determines the 'fate' we voluntarily take upon ourselves as we appropriate the past to shape the future – a fate that Heidegger calls 'destiny' when related to the social community in which one operates. Historicity thus precedes 'history' in the meaning of the 'historical process', because one is already historically positioned before conceptualizing it in terms of unilinear history.

For the Wandervogel, the experience of the solstice fire was, for example, one of those instances where the entire spectrum of German history came together in experience. The fire was 'historical' due to the ancient Germanic origins of the solstice festival. Although history lacks precise information on the origins of the festival, the Wandervögel tended to explain its value out of the closeness of the ancient Germans to nature. In the December solstice the fire symbolized the sun, and carried hope and joy for the nascent spring. This was where they found the universal value of the feast, as even 'in the era of steam heating ... perhaps we do not feel it as deep as our forefathers; still we owe our vitality and zest for life to the great, glorious daystar, which passes over us and penetrates us and fills us with life and joy through a warm beam of light'.[38] Others saw a symbol of life in the fire, as in December the fire was lit as a sign of hope and expectation on the shortest day of the year, and as it was lit on the longest day in June as celebration. Solstice celebrations survived Christianization as the festivities were deeply rooted in the 'dispositional needs' of the people.[39] Subsequently, the summer solstice was reframed by Christian rulers as *Johannisfest*, to celebrate the birth of John the Baptist. But, the author emphasizes, the feast was no longer a place to ruminate on ancient customs, but it had gained actuality as the fire hinted at the current 'brightness in the hearts of German youth', as the Wandervogel had re-established inner bonds with the body and with nature.[40]

The fascination with fire and light as symbols and the solstice feast as a ritual reflect the ongoing irrationalization of the youth movement. The movement stood not alone in this process – in fact, much was inspired by the Lebensreform movement within which the search for a new sacrality had already been firmly established at, for example, the Monte Verità. For the youth movement, the illustration *Lichtgebet* (Light Prayer) by Fidus (the artist name of Hugo Höppener), was perhaps the best visualization of the way light was turned into a cult of the unity of body and soul. The illustration was distributed as a postcard on the Freideutsche Jugendtag and was to become an often reprinted 'cult image' of the youth movement. It had at least the 'gesture of resoluteness and the indefiniteness of goals' in common with the programme of the youth movement, as it was laid down in the Meißner formula.[41] Yet, it must be emphasized that such an image lacked the ideological value for the younger members of the Wandervogel. It is said that at the Meißner, two young Wandervögel saw Fidus's postcard and after a while one reacted plainly: 'Look how the rascal enjoys himself'.[42]

The solstice speeches not only contained explanations about the purpose of the feast, but could contain basically anything relevant to the Wandervogel-chapter who organized the festival. During the war they bore reference to fallen comrades, or to those still serving at the front. Before the war, when the revolt against German historical culture initiated at the Meißner still had momentum, the speeches often connected the ceremony to the youth movement's Fichtean conception of the nation. The Alt-Wandervogel from Birkenfeld emphasized at a solstice fire in June 1914 that 'in this hour, everywhere in the broad German fatherland our brothers gather around burning firewood, loyal to the ancient, ancestral customs. All are filled with the same mysterious weaving and working forces of ancient, legendary folk beliefs'.[43] Forming a broad circle around the fire, they sang a song which was almost obligatory at this event: 'Flamme Empor'. This song recalled the 'Spirit of 1813' as it was written in 1814 by Johann Heinrich Christian Nonne for the first annual commemoration of the Battle of the Nations. Yet, singing 'Flamme Empor' was the only recurrent element of the feast: 'apart from that, the feast is carried by the attunement of the moment'.[44]

The word 'attunement' is the English rendering of the concept *Stimmung*, which refers to a pervasive mood or atmosphere as well as to one's attunement to this atmosphere. It cannot simply be translated as 'mood', for in English, the term 'mood' can be either object-bound (the mood of a landscape), or subject-bound (my mood). In German, however, the concept eludes the subject–object dichotomy, which becomes clear when we take the musical connotation of the word *Stimmung* into account. In a musical performance, individual instruments are *gestimmt* ('tuned'), but the musical piece is not the sum of all individual tones. There is also a *Stimmung* of a musical piece which, as David Wellbery makes clear, has 'massive presence as a semantic resource'.[45] *Stimmungen* therefore form the basis of all our experiences; they 'colour' our experiences and 'embed' them. Attunements like fear, boredom and ecstasy are never just related to specific situations and therefore prelude the detachment of subject and object.[46] This implies that attunement is neither embedded in the subject, nor in the object, but in what in Heidegger's philosophy is called *Dasein*.[47] Attunements that determine our experience can be influenced or steered without creating a situation of 'inauthenticity'. This does not mean that man can consciously choose a *Stimmung* in a way in which he is elevated above the attunement as a transcendental subject. No, life is always embedded in *Stimmungen* – but this does mean that one can learn to deal with them, as one can enforce a certain *Stimmung* and counter unpleasant *Stimmungen* with other attunements.[48]

The attunement of the fire created a situation in which the historical meaning and significance of the solstice festival faded, and in which the self-definition of the Wandervogel as a 'child of the light' and the *völkisch*-Germanic imagery that accompanied it were only of secondary importance. What the experience of 'being attuned' generated was the fading of object and subject, which made the past palpable in the presence of the fire.

## Jewish Experience in the German Countryside

We have seen how *Erlebnis* was conceived as an alternative way to relate to the past. This past was obviously a German past. The temporal distance between past and present and the alterity of the past dissolved in non-rational experience, because the pre-conceptuality and the experience of lived time as 'flow' endorsed the idea of a lived tradition – the idea that history has presence in the totality of our experience, and the idea that we can only put the past at a distance when we reject experience and approach it merely through cognition. The past then becomes objectified as history and lacks any moral imperative for the self-fashioning of one's own life. In Germany the sources of experience were manifold: castle ruins, townscapes, cathedrals, folk culture and folk songs – all already self-evidently German. I will illustrate what the value of experience and living tradition could be when such sources lacked with the case of the Jüdische Wanderbund Blau-Weiß.

In 1912, the Jüdische Wanderbund Blau-Weiß was established at the initiative of the Zionistische Vereinigung fur Deutschland with the aim of educating children from assimilated families into a new sense of Jewishness.[49] Blau-Weiß was named after the colours of the Zionist flag, the current flag of Israel, and quickly gained popularity in the larger cities of Germany and Austria-Hungary. With a thousand members at the outbreak of the First World War, the association grew to more than three thousand in the early 1920s. All came from middle-class and mostly assimilated families. The main reason for the popularity of the movement was that it was modelled after the Wandervogel.

The Wandervogel became a model for two reasons. First, hiking was a good way to overcome the physical degeneration of the Jewish people. They were ashamed of 'the contemporary type (*Typus*) of German youth', whose degenerative mental and physical condition was one of the main arguments to win parents and educators for the case of a Jewish youth movement.[50] This 'shame' had less to do with anti-Semitic caricatures than with the broader social and reform-pedagogical debate on the detrimental influences of modern urban life and the repressive character of the educational system on German youth in general. It was noted that:

> our Jewish youth was in general physically less efficient [*untüchtiger*] and more nervous than the other youths; a relatively larger part suffers under the damaging influences of urban life. In an environment of materialistic thinking and acting adults, in the proximity of sceptical, ironical, joyless people, estranged from nature, grown up in the atmosphere of the Jewish wit and Jewish self-mockery, our boys

and girls are *a generation whose general human attitude to life is already spoiled in the parental home.*[51]

Second, the Wandervogel provided a successful model for the renegotiation of German identity, for in their hikes they had constructed a more 'original' conception of the German people, as a community, opposing the artificial patriotic nationalism of the modern society. The revitalization of a Jewish identity within Blau-Weiß was based on the same unease with political nationalism – both in German historical culture, and in the political Zionism of Theodor Herzl. Added to this was unease with the cultural memory of the Jews as an oppressed and persecuted people in exile. Instead, Blau-Weiß was inspired by the cultural Zionism of Martin Buber. Buber propagated a quest for a Jewish Renaissance, the spiritual revitalization of Jewish life in exile, which aimed at overcoming the legacy of the Jew as a ghetto-being, and at the construction of a new type of strong, active, creative and, most of all, natural Jew. Buber did not want to reject Jewish tradition or heritage, but wanted to revitalize, to resurrect it so to speak – hence the word 'renaissance'. He differed from political Zionists on the idea that the revival of the Jewish people was not only a political solution, but a question of identity. In order to reinstate such a sense of Jewish identity, it was necessary to reattach to lost traditions and reinstate a natural attitude to life.[52] Thus, Zionism for Buber was a cultural Zionism, based neither on religion nor on political nationalism, but on a natural Jewishness. To revitalize the Jews in exile as a strong and creative people, freed from the burden of meaningless and misunderstood traditions, was a question of the same 'historical paradox of progressive return' which Burckhardt identified in the Italian Renaissance.[53]

For Blau-Weiß, wandering was the answer to the regeneration of Jewish identity, as they believed that 'in the mode of hiking [*in der Art des Wanderns*] the whole person can be expressed, and conversely, that the mode of hiking can shape the person' into a new type of strong, creative and authentic Jew. This poses a serious difficulty, for the landscape which functioned as the object of self-identification was the same historical landscape which the Wandervogel used to embed the individual in the vitality of living German traditions.[54] As Blau-Weiß wanted to educate assimilated youth into a renewed sense of Jewishness, they were primarily interested in those elements of folk culture which expressed Jewish presence in the historical landscape. It was stated that the Jewish wanderer had the 'duty to visit sites of Jewish memory, everywhere we go on a hike'.[55] In this way, the half-forgotten and ruined remains of Jewish habitation of pastoral Germany, such as the Jewish cemetery of Worms, served as objects which reflected the historical possibility of a strong and self-conscious Jewish people. However, Jewish heritage lacked the self-evidency of German heritage. Decades of assimilation had made Jewish presence in Germany slowly disappear from the countryside. On a cold December evening in 1913, while strolling around the streets and alleys of the Alsatian village of Weißenburg (now Wissembourg) – where every window was lit by the shining lights of a Christmas tree – three hikers of the Mannheim Blau-Weiß could not but let their memories and their thoughts hark back to the times when 'our people still put small, moderate Chanukah candles in the windows. Who of us wanderers still knows about this custom and who still practices it?'[56]

Nonetheless, the south of Germany was still inhabited by isolated rural Jewish communities, although these were gradually disappearing as well, as youths migrated to Stuttgart or Zurich for work, leaving only the aged and children to populate the synagogues.[57] When Jewish communities were discovered on a hike in the countryside, this came as a pleasant surprise. Hans Oppenheim, a young medical doctor and the leader of a Berlin group, recalled the small village of Edelfingen on the river Tauber, where his group of Berlin hikers accidentally ran into a Jewish community of twenty-five families: 'These people were not like those grief-stricken, nervous Ghetto-creatures of the *Großstadt*, but upright and broad-shouldered, and the smell of sweat of physical labour, the narrow contingence with the soil, was aired by these people. They were farmers.'[58] As such, the Jewish community of Oppenheim was the living proof of the vitality of the Jewish people, perhaps a living anachronism, but a spark of hope for the regeneration of the Jews as a *Volk*. The communal experience of the Berlin youths who were warm-heartedly welcomed in the village was unforgettable. 'This was finally a type of Jewish experience [*Erlebnis*], of which we unfortunately have too few.'[59]

Such testimonies of the vital presence of Jewishness in the German landscape was, however, quite rare. In most places where Blau-Weiß wandered, Jewish heritage was either absent or testified of the history of Jewish suffering. When the München chapter travelled to the Jewish settlements in the Fränkische Schweiz in 1917, they found no lively Jewish community, for migration to the city and to America had reduced the once flourishing Jewish communities in many villages to a family or two. The Jews they did find were mostly cattle traders, who – disappointingly – did not connect with the soil like the farmers from Edelfingen.[60]

The absence of Jewish heritage was partly compensated by the *Erlebnis* of the rooted heritage of other peoples. Memorials of the sixteenth-century *Bauernkrieg*, which showed the self-conscious action of the German *Volk*, could as easily be an object of Jewish experience as the nationalism of the Swiss *Volk*, because both were examples of vital and creative nationhood:

> On the evening before the Swiss National Festival we climbed the Hohentwiel. … We marvelled at all the beauty and rejoiced over the Volk that has so much history to revere. And suddenly we began to speak about our people, who wander homeless around the earth and start to forget their heroes.[61]

Just as the experience of the history of another people could inspire thoughts on Jewish history, landscape too could function as a reminder. In the winter of 1913, for example, the Berlin chapter of Blau-Weiß undertook a three-day *Winterfahrt* through the district of Barnim, north of Berlin. The hikers were mainly struck by the salient way in which the trees 'spread out their branches to provide the falling snow a pleasant sojourn'. For minutes they gazed at the interplay between snow and trees and noticed that 'occasionally a loaded tree leaped in gentle sways to his comrades on the other side of the road. When a tree from the other side met him, a magnificent Gothic arch arose'. On the third day of their trip, they encountered real gothic arches. The ruins of the medieval Cistercian abbey of Chorin, with its tall, ivy-entwined gothic windows, carefully restored and reconstructed in the age of Romanticism, offered a splendid sight. But when gazing at this striking scenery, something dissonant caught the onlookers' attention. Parallel to the lofty arches, there proudly stood a foreign tree, which – despite the trained eye – none of the admiring ramblers was able to recognize. Luckily, a close examination revealed a small sign, stating that the exotic tree was in fact a cedar. They 'looked at each other and were filled with exultation on the fact that our tree was so beautiful'.[62] The tree that beforehand they only knew by name – whether from Biblical narratives or from the Zionist song 'Dort wo die Zeder schlank die Wolke küßt'[63] – did not directly foster Zionist feelings, but the cedar that kissed the German sky at Chorin ironically exalted the young hikers' love for the German forest. At the end of the third day, they 'travelled home, soon to go out again into the forest – which is our true homeland'.[64]

However, the proper working through of *Fahrtenerlebnisse* mainly took place at what was regarded as the second important activity of Blau-Weiß besides the *Fahrt*: the *Heimabend* (social evening). Like the Wandervogel, the different Blau-Weiß chapters established homes (*Heime*) in which evening gatherings were held and Jewish holidays were celebrated. Larger and financially strong chapters also established *Landheime* in rented dwellings in the countryside, which functioned as places of departure or arrival for hikes, as places to welcome visitors and as sites for gatherings. For the Blau-Weiß leadership – which before the war was mainly recruited from the Kartell Jüdischer Verbindungen (KJV), the umbrella organization for Jewish-national Zionist student associations, and which was strongly influenced by the ideas of Martin Buber – the *Heim* was the place where this attempt to overcome the history of the Wandering Jew and the creation of a new type of Jew took place.[65] Emphasis was put on those elements of the Jewish past which witnessed acts of self-conscious Jewry. Old Testament heroes and prophets were introduced in the *Blau-Weiß-Blätter* in a secular and romantically refashioned way. Simon bar Kokhba – the Jewish leader of the revolt against the Romans in 132 – was for Blau-Weiß what Siegfried was for the Wandervogel: the embodiment of heroism and strength, and a substitute for childhood heroes from Karl May's books.[66]

The Maccabees exemplified the strength and the stamina of a community. Religious holidays – many of which were never celebrated in the parental home

– were reappropriated by the Blau-Weiß and were celebrated in the *Heim* or in the open. However, these holidays were not celebrated as religious holidays, but as examples of the vitality of the Jewish nation. Chanukah was among the most popular holidays, as it was based on the heroic history of the Maccabees. The Berlin chapter celebrated Chanukah by putting seven large bonfires up on the top of the Krähenberg near Potsdam, in the shape of a Menorah. The permission for this feast was easily obtained, as the authorities believed the feast to be a sort of Germanic solstice celebration, which the local Wandervogel usually celebrated on the same spot and in a common manner. Sukkot, the Feast of Tabernacles, was an opportunity to emphasize 'that our fathers became strong in simplicity [*Einfachheit*] and in connection with nature, so that many movements in ancient Israel, who wanted simplicity again, followed the treats of this festival'.[67]

Additionally, the *Heim* was the place where books were discussed – certainly not only on Jewish history. From the Bible, to Fichte's *Reden an die deutsche Nation*, to Hans Blüher's history of the Wandervogel – those narratives which emphasized the natural genesis of a nation or the revolt of youth were of interest and liable for discussion. Courses in Hebrew, Jewish history and folk culture were organized and attended. Questions were discussed on topics such as 'Jewish Youth Hiking', 'Blau-Weiß and the School', 'The Life of East European Jewry' and 'Why We should Love Flowers'.[68] This was a unique situation when one takes the fact into consideration that such questions were rarely discussed in the parental home and that the German school system did not formally allow pupils to voice their opinions.

Felix Rosenblüth, one of the initiators of Blau-Weiß, phrased his belief in the ability of the Blau-Weiß education to create Zionists as follows. The basic idea was 'to bring children from the big cities in contact with nature, into the outdoors. A naturally sensitive person had to become Zionist anyhow'. One had to tell the youngsters something about Chanukah and the Maccabees, 'and then everything develops spontaneously'.[69] This project had succeeded to the extent that by the beginning of the First World War, Blau-Weiß members increasingly saw themselves as a distinct group, and not just as Jewish Wandervogel as they initially did. In the end, it were the *Bundestage* – like the one in Lockwitz in 1916 where three hundred of the total of twelve hundred Blau-Weiß members had gathered – which contributed to a sense of belonging:

> When it became entirely dark, we crowded around the flames [of the campfire] in a passionate feeling of belonging together and the impossibility of ever parting again. Never since the Galuth had Jewish youth come together in this way. Never since the time when the unity of our people was broken had Jewish youth dared to feel this free. This was Romanticism, but not the extrinsic Romanticism of the darkness and of the fire, which is borrowed so easily: this was instinctively finding oneself together, the vitalization of the *Blutsgemeinschaft*, which had never before been such a powerful reality.[70]

Although there had always been different vantage points within Blau-Weiß between Zionist and more Wandervogel-oriented leaders, the first serious criticism struck the very principle that both camps shared: the basic connection of hiking and Jewish identity. Between August 1915 and early 1916, the seventeen-year-old Berlin schoolboy Gerhard Scholem (today better known as Gershom Scholem) published a series of pamphlets in his father's printing office under the name *The Blue-White Spectacles* (*Die Blau-Weiße Brille*), which he distributed privately among friends. In them, Scholem critically assessed issues concerning Zionism, including the writings of Martin Buber and the practice of Blau-Weiß and the KJV.[71] Scholem came in contact with Blau-Weiß when friends invited him to join the association, but he left after only two 'trial hikes' (*Probefahrten*). The group culture opposed him, for he preferred to hike in solitude or in the company of a good friend.[72]

The inability to be lonely within the youth movement was exactly the basis on which Scholem attacked the quest for community. 'When community [*Gemeinschaft*] between people is indeed the highest that can be demanded, what use then has Zionism, when it can be realized in Galuth?' In this way, the Jewish youth movement bases its Zionist programme on a *petitio principii*, which is the 'curse of Zionism': the 'pseudo-Zionistic lie of community' [*Gemeinschaftslüge*].[73] And when youth cannot be alone, Scholem continues, it cannot be silent and reflective, but loses itself in a stream of chatter (*Geschwätz*). Neither can youth speak, for it lacks a language of its own, which causes a state of confusion. In Blau-Weiß, Hebrew was only learned superficially and not seen as a necessity for building a new community. Without a proper understanding of the Hebrew language, the construction of a 'whole' Jew would fail, and Blau-Weiß' quest for a strong, creative, acting – indeed Nietzschean – Jew would be futile. Instead, what the Jewish youth movement in general and Blau-Weiß in particular had created was nothing but 'confusion' and 'superficiality'.[74] Large words are spoken about the revitalization of Jewry, but no action was undertaken to put it into practice in aliyah – the 'remigration' to the land of Israel.

With his friend Walter Benjamin, Scholem shared an aversion to the 'cult of experience' ('*Kult des Erlebnisses*'), which Blau-Weiß in its turn shared with Martin Buber, and which in a sense formed the very basis of Blau-Weiß as a *Wanderbund*, as this principle connected hiking to the construction of Jewish identity. Benjamin said mockingly that if it was up to Buber, every Jew would first have to be asked: 'Have you experienced Jewishness yet?'[75] Within the youth movement, the emphasis that was put on *Erlebnis* was born out of poverty: 'as youth could not be silent and could not speak, could not see and could not act, it experienced [*erlebte*]'.[76] In essence, Scholem stated that experience was nothing but a phantasm, which led to an untrue relationship with community. He attacked the very idea that 'to become conscious of one's own Jewishness in wandering, and through wandering, means a deepening of community life'.[77]

In sum, Scholem believed that it was rather naive to believe that someone's Jewishness was cultivated by a hike. Only true 'Hebrewisation' could help youth out of its confusion.

The critique Scholem aired struck Blau-Weiß harder than the predictable arguments that had been voiced by assimilationist critics for several years, for this critique came from within and – ironically – from personal experience. In a reaction, Karl Glaser, one of the most prominent Blau-Weiß leaders, called Scholem the 'true anti-Blue-White' (*'wahre anti-Blau-Weiße'*) and noted that the triumph of his theory would mean the end of Blau-Weiß.[78] However, Scholem forgot that the association was still quite young and it was impossible to construct a 'full Jew' all at once. By now, the *Sehnsucht*, the romantic longing for a yet undefined and unknown *Heimat*, which Scholem refuted, was exactly what kept Jewish youth together.[79] The dogmatism of Scholem's alternative lacked the educational value needed in Blau-Weiß.

*Erlebnis* enabled Blau-Weiß to hike through a German landscape and still educate Jewishness, because experience provided a sense of community. To connect this sense of community to the idea of a culturally and historically shaped nation was, however, more problematic. For the Wandervogel, experience in the German countryside was more easily explained as the experience of Germanness. To translate their communal experience into cultural meaning was more problematic for Blau-Weiß due to the lack of Jewish presence in German towns and landscape. Lacking self-evidency, their *Erlebnis* was vulnerable to critique like Scholem's. In the next section, we will see that translating the lived experience of the heritage of another nation into cultural meaning was less problematic by focusing on the Flanders experience of Wandervogel soldiers in the First World War.

## The Great War and Flanders' Idyllic Soul

When the war broke out in August 1914, it did not halt the youth movement's wandering activities. Although, as the war continued, wandering at home was hampered by a lack of capable leaders and saw a steady decline in hikes, those who served carried the youth movement's young traditions into the army. Despite the movement's fierce opposition to German jingoism, there was almost unanimous support for the war effort. This support is often explained by the fact that the outbreak of the war generated a sense of unity and a sense of shared destiny among the Germans, which jingoism could by no means have generated by itself.[80] This nationwide sense of unity was initially an experience, but would soon become pivotal in the war discourse of the German intellectual elite. In reaction to claims – primarily British – that the German war effort was being driven by a mere zest for power, historians, economists, lawyers and philosophers as close to the youth movement as Paul Natorp would provide a broad range of arguments that basically boiled down to the fact that there was a fundamental difference between German 'culture' and Western 'civilization'.[81] While Germany was presented as the land of introspection, of the soul, of culture and of a true individualism which accounts for the individual's embeddedness in the larger community, the West represented an egoistic individualism, convention and pretence, lacking inner values. More concretely, the German 'ideas of 1914' were posited against the 'ideas of 1789', which included British liberalism and French democracy; 1914 became the world-historical moment in which the German national character was tested and in which the German people had a task far beyond the emperor's imperial politics: the protection of Europe against the dangers of Westernization.[82]

To the youth movement, August 1914 meant the fulfilment of the Fichtean idea of an inner and spiritual nationhood that had already been established before the war. As the social, economic and political differences seemed to dissolve, and absolute nationhood seemed to be fulfilled, the members of the youth movement could participate in the patriotic outbursts, which they had previously despised, without losing their credibility. One member of the Freideutsche Jugend wrote retrospectively in 1919:

> When in August 1914 the war awoke us from quiescence and unconcern and all the minor issues that had appeared to us so deep and important in those days, then we all experienced – for there is hardly anyone among us who can deny this experience – the enthusiasm of unconditional commitment to the Volk and the fatherland. What had before appeared to us as empty tones – echoes dispersing in the wind – suddenly gained meaning, existence and value. We ourselves, however, became valueless – a small part in a totality of millions. And with millions we sang the old patriotic songs; but not, as has been said, behind beer mugs in smoke-filled pubs with the common patriotic zeal – no! We sang these songs – which previously we had hardly sung; yes, which we had despised as artificial, untrue sentiment – we sang them, *because for us every single word of it had turned into an experience*! Now we lived these songs, like the volunteers of Ypres lived them, as the words and rhythm of 'Deutschland, Deutschland über alles ...' ran through their veins as they attacked while singing – the attack that became their death. We *lived* it, and had it died, the times of exaltation would have brought us *death*.[83]

The war was to a certain extent a relief. The youth movement had little trouble identifying the problems of modern life in Wilhelmine Germany, but had not yet found concrete ways to translate this critique into social engagement. The war, which was interpreted as a 'defensive' war, provided the possibility to participate and determine world events in a way similar to the student volunteers of 1813 – a possibility German historical culture had reserved for emperors, kings and generals. In this way, the war provided a way of social engagement and taking social responsibility.[84] The war participation of the movement was significant. By 1916, six thousand members of the Wandervogel e.V. had joined the army – which was half of the number of members they had had at the outbreak of the war.[85] Eventually the Wandervogel e.V. – the largest of the various Wandervogel associations – would alone supply ten thousand soldiers for the entire war – a quarter of whom would not survive it.[86] Walter Laqueur estimated that the total number of Wandervogel soldiers was fourteen thousand, again with a mortality rate of 25 per cent.[87]

Despite the fact that the Wandervögel were absorbed into the large imperial army, romanticized testimonies of how they were able to recognize other Wandervögel in barracks, on the front or during troop movements by their attitude, or by the look in their eyes, abound.[88] Apart from these 'spontaneous' encounters, a network was set up in 1915 connecting some 3,500 Wandervögel on both the Eastern and the Western Front.[89] In the spring of 1917, loose groups of Wandervögel on the Western Front organized themselves as *Feldwandervogel*, trying to continue a Wandervogel lifestyle in the moments they were off-duty. Their journal *Der Zwiespruch* reached approximately 1,300 Wandervogel soldiers in 1918.[90] Over the course of the war some 128 meeting places were established in and behind the trenches, of which some 30 were situated in Flanders.[91] In 1916, teachers at the German schools in Antwerp and Brussels with a background in the youth movement even established Wandervogel departments for their pupils. The fact that the organization and the activities of the Wandervogel soldiers had gained a more permanent character was decisive for their appropriation of Flemish culture, history and landscape. By 1916, the initial conviction that the 'spirit' of 1914 had definitely ended the individualism and social discord of Wilhelmine society had faded. As the habituation to war grew, they realized that the army was not an expression of a new German nationhood, but that it was in fact an institute built upon Wilhelmine social order. News from war profiteers and usurers resulted in a negative image of the *Heimat* among the soldiers, and supported the belief that basically nothing had changed after August 1914. Otto Neumann, a Wandervogel from Osnabrück, wrote from the front that for him the war habituation was the prime cause for losing his initial hopes:

> War habituation: yes, that is the worst and most despicable thing. That a certain equilibrium has got hold of the soul of the people, that one acknowledges the state of affairs as necessary, and that one liberates oneself in this acknowledgement, is not the most detestable thing of all – no, what is detestable is that people repress it: that people again utter and validate the old norms again, that people unconsciously readapt the old egotism of subjecting the world to their will, that people no longer acknowledge the deeper unity. This at least is my image of home.[92]

The loss of the initial belief that in 1914 a *Volksgemeinschaft* had been established that finally gave the idea of nationhood substance rather than empty form was not only visible among the Wandervogel soldiers. From 1916 onwards a sceptical attitude towards the war became common among the German troops, which the army leadership unsuccessfully tried to counter with a propaganda offensive filled with rhetoric on Germanness and arguments on the historical mission of the German nation.[93] In 1916 and 1917, the idea that the war was not the beginning of a new era, but the final struggle of the 'old' Europe gained momentum. With the dissolution of optimism, the pre-war critique of modernity became valuable again and coloured the Wandervogel's engagement with Flanders.

When, by 1916, the soldiers picked up Wandervogel life in their spare free moments, they also took up wandering and subsequently renewed their interest in, and engagement with, folklore and rural life. Soon, rural Flanders was being hailed for its scenic qualities. Peter Zylmann – an Alt-Wandervogel who had taught at the German school in Antwerp since 1912 and became the leader of the Antwerp Wandervogel group after he had returned to this position in 1916 due to a war wound – praised the 'melancholic heathlands' in the north with its beautiful sunsets, as well as the green fields and meadows with the picturesque villages along the river Scheldt and its tributaries.[94] One could wander here for hours 'without getting tired by the constantly changing images'.[95] He equally hailed Flemish culture and society, which he found to be more authentic than German culture, as Flemish social structures appeared to him to be expressions of life, contrary to the rational goal-oriented organizations and associations that dominated German life. When witnessing lower-class Flemish girls dancing in the streets as a group of musicians passed through Antwerp on a sunny summer's day, he recognized 'images of a Breughel or Teniers spilled over in merry life'.[96] The fact that such expressions of life were regarded as old-fashioned by the average German was proof for Zylmann that, in modern German culture, life and expression had drifted too far apart – or had even been disconnected as modern society had become goal-oriented, unspontaneous and artificial. In Flanders, he recognized a reciprocal relationship between expression and experience which served as a proof and an argument that the Wandervogel's turn to folk culture was a legitimate and timely attempt to counter the negative effects of modern civilization.

'When we want to entirely understand a people in its life expressions', the Saxon Wandervogel Otto Schönfelder wrote in an essay on Flanders, 'then we must not only focus on what has been determined historically, but also take into account that which remains ever the same and which eternally returns'.[97] Schönfelder had unconscious attitudes and actions in mind that elude cognition or precede it, and that therefore are basically unhistorical, for history was understood as the domain of the conscious self-constitution of man in thought and action. The joy of life and nature, but also sleeping, eating, drinking and dreaming, are such timeless forces that determine life as much as the change of sun and rain – which means: unmediated, without interference from human reason. The fact that such non-rational factors are often neglected in the study of culture and people had in Schönfelder's opinion to do with the fact that such studies usually only take the products of the human 'spirit' into account: historical constellations such as culture and politics. In his interpretation of Flanders, Schönfelder could not, however, neglect the fact that although social life appeared to be in stagnation due to the war and francophone cultural hegemony, still 'an unparalleled zest for life could develop and remain, which even includes the poorest part of the population – something that in Germany has been lost due to the strong industrialization and the related migration'.[98] For Schönfelder, this zest for life appeared in many expressions of Flemish folk life, from the widespread fishing to the organization of the household.

Schönfelder's vitalist interpretation of Flemish culture was mainly inspired by an article published by the young Jena philosopher and pedagogue Herman Nohl in *Die Tat*.[99] Nohl knew the youth movement quite well through his students, as Jena was a hotbed of the youth movement in the pre-war years, housing Eugen Diederichs' Sera-circle, the Akademische Vereinigung Jena (which had been part of the Deutsche Akademische Freischar and part of the Freideutsche Jugend since 1913), as well as a lively Wandervogel community.[100] Nohl himself was more or less the academic 'mentor' of the Sera-circle, on which he made quite an impression.[101] Rudolf Carnap – the later logician, then member of the Sera-circle – recalled that Nohl 'took a personal interest in the lives and thoughts of his students, in contrast to most of the professors in Germany at that time, because in his seminars and in private talks he tried to give us a deeper understanding of philosophers on the basis of their attitude towards life (*Lebensgefühl*) and their cultural background'.[102] The interest in the philosophy of life, which Nohl inherited from his tutor Dilthey, fitted the ideas on the pre-rational roots of culture that were circulating in the youth movement.

It was with the interest in attitudes to life that Nohl approached Flanders when stationed as part of the German occupational forces in Ghent between 1915 and 1918, as a leg injury made him unfit for front service.[103] In his article he praised what he called the 'idyllic soul' of Flanders: 'the peaceful joy of life in relation to nature, the house and the family' that is proper to all nations.[104] According to Nohl, this joyful acceptance of life was a vital element of human existence, but is commonly overlooked as history is usually interpreted as the domain of human volition. The will is then understood as an expression of the human soul which presents itself in questions of state, science, culture and society. *Dasein* – the simple presence of men and nations, the 'eating, drinking, sleeping, chatting and celebrating, dreaming and strolling, which even according to Plato takes up two-thirds of every day', is regarded in the light of history as un- or pre-historical vegetative and eternally recurring life; simply as a domain beyond history.[105] Nohl regarded this lack of interest in daily unreflective life and habits of man quite unjustified. The rhythmic tensions in the 'idyllic soul' and its spilling over into the totality of life are not only characteristics of every historical existence, but also the primordial sources of historical existence. The everyday existence of idyllic life was for Nohl the precondition as well as the foundation on which man was able to act 'historically' in the first place. But because the dynamics of idyllic life differ from situation to situation, idyllic life was not to be interpreted as an invariable, timeless and transcendent source of life: it was this aspect of historical life that we always tend to forget, because we want to see it as invariable, timeless and transcendent.

With these thoughts, Nohl took stand in the conservative discussion on the role and function of history, which would later evolve into the crisis of historicism. His main point of reference was Friedrich Nietzsche's already mentioned 1874 essay *Vom Nutzen und Nachteil der Historie für das Leben*. Nietzsche concluded that there was a surplus of history, generated by modern society as a counterweight to progress, and that this surplus of history frustrated 'life'.[106] With these remarks, Nietzsche constructed 'history' and 'life' as oppositional categories, in which he did not mean the past per se when referring to 'history', but cultivated historical memory or practised history in its many appearances. He compared life to the unhistorical, vegetative life of the animal. While the animal lives in the happiness of the unreflected moment, man has forgotten to live momentarily as he has been accustomed to apprehend life through historically defined frames of meaning and identities. Man is caught up in the current of becoming, and sees his life being dictated by history. Nietzsche's answer therefore was that the relation between life and history had to be re-evaluated: no longer should life stand in the service of history, but history should serve life. Nohl continues Nietzsche's logic, but also amends it on a crucial point: he does not understand life and history as oppositional categories, but sees life as something that always precedes history and makes history possible. History – both in its meaning as historical representation and as the course of human action – is always carried by life: without life there is no 'history', but there certainly is life without 'history'. Nohl's answer to the problem of history was therefore to learn to live again – to create new history out of the fullness of human existence.

For Nohl, Flanders was the prime example of how life could function as source of power and as carrier of history. Nohl did not relate idyllicness to Flanders' economic backwardness, but overcame the modern logic of history by referring to more or less timeless factors as causes of idylicness. The climate, for example, was a factor which meant that life was lived more on the streets and in the open than in Germany. The Flemish home – the small, tidy, detached house – was the centre of Flemish life, for Nohl as it was a place of comfort, of shelter, of work and of leisure. Because the transition from city to countryside was more gradual in Flanders than in Germany, the answers that the *Lebensreform* movement sought to urban problems, such as the garden city and the family home, were already naturally present here.[107] But while Nohl continued with a laudation on the way Flemish art captured the idyllic soul, the fascination of the Wandervogel soldiers with Flanders remained concerned with the question of German culture. Flanders' bucolically interpreted 'idyllic soul' became a symbol for what Germany ought to become. When Otto Schönfelder used Nohl's article to express the Wandervogel's fascination with Flanders, he made clear that 'without a doubt this way of life had many dark sides, but the sunny sides dominate so strongly that the foreigner continuously asks himself in astonishment if he has not left the world of haste and money behind and entered a legendary land of dreams and wonders, in which pure and healthy feelings, a certain joy of life as well as a quiet cheerfulness of character have been preserved – things that we Germans have unfortunately almost entirely lost over the course of time'.[108]

For the Wandervogel soldiers, Flanders' idyllic soul was in the first place present in the landscape. The idealization of the landscape had much to do with nostalgic memories of pre-war hikes with old comrades through the German countryside. The Flemish landscape was a source of memory – not because it was similar to the German landscape, but because it generated recollections of the *Heimat* as it was also a domain of experience and unburdened wandering. For Wandervogel Walter Hedicke, wandering was as 'sunshine in the darkness of war' and Flanders was a 'blissful land', where he could journey 'singing and laughing as Wandervogel, in the familiar Wandervogel garb'.[109] Herman Nohl wrote in recollection of his 1914-fallen Wandervogel friend Karl Brügmann, that Brügmann went into the war as if it were a Wandervogel hike, 'filled with the beauty of his home and with the great unity of his people in those days; cheerful in the adventurous soldier's life with all its real tasks and in the friendliest contact with the Flemish population'.[110] Entering Flanders was, Brügmann wrote to Nohl, 'as if we entered a Thuringian village by night'.[111]

Gertrud Döring, one of the female leaders of the Antwerp Wandervogel-group, wrote about an experience on the moors in the vicinity of Antwerp in terms of Proust's *souvenir involontaire*: 'We happily stretched out on the soft ground. The knotty pines nodded above us, and for me old times arose: the hours on the Märkische Heide of which I had so often dreamt'.[112] Although she was disturbed in her recollections as the group of girls she led wanted to play a ballgame, the hike would revoke a chain of memories of her own *Heimat* and of fallen friends and acquaintances. Döring taught the group some German folk dances on the spot, but when returning to Antwerp they walked towards the roar of the cannons. But before they reached Antwerp's outskirts, they too met Flanders' idyllic soul. When they passed by a small farm and decided to ask for a glass of milk, they found an old peasant woman in front of a large fireplace, above which a copper kettle hung, with kittens playing at her feet. 'The fairy tale was complete when one of our girls – with a garland in her hair – approached her. "Sleeping Beauty", the others, who witnessed the beautiful scene with astonishment, whispered.'[113] They valued Flanders for its idyllic character – there was no monumental, critical or antiquarian interest. The idyllic was the primal source of history, but it could not therefore be explained in historical terms – only in legendary terms, in analogy to Sleeping Beauty.

The same applied to the experience of Flemish cities. For Enno Narten, the view of the idyllic town of Damme brought up memories of his *Heimat* East Frisia. His recollection, however, was in stark contrast to his experiences in Flanders. It was the village Bant, in the shadow of industrial Wilhelmshaven, which he had in mind when approaching Damme. The existence of picturesque Bant, with its church ruin and its sincere inhabitants, was already threatened before the war by 'the wall of houses and the chimney forest' of Wilhelmshaven – a fate that seemed to be imminent with the expansion of the war industry.[114] Damme on the contrary had retained its charm due to oblivion. Here, the inhabitants had not transformed into industrial labourers who drag themselves along in life without joy, forgetting the pleasure of watching the sky, the sea or the sun. Narten too does not counter the negative effects of progress with the idealization of a specific past, but with an attitude to life that we may call 'idyllic' with Nohl and which is redemptive. Narten found the key to Flanders' idyllic soul in the devotion of the priest who let them enter the Church of Our Lady: 'the tall house of worship, the dimensions of which could only be guessed due to the darkness; the slender columns that rose to unknown heights; the dead silence; the dimly lit choir and the praying priest before the altar – all this had something mystical about it. We continued to look for a long time'.[115]

Connecting mesmerizing to recollections of home was by no means a German phenomenon. Paul Fussell, for example, has pointed out how British war memoirs also tended to counter portrayals of the harshness of war with recollections of a bucolic England.[116] The pastoral idealization of Flanders was, however, not so much accompanied by an idealization of the *Heimat*, but by memories of a pre-war Wandervogel life in Germany. Therefore, the idealization of Flanders was drawn into the discourse of cultural criticism that characterized the pre-war Wandervogel. The feelings of unity, which seemed to have overcome the fragmentation, isolation and individualism of bourgeois life, had become a lost hope when the war efforts stranded and stabilized in the stand-off of the trenches. The Osnabrück Wandervogel Otto Neumann, for example, wrote from the trenches that for him the habituation to war was one of the causes to have lost initial hope:

> What is odious is not that a certain equilibrium of the folk soul has occurred, but that the developments are acknowledged as necessities and are released from pressure in this recognition – but that they are repressed: that the old standards are expressed and given validity again and that unconsciously the old complacency is accepted again that one could influence and determine the world; that the deeper unity is no longer recognized. This, at least, is my image of home. But perhaps we have become idealists with big dreams in our simple life, in burdens and dirt. But better this way than vice versa: appearing to be a man of honour, but rotten inside.[117]

Flemish landscape and culture were thus more than repouse for the horrors of the front: they were objects of hope for the cultural regeneration of Germany.

Although the 'ideas of 1914' initially caught on among the Wandervögel, from 1916 war habituation led to the belief that the belief that modern, bourgeois society had been overcome was actually untrue. Rather than attributing the negative effects of modernity to the West – as had been the case in the discourse on the 'ideas of 1914' – the Wandervögel harked back to the pre-war belief that things such as individualism, formalism and capitalism were part of a worldview and of a specific social structure that were equally present in Germany as in the rest of Europe. In Flanders, the Wandervogel soldiers sought and found answers to these problems. Flanders showed it was possible to act out of life itself, to establish new frames of meaning out of the unmediated tensions of life – frames of meaning that were *expressions* of life rather than determinants that restrain life as the bourgeois culture of Wilhelmine was understood. Idyllic life was not reserved for bygone and unattainable times, as for example Greece had been for Weimar Classicism. Neither was it a Rousseauian domain beyond history. Idyllic life – the unmediated life of man in and with the world – was the prerequisite of historical action. The youth movement wanted more than just a shift in accents. This explains the fact that the Wandervogel soldiers had a strong interest in cultural expressions of Flemish idyllic life. Flanders was a land of hope: here the idyllic soul proved the possibility of gaining a new order of life out of existential *Dasein*. As such, Flanders became a source of inspiration for the regeneration and revitalization of Germany after the war.

## Conclusion

Wandervogel Hans Bohnenkamp once argued that for everything man can comprehend, there is also a mode of immediate apprehension: 'for an object or an event in spatiotemporal reality this is for example the bodily perception of the senses, for a general coherence it is evidence, for a value it is being struck by emotion'.[118] To have such an 'original' encounter with the things around us does not imply that the encounter includes the discovery of something entirely unknown: 'It can also occur that someone else, to whom the matter is already present, opens the eyes, the mind or the heart. In any case – then man "has" the "matter itself"'.[119]

For the youth movement, *Erlebnis* was the prime mode of apprehension of basically everything in life – from friendship, to a painting, to a landscape, to an old city. Yet, although *Erlebnis* appears not to be a category immediately relevant to history, we have seen with Konrad Cramer that, at least conceptually, the rise of *Erlebnis* is related to the rise of the concept of history. While the old concept of experience lost its unified meaning of both the method of inquiry (*historia*) and the substance of inquiry (*res gestae*) in modernity, the concept of history (*Geschichte*) took over this dual meaning – with the main side effect that the subject matter was now temporalized. In other words: in modernity, history meant both the study of human action and the contents thereof, and the study of history that framed the latter meaning as being part of a linear history of collective development. Despite the dual meaning of the concept of history, the object and the subject of historical understanding can be discerned, in which the latter refers to human experience as the source for inquiry and cognition as the method. Now, the Wandervogel's critique against the dominance of cognition over life and history made them turn the tables and prioritize experience over cognition. This solved the problem of historical distance to the extent that in experience the past is not yet objectified and thereby distanced. In experience, the past does not appear as historical, but as part of the lifeworld, and thereby attests to the historicity of man. Only in cognition is historical distance constructed. Yet, for the Wandervogel, *Erlebnis* was not only substance as Cramer contends, but both method and substance. It could be cultivated and did require knowledge. But, because it tapped into pre-rational life, *Erlebnis* could count as the basis for a post hoc cognitive reworking and narrating of history.

In the same way, *Erlebnis* could function as a source of nationhood. For both Blau-Weiß and the Wandervogel, the nation was not something to be constructed through cognition or narrative – it had to be lived before meaning was attributed. The tragedy of Blau-Weiß was that it aimed to revive a culture based on a narrative tradition through *Erlebnis*. The absence of Jewish relics in the German landscape made the project aimless and susceptible to criticism about seeking things that were not there. For the Feldwandervogel, on the contrary, Flanders contained neither relics nor heritage that they could reasonably call their own, but the Flemish attitude towards life at least confirmed their belief that it was possible to constitute culture on the basis of experience.

In sum, *Erlebnis* provided a mode of apprehending the past which precedes cognition. Because in *Erlebnis* subject and object had not yet mutually constituted each other, the past could not count as being qualitatively distanced. Rather, the past 'flowed' into the present in the form of traditions, speech and institutions that constitute the lifeworld. Yet, for the youth movement, the experience of history also had a moral function. By seeking experiences of historical elements that they considered to be genuine expressions of a life lived existentially rather than rationally, they tapped into the sources of life itself rather than those of a specific past. Dialects, folk songs of solstice fires and castles could provide such experiences. This brings us to the point where history is no longer perceived as a linear development. In the next chapter, I will discuss the rise of religiosity during the First World War, and the consequences it had for the youth movement's conceptions of time during the postwar period of revolution and economic crisis.

## Notes

1. Manfred Hausmann, 'Zum ersten Male', in Ziemer and Wolf, *Wandervogel und Freideutsche Jugend*, 166–69: 166.
2. Ibid., 167.
3. Ibid., 167.
4. Ibid., 168–69.

5. Cf. Engelhardt, *Die deutsche Jugendbewegung als kulturhistorisches Phänomen*, 118–19; Hans-Joachim Schoeps, *Zeitgeist im Wandel* (Stuttgart: Klett, 1967), 32.

6. Hans-Georg Gadamer, *Truth and Method* (London: Continuum, 2004), 55. See also: Craig Ireland, *The Subaltern Appeal to Experience: Self-Identity, Late Modernity, and the Politics of Immediacy* (Montreal: McGill-Queen's University Press, 2005), 55.

7. Reinhart Koselleck, 'Transformations of Experience and Methodological Change', in Reinhart Koselleck (ed.), *The Practice of Conceptual History* (Stanford, CA: Stanford University Press, 2002), 45–83: 46.

8. Gadamer, *Truth and Method*, 56.

9. Konrad Cramer, 'Erleben, Erlebnis', in Joachim Ritter, Karlfried Gründer and Gottfried Gabriel (eds), *Historisches Wörterbuch der Philosophie. Vol. II* (Basel: Schwabe Verlag, 1972), 703.

10. Ibid., 703.

11. Wilhelm Dilthey, 'Fragmente zur Poetik (1907/8): Das Erlebnis', in Georg Misch (ed.), *Gesammelte Schriften 6: Die geistige Welt. Einleitung in die Philosophie des Lebens II* (Stuttgart: B.G. Teubner, 1924), 313–17: 313.

12. Schoeps, *Die letzten dreissig Jahre*, 32.

13. § 1 der Satzung des "Wandervogels Deutscher Bund für Jugendwanderungen", wahrscheinlich aus dem Gründungsjahr des Bundes 1907.

14. Anna Hilaria von Eckhel, *Auf der Lenzfahrt des Lebens: Tagebuch eines Wandervogels* (Breslau: Bergstadtverlag, 1922), 38.

15. Hjalmar Kutzleb, 'War Gelegenheit zu einer gewandelten Art des Seins', in Ziemer and Wolf, *Wandervogel und Freideutsche Jugend*, 136–44: 138.

16. Ibid., 138.

17. Max Heilmann, 'Wandervogel und Kunst', in Friedrich Wilhelm Fulda (ed.), *Sonnenwende. Ein Büchlein vom Wandervogel* (Leipzig: Hofmeister, 1919), 16–21: 16–17.

18. Cramer, 'Erleben, Erlebnis', 703.

19. Ibid., 704.

20. See, for example, the *Wandervogel Diary*: Erich Matthes, *Wandervogels Tagebuch* (Leipzig: Matthes, 1915).

21. Karl Binder-Krieglstein, 'Vom Gaublattleiter', *Wandervogel. Gaublatt für Schlesien* 5 (June–July) (1915), 64–66: 65.

22. 'Aus der Bewegung', *Wandervogel* 8(8) (1913), 245–47: 245.

23. Mario Fischer, 'Zwischen Jugendbewegung, Lebensreform und Kriegsbegeisterung. Der Wandel des Erlebnisbegriffs in den Reformbewegungen des ausgehenden Kaiserreichs und der Weimarer Republik', in Gerd Häffner (ed.), *Religiöse Erfahrung II: Interkulturelle Perspektiven* (Stuttgart: W. Kohlhammer Verlag, 2007), 141–55: 146; Eduard Spranger, *Psychologie des Jugendalters* (Heidelberg: Quelle & Meyer, 1929), 341.

24. Alfred Heidenreich, 'Auf der Suche nach neuen Wegen', in Kindt, *Die deutsche Jugendbewegung 1920 bis 1933*, 35–45: 40–41.

25. Frank Fischer, 'Deutsche Vergangenheit', *Wandervogel* 8(9) (1913), 285–89: 285.

26. The idea of the 'acceleration' of history in modernity as the formative event in the rise of modern historical consciousness goes as far back as the rise of this consciousness itself. Fischer is therefore repeating common ideas rather than phrasing his own. Cf. Reinhart Koselleck, 'Time and History', in Reinhart Koselleck (ed.), *The Practice of Conceptual History: Timing History, Spacing Concepts* (Stanford, CA: Stanford University Press, 2002), 100–114: 113.

27. Fischer, 'Deutsche Vergangenheit', 285.

28. Ibid., 287.

29. 'Voigtländers Quellenbücher', *Wandervogel* 8(12) (1913), 379.

30. Cf. Johann Wolfgang von Goethe, 'Von deutscher Baukunst (1772)', in Johann Wolfgang von Goethe and Siegfried Seidel (eds), *Berliner Ausgabe Bd. 19. Kunsttheoretische Schriften und Übersetzungen. Schriften zur bildenden Kunst 1* (Berlin: Aufbau-Verlag, 1985), 29–39; Fischer, 'Deutsche Vergangenheit', 288.

31. Fischer, 'Deutsche Vergangenheit', 288.
32. Hellmut Mebes, 'Auf Fahrt Geschichte erleben', *Wandervogel* 13(9/10) (1918), 193. Mebes' article was a reprint from the local Wandervogel journal of North Thuringia: Hellmut Mebes, 'Auf Fahrt Geschichte erleben', *Fahrtenblatt des Wandervogels Nordthuringgau* 10(4/5) (1918), 30.
33. Mebes, 'Auf Fahrt Geschichte erleben'.
34. Fischer, 'Deutsche Vergangenheit', 287.
35. Mebes, 'Auf Fahrt Geschichte erleben'.
36. Ibid.
37. Eric Hirsch and Charles Stewart, 'Introduction: Ethnographies of Historicity', *History and Anthropology* 16(3) (2005), 261–74: 262; David Weberman, 'Phenomenology', in Aviezer Tucker (ed.), *A Companion to the Philosophy of History and Historiography* (Malden, MA: Wiley-Blackwell, 2009), 508–17: 511ff. See also Veronica Vasterling's dissertation on Heidegger!
38. Schrank and Schuch, *Wandervögel im Hunsrück*, 10.
39. Jahn, 'Eine Sonnenwend-Ansprache', *Wandervogel* 6(7) (1911), 172–73: 172.
40. Ibid., 172.
41. Rolf-Peter Janz, 'Die Faszination der Jugend durch Rituale und sakrale Symbole. Mit Anmerkungen zu Fidus, Hesse, Hoffmannsthal und George', in Thomas Koebner, Rolf-Peter Janz and Frank Trommler (eds), *Mit uns zieht die neue Zeit: der Mythos Jugend* (Frankfurt am Main: Suhrkamp, 1985), 310–37: 310, 323. See also: Meike Sophia Baader, 'Naturreligiöse Gestimmtheit und jugendbewegte Aufbruchsgeste. Bildgedächtnis der Jugendbewegung und mentales Gepäck: Fidus' "Lichtgebet"', in Barbara Stambolis and Rolf Koerber (eds), *Erlebnisgenerationen – Erinnerungsgemeinschaften. Die Jugendbewegung und ihre Gedächtnisorte* (Schwalbach/Ts.: Wochenschau-Verlag, 2009), 153–68; Michael Neumann, 'Fidus – Ikonograph der Jugend', in Gerhard Ille and Günter Köhler (eds), *Der Wandervogel. Es begann in Steglitz* (Berlin: Stapp Verlag, 1987), 256–65. The idea of 'purity' expressed by Fidus's *Lichtgebet* was a common theme in *fin-de-siècle* bourgeois art and culture, and by no means an invention of the youth movement. On 'purity' and *fin-de-siècle* culture, see: Arnold Labrie, *Zuiverheid en decadentie. Over de grenzen van de burgerlijke cultuur in West-Europa, 1870–1914* (Amsterdam: Bakker, 2001).
42. Else Frobenius, *Mit uns zieht die neue Zeit. Eine Geschichte der deutschen Jugendbewegung* (Berlin: Deutsche Buch-Gemeinschaft, 1927), 129.
43. Schrank and Schuch, *Wandervögel im Hunsrück*, 7.
44. Ibid., 8.
45. David E. Wellbery, 'Stimmung', in Karlheinz Barck (ed.), *Ästhetische Grundbegriffe. Historisches Wörterbuch in sieben Bänden. Band 5* (Stuttgart: Metzler, 2003), 703–33: 704.
46. Otto Friedrich Bollnow, *Das Wesen der Stimmungen* (Würzburg: Königshausen & Neumann, 2009), 40–41.
47. Cf. Boris Ferreira, *Stimmung bei Heidegger: das Phänomen der Stimmung im Kontext von Heideggers Existenzialanalyse des Daseins* (Dordrecht and Boston: Kluwer Academic Publishers, 2002); Byung-Chul Han, *Heideggers Herz. Zum Begriff der Stimmung bei Martin Heidegger* (Munich: Fink, 1996).
48. Bollnow, *Das Wesen der Stimmungen*, 133; Martin Heidegger, *Sein und Zeit* (Tübingen: Max Niemeyer Verlag, 1967), 136.
49. Although Blau-Weiß was established in the same period that anti-Semitic controversies occurred in the Wandervogel, the establishment of Blau-Weiß was already planned before these controversies. The establishment of this Jewish hiking association was thus not a direct reaction against these anti-Semitic incidents. Cf. Jörg Hackeschmidt, *Von Kurt Blumenfeld zu Norbert Elias: die Erfindung einer jüdischen Nation* (Hamburg: Europäische Verlagsanstalt, 1997), 47ff. On anti-Semitism in the youth movement, see: Andreas Winnecken, *Ein Fall von Antisemitismus: zur Geschichte und Pathogenese der deutschen Jugendbewegung vor dem Ersten Weltkrieg* (Cologne: Verlag Wissenschaft und Politik, 1991).
50. Siegfried Bernfeld, 'Eine Zeitschrift der Jüdischen Jugend', *Jerubbaal. Eine Zeitschrift der Jüdischen Jugend* 1(1–4) (1918/1919): 3.

51. 'Leitfaden für die Gründung eines Jüdischen Wanderbundes "Blau-Weiss"', in Jehuda Reinharz (ed.), *Dokumente zur Geschichte des deutschen Zionismus 1882–1933* (Tübingen: Mohr Siebeck, 1981), 114–17: 115.

52. Bernard Susser, 'Ideological Multivalence: Martin Buber and the German Volkish Tradition', *Political Theory* 5(1) (1977), 75–96: 81–82. For the influence of Buber's thought on the broader Jewish youth movement, see: Chaim Schatzker, 'Martin Buber's Influence on the Jewish Youth Movement in Germany', *Leo Baeck Institute Yearbook* 23 (1968), 151–72.

53. Asher Biemann, 'The Problem of Tradition and Reform in Jewish Renaissance and Renaissancism', *Jewish Social Studies* 8(1) (2001), 58–87: 64.

54. Joseph Marcus, 'Wanderpflichten (Fortsetzung)', *Blau-Weiß-Blätter* 1, no. 6 (1913–1914) 1–3: 1.

55. Hans Oppenheim, 'Große Fahrten', *Blau-Weiß-Blätter* 4(3) (1916–1917), 55–57: 57.

56. Otto Simon, 'In den Vogesen', *Blau-Weiß-Blätter* 1(11) (1913–1914), 4–6: 4–5.

57. Karl Glaser, 'Unsere Große Sommerfahrt (Fortsetzung)', *Blau-Weiß-Blätter* 1(8) (1913–1914), 2–6: 5.

58. Oppenheim, 'Große Fahrten', 56.

59. Ibid., 57.

60. Eli Steinberg, 'Von unserer Fahrt – Von den Judensiedlungen in der fränk. Schweiz', *Blau-Weiß-Blätter* 5(3) (1917–1918), 105–6.

61. Glaser, 'Unsere Große Sommerfahrt (Fortsetzung)', 5–6.

62. Bernhard Bartfeld, 'Winterfahrt', *Blau-Weiß-Blätter* 1(9) (1913–1914), 5–6: 5.

63. This 'Lied von der Zeder' was written by Leo Feld and was the hymn of the First Zionist Congress in 1897. The song would also be published in the *Blau-Weiß Liederbuch* in 1914. Cf. Bundesleitung des Blau-Weiss, *Blau-Weiss Liederbuch* (Berlin: Jüdischer Verlag, 1918), 166.

64. Bartfeld, 'Winterfahrt', 5.

65. For an analysis on how Blau-Weiß attempted to put Buber's idea of a Jewish Renaissance into practice, see: Ivonne Meyboom, *Erziehung zum Zionismus. Der Jüdische Wanderbund Blau-Weiß als Versuch einer praktischen Umsetzung des Programms der Jüdischen Renaissance* (Frankfurt am Main: Peter Lang, 2009). Meyboom interprets this attempt as an 'invented tradition'. Hobsbawm, however, originally used this term in reference to the nationalist establishment of largely fictive historical continuity by the nineteenth-century middle classes – exactly the type of historical construction that *völkisch* thinkers, including Buber, refuted as being artificial. It would be rather naive to call every construction of traditions 'invented traditions', because it negates the paradox of progressive return. Cf. Eric Hobsbawm, 'Introduction: Inventing Traditions', in Eric Hobsbawm and Terence Ranger (eds), *The Invention of Tradition* (Cambridge: Cambridge University Press, 1983), 1–14.

66. Meyboom, *Erziehung zum Zionismus*, 85–87.

67. Albert Baer, 'Sukkotfeiern II', *Blau-Weiß-Blätter* 3(4) (1914–1915), 85–86.

68. Felix Seidemann, 'Berichte – Teplitz-Schönau', *Blau-Weiß-Blätter* 4(1) (1916–1917), 21.

69. Cited from an interview with Felix Rosenblüth (the later Israeli Minister of Justice Pinchas Rosen) in: Yehuda Eloni, *Zionismus in Deutschland: von den Anfängen bis 1914* (Gerlingen: Bleicher, 1987), 449.

70. Karl Glaser, 'Der Blau-Weisstag in Lockwitz', *Blau-Weiß-Blätter* 4(2) (1916–1917), 23–28: 27. In Lockwitz, Blau-Weiß was transformed from an umbrella organization for individual associates into one national movement.

71. His critique of Blau-Weiß was later printed in: Gerschom Scholem, 'Jüdische Jugendbewegung', *Der Jude* 1(12) (1916–1917), 822–25; Gerschom Scholem, 'Jugendbewegung, Jugendarbeit und Blau-Weiß', *Blau-Weiß-Blätter Führerzeitung* 1(2) (1917–1919), 26–30; Gerschom Scholem, 'Abschied. Offener Brief an Herrn Dr Siegfried Bernfeld und gegen die Leser dieser Zeitschrift', *Jerubbaal. Eine Zeitschrift der Jüdischen Jugend* 1 (1918–1919), 125–30.

72. Gerschom Scholem, *Von Berlin nach Jerusalem* (Frankfurt am Main: Jüdischer Verlag, 1994), 64.

73. Scholem, 'Abschied', 126.

74. Scholem, 'Jüdische Jugendbewegung', 825.
75. Gerschom Scholem, *Walter Benjamin: The Story of a Friendship* (New York: Schocken, 1981), 29.
76. Scholem, 'Abschied', 127.
77. Moses Calvary, 'Blau-weiß. Anmerkungen zum jüdischen Jugendwandern', *Der Jude* 1(7) (1916), 451–57: 452.
78. Karl Glaser, 'Oratio pro domo', *Blau-Weiß-Blätter Führerzeitung* 1(2) (1917–1919), 30–39: 35.
79. Hans Oppenheim, 'Ene Kritik des Blau-Weiß', *Blau-Weiß-Blätter Führerzeitung* 1(1) (1917–1919), 10–12.
80. Cf. Kurt Sontheimer, *Antidemokratisches Denken in der Weimarer Republik* (Munich: Deutscher Taschenbuch-Verlag, 1978), 96–100; Jeffrey Verhey, *The Spirit of 1914: Militarism, Myth, and Mobilization in Germany* (Cambridge, MA: Cambridge University Press, 2000), 72–114.
81. Wolfgang J. Mommsen, 'Einleitung: Die deutschen kulturellen Eliten im Ersten Weltkrieg', in Wolfgang J. Mommsen (ed.), *Die Rolle der Intellektuellen, Künstler und Schriftsteller im Ersten Weltkrieg* (Munich: Oldenbourg, 1996), 1–15: 2.
82. Hans Maier, 'Ideen von 1914 – Ideen von 1939?', *Vierteljahrshefte für Zeitgeschichte* 38(4) (1990), 525–42: 526. See also: Stefan Bruendel, *Volksgemeinschaft oder Volksstaat: die 'Ideen von 1914' und die Neuordnung Deutschlands im Ersten Weltkrieg* (Berlin: Akademie Verlag, 2003); Kurt Flasch, *Die geistige Mobilmachung. Die deutschen Intellektuellen und der Erste Weltkrieg – ein Versuch* (Berlin: A. Fest, 2000); Verhey, *The Spirit of 1914*.
83. Cited from: Friedrich Wilhelm Foerster, *Jugendseele, Jugendbewegung, Jugendziel* (Erlenbach-Zurich: Rotapfel-verlag, 1923), 107.
84. Reinhard Preuß, 'Freideutsche Jugend und Politik. Politische Orientierungen und Manifestationen innerhalb der bürgerlichen Jugendbewegung 1913–1918/19', *Jahrbuch des Archivs der deutschen Jugendbewegung* 16 (1986), 229–40: 235.
85. Gudrun Fiedler, *Jugend im Krieg. Bürgerliche Jugendbewegung, Erster Weltkrieg und sozialer Wandel. 1914–1923* (Cologne: Verlag Wissenschaft und Politik, 1989), 38.
86. Hermann Mitgau, 'Der Feldwandervogel', in Will Vesper (ed.), *Deutsche Jugend. 30 Jahre Geschichte einer Bewegung* (Berlin: Holle & Co., 1934), 63–83: 83.
87. Laqueur, *Young Germany*, 97.
88. Erich Leistner, 'Wie wir uns fanden', *Wandervogel* 12(6/7) (1917), 148–49.
89. Willibald Karl, *Jugend, Gesellschaft und Politik im Zeitraum des Ersten Weltkriegs* (Munich: Stadtarchiv München, 1973), 144.
90. Samm, 'Der falsche "Zwiespruch"-Name', *Der Zwiespruch. Rundbrief der Feldwandervogel im Westen* 14 (1918), 238.
91. Otto Schönfelder, 'Vom Feldgau Nordwest', *Wandervogel* 14(2/3) (1919), 75–76. This article was published in a special issue on Flanders, which had already been in preparation before the war ended.
92. Otto Neumann, 'Feldpostbriefe (1917)', in Ziemer and Wolf, *Wandervogel und Freideutsche Jugend*, 530–33.
93. Anne Lipp, *Meinungslenkung im Krieg: Kriegserfahrungen deutscher Soldaten und ihre Deutung 1914–1918* (Göttingen: Vandenhoeck & Ruprecht, 2003), 311.
94. On Zylmann, see: Martin Tielke, 'Peter Hermann Zylmann', in Martin Tielke (ed.), *Biographisches Lexikon für Ostfriesland III* (Aurich: Ostfriesische Landschaft, 2001), 446–54.
95. Peter Zylmann, 'Vom Wandern in Belgien', *Wandervogel* 14(2/3) (1919), 65.
96. Ibid., 65.
97. Otto Schönfelder, 'Vom flämischen Volkstum', *Wandervogel* 14(2/3) (1919), 37–38: 37.
98. Ibid., 37.
99. Ibid. Cf. Herman Nohl, 'Die idyllische Seele Vlanderns. Das Land der Leie und Albijn van den Abeele', *Die Tat* 8(12) (1917), 1094–1103.
100. Elisabeth Blochmann, *Herman Nohl in der pädagogischen Bewegung seiner Zeit 1879–1960* (Göttingen: 1969), 63 ff.

101. Meike Werner, 'Jugendbewegung als Reform der studentisch-akademischen Jugendkultur. Selbsterziehung – Selbstbildung – die neue Geselligkeit: Die Jenenser Freistudentenschaft und der Serakreis', in Ulrich Herrmann (ed.), *"Mit uns zieht die neue Zeit" – der Wandervogel in der deutschen Jugendbewegung* (Weinheim: Juventa, 2006), 171–203: 196.

102. Rudolf Carnap, 'Intellectual Autobiography', in Paul Arthur Schilpp (ed.), *The Philosophy of Rudolph Carnap* (LaSalle, IL: Open Court, 1963), 3–86: 4. On Nohl's mentorship of the Sera-cirle, see: Werner, 'Jugendbewegung als Reform', 196.

103. Walter Thys and Herman Nohl, *Ein Landsturmmann im Himmel. Flandern und der Erste Weltkrieg in den Briefen von Herman Nohl an seine Frau* (Leipzig: Leipziger Universitätsverlag, 2005), 8.

104. Nohl, 'Die idyllische Seele Vlanderns. Das Land der Leie und Albijn van den Abeele', 1094.

105. Ibid., 1094.

106. Cf. Nietzsche, 'On the Uses and Disadvantages of History for Life'.

107. Nohl, 'Die idyllische Seele Vlanderns', 1097.

108. Schönfelder, 'Vom flämischen Volkstum', 38.

109. Walter Hedicke, 'Frühling in Flandern', *Jung-Wandervogel. Zeitschrift des Bundes für Jugendwandern "Jung-Wandervogel"* 7(7) (1917), 117–18.

110. Herman Nohl, 'Vom deutschen Ideal der Geselligkeit', *Die Tat* 7 (1915), 617–34: 631. On Brügmann, see: Heinrich Gerhard Brügmann, *Karl Brügmann und der freideutsche Sera-Kreis Untersuchung eines Modells von Jugendleben und Geist der Meißner-Generation vor 1914* (Frankfurt am Main: 1965).

111. Brügmann cited in: Nohl, 'Vom deutschen Ideal der Geselligkeit', 631.

112. Gertrud Döring, 'Auf Mädchenfahrt in flämischen Lande', *Wandervogel* 14(2/3) (1919), 67–68: 68.

113. Ibid., 68.

114. Enno Narten, 'Damme', *Wandervogel* 14(2/3) (1919), 50–52: 50.

115. Ibid., 51.

116. Paul Fussell, *The Great War and Modern Memory: The Illustrated Edition* (New York: Sterling Publishing Company, 2009), 298.

117. Neumann, 'Feldpostbriefe (1917)', 530–33. On Neumann, see also: Hanns-Gerd Rabe, *Otto Neumann: Leben und Soldatentod eines Osnabrücker Wandervogels* (Osnabrück: Wegmann, 1980).

118. Hans Bohnenkamp, 'Jugendbewegung als Kulturkritik', in Walter Rüegg (ed.), *Kulturkritik und Jugendkult* (Frankfurt a/M: Suhrkamp, 1974), 24–34: 31.

119. Ibid., 31.

CHAPTER 3

# The Postwar Crisis of Experience and the Religious Turn

Waking from feverish dreams, it took some time before Franz Christ realized he had been shot in the stomach and had awoken in a sickbay far behind the front. While gaining consciousness, he gazed into the eyes of the priest who had just given him the last rites and asked him to confess. Annoyed that the priest was preparing him to depart life, while he had just envisaged re-entering it, Christ recalled that 'all this stuff appeared to me to be such a ridiculous comedy, that I was disgusted. I preferred to cross into the afterlife without a master of ceremony, and therefore tried to burst out in a rather painful laughter and sank into the next unconsciousness'.[1] The experience that in modern society even death was a staged event led Christ to rethink the presumptions of Christianity. It was as if he had unmasked life, including what he had believed himself to be. He found that salvation lies not in participating in the comedy of life, as if it were a reward for good performance, but that it lies in trading the conventional conception of God for the highest motif man could desire to give all his energy and his life for – be it honour, science, youth, love, *Heimat* or the Messiah. Yet, at the same time, Christ was pessimistic about the possibility of contemporary society redeeming itself from its masquerade – for many it would be too tempting to keep playing a role for short-term profit, rather than dedicating life to one's highest principle. In the end, Christ put his hopes in an absolute renewal of society, addressing God himself that his 'salvation has grown old, and a new Incarnation is necessary'.[2]

The Wandervogel and Freideutschen entered the war being generally a-religious. They had renounced ecclesial youth associations for being adult-influenced youth welfare organizations, and both the Catholic and Evangelical churches were met with complete indifference.[3] Sunday was the weekly day for hiking, and although this sometimes incited a conflict with parents, such problems were exceptional. When they came out of the war, the stance on religion had changed significantly to the extent that it has been asserted that the core of the youth movement had become religious.[4] But in the light of Christ's testimony, this religiosity should not be interpreted in terms of a formalized dogmatism, but rather as an existential quest for the eternal.[5] The wave of religiosity that swept through the movement from the late 1910s well into the 1920s, had significant consequences for the comprehension of history, historical memory and historical time in the youth movement. Prospects for the regeneration of 'life' which had been opened by the end of the war, the breakdown of Wilhelmine society and the November Revolution, only endorsed a new conception of history which had developed during the war.

The new understanding of history developed on the level of the numerous individual biographies of the members of the youth movement. Their maturation coincided with a war and later on with a revolution that did not allow a seamless transition into adult life in a stable society. Yet, these individuals shared an experience of the possibility of unmediated community – an experience that would later become the prospect for wider social change, a change which would be phrased in eschatological terms. How the historical orientation changed under the influence of religiosity and metaphysics is best traced in these individual biographies. This chapter will therefore examine two cases: Rudolf Haberkorn and Ernst Wurche. After an analysis of the rise and function of religiosity in their personal development, I will relate the metaphysical questions and positions of the youth movement to what is called the 'crisis of historicism' – the social and scholarly crisis of modern historical consciousness as an explanatory paradigm for human action – which reached its apex after the war. Focusing on the Freideutsche Jugend in the immediate postwar years, I will continue with an analysis of the problem of formulating a coherent collective ideology on the basis of a non-dogmatic religiosity, followed by closing remarks on the role, function and meaning of memory in a 'post-historicist' youth movement.

## Rudolf Haberkorn's Stillest Hour

Rudolf Haberkorn, a Wandervogel leader from Posen and member of the Freideutsche Jugend, showed clear disillusionment about his theology study at Halle before the war. Although he had tried to live up to the expectations of his parents, the prospect of preaching every week to an anonymous congregation, which required you to replace your personal beliefs with the dogmas of the Evangelical Church, instilled strains 'already by the *thought* of the future'.[6]

A reading of Nietzsche's *Vom Nutzen und Nachteil der Historie für das Leben* led Haberkorn to understand that these strains were caused by the burden that the thoroughly historical education placed on youth.[7] What Nietzsche wrote about the historical education of man was what Haberkorn recognized to be the main fault of the Evangelical Church as an institution: the church energetically required its members to subject to its dogmas, but by placing this burden it actually accomplished their estrangement. The church so blatantly lacked confidence in 'the good and the true' in people that it had become an ossified institution that did not serve life, but only served tradition. Haberkorn often wondered 'what their conception of God looks like when they have so little confidence in the divine in man'.[8]

The vitalist ideas that Haberkorn derived from Nietzsche made him aware of the hopeless situation he found himself in. On the one hand he was pushed in the direction of a church that had forgotten life, while on the other hand he was confronted with a bourgeois society in which the main goal was to live a 'tranquil and quiet life', undisturbed by one's neighbours and with a state pension as the ultimate goal.[9] Contemplating these prospects, a vision of a man recovering from a long and troublesome disease, intensely longing for health and labour, filled Haberkorn's heart. In this vision it is the longing of the soul – not the 'rational' mind – which makes life meaningful and gives one the strength to endure. Haberkorn explored the possibilities of a radical act in an equally vitalist way: to break with all the burdens of his historical education and to turn to life itself. He thought about choosing an occupation in which he had economic independence, in which he would not have to compromise his personal values to any historically established authority. However, Haberkorn considered this desire to be a break with his parents. As he found himself unable to cope with such a radical act, he continued his theology study in a state of mental despair.

Shortly before the war, Haberkorn found relief in the Soziale Arbeitsgemeinschaft Berlin-Ost (SAG) – an association inspired by the British settlement movement, dedicated to offering social work to the lower classes in one of the poorest working-class districts of Berlin: Friedrichshain.[10] The SAG offered a broad range of activities, from taking proletarian children to the countryside, to juvenile court assistance, to educational courses.[11] By volunteering for work with the proletariat, Haberkorn hoped to find 'life' in a circle of likeminded people. Although the youth movement had taught him to experience, to Haberkorn's grief the movement had refrained from actual involvement in German society and culture.

It would, however, take the experience of the war before his fragmentary thoughts came together. In August 1914, Haberkorn confessed that he too was enthused by what has often been called the 'spirit of 1914'. He explained the act of volunteering for duty with the 6th Grenadier Regiment in Posen by stating that in times of peace he would 'only have served for the sake of the social *object* "army", but not for the national *subject* 'fatherland'. This however had changed now'.[12] He too was exasperated by the Serbian-nationalist assassination of Archduke Franz Ferdinand of Austria – but once in the barracks, Haberkorn soon found out that Germany's jingoistic enthusiasm was rooted in nothing more than cold, materialistic and selfish calculation. This was Haberkorn's stillest hour. Facing the probability of death, Haberkorn disposed of any belief in state-sponsored nationalism, and started to see the war as an ordeal; an ordeal of self-conquest that he already in 1914 regarded as a necessary step for the 'inner rebuilding after the war – socially and spiritually understood'.[13]

An infection in his right hand prevented Haberkorn from actually going to the front. His slow recovery gave him time to finish his theology examinations at the request of his father, and enabled him to intensify his involvement in the Posen Wandervogel as well. In these days, Haberkorn further developed his ideas on inner reform. Obviously, he was not the only one pondering the possibilities of making the Wandervogel experience – which he interpreted as an experience of the unity of life – the basis of the inner renewal of the broader German people. Shortly before and during the war, the first generation that had 'grown up' in the Wandervogel started to organize themselves in associations that could translate the Wandervogel experience into meaningful goals for adult life.[14] By 1916, two associations of older Wandervögel seeking to expand their reach into society – the mainstream Bund der Landesgemeinden and the short-lived *völkisch* Greifenbund of Otger Gräff and Frank Glatzel – opposed each other. Although both strove to make the Wandervogel experience the basis for a new worldview, the Greifenbund went further than the Landesgemeinden in two respects. First, they wanted to create an entirely new folk culture instead of only a worldview. Second, their efforts were only aimed at those of German blood, thus explicitly excluding Jews. Haberkorn tried to mediate by arguing that not objective, 'scientific' descent should be the point of departure, but that a people's idiosyncrasy should be regarded an idea, a task or a goal in need of realization. 'This understanding does not judge the Jews from above as inferior people; neither does it contravene the idea of human community';[15] rather, it enables the Jews an inner reform of their own people in the light of humanity, without having to denounce their own heritage, or be objectified or even harassed on eugenic grounds.

It was in his idea of humanity that Haberkorn found answers to the crisis of historical education, as well as to the personal solitude which he recognized as being by and large the very consequence of this individuating and demanding historical education. His sketchy thoughts on humanity blended Wandervogel rhetoric with his prime sources: Nietzsche, Meister Eckhart and the New Testament. The Wandervogel provided him with an unequivocal belief in the inner and outer unity of life. Only by living outer life naturally and inner life truthfully can one actually *live*, rather than be lived, and come to true humanity. Humanity, *Menschheit*, is not the humanist ideal of *Humanität* (*humanitas*), but can be read in line with Meister Eckhart as man's nature – that which makes man 'man'. In the youth movement, 'man' (*Mensch*) neither refers to the empirical man – to 'the bourgeois, sated, finite' man, as the German philosopher and theologian Paul Tillich once wrote in a publication on the Freideutsche Jugend – nor to the abstract notion of an 'ideal man'.[16] Rather, the movement reveres what is human in the most general sense in each and every human being. 'It is the metaphysical, the cosmic energy, which constitutes the individual and nonetheless universally human in every person.'[17] Insofar as man is submerged by others or by himself, he is in need of liberation and redemption.

For Haberkorn, the liberation of humanity is the ultimate goal of all human life, thus humanity as a goal is the basis of mutual love. This, it will not surprise, would be something to realize in the coming, postwar, Germany. When the liberation of humanity as an ideal and the Wandervogel ideal of personality converge, true humanity could be accomplished. However, this requires sacrifice: of the ego or self-image, of the quest for wealth, of all forms that constitute bourgeois egoism. Only when one lets all prejudices and perceptions fall can one experience true personality, which is 'the direct experience of personal perpetuity'.[18] This experience is rooted in community, for man is not an autonomous or individual entity, nor a monad, but a relational being. When the eternal unity of personality and humanity is experienced, we experience God. As such, 'humanity as a reality is the end goal of history'.[19]

Expanding these beliefs, Haberkorn pondered the possibilities for a 'new German religion'. His ideas on this new religion were built around what he called a 'guild' – once the denominator for the association of craftsmen in a particular town, but revived by the Feldwandervogel. In the Feldwandervogel, those Wandervögel who were detached by the army in mobile tactical units did not fit in an organizational structure that was based on geographical location, and they therefore organized themselves in 'guilds', which registered at local 'nests' wherever fortune took them.[20] Haberkorn used this concept of close-knit mobile 'guilds' and made them the congregation of the new 'religion'. For him, the guild should consist of eight to twelve members bound together by shared lived experience; faithful and obedient to the inner spirit, loyal to one's companions and brave towards the world. This group was just large enough to establish a deep sense of community, but too small to become an association that could formalize relationships. Because humanity is eternity, the first step for the guild was to prevent experience ossifying as historical memory.[21] For Haberkorn, experience (*Erlebnis*) was a direct gift of life and was thus originally perennial. Holding fast to eternity implied radiating experience back into to the outer world through vivacious action, such as laughter, dance, compassion, fidelity and courage. Turning experience into action meant penetrating life and eternity.

Haberkorn construed his ideas on meaningful action on a paradoxical combination of Christ's doctrine of compassion and Nietzsche's doctrine of the 'bestowing virtue' (*schenkende Tugend*).[22] For Nietzsche's Zarathustra, the highest virtue was the virtue that bestows itself, the virtue in which one sacrifices and gives oneself. It is the highest form of egoism, for it does not subsume life as possession, but subsumes life only in order to be able to give it again as a gift of love. The step to recognize that Jesus sacrificed himself out of the highest selflessness of the bestowing virtue was easily made. The free death of sacrifice for one's brothers was clearly a timely theme in the heat of the Great War, but for Haberkorn it became the core of his own sketchy and thoroughly rudimentary philosophy of history – a philosophy that believed that the goal of history was '*humanity* as an eternal value: the Kingdom of God'.[23] The voluntaristic pure Good of the bestowing virtue was the driving force that went bottom-up and grew out of the close communities from which *Erlebnis* spilled over in life.

Haberkorn would not live to see postwar Germany himself. After taking his examinations, he became dragoon in Lüben, as well as the local Wandervogel leader. But when his platoon was sent to the front in Courland, in early 1917, Haberkorn's shelter took a direct hit from a grenade, mortally wounding the young soldier inside. A friend recalled that even in his last moment, Haberkorn remained a full-hearted Wandervogel by refusing to take alcohol to quell the pain, for 'he did not want to dull his senses'.[24]

Haberkorn died too early to experience the first meeting of the Freideutsche Jugend during the war in the Solling hills in October 1917. This was the meeting where the question of the relationship between 'Christianity and War' was discussed. Here, the younger members took a stand against both the older speakers and the *völkisch* fraction, who tried to reconcile the Christian values with the national '*sacro egoismo*'. 'It was an experience that shocked everybody who was involved,' wrote Knud Ahlborn, 'when one youngster after another confessed to the spirit of atonement, of love, of humanity, and opposed the dogma's of vengeance, of hate, of national self-interest.'[25] When confronted with the argument that the course of history has shown that war cannot be banished, they reacted by challenging the very conception of history that underlined this argument. History, in their words, was 'a pillow on which most sleep their entire life; but for the rest of us it is the transcript of past actions and a demand to accomplish something yourself'.[26] The Solling meeting was a turning point, after which the opinion on the war changed for the majority of the Freideutsche Jugend.

## The Releasement of Ernst Wurche

Haberkorn's case is far from isolated. Much better known is the story of Ernst Wurche, which is told in Walter Flex's autobiographical novel *Der Wanderer zwischen beiden Welten* (The Wanderer between Both Worlds). The novel was not just popular among Wandervögel, but was a main catalyst for popularizing the Wandervogel in broader German society. After its publication in 1917, *Der Wanderer zwischen beiden Welten* became the fourth best-selling German war novel of the interwar period, right after Manfred von Richthofen's *Der rote Kampfflieger*, Erich Maria Remarque's *Im Westen nichts Neues* and Gunther Plüschow's *Die Abenteuer des Fliegers von Tsingtau*.[27]

Walter Flex recalled first noting the striking character of Ernst Wurche when marching up the slopes of the hills of Lorraine, away from the front, early in 1915. Both Flex and Wurche marched in the same column of volunteers that was bound for an officer training course in Posen. The Silesian theology student Wurche had struck up a song that seemed out of place against the background of the Western Front, but that opened Flex's eyes for the morning beauty of the Lorraine valley: 'Wohlauf, die Luft geht frisch und rein! Wer lange sitzt, muß rosten. Den allersonnigsten Sonnenschein läßt uns der Himmel kosten'.[28] Enthralled by the wanderlust the song aired, Flex was caught by the morning sun, which rose behind the church of Hattonchâtel, radiating throughout the valley. 'Perhaps I would not have seen it like this without the twenty-year-old comrade beside me. He had stopped singing, and was completely absorbed in looking and walking.'[29]

Wurche, who was soon to be his friend, embodied the Wandervogel in every facet[30] – literally. Both his physical appearance and his pace were youthful and tender, but also resilient: 'as the lean, handsome man in the shabby grey coat descended the hill as a pilgrim, the bright grey eyes full of splendour and unerring desire, he was like Zarathustra, who comes from the heights, or the Goethian wanderer'.[31] Here, Wurche's physical appearance touched upon the figurative aspect of his appearance. Bound to become an officer, Wurche refrained from any Prussian authoritarianism; the intentionality he posited towards his surroundings, the direct and unprejudiced interest in the given world resonated in his social philosophy. He wanted to *be* a Zarathustra: a wandering teacher. He was convinced that a teacher or a leader had to derive legitimacy for his position not by birth or wealth, but by being a role model in words and deeds. However, to be a lieutenant would not mean that one had to precede one's troops in *death*, as some of Wurche's fellow aspirant officer's believed in an air of patriotic frenzy; no, for Wurche 'being a lieutenant means: to be a living example to one's men, *to precede them in life* [*vorleben*]. … To precede them in death [*vorsterben*] is then perhaps a part of it'.[32] Compared to life, death is an easy option, as much an escape from responsibility as a denial of what war is primarily about: existence.

Wurche was a prime example of what was called a 'Wandervogel personality': someone who stands out from the anonymous masses of modern society by acting in and interacting with the social world on his own premises; an individual who does not allow himself to be subjugated to social conventions. Furthermore, in the field he became a *leading* personality (*Führerpersönlichkeit*), which is – according to the journal *Wandervogel* – a leader 'to whom followers flock voluntarily, for they regard him as a personality, as a "guy", because they trust him, because they sense him to be paramount in knowledge and volition, in experience and worldview'.[33] But more than a factual transmitter of information, the *Führer* was a guide. In the first place a guide when leading a hike, but in a broader sense a guide in the questions of life. The *Führer* was thus an educator by example, an *Erzieher*.

Nietzsche once called Schopenhauer an educator. Not because he excelled in the transmission of knowledge, but because Nietzsche's Schopenhauer stood up against the currents of his age as an individual, and personally exemplified his acknowledgement that true heroism lies in the resistance to regarding oneself as merely belonging to a history of becoming. The everyday understanding of the end to which one lived, which comprised of *becoming* 'a good citizen, or scholar, or statesman', in fact reduced one's life to be 'no more than a point in the evolution of a race or of a state or of a science'.[34] In his historical quest of 'becoming', man had forgotten what it meant to 'be': '[I]n becoming, everything is hollow, deceptive, shallow and worthy of our contempt; the enigma that man is to resolve he can resolve only in being, in being thus and not otherwise, in the imperishable'.[35] Being does not allow an 'ought'.

Now we can understand that the *Wandervogelführer*'s 'knowledge' was rooted in the 'condemnation of everything artsy and corrupt, of everything blasé, garnished, dishonest and artificial' – not the condemnation of modernity or bourgeois society per se, but the condemnation of the predicament that valued appearance over essence.[36] However, when it comes to 'being', the students who made up the leadership of the movement could hardly find the words to explain the sense of vitality that ran through their veins. They were very grateful that Flex captured at least part of it in Wurche's mystical postulate: 'Rein *bleiben* and Reif *werden* – das ist schönste und schwerste Lebenskunst' (To stay *pure* and become *mature*, that is the finest and most difficult art of life).[37] The reception of *Der Wanderer Zwischen beiden Welten* in the Wandervogel movement mingled pride of Flex's acknowledgment that the future deliverance of Germany was to come from the 'spirit of the Wandervogel' with the acknowledgement of the responsibility for such pretensions.[38]

Wurche's existential disposition was as much based on a deep religiosity as was Haberkorn's. More than Nietzsche's Zarathustra, who took off announcing the emergence of a post-metaphysical man, did Wurche listen to those voices that spoke of a God that had never left. 'Prayer', said Wurche, 'is a soliloquy with the divine in us'; it is a 'struggle with the man in us over the readiness of the soul'.[39] The divine cannot be separated from being and the 'man in us' is the self-fashioned man, the man who 'became', and who by becoming had created a God external to him, in need of representation. To Wurche, the Western Front appeared as revelation, for it unveiled man in his ugliness and beauty, in his cowardice and heroism – at the front such appearances could not hold. 'When it is the meaning and purpose of human life to uncover the essence of human form, then we do have our part in life. ... No one has seen so many shells fall, so much meanness, cowardice, weakness, selfishness, vanity; no one has seen so much dignity and nobility of soul as we have.'[40] The utmost he could demand from life was that it unveiled itself, and as the war had provided this purification, Wurche could now only quietly await what life had to demand from *him*. The 'readiness of the soul' now encompassed the ability and peace of mind to quietly await these demands of life. Here we hear the mystic voice of Meister Eckhart, to whom *Gelassenheit* (*gelâzenheit*, releasement) was the highest virtue.[41] *Gelassenheit* is a disposition in which man lets go of will and representation, of self-image and world-image, of all impressions and intentions. This enables the condition of the 'empty spirit' (*ledic gemüete*) which enables the receptiveness for the Godhead to *be* in its pure transcendence: 'Some simple people imagine that they are going to see God as if He were standing yonder and they here, but it is not to be so. God and I: we are one. By knowing God, I take Him to myself. By loving God, I penetrate him'.[42]

For Flex, Wurche primarily exuded his *Gelassenheit* when remaining utmost cool-headed when the train that was to take the newly promoted officers to the Eastern Front was derailed by Russian artillery.

> Ernst Wurche had just been standing at the window shaving. The middle of the track started cracking and breaking. He slightly raised his razor and held on to the luggage rack with his left hand. In the other compartments, we saw comrades – some in shirtsleeves – jumping from the swaying coach. A suitcase and a laundry bag had fallen on my own head and had me thrown forward. I scrambled up again. The train was standing still. I looked at Wurche and had to laugh. He neatly finished his interrupted shave, wiped the lather off his face and said calmly: 'Well, now we can probably get off as well'.[43]

In as far *Gelassenheit* could be a mere attitude as outer form, Wurche would certainly have lost it in these anxious moments. However, for him *Gelassenheit* was no attitude, but an existential disposition that on the one hand enabled him to cope with the anxieties of modern warfare without losing himself, and that on the other hand enabled him to engage with his surroundings in a preconceptual mode. The landscapes he encountered did not appear categorized as 'Romantic' or 'picturesque', but as a marvellous interplay of colours, sounds and shapes, of hopes, dreams and laughter, just as his men appeared not as 'soldiers', but as fellows to him.

Like Haberkorn, Wurche derived the idea that empirical man had to be overcome from *Zarathustra* – and like Zarathustra his soul was always 'patrolling for the eternal'.[44] For him, both man and peoples were 'eternal and ephemeral at the same time'.[45] With the Swiss writer and poet Gottfried Keller, Wurche acknowledged that like individual death, the downfall of a people is eventually inevitable.[46] But exactly this acknowledgement makes life worthwhile, because it enables man to work in the name of his people for the glory of respectful commemoration of successive peoples and civilizations. However, as most nations have succumbed in inertia, the highest achievable goal for a nation is to die a hero's death, which means: while going down, fulfilling its tasks of life to the utmost. Once a nation or civilization has unveiled and consolidated its abilities, there is no need to forcibly prolong its existence; new phenomena 'abide by the gates of time'.[47] Death is ugly and painful, but when a nation receives its death blow at its apex, there is no need to grieve or mourn, because neither the succumbed nation, nor its surviving members are accountable for what comes afterwards. When a nation, or any collective entity, tries to rule the world from the grave, the ossification and historization of life would commence. Here, Wurche sings the song of eternal recurrence.

Wurche died a hero's death himself. When his nightly reconnaissance patrol came under heavy shrapnel fire near Lake Simnas in the south of Lithuania, Wurche advanced on his own to reconnoitre the Russian positions. But when he did not return, his company advanced to find their lieutenant mortally wounded. Wurche died on the way back to camp on Monday 23 August 1915. On hearing the news of his death, Walter Flex felt a deep guilt for not being able to stand by the side of his Wandervogel friend, comforting him and hearing his last words. It was only when standing at his grave that Flex slowly started to realize what dying meant in the light of eternity.

> For great souls, death is the greatest experience. When the day on earth goes to rest and the windows of the soul – the colourful human eyes – bedim like church windows in the evening, then in the dusky temple of the body, the soul blossoms in a dark glow like the Body of Christ blossoms at the altar under the sanctuary lamp, and fills itself with the deep radiance of eternity. Then men's voices have to keep silent. Even the voices of friends ... Therefore, do not search and yearn for last words of the dying! Who speaks to God, no longer speaks to people.[48]

In Wurche we witness a similar development as in Haberkorn. Like the Feldwandervögel we discussed in the previous chapter, they welcomed the war as the possible moment to overcome individualism and to gain for the nation spiritual meaning. Yet, at the same time, while the experience of community and authentic life was put forward as a basis on which to establish such spiritual nationhood after the war, others took the Wandervogel experience to be religious experience. After the war, it was this religious element that would prove to provide possibilities to overcome modern historical consciousness because, rather than taking man's autonomy of action and consciousness as the basis for a worldview, in this religiosity the world and cosmos, God and nature appeared as a unified and eternal whole in a pantheistic way, and the Godhead expressed itself in human life in temporary forms. By interpreting such expressions as the temporal realization of the eternal, the idea that history was the progressive development of human consciousness, morals or technology could be underpinned. This also required an assessment of both the problem of history and the traditional function of experience in the youth movement.

## Historicism and the Crisis of Experience

When, by 1916, the high expectations of August 1914 had faded, the war was interpreted as the ultimate explosion of the state as 'deficient machine', which framed the minds of people not only through the educational system but through the military as well.[49] Now it was clear that not only youth but the entire German people suffered from the same fundamental problem. Haberkorn called this problem, after Nietzsche, the 'historical education' of man. I call it, with Karl Mannheim, the 'worldview' of historicism.[50] Historicism was not just a historiographical school, but the all-encompassing understanding that all human values and ideas are conditioned historically and can only be understood historically. As such, historicism was in fact not an optional point of view, but an inescapable precondition of modern existence, widely carried in bourgeois circles.[51] Within the youth movement, historicism was understood exactly in this way. According to Wandervogel and reform pedagogue Friedrich Schlünz, historicism is 'the younger child of Enlightenment', which 'has intruded all occurrences of our lives. … It asserts that nothing, no action, no event can be understood thoroughly without tracing its historical origins'.[52] Through creating a narrative of historical development, starting from the earliest ages, the present moment is understood, and the path for future action becomes visible. But as man is historically determined, 'youth has been conceptually deviated from the facts of its own direct experience, which', Schlünz argued, 'after all constitute … vivacious transitions from the preceding to the new'. In his view, youth had consequently always been prompted with the experience of the preceding as being essential, and 'never has youth been let to sense what is the development nucleus of a prospect in himself'.[53] According to Ernst Troeltsch, historicism – as the 'fundamental historicization of all our thought about mankind, his culture and his values' – prompted youth with a lack of faith in knowledge, including scientific knowledge, because neither education nor science could provide a sufficient framework for future orientation.[54] Thus, the crisis of historicism was directly linked to the crisis of education and the crisis of science.

With regard to historical understanding, the problem for youth was that the historicist worldview created a feeling that history was external to youth, that it was the domain of great historical characters and quasi-characters such as the state and the nation. Never could one be the carrier of the historical moment oneself – the historicity of the 'I' had been forgotten. The main problem of historicism, Schlünz argued, is that the historicist conceptual understanding of the past has led to a conceptual understanding of the present, 'which depicted the rise of the German Empire, imperialism, the glorification of the monarch, the omnipotence of the state, without sensing the stirring covert vigours of the people in socialism, without sensing the inner hollowness of the platitudes of the glorification of everyday occurrences such as birthdays, centennials'.[55]

Schlünz even contended that the historical education of modern man had obstructed the vast majority of educated Germans in truly experiencing the historicity of the November Revolution in 1918 and the sudden fall of the emperor and numerous dynasties: 'the intellectualism in history has thoroughly suppressed the vivacious emotional experience of historical greatness. Few among our people have fully experienced the fall of the worldly powers as a deep inner liberation for responsible action'.[56]

The development of the youth movement into a 'subculture' with its own mores, own speeches and its own stars, led to an increased acknowledgement that the movement had made the same mistake it accused bourgeois society of – namely that it had created social forms that were now venerated for the sake of form only, while the content in service of which it had been shaped had been forgotten. It had always been a problem that the youth movement attracted new members who fancied its culture over its 'inner' aspects, but now it was the leaders themselves who had forgotten experience.[57] The 'Romanticism' of the Wandervogel was part of a vehement discussion that had raged through the movement since the war. It basically came down to the question what to do with the 'elders' of the youth movement. The return from the front had resulted in a large number of older leaders reclaiming their position in the Wandervogel and Freideutsche Jugend – to great opposition from the young, who feared becoming the subject of a false, sentimental, overemphasized and tirelessly cultivated Romanticism of the older leadership.

At the same time, there was a gender aspect to Wandervogel's waning Romanticism. During the war girls were in the majority in many groups. The fact that they had taken up leadership positions had led, so argued some boys, to an equally false Romanticism that was tied more to cultivated indoor activities or dancing, than to the bodily experience of wandering. These arguments often drew from the anti-feminist thought of Hans Blüher, who had stated that the Wandervogel was in its core a male association in which the Platonic 'eros' was the main binding factor – a factor that should not be challenged by inciting lower drifts of the flesh by mixed-sex wandering.

In 1919, Gerhard Friese noted that the phrase 'Wandervogel spirit' had become 'bleak mockery'. For him the 'Wandervogel experience' had turned into an empty phrase:

> We cannot, yes we can no longer experience it. It has been pre-experienced for us a thousand times, and all of that was traded like horses. All that is sacred, mysterious, has been discussed over and over again; the nightly hikes and nightly fires were desecrated by subversive witty conversations. The mythos has vanished, and what remains are the dead residues; form, meaningless form.[58]

At the same time, Friedrich Schlünz argued that the rapidly expanding body of Wandervogel literature speaking of various *Stimmungen*, such as experiences in nature, but also the 'medieval attunement of the Middle Ages in towns, images and speech', had put a normative mark on how to experience *Stimmungen*, which obstructed the ability of direct experience for the young.[59] Of course the love of historical localities or local sagas is good, Schlünz argued, and obviously many articles in the Wandervogel magazines are inspired by personal experience, but its narrative representation in long, almost scientific treatises diverts experience to sentimentality. Sentimentality, rather than naive experience, has the tendency to forget the present needs in favour of an idealization of the past. Thus, the ossification of the movement led to the ossification of historical experience in sentimental representation, which was done for the sake of form, without the sense of an inner urge to do so. An obligatory relationship with the past forgets the present and the present needs.

In a passionate call, the Jena chapter of the Wandervogel e.V. had claimed the youthful right for an 'insouciant romanticism', stating that:

> We have perched on countless mysterious ruins many a night around crackling fire, and haven't given a damn whether, under the ramshackle remains of walls over which the red glow poured a restless shadow, some treasure was hidden – or if haunted ancestresses wandered there over the decayed stairs on moonless nights. We thought – no, we did not think at all – we felt only very simply, that it was beautiful – unspeakably beautiful.[60]

However, in the end a return to Romanticism proved to be untenable, because it was just as escapist as the flight in theory. In postwar Germany a new Romanticism did not even appear an anachronism; it appeared as a denouncement of historical time and as an absolute negation of all worldly affairs that now affected everybody personally.[61] The greatest challenge regarding historical understanding that the postwar youth movement faced was how to develop a social responsibility that holds true to one's inner experience of both nature and the past, while at the same time encouraging a creative constitution of the future.

The conservative political philosopher Leo Strauss once said that for postwar German philosophy the central problem was '*not* history vs. unhistorical naturalism, or the grown vs. the made', as it had been in nineteenth-century idealism, '*but* life or existence vs. science, science being *any* purely theoretical enterprise. The science criticized in the name of life or existence, comprises of both natural science and history'.[62] The youth movement in its broadest meaning fits neatly in this description and was without any doubt part of the same intellectual current; the struggle with intellectualism both within and beyond the movement was a struggle with the premises of historicism. It was a struggle inspired by one of Haberkorn's favourite works: Friedrich Nietzsche's *Vom Nutzen und Nachteil der Historie*, as well as writings such as Oswald Spengler's monumental *Der Untergang des Abendlandes* (1918). As we have seen, Nietzsche's work attracted revived attention, mainly after 1914. Before the war Nietzsche had been kept far from the Wandervogel, for parents and educators saw him as a corruptor of youth and as a despiser of

Christianity and Germanness.[63] Johann Gottlieb Fichte, Paul de Lagarde or Julius Langbehn were preferred due to their adherence to the German cause. It was only during their university study and notably during the war that Nietzsche drew the attention of the youth movement.

Nietzsche had made it possible for Haberkorn to bring the problems of modernity under one denominator: history. Modern historical consciousness thus functioned as an umbrella concept of a worldview that was based on faith in reason, on the objectivity of social institutions, and on human moral development – thus also on unilinear time. At the same time, Nietzsche led him to understand how to revalue life and *Erlebnis* not as a mere reaction to historicism, but as its cure. Nietzsche's work entailed a strong refutation of historicism based on the objection that when historicism would conquer all aspects of life, this would mean the end of history itself. History, after all, thrives on spontaneous, creative action. However, when man understands himself merely in historical terms, as the product of a historically evolved culture, society, nation or community, the demands put forward by history are a burden that obstructs truly historical action. Truly creative action puts history in the service of life, instead of regarding history as an end in itself.

Whereas Nietzsche provided the youth movement with arguments for a critique of historicism, it was Spengler who, in their view, took historicism to its ultimate consequence. For Spengler, historical consciousness was itself an expression of the spirit of a specific historical epoch – an expression of what he calls the 'faustian' culture of Western society since the tenth century. Taken from Goethe's well-known play, the term 'faustian' refers to the orientation of the Western 'soul' on infinite space – contrary to, for example, the Apollonian soul of the Classical world, which focuses on the materially present world.[64] But just as each epoch has incommensurable spatial orientations, science and mathematics, Spengler emphasizes that historical thought is an idiosyncrasy of – now declining – faustian culture. It makes, he states, 'great difference whether anyone lives under the constant impression that his life is an element in a far wider life-course that goes on for hundreds and thousands of years, or conceives of himself as something rounded off and self-contained'.[65] While all cultures and civilizations partake in the in itself meaningless biological course of events that make up 'human history', faustian culture explains life historically in the modern sense: in reference to direction and progress. Trying not to make the mistake of confusing this Eurocentric explanation with 'reality', Spengler falls back on an organic understanding of history, in which cultural forms rise and decay like all other life forms.

While contemporary historiography tends to interpret Spengler's work as an example of what British analytical philosophers have called the 'speculative philosophy of history', in Weimar Germany, anti-positivist scholars and thinkers saw his work as a philosophy that historicized the philosophy of history itself and was therefore radically historicist.[66] Although in the youth movement Spengler's morphology was generally rejected for its fatalism and pessimism – and his book was even allegedly burned at solstice festivals for these reasons – his radical historicism also opened up a new possibility.[67]

It destructed the burden of historical authority and made clear that, because all is expression, what was once good and true need not be good and true *now*. Spengler freed the youth movement from the fear of being original. At the same time, he explicated that shaping the future did not mean continuing any of the forms of Western life: 'not Fichte or Nietzsche; not Christianity, or socialism: all these are creations of Western life, and can only be adjusted to the new sense of life by random reinterpretation'.[68] The authority of these thinkers or systems of thought would not suffice, because post-historicist thinking would not be concerned with the *historical* interest in their opinions as being constitutive for the present and providing guidance for the future. Rather than being concerned with systems of thought or with opinions of past thinkers, post-historicist thinking would aim at the very content of past thoughts – at the fundamental, essential and metaphysical questions of life. The study and understanding of the past would now be more urgent than ever, and would lead to a new apex within the youth movement. Acknowledging that the Western worldview was apt to end, enabled the possibility that the truth, or the path to truth, could be found in a thorough hermeneutic interpretation (rather than a determination) of sources of wisdom beyond the rational modern epoch.

Thus, even when the Wandervögel denounced Spengler's fatalism, he did encourage them to envisage themselves as the carriers of the world beyond the downfall of the West; he enabled them to think the future as the 'absolutely' new, rather than as the 'historically' new. This not only meant that it would prove to be impossible to let people who still thought historically to understand what the youth movement strove to achieve, but also that the proposed political alternatives for future Germany that had been put forward within the movement would be rejected by the mainstream. Resorting to historical theories of revolution and restoration would mean continuing to think on the premises of historicism. The fundamentally new, however, was not to be thought in terms of historical temporality as the evolving or the revolving. Rather, we could call the pending historical moment with 'Freideutsche' Alfred Peter a 'renovation'.[69] The future was neither thought through the past, as would have been the restorative tendency. Nor was the past thought through the future, as would have been the revolutionary tendency. Renovation however lies 'beyond the borders of this temporality'.[70] It attests only to eternity. Absolute renewal could only be understood on the basis of the Wandervogel's religiosity. Thus, the youth movement's religiosity was their profound answer to the crisis of modernity understood as the crisis of historicism.

## Jena 1919: Passivism versus Activism

The first meeting after the war of the Freideutsche Jugend took place around Easter 1919 in Jena. It was to become a decisive meeting for the youth movement, for its leadership had to seek answers to a number of tensions that had built up during the war. Additionally, the movement had to come to terms with the problems of the day. The revolution, the abdication of the emperor and the proclamation of the German Republic had robbed Germany of its social, political and cultural securities. But more importantly, it had robbed the middle classes of the self-evidency of the idea of social order in general and Wilhelmine social order in particular. Overnight, the secure, bourgeois world had become a feature of a distant past. In a period of just a few months, the armistice had been signed and the revolution had been quenched in blood through intervention by the newly established Reichswehr and *Freikorps* units.

The challenges for the youth movement were tremendous. Still recovering from the loss of a large portion of its leadership, the meeting at Jena ought to have provided a new organizational beginning.[71] The Wandervogel e.V. had already joined the Freideutsche Jugend in 1917, after settling its differences with Gustav Wyneken, and now a start was made to intensify cooperation with the proletarian youth, which delegated representatives to the Jena meeting. A root problem, however, was the rampant politicization within the movement. The *völkisch* wing around Frank Glatzel strongly opposed the revolution, while the Wyneken-oriented leftist circle around the *Anfang* supported the revolution.

Yet, despite the political differences, there was unanimity over the fact that the meeting had a deeply religious character. While the left explored the possibilities for a 'religious Bolshevism', and the right toyed with a *völkisch* appropriation of Germanic mythology, the mainstream sought refuge in a broad variety of religious sources: in the Upanishads, Buddhism, Christian mysticism, Ayurvedic mythology, Taoism and anthroposophy, and also in the teachings of Rabindranath Tagore and in the poetry of Hölderlin and Stefan George. Yet the meeting at Jena was a focal point for the hopes and the prospects of the postwar youth movement. It was felt that the youth movement in general could no longer afford to be a realm of youth separate from society; this was the moment for youth to stand up and define the destiny of themselves and the nation.

However, the 150 people who gathered in Jena were treated 'to the speeches of debating philosophers, the sermons of religious visionaries, and the constructions of alienated theoreticians'.[72] Most disillusioning was the speech by the artist Friedrich Vorwerk, who preached a deeply fatalist religious Bolshevism. Contending that the revolution of the proletariat would only result in a 'negative capitalism', Vorwerk stated that real communism lies in the readiness to give oneself entirely for the other, a state that can only come about when all ties to the intellectual and physical necessities of life are cut.[73]

Only then can there be a 'valuable minimum' on which new life can be built. This state, however, cannot be reached through direct efforts; it is imminent in the decay of modern society. 'Communism will come, whether we want it or not; there remains but one thing for us to do – to go under with this world.'[74] Downfall and renovation were cosmic events – and there is no room for human agency when it comes to the cosmos.

By no means did fatalistic accounts such as Vorwerk's lectures answer the existential crisis of expectation of the youth movement, neither did they appeal to its affirmative attitude. In the end the open renaissance of metaphysical thought had no avail: '[T]hey dug up the deepest secrets of the soul, they gushed quite broadly over the polarity of all occurrences, let themselves float on the stream of life, rather than seize life itself, to permeate it with positive labour, ... out of the abundant powers of youth'.[75] The younger attendees could hardly comprehend the jargon of the lectures and some would claim this display of intellectualism to be treasonous to youth.[76]

When after five days the series of lectures was over, little time was left to discuss the practical issues of the movement, such as the relationship to the proletarian youth movement, the value of rural settlement projects, the idea of *Volksgemeinschaft*, and the movement's expansion. The most fundamental question of the postwar movement remained unanswered: how to overcome the divergent political orientations in a mutual understanding and in a new experience of community?[77] It appeared to be impossible to find a 'common denominator' for the often unclear, unarticulated and contradictory worldviews in this revolutionary age, for every fraction used its own catchphrases – often misunderstood by others.[78]

Disillusioned by the passive fatalism inherent to the potpourri of Christian and Buddhist mysticism, religious Bolshevism and anthroposophy that the lectures displayed, and frustrated by the inaction of the disintegrating youth movement, a small band of revolutionary students strove to set an example. When, on the morning of Monday 14 April, the leaders gathered at the Galgenberg on the outskirts of Jena, a group of left-wing students led by Carl Rieniets, Ernst Castens and Adolf Hansen entered the university building to act spontaneously, rather than to contemplate.[79] Their objective: the 'liberation' of a long-hidden mural.

Between 1907 and 1909 the Swiss symbolist artist Ferdinand Hodler had painted the monumental *Der Auszug deutscher Studenten in den Freiheitskrieg von 1813* (German students setting out for the War of Liberation of 1813) on the wall of the new academy's lecture hall. It was a gift from alumni for the 350th anniversary of the university, and depicted the departure of Jena students for the Napoleonic War, dressed in the black and red tunic of the Prussian Freikorps Lützow's Rifles. The symbolist style of the painting did not lie well with the bourgeoisie of the provincial town, who were more inclined to traditional realist history painting. Although Jena had once known a lively left-liberal circle that had strongly criticized the Bismarck-cult and connected more with the traditions of 1848 and 1849 than with state-sponsored nationalism, after the turn of the century their influence had quickly waned.[80] Contrary to the conservative taste for conventional history painting – which, as exemplified in the paintings of Karl Röchling, Anton von Werner and Wilhelm Camphausen, depicted victorious generals and regiments in frontal assault – Hodler showed war volunteers in departure. It was a tacit correction to the political memory of the age, which overemphasized the leading role of the Prussian king Friedrich Wilhelm III in the mobilization of the German coalition forces, based on the Prussian legend contained in Heinrich Clauren's famous phrase 'Der König rief und alle, alle kamen' (the king called and all came).[81] The symbolism was striking; not only the composition but also the topic signified that the War of Liberation was a people's war, instigated by the German bourgeoisie, rather than by Prussian nobility. The Lützow Freikorps was, furthermore, the regiment that on the return from Waterloo had laid the foundation for the *Burschenschaften*, and thus for the urge of the liberal-democratic unification of the German nation.

Although conservative critique on his painting had been aired before, when Hodler subscribed an open letter condemning the German bombardment of Reims Cathedral in 1914 as an 'act of barbarism', he was publicly regarded to be an enemy of the German Empire, was expelled from German art societies and his art was considered worthless.[82] After a campaign, led by the eighty-year-old zoologist Ernst Haeckel, had demanded the removal and sale of the mural, the university board decided to at least cover the fresco with wooden panels to quell the discussion and to protect the mural from damage by political fanatics. This decision did indeed quell the discussion. But when, after Hodler's death in May 1918, the university board decided not to remove the panels as had been suggested in the press, keeping the mural covered appeared to be much more problematic than during the war. By maintaining the cover, the university was suspected of retrospectively supporting Haeckel's iconoclasm and was subsequently attacked by predominantly leftist commentators who questioned the strange situation of equating the attributed opinion of an artist with the content of his art. The Swiss publicist Victor Snell stated that, in terms of sheer stupidity, the Academic Senate surpassed those French journalists who tended to hold Richard Wagner posthumously responsible for the war.[83] Closer to the youth movement, Ferdinand Avenarius called for the removal of the panels, arguing that after Hodler's death the determination in departure that the expressionist mural depicted should again been seen artistically. 'The human Hodler is dead', he wrote. 'These boards have been standing there to give us time to allow for reflection. Would they remain there longer, they would become an embarrassment – nothing else.'[84] It was a call repeated after war and revolution by students in the Jena Workers and Soldiers Council, but had no avail with the national-conservative university board.

**Figure 3.1** Ferdinand Hodler, *Der Auszug deutscher Studenten in den Freiheitskrieg von 1813*, 1908–09. Wikimedia Commons.

At the Jena meeting of the Freideutsche Jugend, a proposal to send the university a letter requesting the removal of the panels was rejected, because the earlier requests by revolutionary students had been in vain.[85] But when, after lunch on 14 April, the Jena congregation commenced, it started with a 'bang'.[86] The news arrived that the Hodler mural had been 'liberated' and that support was urgently needed to defend the liberation against university officials and in scuffles with nationalist fraternity students.[87] In response to the emergency call, some 150 attendees rushed to the university in support of the 'Hodler liberators'. Although the fraternity students were nowhere to be found, the 'liberation' was a success: the panels were removed, and the removal was sanctioned post hoc by the university board.

The publisher Eugen Diederichs – a prominent figure in the youth movement ever since his neo-Romantic Jena-based 'Sera circle' had joined the Freideutsche Jugend – hailed the action as 'a beautiful symbol of the new spirit to prompt inner sense over ossified life', and called it a wake-up call for universities to step down from merely treating both social and scientific problems objectively, but to be exemplary for humanity.[88] In his view, it was the Freideutsche Jugend that had re-established the forgotten symbolical value of the mural.

Ironically, one eyewitness noted that any understanding of the symbolical value of the fresco was exactly what lacked. Hardly any of the onlookers experienced the 'grand rhythm' of the image. Surprised, and even shocked by their own audacity, the momentum was lost in trivial chatter. 'There was a broad discussion on what to do with the panels from which the painting had been liberated – which laid scattered on the floor. Afterwards on the street they got into a huddle and contemplated the act and the actors: "was it a student prank", "a symbolic deed", "an occurrence with a mystical background" ...?"[89] Some were abhorred that the 'liberated' picture actually depicted a war-related scene, while others were only just prevented from burning the panels on the university's courtyard.[90]

The 'spirit of 1813' that the grand mural depicted, the spirit of self-determination in which the Meißner formula was phrased before the war, remained entirely unnoticed in the struggle for the interpretation of the liberation. The fatalism of the Jena gathering was countered with an even more unclear activism. We can state with Richard Hamann that the 'mixture of humanistic-idealistic, national-religious and vitalist-theosophical trains of thought ... led to an absolute chaos of faith'.[91] The case of the 'liberation' of the mural indicates the inability to grasp the meaning of their own actions, an inability directly related to the loss of traditional frameworks of meaning in postwar revolutionary Germany. With the demise of bourgeois society and Wilhelmine mentality, there was little to rebel *against*. The conservative university board could have been targeted, but as the representatives of what? Something symbolic or even revolutionary had taken place; but with the lack of an established opponent, it was utterly unclear what the value or potential – let alone the meaning – of this act was. Given the spiritual mood in the postwar youth movement and the fact that the historicist 'worldview' was itself deemed to be a thing of the past, answers were sought from a religious stance that related life to the eternal, rather than to the ephemeral. Although this did not provide any clear answers to the meaning of the 'liberation' of the Hodler mural, it raises the question of how the youth movement intended to relate to the past, and what the function of memory was, when the past could no longer be seen as a bygone 'historical' past. This is what we will discuss next.

## Memory as Advent Action

Wandervogel Eduard Lenz – co-founder of the Christengemeinschaft, a movement for religious renewal – clearly recalled a night when he sat together with a local group of Wandervogel friends, speaking about the many mysterious aspects of life. They all attended the higher classes of the gymnasium. But rather than turning to the Classics, the discussion ended in a nightly reading of the Bhagavad Gita. Lenz remembered that they were not the least interested in the teachings of the Hindu epic. No lessons were drawn from the reading, but they were captured by the humanity (*Menschheit*) at work in the Gita. 'Never have I been interested in history in the ordinary sense of the word. But we felt a strong urge always to observe those endeavours of man which touch upon what is most deeply human in himself in the unfolding humanity of the past.'[92] Be it a reading of Lao Tzu, Buddha's teachings, Plato, Goethe, or envisaging personalities such as Alexander the Great, Pericles or Napoleon, it was always a past quest for the inner self which was the object of interest.

Lenz's recollections testify of a new understanding of temporality, in which memory was no longer the recollection of past events, from which one could derive an identity for the present, but was always a creative act that could generate something that goes beyond identity: a present experience of the intrusion of the eternal in the course of events. Man's perennial quest for eternity became at the same time memory's goal and object. Lenz summarizes his understanding of history as follows:

> The gods have released man from their keeping. He should find his kingdom. History is the quest of man for a secret goal. Soul formation is the meaning of history. People in the past – and we ourselves – proclaim in their lives how they have sought themselves and found the mysterious kinship with the gods in the 'I'. How do we become the brothers of the gods? This, I believe, is the question history poses. I want to behold the people who came before us in such a way that we retrieve them in the being of our soul as soul-shaping powers, so that we experience: we were there when the past events occurred. Our soul is the fruit of a sprout of soul in the past.[93]

Another Wandervogel, Erich Trummler, captures this historical understanding in an article in *Freideutsche Jugend* remembering Hölderlin. 'When we have a memory, a sacred remembrance,' he wrote, 'then we act *advent*' – in favour of what is coming.[94] When remembering, people are not struck by what is ordinary but by those historical figures who were most visionary in their age. In the act of remembering, these visionaries are not forebears whose wisdom or heroism reflects upon those who remember because their thoughts and actions have constituted the present, rather they become guiding stars or prophets, whose thoughts, ideas and actions encourage those who remember to tackle their own fate. In remembering, man – he argued – foreshadows the acknowledgment of his own fate. Defined as 'advent action', I would like to emphasize that memory was conceived differently from what is commonly regarded to be the function of memory. Commonly, memory is understood as the recollection of past events (either individually or collectively) in order to establish an understanding of an identity in the present and expectations for the future. Memory thus carries the past into the future, on which it is projected as expectation. Now, the notion of 'memory as advent action' indicates a different constellation: memory is not projected into the future, but basically comes from the future towards the present and presents itself as destiny – its direction and function are reversed. How could memory present itself as destiny? Because when one is confronted with a future that is not regarded as fully malleable, but that is destined, memory does not need to provide prospects for what man can and needs to achieve. What it can do is recall how people in previous times dealt with their destiny. This, after all, also shaped the present, and an awareness of it could generate a readiness to deal with destiny, which was both symbolically and practically useful for members of the youth movement in the turbulent years after the war.

By understanding memory as advent action, the youth movement followed Nietzsche's answer to the crisis of historicism: it attested to eternity. Nietzsche called those powers supra-historical 'which led the eye away from becoming towards that which bestows upon existence the character of the eternal and stable, towards art and religion'.[95] However, contrary to the early Nietzsche, the youth movement did not understand eternity as a quality that could be bestowed upon existence, but as the very essence of existence itself. Therefore, religion was not an object of their interest, but the immediacy of religious experience was the very prerequisite for their existential understanding of the world.

It was often asserted that a religious apprehension of the world was natural to youth. After all, had youth not left the securities of childhood behind and did it not stand on the brink of an insecure and unknown future? Did not innumerable possibilities open up; was not youth the age to transgress the horizon of the known and comfort? Thus Paul Tillich could argue that it was in the infinite that youth could find itself:

> Whether on the wings of speculative imagination, whether through a solitary contemplation of the depths of one's own soul, whether through the mysticism of friendship or unrequited love, whether through the world-reforming urge to act and to create man ... always, the infinite is the element, in which the soul of youth finds itself.[96]

It was only through an awareness of infinity that the postwar youth movement apprehended the past. According to female Wandervogel Else Stroh, not only timelessness (not-time) stands vis-à-vis time, but also time-infinity; this is the time in which God shapes himself.[97] Whereas *subjectivity* relates to the ephemeral, to a historical understanding of the 'I' as a moral being that is part of the chain of history, it is *individuality* which Stroh relates to the eternal. She perceives individuality as the soul, which is the incarnation of the eternal in the self. When regarded in the light of eternity, 'no longer the indifferentiation of history, but entering into it for the future's sake is the watchword'.[98]

The metaphysical longing in the youth movement – which was called an 'immanent mysticism' or even 'pantheism' – showed a clear resonance when it came to the position of history in regard to the manifold forms in which it was understood.[99] Wandervogel Anni Wächter argued:

> The difference is that all of us, regardless of what we think of God and the beyond, see the goal of a new humanity in this world. Thus our mysticism is not from above but from within. It does not distance itself from the struggle but it is the driving, supra-rational force that stands behind our life purpose. If this were not the case, our new formation of human life would be merely a material, superficial improvement of the world.[100]

The task of the movement was to find these inner powers and bring them to full fruition. Only then could an entirely new future be established. But beyond seeking these powers through inwards reflection alone, she stated, they could be found in the thoughts and deeds of people in earlier times as well. By looking at the ways people in the past answered to the demands of life could memory function as 'advent action'.

For Trummler, Hölderlin was such an exemplar because his poetry reconciled the Dionysian Godhead of the Gothic masters with the Apollonian gods of the ancient Greeks.[101] Lenz recognized that he felt a much deeper inner connection with 'his' highest exemplars – ranging from Lao Tze to Napoleon, who he regarded to be the 'personifications of the eternally human' – than with any person in the present. One of the goals he set for himself was 'to experience history in this way: that through the observation of the becoming of humanity, man always experiences the unfolding of the eternally human in his own soul'.[102]

However, at the same time he acknowledged having had a strong longing for an exemplar in the present; a longing for an older leader who was initiated in the secrets of the soul. It was the same longing Haberkorn once felt in one of his moments of despair, when he confessed to having wanted a person near him, 'whose entire being is triumph and clarity and purity. In his silent presence I would like to weep until the soul has been released entirely and peace has come, just as peace drapes itself over the silent pine forest when the sun pours its last golden affluence over it'.[103] The experience of immediate intersubjectivity between the 'I' and the 'thou', which lies at the root of communal experience, could thus be a gateway to releasement of the I as long as the thou is himself 'released'. In the immediate proximity of a thou who does not attest to the will or to the fatalist not-willing of the I, who neither requires the I to act nor to behave, nor requires the I to refuse the will by not-acting, by passively awaiting fate, the I could find the *Gelassenheit* at peace and the eternal could be born in the I. In this way, the identical ground of the ephemeral I and the eternal Godhead or humanity could be experienced.

The risk of seeking infinity of the soul was becoming passive, as became clear at Jena. Paul Natorp recognized in this passivism a far greater danger than in politization, because it touched the most fundamental question of the inner life of the movement. 'Obviously,' Natorp said, 'seeking soul starts with solitary introspection.'[104] However, cherishing the deepest 'inner' personality or individuality and protecting it from the outer world has as a consequence that the inner ground can never transcend the communal world, and thus becomes an idol and mere theory. In this way, undivided humanity can never be achieved, because when the soul is understood to be found in the inner self, in personality so to speak, the rift between the personal and the collective is only endorsed. The absolute ground, on which the relativity between individual and community rests, can, however, never be derived from either of these two poles.

Instead, it can only be disclosed. Then it becomes clear that true individuality, as the exclusion of all duality, is the last ground, the one and the same, the identical – and as such, true individuality always implies true community. This ground can then be disclosed through 'the *Word*, the Logos; the word that was in the beginning and was with God and was the origin, was God itself. The Word – which had entered the world as if it had entered its own property, and in *us* had wanted to dwell – becomes vivacious in us once we let it in, once we are willing to hear its inaudible voice in the last, silent ground of our soul'.[105]

Such an amalgam of the Gospel of John and Eckhart's mysticism was the basis of the new religiosity for Haberkorn and Wurche as well. By adhering to the mystic experience of the unity of man and God as a theology that opposed traditional eschatology, it became possible for Haberkorn to frame the 'Wandervogel experience' as the experience of the unity of life, which opposed the modern worldview of historicism. From this perspective, the concept of *Erlebnis* could now be understood as Meister Eckhart's 'exposure of the last ground and thereby the innermost core elements of human life in the highest sense'.[106]

This, however, was an ideal situation. Often more clear and concrete answers were sought to the questions of life in the postwar years, which made members of the youth movement susceptible to a great variety of ideas and belief systems: 'Instead of leaders, they followed prophets ..., windbags were mistaken for heroes, formulas were mistaken for form. Instead of striving for the consummation of their humanity, they strove for points of view and worldviews'.[107] They visited speeches of Rabindranath Tagore, seeking 'answers, or at least an affirmation of the cleverness of their ideas'.[108] Others turned to Rudolf Steiner's anthroposophy in search of a bridge between the sensed possibility of redemption and practical life.[109] The attraction of some to Rudolf Steiner's anthroposophy was followed with suspicion by others, fearing that such devotion to a single doctrine and a single leader would grow into a dogmatic 'anthroposophical Catholicism under Steiner's papacy'.[110] However, the fact that the older leadership was unable to provide such exemplars certainly strengthened the urge to find inspiration (*inspiratio*) in historical sources.

## Conclusion

The First World War was a crucial event for the youth movement's conception of time and history. Initially it provided a possibility to become involved in history. While school history and state nationalism had presented the past as something venerable but distanced, the war opened the opportunity for the young to participate in an event that could shape history and German destiny. In August 1914, the war seemed to have provided German nationhood with spiritual content and a sense of purpose. This made participating in the war effort especially attractive for members of the youth movement: the moral predicaments of the Meißner formula could now be put to the service of society. This explains Haberkorn's enthusiasm for the war, as well as Wurche's attempts to be a morally exemplary leader for his troops.

But once the aura of August 1914 had faded, it became clear that in broader German society the initial outburst of 'spiritual' unity had not resulted in changed culture, morals or relationships. While the soldiers from the youth movement assured themselves that death was the greatest act of life, they were met with a society that instrumentalized even this ultimate act for mundane causes – be it the fatherland, or religious dogmas. This is what Franz Christ realized after being shot: it was too difficult for society to change itself, because many would not be able to reject short-term profit for long-term ideals. He was not alone in his disappointment in man's moral capability to change society. During the war, more and more voices in the youth movement sought salvation in a domain beyond human action – a non-dogmatic, experience-inspired religiosity got hold of the movement.

This religiosity was the basis for an important shift in the understanding of history, which would become increasingly apparent in the years after the war when the question of social change was most urgent. By replacing the focus on human agency with an orientation on the 'eternal', history was no longer what it used to be. We have seen with Reinhart Koselleck that, in the nineteenth century, 'history' had become a term that denoted both the representation of human actions, and the course of these actions itself. In the latter connotation, history was understood as the process of human moral progress – progress based on a belief in human agency and rationality. The loss of faith in human agency and the rise of religiosity led to the loss of the self-evidency of 'history' and the unilinear conception of time on which the modern idea of history was based. Before the war, the youth movement had still adhered to this traditional concept of history. It did criticize German historical culture, but not the underlying conception of time. Insofar as lived experience was cultivated, it had been an alternative mode of appropriating the past, but this past was still *in need* of appropriation because it remained historically, temporally and qualitatively different from the present. In testimonies of experiences, references to religious or cosmic temporality had already been present, but only during the war did these references started to dominate the self-narrative and self-explanation of the movement.

In the internal struggles between the boys and the girls and between older and younger members, which had intensified after 1917, the deliberate cultivation of experience was rejected as a template to which hikes and events had to adhere. This self-reflection on the movement's activities went hand in hand with the critique of historicism. Ironically, both historicism and the 'cult' of experience were now historicized – they were attributed to Wilhelmine society, which was now officially a thing of the past. A new Germany had become reality, or was expected to become a reality in the near future. However, the basis on which the advent of this new reality could come about was not clear, and was the subject of fierce disputes within the movement. Yet, it is clear that 'historicism' as a worldview was no longer a self-evident template for interpreting and explaining events. This is made painfully clear by the incapability of the members of the Freideutsche Jugend to interpret their own 'liberation' of the Hodler mural. Faith in moral self-determination had been replaced by an unclear but deeply experienced religiosity. Richard Braun strikingly called this development from the pre-war youth movement to the postwar youth movement a development from 'autonomy' to 'theonomy'.[111]

Both the Wandervogel and Freideutsche Jugend would disintegrate as a result of disputes in the early 1920s, but although ideas and ideologies clashed, the members of the youth movement had gained awareness that a meta-critique of historicism and historical consciousness was needed to gain a truly new society. History and memory were understood in relation to the absolute, and memory became advent action: an incentive for the genuine constitution of a new man and a new society.

In the next chapter, I will analyse what the role of the past was in the non-historicist strife to realize the eternal in the temporal world by focusing on the Middle Ages as an object of 'memory as advent action'.

## Notes

1. Franz Christ, 'Religiöse Erlebnisse und Betrachtungen an der Somme', *Freideutsche Jugend* 2(12) (1916), 362–64: 363.

2. Ibid., 364.

3. O. Neuloh and W. Zilius, *Die Wandervögel. Eine empirisch-soziologische Untersuchung der frühen deutschen Jugendbewegung* (Göttingen: Vandenhoeck und Ruprecht, 1982), 133–34.

4. Wilhelm, 'Der geschichtliche Ort der deutschen Jugendbewegung', 27.

5. Cf. Achim Reis, *Die Jugendbewegung als religiöses Phänomen* (Frankfurt am Main: Johann-Wolfgang-Goethe-Universität, 1994), 36.

6. The following is based on letters from Haberkorn to Friedrich Siegmund-Schultze, theologist and founder of the Soziale Arbeitsgemeinschaft Berlin-Ost, written between 1914 and 1917. Friedrich Siegmund-Schultze, *Ver sacrum: was die im Kriege gefallenen Mitarbeiter der sozialen Arbeitsgemeinschaft dem deutschen Volk zu sagen haben. Mitteilungen und Aufzeichnungen* (Berlin: Furche-Verlag, 1919), 135.

7. Cf. Nietzsche, 'On the Uses and Disadvantages of History for Life', 116–23.

8. Siegmund-Schultze, *Ver sacrum*, 134.

9. Ibid., 131.

10. On the SAG, see: Christoph Sachße, 'Friedrich Siegmund-Schultze, die "Soziale Arbeitsgemeinschaft" und die bürgerliche Sozialreform in Deutschland', in Heinz-Elmar Tenorth et al. (eds), *Friedrich Siegmund-Schultze (1885–1969): ein Leben für Kirche, Wissenschaft und soziale Arbeit* (Stuttgart: Kohlhammer, 2007), 35–49.

11. Jens Wietschorke, 'Der Weltkrieg als "soziale Arbeitsgemeinschaft". Eine Innenansicht bildungsbürgerlicher Kriegsdeutungen 1914–1918', *Geschichte und Gesellschaft* 34(2) (2008), 225–51: 229.

12. Siegmund-Schultze, *Ver sacrum*, 137.
13. Ibid., 138.
14. Cf. Werner Kindt, 'Die Älterenbünde des Wandervogels bis zum Ende des Ersten Weltkrieges', in Kindt, *Die Wandervogelzeit*, 949–54.
15. Rudolf Haberkorn, 'Naumburger Nachklang', in Kindt, *Die Wandervogelzeit*, 988–89: 988.
16. Paul Tillich, 'Die Jugend und die Religion', in Adolf Grabowsky and Walther Koch (eds), *Die Freideutsche Jugendbewegung. Ursprung Und Zukunft* (Gotha: Perthes, 1921), 8–13: 11.
17. Ibid., 12.
18. Rudolf Haberkorn, 'Die Einheit des Lebens als Wandervogelerlebnis', in Siegmund-Schultze, *Ver Sacrum*, 152–53: 153.
19. Ibid., 153.
20. 'Die Gilden', *Der Zwiespruch. Rundbrief der Feldwandervogel im Westen* 6 (1917), 98–99.
21. Haberkorn, 'Gedanken zur neudeutschen Religion', in Siegmund-Schultze, *Ver Sacrum*, 153–63: 153.
22. Friedrich Nietzsche, *Thus Spoke Zarathustra* (Cambridge: Cambridge University Press, 2006), 55–59.
23. Haberkorn, 'Gedanken zur neudeutschen Religion', 158.
24. Helmut Pohl in a letter to Friedrich Siegmund-Schultze, 6 March 1917. Siegmund-Schultze, *Ver sacrum*, 151.
25. Knud Ahlborn, 'Freideutsche Jugend und Menschheitsgedanke', in Kindt, *Grundschriften der Deutschen Jugendbewegung*, 195.
26. Ibid., 195.
27. Thomas S. Schneider et al., *Die Autoren und Bücher der deutschsprachigen Literatur zum 1. Weltkrieg 1914–1939* (Osnabrück: Universitätsverlag Osnabrück, 2008), 10.
28. Joseph Victor von Scheffel's *Frankenlied* (approx. 1870). Cf. Walter Flex, 'Der Wanderer zwischen beiden Welten. Ein Kriegserlebnis', in Walter Flex (ed.), *Gesammelte Werke, Band 1* (Munich: C.H. Beck, 1925), 185–266: 190.
29. Ibid., 191.
30. Although being called a Wandervogel by Flex, Wurche was in fact a member of the academic Freischar *Skuld*. Although *Skuld* initially developed out of the Berlin chapter of the *Deutscher Bund abstinenter Studenten*, the association operated in the youth movement's sphere of influence, and took up hikes and physical culture shortly after its re-establishment in 1907. *Skuld* maintained a close relationship with the Wandervogel of Berlin-Friedrichshagen and was present at the *Freideutsche Jugendtag* at the Hohe Meißner in 1913. Cf. Gerda Voß, 'Aus der Geschichte der "Skuld"', in Kindt, *Die Wandervogelzeit*, 452–53. Wurche himself was preparing for his first *Große Fahrt* with *Skuld* when the war broke out. See the letter by Margarete Wurche printed in: Hinrich Jantzen, *Namen und Werke 1. Biographien und Beiträge zur Soziologie der Jugendbewegung* (Frankfurt a/M: Dipa-Verlag, 1972), 318.
31. Flex, 'Der Wanderer zwischen beiden Welten', 191.
32. Ibid., 194.
33. G.S., 'Führer sein!', *Wandervogel* 13(9/10) (1918), 185.
34. Nietzsche, 'Schopenhauer as Educator', in *Untimely Meditations* (Cambridge: Cambridge University Press, 1997), 125–94: 155.
35. Ibid., 155.
36. G.S., 'Führer sein!'
37. Flex, 'Der Wanderer zwischen beiden Welten', 216.
38. Wilhelm Hagen, 'Vom Geist des Wandervogels', *Wandervogel* 11(11) (1916), 230.
39. Flex, 'Der Wanderer zwischen beiden Welten', 213.
40. Wurche cited by Flex in: Walter Flex, *Briefe von Walter Flex*, eds Walther Eggert-Windegg and Konrad Flex (Munich: C.H. Beck, 1927), 184–85.
41. Although Flex does not mention Eckhart, associating Nietzsche's Zarathustra with Eckhart's mysticism was not uncommon in circles around the Freideutsche Jugend. Cf. Paul

Schulze-Berghof, 'Zarathustra-Deutsche-Mystik-Deutscher Glaube', *Der Vortrupp. Halbmonatsschrift für das Deutschtum unserer Zeit* 5 (1916), 297–303.

42. From Eckhart's sixth German sermon, *Iusti vivent in aeternum*: 'Sumlîche einveltige liute wænent, sie süln got sehen, als er dâ stande und sie hie. Des enist niht. Got und ich wir sîn ein. Mit bekennenne nime ich got in mich, mit minnenne gân ich in got'. English translation cited from: Karen J. Campbell, *German Mystical Writings* (New York: Continuum, 2002), 131.

43. Flex, 'Der Wanderer zwischen beiden Welten', 201–2.

44. Ibid., 214.

45. Ibid., 214.

46. Cf. Gottfried Keller, 'Das Fähnlein der sieben Aufrechten', in Gottfried Keller (ed.), *Gottfried Keller's gesammelte Werke* (Berlin: Wilhelm Hertz, 1891), 258–334: 277.

47. Flex, 'Der Wanderer zwischen beiden Welten', 215.

48. Ibid., 249.

49. Albert Kruse, 'Jugendbewegung und Zeiterlebnis', in Kindt, *Grundschriften der Deutschen Jugendbewegung*, 202.

50. Karl Mannheim, 'Historicism', in *Essays on the Sociology of Knowledge* (London: Routledge & Kegan Paul, 1952), 84–133: 85.

51. Friedrich Jaeger, 'Theorietypen der Krise des Historismus', in Wolfgang Bialas and Gérard Raulet (eds), *Die Historismusdebatte in Der Weimarer Republik* (Frankfurt am Main: Lang, 1996), 52–70: 52. See for a detailed study on the radical ways in which historical thought started to dominate all facets of life in modern society: Peter Fritzsche, *Stranded in the Present: Modern Time and the Melancholy of History* (Cambridge, MA: Harvard University Press, 2004).

52. Friedrich Schlünz, 'Intellektualismus und Historizismus', in Fritz Jöde (ed.), *Pädagogik deines Wesens. Gedanken der Erneuerung aus dem Wendekreis* (Hamburg: Freideutscher Jugendverlag Adolf Saar, 1919), 41.

53. Ibid., 41–42.

54. Ernst Troeltsch, *Gesammelte Schriften 3: Der Historismus und seine Probleme* (Tübingen: J.C.B. Mohr, 1922), 102. Translation derived from: John Roderick Hinde, *Jacob Burckhardt and the Crisis of Modernity* (Montreal: McGill-Queen's University Press, 2000), 143.

55. Schlünz, 'Intellektualismus und Historizismus', 42.

56. Ibid., 42.

57. Cf. Georg Schmidt, 'Ein Sendschreiben, zur Tröstung und Erbauung der korfhänger-ischen Schwarzfeher, so wo einen stolzen, sonnenwärts strebenden Vogel sich umwandeln sahen in ein klumpig träges Federvieh', *Wandervogel Führerzeitung* 2 (1913), 23–26: 24.

58. Gerhard Friese, 'Bemerkungen zur "Bewegung"', *Wandervogel* 14(7) (1919), 126–30.

59. Friedrich Schlünz, *Wandervogel wach auf!* (Hamburg: Freideutscher Jugendverlag Adolf Saal, 1919), 3.

60. Walter Männel and Adolf Hansen, 'Wandervogelrevolution. Ein Flugblatt', in Kindt, *Die Wandervogelzeit*, 857–59.

61. Hertha Niehaus, 'Zum Aufruf der Ortsgruppe Jena im Frühjahr 1919', *Wandervogel* 14(6) (1919), 160.

62. Leo Strauss, 'The Living Issues of German Postwar Philosophy', in Heinrich Meier (ed.), *Leo Strauss and the Theologico-Political Problem* (Cambridge: Cambridge University Press, 2006), 115–40: 116.

63. Niemeyer, "Plündernde Soldaten"; Niemeyer, 'Nietzsche als "Prophet der Jugendbewegung"', 186–87. See also: Ulbricht, 'Nietzsche als "Prophet der Jugendbewegung"?

64. Frits Boterman, *Oswald Spengler en "Der Untergang des Abendlandes". Cultuurpessimist en politiek activist* (Assen: Van Gorcum, 1992), 103.

65. Oswald Spengler, *The Decline of the West: Form and Actuality* (London: George Allen & Unwin Ltd., 1926), 8.

66. For the concept 'speculative philosophy of history', see: Rolf Gruner, 'The Concept of Speculative Philosophy of History', *Metaphilosophy* 3(4) (1972), 283–300. For this interpretation of Spengler's works, see: Strauss, 'The Living Issues of German Postwar Philosophy', 118ff.

67. Hans Schlemmer, *Der Geist der Deutschen Jugendbewegung* (Munich: Rösl & Cie., 1923), 100. On their disappointment that Spengler could not answer the question, see: 'What shall we do?', in Marianne Weber, *Max Weber: A Biography* (New Brunswick: Transaction Publishers, 2009), 674.

68. Friedrich Cornelius, 'Was kann uns Spengler sein?', *Freideutsche Jugend* 6(8/9) (1920), 261. Cf. Hans Hartmann, *Oswald Spengler und Deutschlands Jugend* (Rudolstadt: Greifenverlag, 1925).

69. Alfred Peter, 'Logos und Eros', *Freideutsche Jugend* 5(12) (1919), 521–27: 521.

70. Ibid., 521.

71. Some 3,500 of 14,000 Wandervogel soldiers did not survive the war.

72. Albrecht Merz, 'Die Freideutsche Führertagung in Jena', *Die Tat* 11(3) (1919/20), 229–32: 229. For the speeches, see: Knud Ahlborn, *Krieg, Revolution und Freideutsche Zukunft. Die Reden und Aussprachen der Jenaer Tagung 1919* (Hamburg: Freideutscher Jugendverlag Adolf Saal, 1919).

73. Ahlborn, *Krieg, Revolution und Freideutsche Zukunft*, 49.

74. Elisabeth Busse-Wilson, *Stufen der Jugendbewegung – Ein Abschnitt aus der ungeschriebenen Geschichte Deutschlands* (Jena: Eugen Diederichs, 1925), 39. Translation cited from: Laqueur, *Young Germany*, 114.

75. Merz, 'Die Freideutsche Führertagung in Jena', 358.

76. Eckart Peterich, 'Aus einem Brief an einen dreizehnjährigen Freund', *Freideutsche Jugend* 5(8/9) (1919), 393–94: 394.

77. *Bericht über die Ostertagung der Freideutschen Jugend in Jena (11.-19.4)*, ed. Georg Steiger, *'Fall Hodler': Jena 1914–1919: Der Kampf um ein Gemälde* (Jena: Friedrich-Schiller-Universität, 1970).

78. Georg Kötschau, 'Erinnerungen an den Freideutschen Jugendtag 1919 in Jena, die Befreiung des Hodler-Bildes und die Solidarität mit geflüchteten Revolutionären nach dem Niederschlagen der Bayerischen Räterepublik', in Georg Steiger ed., *'Fall Hodler': Jena 1914–1919: Der Kampf um ein Gemälde* (Jena: Friedrich-Schiller-Universität, 1970), 121.

79. Pamphlet by Ernst Castens, Eckart Peterich, Paul Reiner, Carl Rieniets and Hermann Schüller. AdJB, Freideutsche Jugend, A 104/9.

80. Hans-Werner Hahn, 'Zwischen Freiheitshoffnung und Führererwartung: Ambivalenzen bürgerlicher Erinnerungskultur in Jena 1870 bis 1930', in Jürgen John and Justus H. Ulbricht (eds), *Jena. Ein nationaler Erinnerungsort?* (Cologne: Böhlau-Verlag, 2007), 73–92: 73–74; Manfred Hettling, 'Die Nationalisierung von Kunst. Der "Fall Hodler" 1914', in Manfred Hettling (ed.), *Was ist Gesellschaftsgeschichte? Positionen, Themen, Analysen (Hans-Ulrich Wehler zum 60. Geburtstag)* (Munich: C.H. Beck, 1991), 215–24: 217.

81. Günter Steiger, 'Feierstunde anläßlich der 50. Wiederkehr der Enthüllung des Gemäldes von Ferdinand Hodler "Aufbruch der Jenaer Studenten 1813"', *Sozialistische Universität* 12(8) (1969), 6.

82. Cited in: Georg Steiger, *'Fall Hodler'*, 71.

83. Victor Snell, 'Les planches vengeresses', *l'Humanité*, 22 August 1918.

84. Ferdinand Avenarius, 'Hodlers Jenaer Bild', *Deutscher Wille des Kunstwarts* 31 (1918), 53. As early as 1914 Avenarius had uttered the hope that after Hodler's fall from grace his art would be valued for its contents rather than for the popularity of the artist. Cf. Ferdinand Avenarius, 'Vom Fall Hodler', *Kunstwart* 28(5) (1914), 185–86.

85. Ahlborn, *Krieg, Revolution und Freideutsche Zukunft*, 50.

86. Kötschau, 'Erinnerungen an den Freideutschen Jugendtag 1919 in Jena, die Befreiung des Hodler-Bildes und die Solidarität mit geflüchteten Revolutionären nach dem Niederschlagen der Bayerischen Räterepublik', 120.

87. Albrecht Merz, 'Zur Jenaer Tagung', *Freideutsche Jugend* 5(8/9) (1919), 354–58: 354; Walther Victor, 'Freideutsch. Zur 25. Wiederkehr des Jugendtages auf dem Hohen Meißner', *Das Wort* 3(10) (1938), 95–102: 102.

88. Eugen Diederichs, 'Die befreiung Hodlers', *Die Tat* 11 (1919/1920), 233. On Diederichs' involvolvement in the youth movement, see: Gary D. Stark, *Entrepreneurs of Ideology: Neoconservative*

*Publishers in Germany, 1890–1933* (Chapel Hill, NC: University of North Carolina Press, 1981), 103–10; Erich Viehöfer, 'Der Verleger als Organisator: Eugen Diederichs und die bürgerlichen Reformbewegungen der Jahrhundertwende', in Reinhard Wittmann and Marietta Kleiss (eds), *Archiv für Geschichte des Buchwesens. 30* (Frankfurt a.M.: Buchhändler-Vereinigung, 1988), 1–148: 73–94.

89. Merz, 'Zur Jenaer Tagung', 355.

90. 'Das Hodler-Bild frei!', *Jenaer Volksblatt*, 16 April 1919; Kötschau, 'Erinnerungen an den Freideutschen Jugendtag', 121.

91. Richard Hamann, *Stilkunst um 1900* (Frankfurt a.M.: Fischer, 1977), 132.

92. Eduard Lenz, 'Jugendbewegung und Zeitenwende II', in Kindt, *Die Wandervogelzeit*, 842–44: 842.

93. Ibid., 842–43.

94. Erich Trummler, 'Der Sternenstand. Dem Gedächtnis Hölderlins', *Freideutsche Jugend* 6(4) (1920), 121–24: 121. Trummler was a member of the Aschaffenburg Wandervogel and of the Werkschar in Munich, and had a clear interest in anthroposophy. Cf. Ulrich Linse, *Zurück, o Mensch, zur Mutter Erde: Landkommunen in Deutschland, 1890–1933* (Munich: Deutscher Taschenbuch Verlag, 1983), 277ff.

95. Nietzsche, 'On the Uses and Disadvantages of History for Life', 120. Cf. Wolfgang Koch, 'Jugend und Geschichte', in Grabowsky and Koch, *Die Freideutsche Jugendbewegung*, 59–62: 60.

96. Tillich, 'Die Jugend und die Religion', 9.

97. Else Stroh, 'Das völkische Problem. Die Völkischen und die Kulturellen', *Freideutsche Jugend* 6(1) (1920), 14–19: 17.

98. Heinz-Dietrich Wendland, 'Das religiöse Problem in der Jugendbewegung', in Carl Schweitzer (ed.), *Das religiöse Deutschland der Gegenwart. Band I: Der allgemein-religiöse Kreis* (Berlin: Hochweg, 1928), 209–38: 228.

99. August Messer, *Die freideutsche Jugendbewegung: Ihr Verlauf von 1913 bis 1923* (Langensalza: Hermann Beyer & Söhne, 1924), 96; Wendland, 'Das religiöse Problem in der Jugendbewegung', 216.

100. Marianne Wright and Erna Albertz, *Anni. Letters and Writings of Annemarie Wächter* (Rifton, NY: Plough Publishing House, 2010), 24.

101. Erich Trummler, *Der kranke Hölderlin, Urkunden und Dichtungen aus der Zeit seiner Umnachtung* (Munich: O.C. Recht, 1921), 8.

102. Lenz, 'Jugendbewegung und Zeitenwende II', 843.

103. Siegmund-Schultze, *Ver sacrum*, 135.

104. Paul Natorp, 'Hoffnungen und Gefahren unserer Jugendbewegung. Zur dritten Auflage 1920', in Kindt, *Grundschriften der Deutschen Jugendbewegung*, 143–47: 144.

105. Paul Natorp, *Individuum und Gemeinschaft* (Jena: Diederichs, 1921), 26. 'Property' here is the English translation of *Eigenschaft*, the term Natorp uses after Meister Eckhart as the translation of 'proprietas' – all qualities that are a person's own.

106. The words of Paul Natorp at the 'Freideutsche Woche' at Solling, autumn 1917: Paul Natorp, *Deutscher Weltberuf: geschichtsphilosophische Richtlinien. Vol. 2* (Jena: Eugen Diederichs, 1918), 83.

107. Georg Götsch, 'Abkehr vom gedanken des Jungenbundes – der Lebensbund als Aufgabe – Rückblick und Ausblick auf eines Bundes Weg und Wille', in Kindt, *Die deutsche Jugendbewegung 1920 bis 1933*, 61–66: 63.

108. W.E.B., 'Tagore, der Weg zur Vollendung', *Freideutsche Jugend* 7(9) (1921), 298–300: 299.

109. Rudolf Steiner, *Die Erkenntnis-Aufgabe der Jugend (GA 217a)* (Dornach: Rudolf Steiner Verlag, 1981), 41–49.

110. Emil Engelhardt, *Jugendbewegung gegen Anthroposophie: Eine Absage an Dr. Rudolf Steiner* (Rudolstadt: Greifen Verlag, 1922), 48. See also: Jakob Wilhelm Hauer, *Werden und Wesen der Anthroposophie. Eine Wertung und eine Kritik* (Stuttgart: Kohlhammer, 1922).

111. Richard Braun, *Individualismus und Gemeinschaft in der deutschen Jugendbewegung* (Erlangen: Karl Döres, 1929), 120.

CHAPTER 4

# Immanent Eschatology and Medieval Forms

We have seen how after the war a new conception of history arose in the postwar youth movement. Yet, as the conception of history changed, the entire constellation of historical time changed as well – and with it the role and position of the future. In an essay written in a volume on the history and prospects of the youth movement in 1921, Paul Tillich argued that the ideals of the establishment of a new humanity, which the new historical consciousness served, implied the establishment of a new eschatology.[1] When youth is so obsessed with a new spirit – with a humanity that expresses itself in the individuality of every single human as the highest ideal – then man can only be free when the social order he lives in is, in its turn, a reflection of the spirit of humanity. However, such a new social order was not expected to come from the intervention of a transcendent God, but only through creative action. This is why the eschatology of the youth movement was called an 'immanent eschatology' – it was eschatology 'of this world, of the realization of history and the world'.[2] Where a 'transcendent eschatology' would reiterate dualism by foretelling the coming of a new world after this world, 'immanent eschatology' foretold the completion of history by humanity as the unity of man and God in the very world we inhabit. It was the deep lived experience of nature, history and community which foretold the coming of a new man, the salvation of whom was not a matter of penance and sacrifice, but of liberation on the basis of one's own inner laws, of one's own vitality.

Heinz-Dietrich Wendland, a leading figure of the Jungnationale Bund, called the religiosity of the youth movement a 'religion of feeling', which was

---

Notes for this section begin on page 151

based on the experience of the cosmic cohesion of the body in the metaphysical unity of the universe.[3] Yet the supernatural has presence in nature – a presence of which many *Fahrtenberichte* testify. Out of the 'cosmic-metaphysical' or 'mystic-pantheistic' experience of the ordered position of life in the totality of the universe, natural life emerged; not as a finding, but as an ethical ideal. Nature changed from being a redeemer from the problems of modern civilization to being an educator.[4] Connected to the youthful urge to discover, explore, and shape the world, the ethical idealism of the youth movement seeks natural life and the constitution of a 'new man' according to it: 'a man of purity, benevolence, moral freedom and personal responsibility; a man who lives in loyalty and commitment to the values he is struck by'.[5] This non-systematic Fichtean idealism is never a pure idealism, because it is always circumscribed by the youth movement's mysticism. Idealism and mysticism thus define and confine each other. The youth movement's mysticism, Wendland states, lacks the asceticism of the great historical mystics, and its idealism lacks the confidence in life and humanity of the German idealist tradition. Rather, their idealism 'is deepened by a mystical element of the unity with the divine *in* this world as one of divine life and divine powers, in the rhythm of which individual man is integrated'.[6] It is a mysticism of attunement (*Stimmung*) that lacks dogmatism and a concrete set of religious beliefs.

Yet, according to Wendland, the tension between the 'quiescent infinity of mysticism and the striving infinity of the ethical idealism' is suspended in the immanent eschatology of the youth movement.[7] This eschatology entailed the promise of the coming of a new man, a new empire, a new order, which is heavily indebted to the new understanding of history we analysed in the previous chapter: the coming era is not a historical era that fades with time, but it is fulfilled time, nascent eternity. It grows with the constitution of a new man, of which those involved in the youth movement were both the announcers and the embodiment.

In this chapter I will first exemplify the chiliastic spirit of the postwar youth movement by focusing on the 'summer of dance' which the youth group 'Neue Schar' triggered in Thuringia in 1920. Then I will discuss three concepts central to the eschatology of the Bündische Jugend: *Bund*, Knighthood and Order. I will show that the turn to the medievalism inherent in these concepts was not just symbolic, but implied concrete action. The cases of the *Laienspiel* and the *Bauhütte* will illustrate how the youth movement tried to put their thoughts to bring about a new era in practice.

## 'Swinging on the Rhythm of Eternity': The Neue Schar

In the summer of 1920, a band of approximately twenty-five young men and women, called the 'Neue Schar', journeyed through Franconia and Thuringia by foot. They came from Wandervogel circles and were led by the *völkisch*-oriented Wandervogel and wood turner Friedrich Lamberty (nicknamed 'Muck').[8] To many, Muck appeared as a Christ-like figure, bringing redemption from the faults of their time and preaching reflection, asceticism, fasting and abstinence. The sight of his Neue Schar only strengthened such ideas, as the girls wandered in white linen dresses, wore their long hair in milkmaid braids, and wore decorative floral wreaths. The boys, dressed in colourful tunics, combed their relatively long hair back. All went barefooted or wore self-manufactured sandals. The way in which the exhilarated crowds accompanied Muck's flock to the city only strengthened his messianic image.

The Neue Schar was more radical in its rejection of modernity than the Wandervogel had been, and Muck Lamberty vehemently agitated against the 'depravity of modern society'.[9] The close inner life of the wandering circle was embellished with a *völkisch* emphasis on pure Germanism, but without becoming militant. The destination of their journey of 1920 was Wartburg Castle – an important site in German memory, because it was the symbol of the national regeneration of the Burschenschaften in 1817. It had been Luther's refuge between 1521 and 1522, and was the site of the legendary 1207 Minstrels' Contest. In 1913 a visit to Wartburg Castle would have been linked to the pedagogical idea of self-education. In 1920, Lamberty defined the goal of his journey as the 'gathering of all honest young people, and strife for the *Volksgemeinschaft* against everything common, against exploitation'.[10]

Lisa Tetzner, a storyteller who wandered through Thuringia at the same time, vividly captured how Muck's band drew thousands of citizens from Thuringia's small towns, eager for redemption in an era of national despair and hyperinflation:

> When I plan to descend the hill to walk towards the town in front of me, I am taken aback by the appearance of an unusual sight. A huge crowd comes up the mountain. It seems as if the entire town is in advance. A small band of strangely clad boys and girls walks in front. They wear colourful, rough tunics, go barefooted or in sandals, and carry heavy loads on their shoulders, as if they were carrying all their belongings. ... Numerous children hold on to them and hold their hands ... – but it is not only children, it is an entire colourful flock which follows. I feel something radiating from this tramping flock, as if they have just learned about a great propagation, and want to move out now to seek salvation. ... The leader of the flock stops at the turn of the road below me. ... Suddenly – the gesture of the man, the impression of the moving crowd, the number of children around him – I see the image of the Nazarene, who is accompanied by the people to Jerusalem and to whom they sing Hosanna, before my eyes. Has he returned in the form of a new prophet? Has the time come in which new signs and wonders will appear?[11]

The Neue Schar sang and danced in the marketplaces of numerous towns, and strategically prepared their arrival through the dispersion of pamphlets which promised 'healthy, heartily cheerfulness' and 'true folk life'.[12] Their manifestation in a marketplace would quickly attract the curious, critics and young enthusiasts. They usually started to dance with experienced members of a local youth movement, after which more and more adults and children would participate:

> They laugh; they participate; they find it quite amusing. Some take it as a joke, others take it seriously. On the second, on the third day, the entire city is in frenzy. The circles have grown. Here in Erfurt the gathering place was the Riesenplatz in front of the cathedral. It was busy with dancing, swinging circles. Thousands gathered to see it. The experts arrive, the critics, the highest authorities, but primarily the teachers of all schools – no, primarily the children.[13]

The choreomania – the outbreak of mass communal dancing – which took hold of Thuringia reminded of the dancing plagues which spread over continental Europe in the sixteenth century. In these often spontaneous outbursts, many danced frantically in a state of ecstasy, which caused many to collapse from exhaustion. Although the causes of the medieval dancing plague are still subject to academic debate, and range from neurological and social-psychological explanations to explaining the phenomenon as a cultural reaction to the depravities of economic hardship, natural disasters and the Bubonic Plague, the choreomania of the inflation period was explained by contemporary physicians as a discharge of repressed eroticism during the war.[14] For those involved, however, it was a positive enthusiasm with a millennialist undertone rather than a psychological reflex. In his *Morgenlandfahrt*, Hermann Hesse explained the susceptibility of the postwar German population for millennialism and its prophets in reference to the situation of despair which had struck the country: 'Shattered by the war, in despair as a result of deprivation and hunger, greatly disillusioned by the seeming futility of all the sacrifices in blood and goods, our people at that time were lured by many phantoms, but there were also many real spiritual advances'.[15] Not surprisingly, Hesse's novel was inspired by the persona of Muck's teacher Gusto Gräser, and by the same spirit of awakening that had accompanied the journey of the Neue Schar.

In these days, Germany was on the brink of collapse and suffering from political instability, rising inflation and the disintegration of bourgeois society and the middle classes. Wandervogel Albrecht von Fritsch recalls that the decisive blow which made the general public receptive to Muck's spiritualism was the fact that the 'last bulwark of reliability' – the middle classes – suffered from a strong depreciation in the value of private property.[16] It had become known that the government would barely compensate for private German property confiscated as war reparation by the Allies. To make matters worse, the government broke the promise to repay the value of private shares in 'enemy' companies which had been used as a compulsory loan to pay for the German war effort. New legislation, such as the fixation of rents, obstructed the private development of real estate, resulting in an unprecedented housing shortage. Furthermore, rising inflation enforced the belief that change could not be brought about by the political parties. In this 'Alice-in-Wonderland state', no one could offer comfort;

the church had lost credibility by supporting the disastrous war, but now their 'German God' seemed to have been defeated or seemed to have 'deserted the country together with the Head of His church, the Kaiser'.[17]

Added to the lack of security and faith, Von Fritsch mentioned the lack of trust. In a situation where dozens of political parties claimed to have the sole solution to Germany's problems and portrayed their opponents as traitors who wilfully drove the country into the abyss, there was no way of telling that your countrymen had more moral sense than the politicians they voted for. Such a constellation made the public receptive to prophecy. The Neue Schar, with their sense of mission, their belief to be the 'pioneers of a new age', and Muck's self-understanding as the 'voice that crieth in the wilderness', was perhaps not the only prophetic movement, but it was certainly the one which carried the redemptive spirit of the youth movement to the broader public at a time when the Wandervogel and Freideutsche Jugend were primarily occupied with the reinvention of their own organizations.[18]

The 'Muck psychosis' and the number of participants soon reached an apex.[19] The circle dances which they invited the public to participate in were cheerful and had the unifying effect of community. Of course the circle was a symbol of unity, but the dance itself, the rhythm of the movements, did incite a primordial, cosmic, experience. Adam Ritzhaupt, a protestant minister from Erfurt, explained in a fascinating report on the Neue Schar's 'summer of dance' how the rhythm of the dance itself was something vigorous which could only be grasped spiritually through unmediated experience: 'In this kind of experience, one feels oneself as being woven into a sense of life which makes us aware of the totality of life – cosmic life – around us, through us and with us'.[20] He goes on to explain that the primordial natural rhythms of human life had been obfuscated by modern, calculated time, and that dance could be called a sacrament for the Neue Schar – a festive rite of bodily expressions.

It is clarifying to recall that Gumbrecht explained the relation between man and world in 'presence cultures' to be one of inscribing the body into the rhythms of a cosmology. Whereas 'meaning cultures' see the transformation of the world as their vocation, and urge to realize a better society in time through agency based on human knowledge of the world, 'presence cultures' lack this concept of agency and therefore challenge unilinear time by spatially bringing to presence what is otherwise absent – in this case the abstract, yet very tangible sense of community among man and unity with the cosmos.[21] Now we can understand why the dance as a 'presence effect' in a meaning-driven society had such a redemptive power. The dances of the Neue Schar did not urge the people to believe in yet another political theory, based on another interpretation of Germany's deplorable situation, inciting another path of action – no, it constituted a bodily experience of being part of an overarching totality which demanded nothing from people as acting individuals, but which did offer comfort and relief. Ritzhaupt called the dance the expression of a 'naive,

**Figure 4.1** The Neue Schar in Eisenach. Photo by Julius Groß, Archiv der deutschen Jugendbewegung, 1920.

pantheistic naturalism'. However, to speak of an '-ism' makes the dance sound like a belief system, while for those present it was an entry into communal or cosmic experience.[22]

Up to twenty thousand men and women are said to have danced in Erfurt in August 1920.[23] Eyewitness accounts emphasize the release of the remnants of Wilhelmine social order and social status in the dance. The Erfurt schoolboy Otto Rudolf Wiemer recalled his astonishment when he noticed his own headmaster in the dancing masses:

> What had got hold of the older generation? Never had we expected any musical inclinations in him. He was a man full of dry harshness, uncommunicative and rejective. Now we saw him truly dancing: with flying coat-tails and a grimly smiling face! We mocked him and made coarse jokes, also about the other teachers who seemed to have lost their professional dignity overnight. But strangely, after half an hour we were dancing ourselves … Finally we sang along enthusiastically, our faces became red and our voices hoarse; we laughed, we waved – intoxicated, but yet peculiarly sober – an audacious, adventurous condition.[24]

In the evening, the Erfurt Barfüßerkirche opened its doors to the Neue Schar. The Evangelical church had been decorated with flowers for an evening service by the Neue Schar. This eclectic service commenced with the singing of Luther's *Ein feste Burg ist unser Gott*, followed by a confession to the absolute confidence in the higher power of God. One young member of the Neue Schar confirmed to the overcrowded church that 'we let ourselves be carried by the vibrations [*Schwingungen*] of eternity'.[25] Swinging was one of the favourite words of the Neue Schar. It referred to more than the dance movements: 'something is swinging when two souls take delight in each other; something is swinging when a community is together in peace and freedom. A soul that swings, however, feels the rhythm of eternity in itself'.[26]

When the Maria song *Meerstern, ich dich grüße* was sung, Ritzhaupt noted with a quiet acclaim:

> A song to the virgin Mary in our Evangelical church! Won't the spirits of pre-Reformation times waken? How would the Catholics laugh about these Protestants, who sing medieval songs about Mary with aesthetic delight. And a silent satisfaction for the Catholics: 'Just wait for the time – the lost will return'.[27]

Suddenly Ritzhaupt was struck by the Gothicism of his church. While in ordinary evening services the Gothic elements were suppressed by gas lanterns, the mood brought about by candles the Neue Schar had lit throughout the church made Ritzhaupt receptive to the direct experience of the Gothic.

Yet, it was striking to Ritzhaupt that all these impressions were so strong emotionally that he had to conclude he was living in a 'time of feelings'.[28] When Muck started a one and a half hour sermon – not from the pulpit, but just standing at the front – many headmasters shook their heads at its rather poor content. The majority of the congregation, however, were captured by the mood and the atmosphere of the candle-lit church and absorbed Muck's ecstatic sermon enthusiastically. 'They sensed real zealousness' in the exploding words of Muck Lamberty, who in his turn found a deeper religious tone in the atmosphere of the church than on the street.[29] His motifs became clear in the confessions he made: 'We are precursors. If we say on whose behalf we arrive, we cannot say anything but "on God's behalf". We feel ourselves called by God's grace'.[30] In the circumstances of postwar Germany it was again possible and even plausible to be called by a higher order – yes, by *the highest* order. Their meaning of the concept of vocation now harked back to the connotation the term had before the Reformation – it was not vocation as dedication to God through labour, but vocation as the divine calling to salvation. Such vocation reinstalled the notion of fate as a defining historical category. Yet, the 'revolution of the soul' that Muck announced was not merely a religious phenomenon: it became exactly historical where swinging – understood as sensing the rhythm of eternity – was the basis for a non-political and non-violent socialism.[31]

In the winter of 1920/21, the Neue Schar settled at Leuchtenburg Castle near Kahla, previously used as a prison but now home to a small Wandervogel youth hostel. Here, the Neue Schar formed a settlement in which it tried to put communal life into practice, making a living by selling self-manufactured wooden candlesticks and other objects. But before the winter was over and they could wander through the countryside again, rumours circulated that Muck strove 'to beget the German Christ with a blonde girl'. He was publicly condemned for sexual escapades, free love and immoral behaviour.[32] Due to the scandal, support for the Neue Schar dwindled in the youth movement, and a new summer of wandering and dancing was no longer an option.

After the fall of the Thuringian messiah, a stream of pamphlets were published – often of an apologetic nature, written by those who were caught in the spell. The limits between a spiritual Eros and its carnal counterpart were contemplated, as well as the question whether Muck had been a false prophet. Had the movement not been too focused on the ecstatic moment and lost touch with practical life?[33] What remained was the memory of a small upsurge of chiliastic choreomania. For many, Muck was the herald of a new way of life, and – this is perhaps the most crucial element – the moments of exaltation with the dancing fever provided the belief that it was within their grasp.

## Bund

The youth movement of the 1920s had found a term to denote the secret unity of the 'swinging' souls: *Bund*. *Bund* was to become the central concept of the youth movement in the 1920s and gave its name to what is generally regarded the second phase of the German youth movement: the Bündische Jugend. This phase set in after the dissolution of the Wandervogel e.V. and the Freideutsche Jugend, and was characterized by a move from the rather anarchistic organizational structure of the Wandervogel to authority, order and allegiance. Yet, order and allegiance were never understood as *imposed* order and allegiance. When Reinhart Koselleck calls the concept of *Bund* in the youth movement a 'voluntaristic concept of action', he forgets its mystic and eschatological undertone.[34] As Wendland noted, there is a strong continuation of idealism between the two 'phases' of the youth movement, and the value of individual liberty was never contested – not even in the most conservative circles. This was different from the experience of unmediated intersubjectivity in community that had given way to the 'mysticism' of individual integration in supra-personal order. This is where the term *Bund* comes in.

*Bund* is not easily defined. Perhaps it defies any definition because of its reference to something that cannot be conveyed. Karl Otto Paetel, in the 1920s a member of the Bund der Köngener – a *Bund* that was established by members of the Evangelical youth association Bibelkreis who in 1920 broke with what they found to be a too patronizing and too pietistic association – confirmed that it was virtually impossible to explain to an outsider what *Bund* meant.[35] Its 'imponderable undertones' were clear to those who were 'struck' by it, and who were thereby 'bound' to it:

> A *Bund* in the language of the Bündische Jugend was not an association of young people that pursued any kind of aim; it was never an ideological organization in the sense that it pursued clear-cut ideological goals. It was a site where people of a specific type found each other, from which they obtained inner support (like Christ did out of belonging to the community of believers).[36]

The rise of the idea of *Bund* was directly related to organizational reformations in the youth movement. The Freideutsche Jugend disintegrated after 1921; the same happened to the Wandervogel e.V. in 1923 after several years of fierce debates on its organizational form. The discussion basically focused on the prerequisites for a *Bund* to be shaped. The question of age was resolved. Nonetheless the older Wandervögel and many Feldwandervögel organized themselves in the Kronacher Bund in 1920. In the gender discussion the majority of the Wandervogel e.V. voted to be a *Bund* that included both sexes, after which advocates of an all-male model established the Wandervogel-Jungenbund. The opposite occurred in the Alt-Wandervogel, which forced a split between boys and girls in 1921, after which opponents founded the Deutsch-Wandervogel. In 1921, the Wandervogel e.V. changed its full name from 'Wandervogel, Bund für deutsches Jugendwandern' to 'Wandervogel, Deutscher Jugendbund' in order to reflect its position as a *Bund* and to emphasize that it was not just an association for the promotion of youth hiking.[37] However, out of the revived friendships between local leaders soon grew the idea that personal trust and favour should be the actual foundation of a *Bund*, which undermined the central organizational structure of the 'Wandervogel, Deutscher Jugendbund'. It ultimately led to the association's collapse in 1923, after which the local branches went their own ways, and many new organizations were established, such as the Wandervogel-Wehrbund and the Schlesischen Wandervogel-Jungenbund. Out of the national-conservative branch of the Wandervogel, the Jungdeutsche Bund arose, and the girls organized themselves in the AWV-Mädchenbund (1920) and the Wandervogel-Mädchenbund (1924).[38]

However, the Bündische Jugend entailed more than just this patchwork of old Wandervogel organizations. In national-conservative circles the Jungnationale Bund and the Adler und Falken were founded, and at the far right the radical-*völkisch* settlement-oriented Artamanen.[39] Most influential for the development of the Bündische Jugend, however, were several organizations that had split off from the scouting movement. In the immediate postwar years, unease with the hierarchical structure of the scouting movement resulted in the establishment of a number of small, new Boy Scout organizations such as the Neupfadfinder and Ringpfadfinder.[40] These new organizations hoped to spark a reform of the scouting movement from an adult-led youth welfare organization to a genuine youth movement. Inspired by the Wandervogel, they too embraced a more spiritual interpretation of what scouting had to be, and spoke about ideals of purity and 'chivalrousness of disposition'.[41] Subsequently other topics of the youth movement such as school reform, and a conception of Volk and humanity that crosses class differentiation were supported. It was in these organizations that a fusion between Wandervogel principles, such as the open choice of leadership and the autonomy of local chapters, and topics from the scouting movement merged and crystallized into a programme for what was to become the Bündische Jugend. The Neupfadfinder in turn would introduce camping and uniforms in the youth movement, but more crucial were its ideological innovations.[42]

In the Bündische Jugend, the idea of *Bund* was discussed on two levels. First, *Bund* as the new social organizational principle of the youth movement was generally believed to convey incorporation of the own space of experience and sense of life. Questions were, for example: was the *Bund* a final stage or a preliminary stage for a new church; did it imply the readiness of a hermeneutic change of position, or did it imply a principle (Christianity, 'Stefan Georgianism', paganism, etcetera); was it a shared disposition or a shared fate that held the *Bund* together;[43] and was the *Bund* in its organizational form meant to be a *Bund* for youth only, or a *Bund* for life?[44] Such questions gave rise to many conflicts, which in turn resulted in the many organizational changes within the loose conglomerate of the Bündische Jugend. It was not uncommon for local chapters to join another *Bund* after an internal conflict, or to establish a new one – as it was the principle of inner conviction rather than reason or pragmatism that mattered, conflicts could only be resolved by restoring trust or by a radical split. The fact that arguments and settlements were often useless in conflicts partially explains the explosion of associations in the Bündische Jugend.

Second, *Bund* was discussed as an ordering principle for broader social reform. Ideas of a *Bündische* state structure were explored as alternatives to the party system of the Weimar Republic, both in the youth movement and beyond. Peter Schröder has argued that this understanding of *Bund* transcended Ferdinand Tönnies dualism between '*Gemeinschaft*' and '*Gesellschaft*'.[45] In 1922, the philosopher Herman Schmalenbach had defined '*Bund*' as a third social realm besides community and society.[46] Because society and community were regarded as antithetical in the youth movement, *Bund* entailed the promise of a synthesis.[47] This synthesis would be – as it was called in national-conservative circles – the final spiritual-religious empire: the 'third' or 'new' empire, a 'divine empire on earth'.[48]

Empire or *Reich* was a disputed concept within the youth movement. The sources to draw from to imagine a *Reich* were plentiful. Besides the chiliastic image of the Third Testament (in German, 'testament', or the covenant between God and man, translates as *Bund*), there was the image of the medieval Holy Roman Empire as a political entity, and in the writings of authors such as Arthur Moeller van den Bruck the term was used in reference to a third Empire beyond the political system of Weimar Germany.[49] On the right wing of the youth movement, the journal *Die Kommenden* used the term to denote a concrete political answer to the Treaty of Versailles and the dominance of the West. *Die Kommenden* was established in 1926 by Wilhelm Kotzde – a *völkisch* author and the leader of the *völkisch Bund* Adler und Falke – to counter the 'mainstream' journal of the Bündische Jugend – *Der Zwiespruch* – in order to support a politicalization of the youth movement towards the right. In their analysis of the vocabulary of *Die Kommenden*, Stefan Breuer and Ina Schmidt state that the 'lowest common denominator' discernible in the use of the term *Reich* in the *völkisch*-oriented part of the Bündische Jugend was the 'territorial and power-political aspect'.[50] In accordance with standpoints aired in other right-wing organizations such as the Stahlhelm, some authors argued in favour of a constitutional unification with Austria, while others dreamt of a Greater Germany as a Central European force to counterbalance the West. Only a minority of these authors had militant ideas, but it is clear that they operated in the *völkisch* discourse.

The 'mainstream' of the Bündische Jugend – to denote those who tried to carry on the legacy of the Wandervogel – had quite a different opinion when it came to the idea of *Reich*. Authors who had themselves been members of the youth movement and identified with the 'experience' of the movement had a less concrete concept of *Reich* than the *völkisch* authors who tried to mobilize more recently established *Bünde* for their political ideals. Reasoning out of the experience of the youth movement, and carrying forward the autonomous tradition of the Wandervogel, mainstream authors saw the youth movement as a social environment that enabled a new mode of being and a social order to be derived from this mode of being, rather than the political understanding of the Third Reich which was phrased at the same time by authors such as Arthur Moeller van den Bruck. In this view, *Bund* became a key eschatological category, a category that hinted at the coming order – an order which was not simply ideological, because it was based on the concrete experience of irrevocable friendship, loyalty and commitment within their own groups and their own *Bund*. Everything that could contribute to this constitution gained the adjective '*bündische*' (i.e. youth or the attitude to life). Even those who were involved in *Bünde* which lacked the general 'mysticism' (and took pride in it after the Second World War) had to admit that the category of *Bund* had eschatological value. Karl Epting, a member of the *Reichsstand, Gefolgschaft deutscher Wandervögel* recalled that, in their circles, *Bund* was understood quite pragmatically and denoted the value of mutual friendship, but nonetheless they took the *Bund* to be 'a necessary form of consolidating people to the preservation of the individual and to ensure a deeper spiritual knowledge countering the superficial and equalizing forces of politics, propaganda and economy'.[51] For all, the term *Bund* carried the mystical promise of cohesion, allegiance between masters and followers, a heroic life, and loyalty to death. *Bund* transcended the individual to the degree that it was itself 'an Idea', of which the different guilds and orders of the Bündische Jugend were practical forms. Yet, in turn the *Bund* 'reflects the Reich, which stands above us all, like a dew droplet reflects the sun'.[52]

Eschatology necessarily implied a new interpretation of the past. The youth movement's idealism made that historical memory functioned as advent action; remembering was an essential part of the immanent constitution of the coming empire. However, the experienced issues with historicism made it impossible to interpret history in a linear fashion. Not believing in historical progress, but being aware of the constant risk that man will forget to live life out of inner experience as he takes the world of social norms, values, consensus, pressure and institutions to be the only reality, the youth movement focused on historical eras which showed the possibilities for natural growth and true community. Neupfadfinder Franz Ludwig Habbel, for example, advised the movement's members to 'let their community grow from the within, out of the pure experience of the other', so they could work in love and piety for the salvation of man.[53] The historical examples that Habbel had in mind when writing this advice were the community of early Christians and the 'gothic man' of the Middle Ages.

## Männerbund and Knighthood

The Evangelical theologian Friedrich Niebergall remarked in 1921 that it would have been a miracle if the combination of Romanticism and the search for a higher authority in the youth movement had *not* led to the rediscovery of the Middle Ages.[54] Or perhaps he should have said: the re-rediscovery. Already in the first decades of the nineteenth century the Middle Ages had become an example of authentic humanity, interconnectedness and strong communal responsibility.[55] After all, the Middle Ages were times that combined those three elements. The Middle Ages 'had the imperturbability that we in our state of defibration seek: the religious European Idea of the universal church'.[56] Niebergall was quite right in his expectation, for the High Middle Ages became the central age of reference in the youth movement in the 1920s. It was the age of Meister Eckhart, the age of Gothicism, which contained an unequivocal consciousness of the omnipresence of the eternal. Meister Eckhart represented unity – the unity of body and soul, of culture and nature, of form and life, of freedom and authority. The Middle Ages symbolized a world before modernity had set in and before reason had made binary oppositions the source of a new logic. The transcendentalism of the art and architecture of High Medieval Gothicism, for example, tried to dispose of all spatio-temporal constraints to attain the effect of presenting the irrepresentable highest powers. The turn to the Middle Ages also meant disposing of the last remnants of the idealist tradition, for the Kantian emphasis on rationality, moral principles and the morality of deed could again be traded for the avowal of creed.

Books about Gothicism were widely read in the postwar youth movement. Not because this age somewhat resembled the conditions of postwar Germany, but exactly because the memory of the High Middle Ages prompted the expectation of an age beyond rationalism, beyond nineteenth-century intellectualism. The youth movement saw the universality of its understanding of humanity mirrored in the gothic unity of science, art and religion. Re-reading medieval sources enabled them to understand the word '*Geist*' again in its original meaning as *spiritus* or the vivid soul, as that 'truly creative thinking, which comes from the whole man with his love and hate, rather than from the intellect alone; which becomes one with the spiritual meaning of the world, or rather, which is immediately certain of its truth out of this last oneness'.[57] According to Max Bondy – a member of the Deutsche Akademische Freischar and a leading figure in the Freideutsche Jugend – 'the new mental disposition we first experienced is a new bond with nature, a new bond with the people, a new bond with God; it is the synthesis of the medieval and the modern, of Gothic bondage and modern individualism'.[58] It is this holistic point of view that meant that in the youth movement ideals of new man and new society were increasingly modelled after medieval topics.

Medieval patterns such as the relationship between knight and vassal, the guilds and the estates became testimonies of the existence of an ordered age. In order to appropriate such topics, the youth movement drew heavily from national-conservative and also *völkisch* sources. Important for the youth movement's conception of the Middle Ages was *Männerbund* – a concept introduced in 1902 by the folklorist Heinrich Schurtz to refer to a hierarchically structured male community of oath, serving a common goal and held together by rules and rituals.[59] Although predominantly present in traditional societies, Schurtz argued that these social structures had survived modernity in, for example, student fraternities and Freemasonry. The concept gained popularity in the ranks of the youth movement through the writings of Hans Blüher.[60]

Blüher's intellectual development also reflected the turn to metaphysics. In his pre-war history of the early Wandervogel, he had created the myth that the Wandervogel had its origin in a 'revolt' against school, state and the parental home. Part of his analysis was the controversial theory that the Wandervogel's success was rooted in same-sex bonds, which he interpreted in terms of Freudian drives.[61] During and after the war, he increasingly understood the concept of Eros in a Platonic sense, as that Idea on which all human instincts and drifts are based. Eros is the 'affirmation of a person regardless his worthiness', which means: apart from all meaning that man retrospectively attributes to a relationship, the first act of this relationship is acceptance apart from the value systems in which man interprets the world.[62] As such, he turned Eros into the irrational principle on which states – as formalized structures of human sociability – ought to be based. This is where Blüher's anti-historicism becomes clear: he criticized traditional conservatism for 'rationalizing' the Eros by trying to vindicate a certain social order by attributing rationality to it, by emphasizing it to be the product of history – specifically, the product of a progressive history of rational or moral development. This was the 'deepest and most infatuated form of corruption of thought', because '*no* situation is holy because of spirit and every situation loses its millennia old authority the moment it is proven unapt'.[63] For Blüher, the state was a sacred principle, which drove on the erotic will 'to commit to a superordinated community'.[64] He therefore dismissed economic, rational and liberal-pragmatic conceptions of state, as these were all post hoc theories that did not explain why man came to form states in the first place.

Blüher's answer to the question of the constitution of state was the *Männerbund*. Remaining anti-feminist, Blüher bypassed the family – that other social core in which Platonic Eros worked so prominently – as being a mere realm of procreation that was of value to the constitution of the state but nothing more. The *Männerbund* on the other hand was a mystical communion based on an inner, spiritual, eroticism known to the initiated. From this class of men, spiritual leaders could be drawn who could creatively generate a state out of the Eros. The women's femininity, Blüher contended, meant that women were bound to the spatiality of the Eros, while men could transcend it to generate a synthesis between Eros and the spiritual logos. In 2008, Claudia Bruns concluded that Blüher did not pose the 'ideal of a soldierly and purely reason-oriented masculinity', but the 'passionate lover, the romantic artist, and the divine priest in opposition to the bourgeois model of the modern, rational man'.[65] Although the qualification 'romantic artist' is perhaps ill-chosen because of Blüher's objections to the metaphysics of spirit in German idealism, it indicates how we have to understand the idea of knighthood in the Bündische Jugend. The knight was not a conqueror, oppressor or hero in his own right, but a servant to higher ideals, humble in acknowledgement of his fate and responsible to his followers.

However, during the war, it had not so much been the knight, but the *Landsknecht* that was the subject of the youth movement's historical imagination. Small groups of Wandervogel in the army named themselves after the *Landsknechte* – the medieval mercenaries who were the topic of many of their folk songs. Together with the image of the *Freikorps* – the volunteer corps of the Napoleonic Wars – the *Landsknecht* was the best the youth movement's historical imagination had to offer when it came to soldiery out of volition. Yet, it seems that imitating *Landsknecht* soldiers and writing correspondence in an archaic *Landsknecht*-like style was primarily play, and had little ideological meaning.[66] The *Landsknechte* were interpreted as jolly wanderers, regardless of the harshness of historical reality, and were a world apart from the way in which Ernst Jünger – who had himself briefly joined the Wandervogel in 1911 – had depicted the ordinary soldier as an unreflective, crude and hardened *Landsknecht* in *Der Kampf als inneres Erlebnis*.[67]

After the war, affiliation with the *Landsknechte* was increasingly overhauled by association with the image of the knight. In the 1920s, the idea of knighthood became a symbol of order and an indicator of the rising conservatism of the youth movement. The turn from unclear ideology to the acknowledgement of the subjugation of life to eternal principles, which characterized the youth movement's 'transition period' in the early 1920s, is thus reflected in the turn from the *Landsknecht* as a representation of the unrestricted and volatile wanderer, a hero of the 'older' generation of the youth movement, to the knight as the hero of the 'younger' generation. '"Knighthood"', a member of the short-lived Wandervogel, Wehrbund deutscher Jugend wrote, 'means initially nothing more than an accentuation of the basic idea: we are not a multiplicity of individuals, where everyone lives his own life – we are rather a community, a community of coequals, who are strong enough and big enough to fit ourselves into a larger order'.[68] The knight as a combatant became the personification of the youth movement's idealism. The image of the knight had nothing to do with historical analogy, with nostalgia or historical representation; it was rather a symbol that stood for a large array of associations that hinted at ordered society, at mysticism and God. Due to its symbolic nature, ideal knighthood could easily be infused with themes from historical epochs not directly related to feudal chivalry.

Knighthood was one of the historical images in which ideas of *Männerbund* concretely shaped both the imagination and the organization of the Bündische Jugend. The Nerother Wandervogel, for example, was one of those new *Bünde* hierarchically modelled after Blüher's ideas of *Männerbund*. It was designed to be only for the young and only for boys. The Nerother split off from the Alt-Wandervogel in 1920, stating that the Wandervogel movement had become a business-like organization; this became most clear in its democratic structure, which resulted in endless discussions without significant progress. Searching for new meaning, this new *Bund* was based on an aristocracy of spirit, in which those born with qualities to lead were put in positions of leadership. This was not based on authoritarian leadership, but on the reciprocity of values such as 'loyalty, courage and knighthood'.[69]

This *Bund* was mythically established on New Year's Eve 1919, in a cave in the Neroter Kopf in the Eifel mountain range, when a group of eight members of the Wandervogel e.V. pledged loyalty to each other and to the initiator Robert Oelbermann. The idea of knighthood became a central theme in the organizational structure of the movement, in which a leader for life appointed trustees as *Bundesritter*, who in turn led different semi-independent chapters ('orders'), which were given names such as the 'Order of Landsknechts' or the 'Order of Robber Knights'.[70] And although this chivalric phraseology must have spurred the imagination of its youngest members, the leadership of the Nerother was quite clear in its conviction that knighthood was meant to be a symbol rather than a representation:

> For us knighthood is the symbol of our will. All that occurs in human life is determined by inner laws, which always prevail and remain the same in its deepest ground. ... For us knighthood is only a symbol and an expression of our way of being. We do not want to stick to the past, but for us the knightly example, which probably arose out of the same inner drives as our contemporary youth movement, can become a combative sign.[71]

Another Nerother emphasized that the value of knighthood depended not on chivalric ideas but on the practice of action. Knighthood primarily had performative value, because it was easy to bestow the title 'knight' upon someone. Whether or not such an appointment had effect depended on the way in which the appointee lived up to the title.[72]

In the transition from the Wandervogel to the Bündische Jugend, the source of many ideas on order, knighthood and *Bund* came from the Neupfadfinder. One of the main journals of the Bündische Jugend was the innovative *Der Weiße Ritter*, a journal named after St George, the English patron saint whose veneration was directly inherited from the British Boy Scouts.[73] It was Baden-Powell himself who had made St George the patron saint of the Boy Scouts and who made him the symbol of the main values of the movement, such as bravery, physical fitness, and the willingness to serve. For Baden-Powell, St George's slaying of the dragon symbolized the determination to fight and overcome evil. Among the Neupfadfinder neither St George nor the idea of knighthood in general were understood in the patronizing and nationalist way that Baden-Powell used them. The knight was a *chiffre* for the new man. The knight in Albrecht Dürer's iconic copperplate engraving *Ritter, Tod und Teufel* (1513), for example, which depicted the *vita activa* of the knight under consequent admonition of *memento mori*, appealed to the Wandervögel for his resoluteness of faith.[74]

For Martin Voelkel, an Evangelical minister in Berlin and a leader and main ideologist of the Neupfadfinder, knighthood was the profound answer to the most basic problem of human life: the problem of man's universal need for redemption. In answering to the 'suspicion of man's incompleteness and the perception of his agonizing position in the complete world as a result of that incompleteness', Voelkel discerns a number of types in which man has sought redemption throughout the ages.[75] The priest, for example, provided redemption by leading a cult through which atonement with the gods could be established; the artist found redemption in participating in nature's creative genesis of new attributes. The irony of history is that the masses reduce the tools of redemption – wisdom, art, reign – so often to the domain of practicality. Thus, commoditization, for example, generates a disenchantment that impedes redemption altogether.

There are, however, two types of saviours who do not allow for this reduction, simply because they do not link redemption to a higher order of being: Christ, and the Germanic knight. Christ typifies the man who is no longer in need of redemption, because he *is* redemption; the knight typifies the man who finds not himself, but the world and the gods in need of redemption. The knight 'exists as he just simply is, and goes as he must, without remorse, without complaint, without fear; yes, he prepares himself time and again to redeem the world, in which he self-evidently always perishes'.[76] In the myth of the holy empire, the promised messiah and the victorious knight meet: the holy empire is the merger and marriage of both the German's heroic works and the grace of God. The tone of struggle and strife in Voelkel's thought is obviously not related to street fights or the battlefield, but to the inner struggle for the acceptance of one's faith.[77] For Voelkel, it is the myth which is the holy sanctuary of a true community – a group of people who have not come together for profit or benefit, but who are intertwined with 'heart and soul'.[78]

Although Voelkel's *völkisch*-Germanic phraseology was not commonly shared, the Neupfadfinder's attempt to reform the scouting movement had its impact on the broader youth movement. It resonated with anti-democratic ideas on the rule of nobility which became popular in some circles in reference to Hans Blüher's or Stefan George's elitist thought. Furthermore, the Neupfadfinder provided new organizational forms that became models for many in the Bündische Jugend. They made a division in ages, in which the *Jungenschaft* consisted of those aged under 17, the *Jungmannschaft* of those aged 17 to 25, and the *Mannschaft* of the adults. Although *Jungenschaft* entailed more or less a continuation of the life of the young as it had been in the Wandervogel, the *Jungmannschaft* was the innovative stage; after all, this was the phase of life in which experience had to be transposed into action; this was the age in which one had to acknowledge fate. Organizing adolescents under the banner of the legends of King Arthur, of St George, or of the Holy Grail intended to create a community of fate. Thus the *Jungmannschaft* could become the elitist knights of the new empire.[79]

## Medievalism and Ordo-consciousness

In the 1920s, the Middle Ages became a past in which the future was read. However, to be able to attain the longed for unity of life, a cosmological worldview had to be reinstated. How ideas on order (cosmos) developed is perhaps most clearly documented in Paul Ludwig Landsberg's *Die Welt des Mittelalters und wir* (1922).[80] Landsberg, a 21-year-old student of the philosophers Edmund Husserl and Max Scheler with an active involvement in the Freideutsche Jugend, was not interested in the historical aspects of the Middle Ages, but wanted to show what was timeless about it.[81] The book he wrote uninterruptedly in a few weeks, driven by an 'inner urgency', took the form of a cyclical philosophy of history.[82] Landsberg's work taught that the history of the West developed along the stages of order, habituation and anarchy. Order is the situation in which 'a part of the objective, divine world order has become a notion and a life form'.[83] It is the situation in which people are obedient to God in a prime commitment that grounds and guides. In the Middle Ages, nature and society were thought to be elements of a God-given, metaphysical order. In the medieval cosmos plants, minerals and animals served man, while man in his turn lived in the social order of the estates, served one another and worked for the common good. Yet, all served God's glory, and all were reflections of God's glory. In the stage of habituation, the meaningless remnants of the former order become ossified and are maintained at random in a state of anxiety. Anarchy at last denotes the liberation from this anxiety and thus liberation from the curtailments of dead forms. Anarchy is creative, calls for action, and is grounded in a longing – a *Sehnsucht* – for the dawn of a new order. The cycle of order, habituation and anarchy was twice repeated in the course of history. Once, the order of antiquity became customized in Late Antiquity, only to fall into the anarchy of the transitory era of the Early Middle Ages. Out of this anarchy, a new order arose in the High Middle Ages, which again became habitual in bourgeois modernity.[84]

For Landsberg, the youth movement embodied the new anarchy, which was not so much a nihilist rejection of all empty and lifeless bourgeois forms, but the start of a search for new forms. After all, this is what distinguishes movements in a period of anarchy from movements in the period of habituation: a positive instead of a negative attitude. According to Landsberg, this distinguished the youth movement and other apostles of a new age such as Wyneken and Stefan George from the likes of Schopenhauer and Nietzsche.

More explicitly, Landsberg's thesis entailed a revision of Jacob Burckhardt's rather optimistic and thoroughly nineteenth-century thesis that the Renaissance had laid the foundations of modernity, as it encompassed the double emancipation of the individual from the bonds of family and community, and from the subjugation to the authority of faith.[85] Contrary to Burckhardt, what modernity represented for Landsberg was not the dawn of a new individual consciousness, but the demise of the high-medieval 'ordo-consciousness', the loss of the idea that all phenomena resemble universal order.[86] Landsberg did not situate the turning point in the Renaissance, but in fourteenth-century nominalism. The genesis of modernity thus harks back to the much debated problem of universals, in which the classical question of how universal concepts relate to the individuality of the contents of our experience was overcome by the nominalist rejection of scholastic realism. Contrary to Aristotelian scholastics such as Thomas Aquinas, who held that universals had real existence independent of our thought, nominalists – of which Landsberg sees William of Ockham as the prime representative – contended that universals were but names (*nomina*) given to the contents of experience, and that only concrete, individual things held reality. The victory of nominalism over realism would pave the way for modern philosophy and for the modern worldview in the broadest sense. Cartesian rationalism, empiricism, German idealism, positivism, and even Neo-Kantianism were deeply indebted to the nominalist turn to epistemology. The modern world forgot metaphysics in favour of epistemology, forgot being in favour of thought, and forgot eternity in favour of temporality. Henceforth, in modernity the universal could only be thought as a derivative of the individual, and eternity could only be understood as a derivative of time.

However, Landsberg did not postulate a 'return' to medieval metaphysics – he deemed the idea of a return 'impossible' and 'unjoyful', but noted in line with the youth movement's concept of historical memory that 'we can only learn from another era, where it is more than itself, where it protrudes into the eternal'.[87] For him, the 'Middle Ages' do not primarily denote the specific historical era, but a fundamental 'possibility of being' that once appeared most vividly and meaningfully structured in life.[88] The 'Middle Ages' are therefore not remote and unattainable, as historicism learned, but a form ever awaiting realization – a future epoch beyond modernity in which historicism is overcome. This is an era in which no longer history, but the question of 'being' is the basic principle: modern historical thinking was to be replaced by 'medieval' cosmology. The dawn of the new order was what Landsberg called the 'conservative revolution' or the 'revolution of the eternal' – it was the 'becoming and already being in the present hour'.[89] Those who stand in the present hour make up the 'we' of his book title. He explicitly called it *The World of the Middle Ages and We* because the intersubjectivity and community, which youth had experienced as something immediate, was the foundation of individual being. This 'we' was the guarantee of the leap towards eternal order, and the guarantee of a good future. But – and this is where idealism and mysticism merge – order was not to be expected to be derived from a realm beyond the world. It required a personal commitment to bring order about.

Landsberg noted that in the Middle Ages 'form' was a principle of life. Without form, there could be no life, and life required form. The Aristotelian scholastic worldview presupposes the unity of form and life. In modernity, form and life have become antithetical; order appears as custom and life as anarchy. To overcome modernity's 'ordered disorder' the youth movement would indeed aim to generate new forms that were drawn from life, from inner experience, and were thus believed to contribute to the establishment of a new order.[90] The urge for new forms was not only visible in the internal reorganization in the Bündische Jugend, but also in the cultural attributes through which it wanted to radiate into broader society. One of the most innovative and widespread forms was the *Laienspiel*.

## Laienspiel

Munich had many faces in 1923. It was the scene of street fights and mass demonstrations, of an endless stream of published pamphlets, of brawling politicians in beer halls, and of Hitler's failed Beer Hall Putsch. At the same time it was the scene of lively bohemian artistic circles, of expressionism and cubism. In this turbulent public arena, many youth groups operated on a small scale for the constitution of their own visions of a new social order, based on the direct experience of community. Their idea of *Volksgemeinschaft* could not be forced onto people by using arms; neither could it be constituted through the art of persuasion – it could only come about through an inner conviction triggered by sharing the wonders of immediacy and intersubjectivity with one another. Many youth groups envisaged themselves to be the priests that could stage the initiation of the people in the secret commitment of the *Bund*.

Close to Christmas 1923, a small circle of young performers entered the Speisehalle III – a soup kitchen for the victims of hyperinflation, for pensioners, for the jobless and for the homeless in a backstreet of the Theresienstraße in Munich. The procession of the young performers led through the dim and unaired hall, and invited the impoverished middle class to cast away their daily nuisances and attend a Christmas play, which was staged in the middle of the hall in a circle of fir sprigs and candles. It was a sacred place in what was regarded to be the most uncomforting of all of Munich's soup kitchens. The sacrality of the circle radiated into the hall, merging the environment into an irrelevant amorphous background. As the procession was welcomed in the circle by a small ensemble of fiddlers, flutists and guitarists, the leader of the performance group recited, in a solemn voice, the first sentences of the medieval Christmas play *Weihnachtsspiel aus dem baierischen Wald* – expressing the inner certainty and releasement with which they wanted to work in society.[91]

The performance group was named the Mirbt-circle, after its leader Rudolf Mirbt, and consisted at that moment of students, young workers, salesgirls, social workers and a tram conductor – all of whom either came from the youth movement or had been caught in its spell. They performed in orphanages, preschools and inns, in Munich's English garden, and for socialist youth groups; in sum, for everyone who wanted to pay attention. Mirbt, the 'uncrowned king of Munich's youth', was to become one of the prime inspirers of the revival of the specific form of amateur dramatic performance he displayed in the Munich soup kitchen: the *Laienspiel* (layman's play).[92]

As described earlier, the Wandervögel had already rediscovered the folk song and folk dance on their hikes through the German countryside before the war. They had made the revival of these elements of folklore one of the central traits of the movement. Historical interest focused on the sixteenth century, for many folk songs originated from the turbulent era of the Peasants' War and the Reformation.[93] The little interest there was in dramatic performance before the 1920s was directed at the same era, and especially at the work of Hans Sachs (1494–1576). But when dramatic performance really caught on as a new type of performance beside the folk song and the folk dance, Sachs's comedies and similar plays, such as the dark comedy of Pyramus and Thisbe from Shakespeare's *A Midsummer Night's Dream* (1600) and Andreas Gryphius's *Absurda Comica oder Herr Peter Squenz* (1657), were considered to be unfit for individual and collective direct experience. These plays sufficed for lowbrow events such as a performance for the parents or a summer festival, but 'the tension posited by the self to the extrinsic thou, by the individual to the whole, the attachment of the spirit to the body, of the soul to the body, of the voice to the gesture, the excitement of the motion' were all deeply missed in the early modern comedy.[94]

In the *Laienspiel* the youth movement found a way of dramatic expression better suited to its demands. The term *Laienspiel* came up somewhere between 1919 and 1922, and referred to medieval dramatic performance by laymen, as it was performed at markets and in inns, well before the professionalization of the theatre in the sixteenth century. The *Laienspiel* developed out of the ecclesial mystery and miracle plays, which staged, for example, the Passion of Christ as *tableaux vivant* throughout a city. Who first coined the term *Laienspiel* remains unsure. Some attribute it to Martin Luserke, a teacher at and later leader of Wyneken's Freie Schulgemeinde Wickersdorf, others to Mirbt himself.[95] Fact is that the reform educator Luserke used it in its strict connotation as a non-clerical performance by laymen, and opposed the priestly atmosphere of annunciation that often accompanied performances in the youth movement in the early 1920s.[96] The old Wandervogel Mirbt, however, interpreted the *Laienspiel* in strict opposition to the professional theatre.[97] For him, the layman was the non-professional performer, and the *Laienspiel* was not an end in itself, but a specific social form apart from actual working life.

The revival of dramatic performance in the youth movement was to a large extent inspired by the work of Gottfried Haass-Berkow. Haass-Berkow came from the ranks of professional dramatists, and was drawn to amateur theatre through the influence of the well-known anthroposophist Rudolf Steiner.[98] In anthroposophical circles, Steiner had staged then largely unknown medieval mystery plays, such as the Oberufer Christmas play – a cycle of plays depicting biblical events with roots traceable to the fifteenth and sixteenth centuries, discovered by Steiner's teacher Karl Julius Schröer in a village near Bratislava, where isolated Swabian settlers still staged it in the mid-nineteenth century.[99] Haass-Berkow had participated in the performance of the play in 1912 and formed a circle with whom he took up these performances on request of the Red Cross during the war. He would become most famous for his rendering of the *Totentanz* (danse macabre), which he compiled out of a number of fifteenth-century texts and pictures. In the Late Middle Ages, the *Totentanz* had been a prolific theme in literature and in the visual and performing arts, for it was as an allegory of the unifying universality of death, reflecting the devastating impact of the Black Death. In the allegory, a personification of death summons representatives of various walks of life to dance in a cemetery, churchyard or church. In dramatic form, the play usually opened with a sermon from a monk, preaching about the certainty of death and the vanity of earthly life, after which figures representing death came from a charnel house. The first victim who Death addressed was usually the pope or the emperor, whose arguments for declining Death's invitation to follow him into the afterlife all prove to be insufficient. The second victim was a prince or a cardinal, and the following victims represented all social strata. The end of the play consisted of a second sermon, with the monk reinforcing the lessons of the allegory.

Since the summer of 1919, Haass-Berkow led a wandering performance group consisting of amateurs from the community college of Thuringia. As part of the summer tour, they performed at the Bundestag of the Wandervogel e.V., staging the catholic play in the protestant church of Coburg. The performance made a deep impression on those present.[100] Haass-Berkow himself noted that the 'attunement and relevance of the enactment reached into the sublime for spectators and performers'.[101] One Wandervogel was so enthralled by the plays *Sündenfall* and *Totentanz* – which Haass-Berkow performed together with Wandervögel and professional performers – that he encountered the limits of representation:

> We sat in the house of God in which Luther once preached, and sang, and then the plays of the 'Fall of Man' and the 'Totentanz' (composed after old woodcuts) were performed. No small words should be spoken about the act of experiencing.[102]

In the youth movement, it was sensed that the *Totentanz* produced exactly the immediate mystic effect that was necessary for the education of a new man. One Wandervogel witnessed in 1920 how a performance of Haass-Berkow's group flooded the Gothic Wiesenkirche in Soest with a public that did not visit the church anymore. The procession of Death and its subjects, performed on the rhythm of a monotonous melody in the 'middle of all those clever and reasonable ordinary people, who know so well who is better and who is less than they are', was striking:

> Under the spell of eternally equal, monomorphous flute tones, an old truth slowly comes to their consciousness, the truth that in the hereafter all men are equal. They hear this every Sunday at the same place, and it weekly slips their mind – but now it grasps so sensibly their inner being that they have to believe – whether they like it or not.[103]

The *Totentanz* proved to be the 'gothic' form the youth movement could apply in its avant-garde quest for the regeneration of society. Subsequently, Haass-Berkow was invited to perform for many youth groups. These consequently took over his themes and imitated his plays and style – usually forgetting the anthroposophical backdrop against which Haass-Berkow operated, and taking the *Totentanz* as an expression of the spirit of the youth movement, as a form of the spirit of the new age.[104]

There was, however, more to performance than the play as a dramatic piece of art containing meaning, references and symbolism. Performing itself was a mode of 'playing'. When we bear in mind that the German word *Spiel* translates both as play and game, we can understand that the English word play does not capture the entire dynamics of a dramatic performance, of performing a play. After all, a game must be played, and play – including dramatic performance – is always a game.[105] The Dutch historian Johan Huizinga famously distinguished several formal characteristics of 'play' (in its broadest meaning, as both activity and action, as ritual and performance, as game and play). First, play is not compulsory; it is a voluntary and therefore free activity. Second, play does not happen in 'real' life – it creates a temporary sphere of activity of its own, with a beginning and an end, but also with a repetitive temporal structure. Third, play also has its own spatial limitations and rules; it has its own arena or stage, and it has its own sacred spots – much like the ritual, which is itself a form of play. Fourth, play creates (and even is) an absolute order. Deviation is not possible without spoiling the entire game. Fifth, play has its tensions and anxieties. It tests the player's prowess and spiritual capacities, which – although play lies beyond good and bad – gives it an ethical character. Sixth, play creates a community of players that extends beyond the duration of the play as they share the experience of being initiated in the play. They understand each other and gain an intimate bond.[106] Culture, Huizinga concludes, arises from play, and never leaves its play element behind.[107]

Bearing Huizinga's remarks in mind, we can focus on the socio-cultural relevance that the play element of performance had for the youth movement. The movement aimed at constituting new culture and community by means of play. While Haass-Berkow primarily focused on reforming professional theatre, the youth movement's *Laienspiel* developed in stark contrast to the theatre as a feature of the constitution of *Volk*. Although the danger of performing for the sake of form only was omnipresent among youth groups, the movement actively attempted to use performing – i.e. 'playing' – plays to achieve the aforementioned aims. After all, play generated community based on an absolute – and therefore eternal – order. Dramatic performance remained the most prolific form of play and was regarded as a microcosm of the ideal community; for, as Wandervogel Richard Poppe argued, play required 'the performer to lose himself in his task, and required the individual to lose himself in interaction'.[108] Let us focus on the community-constituting function of play for the youth movement – bearing in mind that I will from now on use the word 'play' in Huizinga's broad meaning, referring to both the drama and its performance, to both 'game' and 'play'.

## The Binding Character of Play

Rudolf Mirbt once wrote that no *Volk* actually 'is'. It was the core experience of the postwar youth movement 'that no people are, and thus no bondage, neither with God, nor with the people' pre-exists.[109] This was a big claim, but it did explain youth's longing for the constitution of bonds. Mirbt found the fulfilment of this longing in play. It is in play that daily routines and distinctions are cast away and that all involved necessarily have to establish a new relationship with each other. Play thus shapes a hermeneutic situation.[110] As Hermann Kaiser would later put it: by playing, man 'lives by answering the word of his fellow man and knows that life is a continuous dialogue with his brethren'.[111]

A fine example of how play practically worked to establish community was given by Karl Reichhold – an economy student from Munich and one of the most active members of the Mirbt circle – when he recalled that during the rehearsal of a play he found one fellow player so deeply unsympathetic that he had to pull himself together not to disturb the atmosphere by expressing his aversion. But when the rehearsals were over and the play was actually staged, interdependency gave way to reciprocity:

> Under the power of the poetic word his figure was suddenly 'objectified'. Beyond the clear contours of his role in the play, I suddenly realized his generally human task of life, which he could not divest of any more than I could of mine. The opposition led to individuation. Within the hour, I found ourselves on the same level. I could no longer look down upon him or overlook him, because I needed him for self-realization. We had become true partners, one indispensable to the other: the road to respect was revealed, from which access to affection was not far away.[112]

Reichhold emphasized that such liberation from solitude by subordinating the self to the meaningful totality of play was not incidental, but typical of the *Laienspiel*. Once caught in the fate of the play, individual aversions are overcome by the play's objective or absolute totality. When the individual encounters the limits of his ability or the limits of his personality when performing, he learns to regard the alien qualities of the other as a 'free gift' and can consequently regard the combined qualities as the totality.[113] Class differences could thus be overcome, as play was seen as the crucial binding factor for community. Mirbt himself thought of play as the 'reflection of human cooperation and all common behaviour in a transforming order'.[114]

In the Munich Mirbt circle, youth from all denominations, political affiliations and different youth movements participated.[115] By the time he came to Munich in 1920, Mirbt had parted with the Wandervogel (he had been leader of the merged Alt-Wandervogel and Wandervogel e.V. in Swabia) for he increasingly felt uneasy with the elitist self-understanding that was rampant in the postwar Wandervogel. Rather than adhering to the aristocratic elitism inspired by Hans Blüher or Stefan George, Mirbt took the initiative to establish a 'Jugendring' in Munich. The Jugendring was a loose organization, which drew members from all of Munich's youth associations, from the Catholic Quickborn to the national-conservatives. It was from the Jugendring that

Mirbt recruited his performers. For Mirbt, the circle was a microcosmic community in which individuality and universality were in balance. In his own circle, he enforced the expressionist stance that all participants could voice their concerns as individuals, but never as commissioners of a political or ideological party.[116]

In performance, Mirbt used some basic rules to guarantee the communal effect of play. Most important was the principle of order. This was crucial for the performance group, because during the play every performer had to take up the character that most adequately fitted his personality. It was striking that the group and the individual performer so often agreed on one's position. The knowledge that even the smallest part was of crucial importance for the totality of the play, made it possible to acknowledge the natural order of the community.[117] It was important to acknowledge that there is no principle that orders play outside play itself. In play, the form is a direct and unmediated expression of the idea, for play itself is not the subject of goal or purpose.

Robert Grosche, chaplain of the University of Cologne and affiliate of Quickborn, summarized this position by stating that the subject of play was not the individual but transpersonal community itself. In play everything ephemeral, coincidental and local is pushed back; the specific is replaced by the general, which is in turn perceived symbolically. When someone plays a role fit for him, he does not play his individual self, but he plays a general type in which he recognizes himself. The type is the stylization of the grand contours of a set of individual examples. When play becomes symbol we can understand that the *Laienspiel* was not appreciated for its 'historical' value. The historical, after all, conveys exactly the individuation that is transcended in play. According to Grosche, in play 'the moment, only the eternal moment, is experienced'.[118]

Nonetheless, there were two basic dangers when it came to the position of history in play. First, the restorative tendency of playing for the sake of the revival of past forms could not be ruled out. Second, there was the danger of using the play as an allegory in service of moral education, rather than as a symbol. Hugo von Hoffmannsthal's play *Jedermann* (1911) for example – inspired by medieval mystery plays and morality plays such as the fifteenth-century Dutch *Elckerlijc* – clearly contained a moral lesson on the idolatry of money, and was therefore deemed unfit as a *Laienspiel*.[119] Not the moral improvement of mankind but its redemption was the object of youth's longing. This, obviously, was the reason that they traded historicism for eschatology.

Mere mimicry always remained a danger in inexperienced performance groups, and plays entailing lessons of individual morality rather than God, fate or community were indeed incidentally performed. Nonetheless, the basic principle of the *Laienspiel* remained what I called the idea of 'memory as advent action': performing a *Laienspiel* was a form of cultural memory which neither served a zest for history, nor the construction of a present identity, but which served the coming of the eschaton, the overhauling of historical thought and the establishment of a new man. The performance group of the Akademische Vereinigung Marburg, for example, noted that when performing the *Oberufer Paradeisspiel*, Shakespeare's *Tempest* or the *Totentanz*, gathering and rearranging these plays was not inspired by an antiquarian curiosity; 'rather, for us it was decisive that the vital ideas in the plays are just as actual today as they were in the times in which they were created'.[120] Alwin Müller regarded the *Totentanz* a text that 'had no poet, because it wanted nothing more than to turn the frescoes of the medieval cathedrals and the woodcuts of Holbein's portfolios into words and gestures, into pace, singing and dancing'.[121]

Another crucial element for the *Laienspiel* was attunement, which was considered to be a crucial prerequisite for the play to be a community-generating *Erlebnis*. Walter Eckart noted that only by attuning individual performers to one another could plays be performed successfully. Performers should therefore have previous acquaintance – they should be friends who can drive one another to greater heights, rather than having the routine of a professional who regards the play as a mere piece of art, and not as an expression of life.[122] From this perspective, technical aspects of performing were not considered to be of crucial importance. As long as the part fitted the personality of the performer, and as long as the attunement was right, they believed that the theatrical form would grow naturally out of the immediacy of expression.[123] But attunement was not simply a matter of a general mood among the performers. For Richard Poppe, one of the founders of the youth music group Finkensteiner Bund, the first requirement for every performer was to sense the *Grundstimmung* (fundamental attunement) of the poetry of the play. Christmas and Easter plays ostensibly have a religious *Grundstimmung*, to which the modern individual who lacks the childlike naivety of faith has to be attuned, would the performance 'not simply be a lie'.[124] Only then can bodily gesticulation be an immediate expression of inner coherence rather than a representation of thought, as it was in the theatre.

Yet, the purpose of performing was not primarily to constitute community among one's own ranks; this was more a prerequisite than an aim. The main goal was to let the sense of community spill over into the audience and thus contribute to the genesis of a broader *Volksgemeinschaft*. Contrary to the ordinary theatre, the *Laienspiel* offered the possibility to establish a reciprocal relationship between players and audience through singing, and thus the possibility for direct participation during the performance. The absence of a stage and a curtain are important elements. Mirbt, however, noted that the performance group was not in control of the community-constituting power of the *Laienspiel*. Play primarily was a stimulus for the individual to carry a disposition into the world of everyday life:

> The certitude of the performer, of once again having shared a common fate with other people in a joint effort – just this consciousness transforms these people. The same happens to the spectator, who has once forgotten himself at a play and

merged in a very strange new condition, which one can perhaps best describe as a consciousness of community. But in all these questions it comes down to the few, to the individual, rather than to the many.[125]

It is the individual's responsibility to carry this experience into his daily life and make the receptiveness for the other a precept, an attitude or disposition in social relationships. For Mirbt, community is always a matter of individual responsibility – the magic of the experience is only a beginning. For him, performance was a pedagogical tool for the educative constitution of a *Volk*.

In the course of the 1920s, many youth groups performed *Laienspiele* during their hikes. They would put up a booth in the marketplace of a provincial town they were passing, or entertain a local audience in a school building with a mystery play, a comical play by Hans Sachs, a *Laienspiel*, or an improvisation of their own. The fee would be nominal, and since there was no stage the distance between actors and public was bridged to the extent that the play became a communal enterprise as it once had been for the peasants in Oberufen. Many groups additionally cultivated singing, and sang in parish churches on Sunday mornings. Performance groups propagated polychoral ecclesial songs by Hans Leo Hassler, Michael Praetorius and Heinrich Schütz, as well as the older Passion music.[126] The Holsterwitz Wandervogel, for example, had already established a wandering performance group for a hike through Pomerania in the summer of 1920. A conscientious preparation in the library had learned that Haass-Berkow had done a thorough job, for they too found that the Oberufer plays were by that time the most suited *Laienspiele*. They added Saint Francis of Assisi's 'Canticle of the Sun' (1224) to their repertoire – accompanied by several girls with Dalcroze-style rhythmic movements in angel suits.[127] Unfortunately their trip was rather unsuccessful as it lacked the mobilizing effects of Muck Lamberty. As a result, they could hardly make ends meet, but they could luckily rely on local Wandervogel for their basic needs. Yet, 'all materialistic needs could not take away the fact that for us every new performance was a new, great experience'.[128]

From 1923 onwards, the youth movement would produce its own plays.[129] Mirbt published a series *Münchener Laienspiele*, which included reworkings of folkloristic narratives and plays such as *Beowulf* and the *Burghers of Calais*, sagas and fairy tales such as the *Nibelungen* and Grimm's *Godfather Death*, Biblical plays and Advent, Christmas and Passion plays.[130] Medieval plays such as Johannes von Tepl's *Der Ackermann aus Böhmen* (± 1400), the Tell Play of Uri (1512/1513) and the *Weihnachtsspiel aus dem Baierischen Wald* were modernized and rewritten. New plays were also written in the spirit of the *Laienspiel*.[131] Death plays symbolized the resignation to one's fate, while miracle plays displayed the saviour of the repentant sinner. Fairy-tale plays had a comical note, as man's weaknesses were ridiculed, while folkloristic plays such as Mirbt's reworking of the *Burghers of Calais* 'signifies "Volk" as a task for all – not as reposure of bygone times'.[132]

Mirbt's conception of *Volk* as something that never *is* but as something that has to be constituted in the intersubjectivity of the 'thou' was not generally shared among the performance groups that became part of what was now known as 'the Laienspiel movement'. The great array of small performance groups of the youth movement that were established in the 1920s found an organizational refuge under the wings of the Bühnenvolksbund, originally a conservative Catholic association for the promotion of amateur theatre. The Bühnenvolksbund opened its ranks for youth performance groups of all denominations and political affiliations in 1922. It represented performance groups way beyond the Bündische Jugend, from the right-wing Jung-Stahlhelm to the Evangelical Christdeutsche Jugend.[133] It was due to the lack of organizational coherence of the Bündische Jugend that the Bühnenvolksbund filled the organizational gap.

But the attempt to unite all performance groups would evidently lead to issues. When the Bühnenvolksbund organized a demonstration of youth performance groups in 1927 at the Deutsche Theater-Ausstellung in Magdeburg, the event resulted in a scandal when the display of the black–red–gold tricolour of the German Republic by republican youth resulted in the departure of the provoked Jung-Stahlhelm and Bismarckjugend, who were denied permission to carry the black–white–red flag of the monarchy. Although the performance groups of the Bündische Jugend had nothing to do with the flag incident, they heavily objected to being put on display by the Bühnenvolksbund. Contrary to their expectations, the event was not a feast of youth, but a politically laden 'desecration' of the *Laienspiel*.[134] 'There was a neat spectacle before the city theatre on Sunday', wrote the correspondent of the social-democratic newspaper *Volksstime*:

> There, the Wandervögel of the Kronach branch had gathered to march off to the exhibition site. A Stahlhelm music band came to trumpet the youths to the exhibition. The youths thanked them for the honour; laughed at the black–white–red trumpeters without respect or deference; the latter then took their trumpets, played a funeral march and strode away sorrowfully.[135]

The political provocations between the left and the right as a result of the incapability of the Bühnenvolksbund – now called an improper organization which put youth 'in an unsympathetic environment, under the shouting of ticket sellers, the playing of military bands, the croaking of an enormous speaker and the other manifold noises of such an exhibition' – resulted in a break with the Bündische Jugend.[136] The Bühnenvolksbund was dubbed a 'youth welfare organization old-style' that denied pedagogical principles such as performing out of inner experience, free choice of leadership and the genesis of community, which had been recognized as best practice in the development of the youth movement.[137] Performing the *Laienspiel* nonetheless continued within the *Bünde*.

## Bauhütte

The turn to the 'Gothic' Middle Ages resulted not only in a revitalization of medieval cultural forms, but also in a renewed interest in cultural property. The 'guild of architects' in the Kronacher Bund of older Wandervogel had turned to 'Gothicism' and to the 'Middle Ages' on the same precept as the *Laienspiel* performers. The 'guild' was a postwar invention that was – just as the 'teacher's guild', 'doctor's guild' or 'technician's guild' – meant to support youth movement members of the same profession in the difficulties of finding a job after the war, as well as to carry the Wandervogel ideals into the professional sphere. This was an idealistic endeavour. Because of the refusal to turn into an interest group and because of the primary commitment to the spiritual domain and to inter-human relations, efforts to structurally change a profession or the economy had little effect.[138] Experiments with alternative labour relations were therefore often restricted to the confinements of the youth movement. This is where, for the 'guild of architects', the value of the Gothic came in. For them, Gothicism was way more than a distinct current in architectural history; it was a symbol for disinterested cooperation of different crafts – a proof of the possibility that architects and craftsmen could surpass current profit-oriented labour divisions in a joint effort.[139]

The *Bauhütte*, the medieval workshop or tool shed on the building site of a cathedral, became the concept for bridging the gap between academic architecture and the traditional craftsmanship that was suffering a lot from the rise of capitalism and the economic situation of postwar Germany.[140] Karl Theodor Weigel and Dankwart Gerlach's call for cooperation between those Wandervogel who were working in construction and those who were working as architects remained unanswered. Hence they feared having estranged intellectual and academic architects with their plans. Their idea of a *Bauhütte*, which grew organically as a community working on a single project, fitted well in the postwar logic of community. Their hopes focused on the restoration of Ludwigstein Castle in Hesse.

Ludwigstein Castle had occasionally been a hiking destination for the youth movement before the war, but when the war was over, the possibility of purchasing the desolate ruin created a chance to fulfil an idea that had evolved during the war. As early as Christmas 1914, when serving at the front at St Quentin, Enno Narten had envisioned renovating the ruin as a monument to the fallen Wandervögel. Ludwigstein Castle was to have a double function: it was to be a memorial for fallen comrades, but it had to go beyond the status of a site of commemoration. It had to point towards the future as well, so it would also become a meeting place of the many associations of the German youth movement: it would become a youth hostel. The purchase in 1920 required strong fundraising efforts, which included collections, Christmas bazaars, slide lectures, recitals, *Laienspiele*, and the sale of letter seals and handmade artefacts.

Narten, an educated civil engineer, took up the supervision of the renovation himself. In times of economic distress, many unemployed members of the youth movement found meaningful occupation in renovating the castle, and many groups offered help when visiting the castle on a hike. From 1922 onwards, the castle became what Winfried Mogge called a 'sacred site' of the youth movement.[141] It became a place of hope and expectation where meetings were held to discuss actual topics, where a hostel was established and where the archives of the youth movement found shelter.

At the same time a 'competing' project was initiated at Waldeck Castle in the Rhineland Hunsrück by the Nerother Wandervogel. Their idea to turn Waldeck Castle into a youth castle came from Gustav Wyneken, who had already posted an advertisement in June 1918 seeking to rent an old castle, cloister or manor in a nice landscape in the Berlin *Volkszeitung*, intending to turn it into a meeting place for the youth movement.[142] It was a wish he had for two years. After his departure from Wickersdorf in 1914, Wyneken came up with the idea of a *Jugendburg* (youth castle) in early 1916. The *Jugendburg* had to become a centre for the spread his ideas on youth culture.[143] Although Wyneken failed to purchase the Castle of the Order of St John in Kühndorf and soon focused on other projects, the idea for a *Jugendburg* remained.[144]

The Nerother Wandervogel took over Wyneken's idea, replaced its educative purpose and started fundraising for the project, for which they chose Waldeck Castle. The possibility of the realization of Waldeck was questioned because, contrary to Ludwigstein, it was a ruin of which only the foundations had survived. It would be virtually impossible to find enough funds for a restoration.[145] But restoration was not exactly the plan. The Rheinische Jugendburg was not to be a 'patchwork' of an ancient building rebuilt with modern materials – it rather had to be an 'entirely new piece of work which points into the future and corresponds to the state of German youth'.[146] What the cathedral was for the Middle Ages, the Rheinische Jugendburg had to become for German youth: embodiment and symbol of the purposeful life of youth.[147] Therefore the ruin was not to be restored, but to be rebuilt in a way which directed towards the future and at the same time gave homage to the past. The architect, Karl Buschhüter, made a design and was willing to supervise the construction.

For the construction, they aimed to establish a *Bauhütte*, consisting of volunteer artisans from the youth movement – when necessary replenished with local professionals. The construction was planned as a long-term project. Therefore the first task was to build accommodation for the artisans and a youth hostel for visitors. The Rheinische Jugendburg was to become 'a kind of settlement for farmers and artisans', of which the latter would work on a basis of apprenticeship, and the former would have to provide income for the project.[148] In the first years, the project would have to be financed by donations, after which farming, and the sale of books and handmade art would generate income.

But, like critics had contended, the project for a youth castle at Waldeck did not succeed. The reason was not primarily financial: the monument preservation authorities did not allow the ruin to be rebuilt. So in 1921, after two years of preparation, another site had to be found. It was decided that the bluff of a nearby ridge which overlooked the castle ruins would be more suitable for their plans. This was a site the authorities approved of, and with slight alterations in the construction plans, the *Bauhütte* commenced with clearing the premises. However, soon after laying the foundation stone in August 1922, hyperinflation made it impossible to purchase construction materials. When the French occupied the Ruhr in 1923, the entire Rhineland economy came to a halt, which resulted in a collapse of the *Bauhütte* community. A new source of income was found in (slide) lectures about the many foreign hikes the Nerother Wandervogel made. With these funds the reinstated *Bauhütte* built a wooden cabin for accommodation – which tragically burned down in 1926. In the end, of the original project only one building would be built before the dissolution of the Nerother Wandervogel by the Nazis in 1933.[149]

Despite the partial success of the youth castle projects in the youth movement, the idea of the *Bauhütte* as a community of artisans putting their labour in service of the eternal, and youth castles as outposts of the coming age, testify of the significant importance of the typified medieval imagery as a fundamental category of the youth movement's eschatology. Back when it had started, their line of thought had been: if this belief could catch as many devout and committed souls as possible, 'then the castle will fulfil its noble tasks in the service of youth, then it will become a source of pure, powerful young life like a grail castle, and will be a fountain of youth, of new, healthy nationhood'.[150]

## Conclusion

In the 1920s, the youth movement developed a great array of future expectations. Although there neither was a clear-cut ideology, nor a coherent discourse reflecting the development of these expectations, these youngsters shared a common logic. The Bündische Jugend did not dispose of the idealist thought of the Freideutsche Jugend. In fact, they continued to believe that the disenchanted modern world curtailed the self by its emphasis on custom, status and career. The self still required self-cultivation out of inner experience, as opposed to external definition. However, the turn to a mystic-pantheistic religiosity implied that idealism had to become part of eschatology. The combination of idealism and mysticism produced an 'immanent eschatology'.

The youth movement's immanent eschatology learned that the new man, the new empire or the new world was to be grounded in *this* world. Because the image of a transcendental God was rejected, the youth movement not only challenged the modern conception of history, but also the linearity of traditional Christian eschatology, which saw time as the void between creation and the Day of Judgment as a one-time occurrence. While the modern linear conception of time was made possible by a transcendental image of the subject, and while Jewish and Christian linear eschatology was made possible by the transcendence of God, the various formulations of radical immanence which were phrased in the youth movement in the 1920s enabled a new conception of time exactly through the negation of the idea that that either a personal God or man himself is responsible for the order of the world. What we have ideal-typically called the 'immanent eschatology' was based on a cyclical conception of time – or what Armin Mohler even more precisely called the 'spherical' conception of time of the 'Conservative Revolution'.

According to Mohler, the image of a circle is too indebted to Christian and modern 'linear' language because it still fosters the idea that when a point on the (circular) line is passed, this point is done with. This image neglects the interconnectedness of multiple dimensions. For those who endorse a cyclical temporality, the sphere displays 'that in every moment everything is enclosed, that past, present and future coincide. In its sign the emptied world is filled again and the volatized being includes itself in the fulfilled moment'.[151] Although Mohler has been criticized for basing his thoughts on the 'Conservative Revolution's' spherical conception of time only on Nietzsche's *Zarathustra*, the case of the Bündische Jugend supports his thesis to the extent that the movement facilitated a social environment in which experiments with 'spherical' temporalities were in place.[152] We recognize it in the Neue Schar, for whom dance was not recurrent movement in Euclidean space – circular motion so to speak – but the bodily coalescence of individuals in a divine cosmic rhythm. We can also recognize it in the *Laienspiel*, which – rather than being a representation of a bygone tradition – was an attempt to establish community on non-rational grounds. In a same way, the uniforms, banners and emphasis on loyalty and allegiance were not representations of a specific 'heroic' historical past – be it the First World War, Medieval or Germanic Germany – but symbols that referred to the irrepresentable: the overarching powers of metaphysical order.

Spherical time is also recognizable in domains we did not discuss. For example, in the youth movement's memory of the First World War, the fallen Wandervogel soldiers were not remembered as heroes of the old empire, but as personifications of the New German. They were in both memory and art depicted as fellow travellers rather than fallen pioneers. In the same vein, Marion de Ras has demonstrated in *Body, Femininity and Nationalism* that the discourse on *Bund* (in the female *Bünde*) revolved around concepts such as 'flow', 'wave', 'bloodstream', 'heartbeat' and 'cycle', which denoted a cosmic rhythm or pulsation, and were as such constitutive for both their body culture and conceptions of state and nation.[153]

Although the self-narratives of the youth movement often stress that coherence was not found in *meaning* but in a specific *experience*, which never culminated in a shared worldview, we may conclude that at least the understanding of time and history that was derived from experience was quite coherent. When memory was 'advent action', idealist action aimed at the immanent constitution of a new man, a new empire. The possibilities of such a new state were not hard to imagine, as they were experienced in the 'swinging' of souls, as the Neue Schar put it, or in play. Just as play rests in itself, men only needed to experience that the world actually already rests in itself. Redemption, the fulfilment of eschatology, would require nothing more than to live life out of inner experience, in communal harmony and with a constant eye on eternity. When man attains this 'Gothic' attitude towards life, then man has already redeemed himself.

In the next chapter I will look at the consequences of this immanent eschatology for the youth movement's interpretation of space by focusing on the foreign hikes, which became very popular in the 1920s.

## Notes

    1. Tillich, 'Die Jugend und die Religion', 12.
    2. Wendland, 'Das religiöse Problem in der Jugendbewegung', 221–22.
    3. Ibid., 216. On Wendland and the youth movement, see: Rüdiger Ahrens, 'Heinz-Dietrich Wendland (1900–1992)', in Barbara Stambolis (ed.), *Jugendbewegt geprägt. Essays zu autobiographischen Texten von Werner Heisenberg, Robert Jungk und vielen anderen* (Göttingen: V&R unipress, 2013), 725–37.
    4. Wendland, 'Das religiöse Problem in der Jugendbewegung', 216.
    5. Ibid., 218.
    6. Ibid., 221.
    7. Ibid., 221.
    8. Lamberty gathered his band after the meeting of the older Wandervogel soldiers at Easter 1920. Cf. Viehöfer, 'Der Verleger als Organisator', 90–91.
    9. Ulrich Linse, *Barfüßige Propheten. Erlöser der zwanziger Jahre* (Berlin: Siedler Verlag, 1983), 99.
    10. Cited from: ibid., 97.
    11. Lisa Tetzner and Hans Pape, *Im Land der Industrie zwischen Rhein und Ruhr. Ein buntes Buch von Zeit und Menschen* (Jena: Eugen Diederichs, 1923), 113–14.
    12. Cited from: Linse, *Barfüßige Propheten*, 107.
    13. Adam Ritzhaupt, *Die 'Neue Schar' in Thüringen* (Jena: Eugen Diederichs, 1921), 8.
    14. Paul Albrecht, *Geschlechtsnot der Jugend* (Berlin: Verlag Junge Anarchisten Hans Strempel, 1926), 11; Lisa Tetzner, 'Selbstlose Brüderlichkeit', *Die Tat* 12 (1920), 773–76: 773. Psychological interpretations of the medieval 'dancing plague' understand the phenomenon as an example of an invariable 'mass psychogenic illness' – a collective delusion resulting from disturbances in the nervous system. In this case it was an incited ecstatic trance sparked by pious fear and anxiety which resulted from various catastrophes such as famine and floods that preceded the choreomania. Cf. John Waller, *The Dancing Plague: The Strange, True Story of an Extraordinary Illness* (Naperville,

IL: Sourcebooks, 2009), 203–31. Others emphasize the historicity of the phenomenon, and especially the religious connotation omnipresent in the phenomenon. Cf. H.C. Erik Midelfort, *A History of Madness in Sixteenth-Century Germany* (Stanford, CA: Stanford University Press, 1999), 49ff.; G. Rohmann, 'The Invention of Dancing Mania Frankish Christianity, Platonic Cosmology and Bodily Expressions in Sacred Space', *The Medieval History Journal* 12(1) (2009), 13–45.

15. Hermann Hesse, *The Journey to the East* (New York: Farrar, Straus & Giroux, 1968), 10.

16. George Reneé Halkett (pseud. Albrecht von Fritsch), *The Dear Monster* (London: Jonathan Cape, 1939), 201.

17. Ibid., 202. On the crisis of both the Protestant and the Catholic church in postwar Germany, see: Klaus Scholder, *Die Kirchen und das Dritte Reich I: Vorgeschichte und Zeit der Illusionen, 1918–1934* (Frankfurt am Main: Propyläen, 1977), 3ff.

18. Linse, *Barfüßige Propheten*, 108. Muck called himself a 'Prediger in der Wüste' after the Luther translation of Isaiah 40:3.

19. 'Dies und das', *Der Zwiespruch* 2(20a) (1920).

20. Ritzhaupt, *Die 'Neue Schar' in Thüringen*, 27.

21. Gumbrecht, *Production of Presence*, 82–83.

22. Ritzhaupt, *Die 'Neue Schar' in Thüringen*, 28.

23. Walter Jacobi, 'Über eine Tanzepidemie in Thüringen', *Psychiatrisch-Neurologische Wochenschrift* 26(3–4) (1924), 14–17.

24. Wiemer cited from: Linse, *Barfüßige Propheten*, 104.

25. Ritzhaupt, *Die 'Neue Schar' in Thüringen*, 11.

26. Ibid., 18.

27. Ibid., 11.

28. Ibid., 11.

29. Ibid.

30. Ibid.

31. Linse, *Barfüßige Propheten*, 106.

32. Wilhelm Siegmeyer, 'Muck-Lamberty', *Junge Menschen* 2(2) (1921).

33. On the 'eroticism' of the Neue Schar, see: Emil Engelhardt, *Gegen Muck und Muckertum. Eine Auseinandersetzung über die höhere freie Liebe mit Muck-Lamberty und Gertrud Prellwitz* (Rudolstadt in Thüringen: Greifenverlag, 1921); Ritzhaupt, *Die 'Neue Schar' in Thüringen*. In 1923, Paul Mämpel, a former follower of Muck, noted in a circular that retrospectively he felt that there had been too much reverie and emotionalism in the movement, as well as a complete lack of understanding the socio-economic situation of the 'Volk' they wished to reinvigorate. He himself therefore turned to the proletarian youth movement. See: Linse, *Barfüßige Propheten*, 242.

34. Reinhart Koselleck, 'Bund', in Otto Brunner, Werner Conze and Reinhart Koselleck (eds), *Geschichtliche Grundbegriffe. Historisches Lexikon zur politisch-sozialen Sprache in Deutschland. Vol. I* (Stuttgart: 1972), 583–671: 670.

35. The early development of the Bund der Köngener is well documented in: *Unser Weg.: Stimmen aus dem Bunde der Köngener. Sammelband aus drei Jahren* (Berlin: Der Weiße Ritter, 1923).

36. Karl O. Paetel, *Das Bild vom Menschen in der deutschen Jugendführung* (Bad Godesberg: Voggenreiter, 1954), 75.

37. Werner Kindt, 'Wandervogel, Deutscher Jugendbund E.V. Kurzchronik', in Kindt, *Die deutsche Jugendbewegung 1920 bis 1933*, 81–87: 84.

38. For the history of these female Bünde, see: Marion E.P. de Ras, *Body, Femininity and Nationalism: Girls in the German Youth Movement 1900–1933* (New York: Routledge, 2008).

39. It is impossible to paint a complete picture of the Bündische Jugend due to the many splits, foundings and refoundings. Rudolf Kneip has given a 'concise' overview of the entire spectrum of Bünde in Weimar Germany in almost 400 pages, in: Kneip, *Jugend der Weimarer Zeit*.

40. For the history of these organizations, see: Felix Raabe, *Die bündische Jugend: ein Beitrag zur Geschichte der Weimarer Republik* (Bonn: Studienbüro für Jugendfragen, 1961); Karl Seidelmann, *Die Pfadfinder in der deutschen Jugendgeschichte* (Hannover: Schroedel, 1977); Hermann Siefert,

*Untersuchungen zur Entstehung und Frühgeschichte der Bündischen Jugend* (Erlangen: Friedrich-Alexander-Universität, 1964).

41. Franz Ludwig Habbel, Karl Sonntag and Ludwig Voggenreiter, 'Ein Geleitwort', *Der Weiße Ritter* 2(1) (1919), 4–6: 4.

42. This was mainly due to the translation of the works of John Hargrave, which were published in the series *Bücher der Waldverwandtschaft*.

43. Karl Erdmann and Helmuth Kittel, 'Vom Wesen des Bundes (1927)', in Karl Seidelmann (ed.), *Gruppe – soziale Grundform der Jugend; Teil 2. Quellen und Dokumente* (Hannover: Hermann Schroedel, 1971), 75–79: 76.

44. Werner Hahn, 'Um die Grenzen des Bundes', *Deutsche Freischar* 1(4) (1928–1929), 8–11: 8.

45. Peter Schröder, *Die Leitbegriffe der deutschen Jugendbewegung in der Weimarer Republik: Eine ideengeschichtliche Studie* (Berlin: Lit, 1996), 48–49.Cf. Ferdinand Tönnies, *Community and Society* (New York: Courier Dover Publications, [1887]2002).

46. Herman Schmalenbach, 'Die soziologische Kategorie des Bundes', *Die Dioskuren. Jahrbuch für Geisteswissenschaften* 1 (1922), 35–105.

47. Schröder, *Die Leitbegriffe*, 49.

48. Heinz-Dietrich Wendland, 'Die jungnationale Bewegung', in Richard Thurnwald (ed.), *Die Neue Jugend* (Leipzig: C.L. Hirschfeld, 1927), 145–59: 155.

49. Arthur Moeller van den Bruck, *Das dritte Reich* (Berlin: Der Ring, 1923).

50. Stefan Breuer and Ina Schmidt, *Die Kommenden. Eine Zeitschrift der Bündischen Jugend (1926–1933)* (Schwalbach/Ts.: Wochenschau Verlag, 2010), 263.

51. Karl Epting, 'Führertum im Bund (1968)', in Seidelmann, *Gruppe – soziale Grundform der Jugend*, 136–37.

52. *Grenzfeuer der vereinigten deutschen Jugendbünde im Fichtelgebirge am 3. u. 4. Erntings 1923* (Regensburg: Heinrich Schiele, 1923).

53. Franz Ludwig Habbel, Karl Sonntag and Ludwig Voggenreiter, 'Etwas ganz Einfaches', *Der Weiße Ritter* 1(3) (1919), 56–58: 57.

54. Friedrich Niebergall, 'Die Jugendbewegung im Rahmen der gegenwärtigen Kulturkrise', *Westermanns Monatshefte* 66 (1921), 82–86: 86.

55. Cf. Peter Raedts, *De ontdekking van de Middeleeuwen. Geschiedenis van een illusie* (Amsterdam: Wereldbibliotheek, 2011).

56. Niebergall, 'Die Jugendbewegung', 86.

57. Wilhelm Stählin, 'Fieber und Heil in der Jugendbewegung', in Kindt, *Grundschriften der Deutschen Jugendbewegung*, 374–428: 383.

58. Max Bondy, 'Zum Aufruf an die freideutsche Jugend', *Freideutsche Jugend* 5 (1919), 70–73.

59. Cf. Heinrich Schurtz, *Altersklassen und Männerbünde* (Berlin: Georg Reimer, 1902).

60. On Blüher's understanding of *Männerbund*, see: Ulrike Brunotte, *Zwischen Eros und Krieg. Männerbund und Ritual in der Moderne* (Berlin: Klaus Wagenbach Verlag, 2004), 70–117; Bruns, *Politik des Eros*, 267–330; Ulfried Geuter, *Homosexualität in der deutschen Jugendbewegung* (Frankfurt a/M: Suhrkamp Verlag, 1994), 163–79.

61. He phrased this theory in the third volume of his Wandervogel history: Hans Blüher, *Die deutsche Wandervogelbewegung als erotisches Phänomen; ein Beitrag zur Erkenntnis der sexuellen Inversion* (Tempelhof-Berlin: B.Weise, 1914).

62. Hans Blüher, *Die Rolle der Erotik in der männlichen Gesellschaft I: Der Typus Inversus* (Jena: Eugen Diederichs, 1919), 226. See also: Claudia Bruns, 'The Politics of Eros: The German Männerbund between Anti-Feminism and Anti-Semitism in the Early Twentieth Century', in Katherine M. Faull (ed.), *Masculinity, Senses, Spirit* (Lewisburg, PA: Bucknell University Press, 2011), 153–90: 168–70.

63. Blüher, *Die Rolle der Erotik*, 230.

64. Ibid., 4.

65. Bruns, 'The Politics of Eros', 170.

66. Cf. 'Rundbrief der "flandrischen Landsknechte"', AdJB, Feldwandervogel, A11/2.

67. Ernst Jünger, *Der Kampf als inneres Erlebnis* (Berlin: E.S. Mittler & Sohn, 1926), 50–57. For Jünger's involvement in the Wandervogel, see: Thomas R. Nevin, *Ernst Jünger and Germany: Into the Abyss, 1914–1945* (Durham, NC: Duke University Press, 1996), 25–28.

68. Georg Weber, 'Ritterschaft', in Kindt, *Die deutsche Jugendbewegung 1920 bis 1933*, 109.

69. Robert Oelbermann, 'Die Verfassung (Adelsherrschaft oder Demokratie)', *Wandervogel* 15(1) (1920), 20–21: 21.

70. On the organizational structure of the Nerother, see: Stefan Krolle, *Musisch-kulturelle Etappen der deutschen Jugendbewegung von 1919–1964: Eine Regionalstudie* (Münster: Lit, 2004), 57.

71. Robert Oelbermann, 'Die Aufruf zur Gründung des Nerother Bundes. Vom 16. Januar 1921 (Urtext)', *Der Herold. Bundeszeitschrift der Nerother* 13–14 (1930), 9–13: 12.

72. 'Ritterlichkeit', *Der Herold. Bundeszeitschrift der Nerother* 13–14 (1930), 59–60.

73. For the history of *Der Weiße Ritter* and the publishing house with the same name, see: Justus H. Ulbricht, 'Ein "Weißer Ritter" im Kampf um das Buch. Die Verlagsunternehmen von Franz Ludwig Habbel und der Bund Deutscher Neupfadfinder', in Walter Schmitz and Herbert Schneidler (eds), *Expressionismus in Regensburg. Texte und Studien* (Regensburg: Mittelbayerische Druck.- und Verlag-Gesellschaft, 1991), 149–74.

74. Schorsch Walling, 'Albrecht Dürer: Ritter, Tod und Teufel', *Der Weiße Ritter* 2(1) (1919), 30. On the reception of Dürer in the youth movement, see: Autsch, *Erinnerung – Biographie – Fotografie*, 189–92. Autsch stresses that it was not only Dürer's art, but also his person that was held in high esteem, as Dürer was regarded as a creative personality.

75. Martin Voelkel, 'Hie Ritter und Reich!', in Kindt, *Grundschriften der Deutschen Jugendbewegung*, 368–73: 368.

76. Ibid., 369.

77. Cf. Hans Dieter Fritzsche, 'Offener Brief an Jochen Hahn', *Der Weiße Ritter* 2(3) (1919), 87–91: 91.

78. Siefert, *Untersuchungen zur Entstehung und Frühgeschichte der Bündischen Jugend*, 140–41.

79. Ibid., 169.

80. Paul Ludwig Landsberg, *Die Welt des Mittelalters und wir. Ein geschichtsphilosophischer Versuch über den Sinn eines Zeitalters* (Bonn: Cohen, 1923).

81. For Landsberg's involvement in the youth movement, see: Elisabeth Korn, 'Das neue Lebensgefühl in der Gymnastik', in Elisabeth Korn, Otto Suppert and Karl Vogt (eds), *Die Jugendbewegung: Welt und Wirkung; zur 50. Wiederkehr des freideutschen Jugendtages auf dem Hohen Meißner* (Düsseldorf: Eugen Diederichs Verlag, 1963), 101–19: 110; Ernst Landsberg, Anna Landsberg and Paul Ludwig Landsberg, *Gedächtnisschrift für Prof. Dr. Ernst Landsberg (1860–1927), Frau Anna Landsberg geb. Silverberg (1878–1938), Dr. Paul Ludwig Landsberg (1901–1944)* (Bonn: Rechts- und Staatswissenschaftlichen Fakultät der Rheinischen Friedrich Wilhelms-Universität, 1953), 7; Eduard Zwierlein, *Die Idee einer philosophischen Anthropologie bei Paul Ludwig Landsberg: zur Frage nach dem Wesen des Menschen zwischen Selbstauffassung und Selbstgestaltung* (Würzburg: Königshausen & Neumann, 1989), 16. Landsberg's direct involvement in the youth movement was limited to a polemic with Hans Blüher: Paul Ludwig Landsberg, 'Hans Blühers politische Irrlehren', *Freideutsche Jugend* 6(10) (1920), 287–89. Later, Landsberg would befriend Romano Guardini, a leading figure in the Catholic youth movement Quickborn.

82. John M. Oesterreicher, *Walls are Crumbling: Seven Jewish Philosophers Discover Christ* (New York: Devin-Adair, 1962), 203.

83. Landsberg, *Die Welt des Mittelalters und wir*, 114.

84. Ibid., 114.

85. Cf. Jacob Burckhardt, *The Civilization of the Renaissance in Italy* (New York: The New American Library of World Literature, 1960). On Landsberg's critique of Burckhardt, see also: Otto Gerhard Oexle, 'Das Mittelalter und das Unbehagen an der Moderne. Mittelalterbeschwörungen in der Weimarer Republik und danach', in Otto Gerhard Oexle (ed.), *Geschichtswissenschaft im Zeichen des Historismus: Studien zu Problemgeschichten der Moderne* (Göttingen: Vandenhoeck & Ruprecht, 1996), 137–62: 143–45.

86. Otto Gerhard Oexle, 'German Malaise of Modernity: Ernst H. Kantorowicz and his "Kaiser Friedrich der Zweite"', in Robert L. Benson and Johannes Fried (eds), *Ernst Kantorowicz. Erträge der Doppeltagung* (Stuttgart: Steiner, 1997), 33–56: 40.

87. Landsberg, *Die Welt des Mittelalters und wir*, 12.

88. Ibid., 7.

89. Ibid., 112.

90. Ibid., 112.

91. Alwin Müller, 'Drei Blätter der Erinnerung. Aus einem Kranz für die "Münchener Laienspiele"', in Hermann Kaiser (ed.), *Begegnungen und Wirkungen: Festgabe für Rudolf Mirbt und das deutsche Laienspiel* (Kassel: Bärenreiter-Verlag, 1956), 18–22: 21. Cf. Wilhelm Dörfler and Hans Weinberg, *Weihnachtsspiel aus dem baierischen Wald* (Munich: Chr. Kaiser, 1923).

92. Müller, 'Drei Blätter der Erinnerung', 20.

93. Alwin Müller, 'Die Laienspiel-Bewegung. Kurzchronik', in Kindt, *Die deutsche Jugendbewegung 1920 bis 1933*, 1672–75: 1673.

94. Ibid.

95. Andreas Kaufmann, *Vorgeschichte und Entstehung des Laienspieles und die frühe Geschichte der Laienspielbewegung*. Dissertation (Stuttgart: Universität Stuttgart, 1991), 14–15; Rudolf Mirbt, *Laienspiel und Laientheater: Vorträge und Aufsätze aus den Jahren 1923–1959* (Kassel: Bärenreiter, 1960), 10.

96. Herbert Giffei, *Martin Luserke und das Theater* (Recklinghausen: Landesarbeitsgemeinschaft für Spiel und Amateurtheater Nordrhein-Westfalen, 1979), 113.

97. Mirbt had been leader of the AWV in Stuttgart and the Wandervogel e.V. in Swabia before coming to Munich in 1920. See: Klaus Vondung, 'Der Münchener Jugendring', in Kindt, *Die deutsche Jugendbewegung 1920 bis 1933*, 31–33: 31.

98. Gottfried Haass-Berkow, 'Experiences in the Realm of Dramatic Art', *A Man before Others. Rudolf Steiner Remembered: A Collection of Personal Memories from the Pages of The Golden Blade and Other Sources* (Bristol: Rudolf Steiner Press, 1993), 34–45: 34–35.

99. Cf. Karl Julius Schröer, *Deutsche Weihnachtspiele aus Ungern, geschildert und mitgetheilt* (Vienna: Wilhelm Braumüller, 1862).

100. Haass-Berkow had already performed at a meeting of the Bund Deutscher Wanderer in 1917, but the impulse to appropriate such forms of play as an expression in the youth movement only came about in the troublesome situation in postwar Germany. Cf. Kaufmann, *Vorgeschichte und Entstehung des Laienspieles*, 68.

101. Hass-Berkow cited in: ibid., 68.

102. 'Die Bundestage der Wandervogel-Bünde', *Der Zwiespruch* 1(6) (1919).

103. Ernst Berghäuser, 'Totentanz', *Wandervogel* 15(7/8) (1920), 166–69: 166.

104. Andreas Kaufmann, '"Der Gottesdienst der neuen Zeit": Laienspiel und neue Religiosität', *Jahrbuch des Archivs der Deutschen Jugendbewegung* 20 (2002), 111–22: 118–19.

105. Johan Huizinga, *Homo Ludens: A Study of the Play-Element in Culture* (London: Routledge & Kegan Paul, 1949), 37ff.

106. Ibid., 7ff.

107. Ibid., 175.

108. Richard Poppe, 'Spielgemeinden', *Der Zwiespruch* 3(4) (1921).

109. Rudolf Mirbt, 'Laienspiel', in Rudolf Mirbt (ed.), *Laienspiel und Laientheater: Vorträge und Aufsätze aus den Jahren 1923–1959* (Kassel: Bärenreiter, 1960), 9–18: 9.

110. For the hermeneutical application of the concept of play, see: Gadamer, *Truth and Method*, 102–30.

111. Hermann Kaiser, 'Zur Freiheit berufen', in Hermann Kaiser (ed.), *Begegnungen und Wirkungen: Festgabe für Rudolf Mirbt und das deutsche Laienspiel* (Kassel: Bärenreiter-Verlag, 1956), 46–48: 48.

112. Karl Reichhold, 'Laienspiel – Kleine Schule der Menschenliebe', in Hermann Kaiser (ed.), *Begegnungen und Wirkungen: Festgabe für Rudolf Mirbt und das deutsche Laienspiel* (Kassel: Bärenreiter-Verlag, 1956), 132–34: 133.

113. Ibid., 134.

114. Alwin Müller, 'Laienspiel – Spiel der Gemeinschaft', in Elisabeth Korn, Otto Suppert and Karl Vogt (eds), *Die Jugendbewegung: Welt und Wirkung; zur 50. Wiederkehr des freideutschen Jugendtages auf dem Hohen Meißner* (Düsseldorf: Eugen Diederichs Verlag, 1963), 67–84: 74.

115. Alwin Müller, *Als München leuchtete: der Jugendring und der Spielkreis Mirbt, 1920–1925: Blätter zur Erinnerung an Rudolf Mirbt und an den Mirbtkreis* (Weinheim: Deutscher Theaterverlag, 1974).

116. Rudolf Mirbt, *Möglichkeiten und Grenzen des Laienspiels: ein Vortrag* (Munich: Kaiser, 1928).

117. Walter Eckart, 'Intuition und Stimmung als Spielgesetz', in Walter Frantzen (ed.), *Laienspiel in der Weimarer Zeit* (Münster: Landesarbeitsgemeinschaft für Spiel und Amateurtheater im Land Nordrhein-Westfalen, 1969), 41–47: 42.

118. Robert Grosche, 'Gemeinschaftserlebnis und Spiel', in Wilhelm C. Gerst (ed.), *Gemeinschafts-Bühne und Jugendbewegung* (Frankfurt a.M.: Verlag des Bühnenvolksbundes, 1924), 10–14: 12.

119. Ibid., 13. Cf. Mirbt, *Möglichkeiten und Grenzen des Laienspiels*, 16.

120. Cited from an invitation to a performance of the 'Spielschar der Akademischen Vereinigung Marburg'; AdJB, Akademische Vereinigung Marburg, A102/4.

121. Müller, 'Die Laienspiel-Bewegung. Kurzchronik', 1673.

122. Eckart, 'Intuition und Stimmung als Spielgesetz', 44–45.

123. Erich Scharff, 'Neues Pathos: "Das Wesentliche"', in Walter Frantzen (ed.), *Laienspiel in der Weimarer Zeit* (Münster: Landesarbeitsgemeinschaft für Spiel und Amateurtheater im Land Nordrhein-Westfalen, 1969), 67–68.

124. Poppe, 'Spielgemeinden', 2. For Poppe and the Finkensteiner Bund, see: Charlotte Wäsche, *Vom Singen im Volke: Richard Poppe (1884–1960) und die Ideale des Finkensteiner Bundes* (Weikersheim: Margraf, 2007).

125. Mirbt, *Möglichkeiten und Grenzen des Laienspiels*, 33.

126. Margaret Hayne Harrison, *Modern Religious Drama in Germany and France: A Comparative Study* (Boston, MA: The Stratford Company, 1936), 82.

127. The 'Canticle of the Sun' had just been translated into German: Saint Francis of Assisi, Karl Josef Friedrich and Willi Geißler, *Der Sonnengesang des heiligen Franziskus von Assisi* (Hartenstein: Greifenverlag, 1920).

128. Helmut Rauner, 'Spielfahrten und Arbeit am Volk', *Der Zwiespruch* 3(1) (1921), 3–4.

129. Kaufmann, *Vorgeschichte und Entstehung des Laienspieles*, 70.

130. For an overview, see: Rudolf Mirbt, *Münchener Laienspielführer: eine Wegweisung für das Laienspiel und für mancherlei andere Dinge* (Munich: Kaiser, 1931).

131. Gerst, *Gemeinschafts-Bühne und Jugendbewegung*, 32.

132. Mirbt, *Münchener Laienspielführer*, 34. Cf. Rudolf Mirbt, *Die Bürger von Calais: Das Spiel eines Volkes* (Munich: Kaiser, 1925).

133. Gaetano Biccari, '*Zuflucht des Geistes*'? *Konservativ-revolutionäre, faschistische und nationalsozialistische Theaterdiskurse in Deutschland und Italien, 1900–1944* (Tübingen: G. Narr, 2001); Ehrenthal, *Die deutschen Jugendbünde*, 151.

134. Gregor Kannberg, *Der Bühnenvolksbund: Aufbau und Krise des Christlich-Deutschen Bühnenvolksbundes 1919–1933* (Cologne: Ralf Leppin, 1997), 69 ff.; Fiede Schleicher, *Jugendbewegung gegen Bühnenvolksbund. Eine Dokumentensammlung* (Hamburg: Die Fahrenden Gesellen, 1927), 2.

135. 'Rebellion der Jugend', *Volksstimme: Tageszeitung der Sozialdemokratischen Partei im Regierungsbezirk Magdeburg*, 9 August 1927.

136. Schleicher, *Jugendbewegung gegen Bühnenvolksbund*, 3.

137. Eberhard Wellmann, 'Absage an den Bühnenvolksbund!', *Der Zwiespruch* 9(58) (1927), 255–56: 255.

138. Gudrun Fiedler, 'Beruf und Leben: die Wandervogel-Idee auf dem Prüfstand', in Joachim H. Knoll and Julius H. Schoeps (eds), *Typisch deutsch: die Jugendbewegung: Beiträge zu einer Phänomengeschichte* (Opladen: Leske & Budrich, 1988), 71–100: 90–92. Fields in which the beliefs

of the youth movement did have considerable effect were pedagogy and education. But here too, the structural changes had to come from outside the movement. Especially the educational reforms, pressed by the Prussian minister of cultural affairs Carl Heinrich Becker in the mid-1920s, offered a wealth of opportunities for bringing reform pedagogical ideas to practice. Becker himself gladly drew personnel from the ranks of the youth movement to staff his pedagogical academies. See: Christine Hohmann, *Dienstbares Begleiten und später Widerstand: der nationale Sozialist Adolf Reichwein im Nationalsozialismus* (Bad Heilbrunn: Klinkhardt, 2007), 58–59.

139. Dankwart Gerlach, 'Zusammenschluss der Bauleute und Handwerker', *Der Zwiespruch* 2(14) (1920).

140. Hans-Ulrich Wehler, *Deutsche Gesellschaftsgeschichte. Vom Beginn des Ersten Weltkriegs bis zur Gründung der beiden deutschen Staaten, 1914–1949. Vol. IV, VII. Teil* (Munich: Beck, 2003), 299ff.

141. Winfried Mogge, 'Oberdada und Wandervögel. Johannes Baader, Burg Ludwigstein und die Jugendbewegung 1922/23', *Jahrbuch des Archivs der deutsche Jugendbewegung* 18 (1999), 233–316: 242.

142. Gustav Wyneken, 'Jugendburg!', *Volkszeitung (Berlin)*, 30 June 1918.

143. Almut Körting, 'Jugendkultur und Jugendburg-Idee', *Köpfchen* 3–4 (2000), 4–9.

144. Cf. Gustav Wyneken, 'Die Jugendburg', in Kurt Hiller (ed.), *Tätiger Geist. Zweites der Ziel-Jahrbücher* (Munich: Georg Müller, 1918).

145. For the criticism, see: Ludwig Tschuncky, 'Eine rheinische Jugendburg?', *Der Zwiespruch* 2(16) (1920).

146. Robert Oelbermann, 'Die Rheinische Jugendburg', *Der Zwiespruch* 2(19a) (1920).

147. *Baustein für Rheinische Jugendburg*, AdJB, Nerother Wandervogel, A19/3.

148. Robert Oelbermann, *Eine Jugendburg als Ehrendenkmal für unsere gefallenen Helden*, AdJB, Nerother Wandervogel, A19/3.

149. The history of Waldeck Castle is well documented in: Hotte Schneider, *Die Waldeck: Lieder – Fahrten – Abenteuer; die Geschichte der Burg Waldeck von 1911 bis heute* (Potsdam: Verlag für Berlin-Brandenburg, 2005).

150. Robert Oelbermann, 'Die Entstehung des Jugendburggedankes', *Werbeschrift für die Rheinische Jugendburg* (Bonn: Bund zur Errichtung der Rheinischen Jugendburg, 1921). In: AdJB, Nerother Wandervogel, A19/3.

151. Mohler, *Die konservative Revolution*, 85.

152. For this criticism, see: Breuer, *Anatomie der konservativen Revolution*, 37; Nadja Thomas, *'Der Aufstand gegen die sekundäre Welt': Botho Strauss und die 'Konservative Revolution'* (Würzburg: Königshausen & Neumann, 2004), 200.

153. Ras, *Body, Femininity and Nationalism*, 85–86.

CHAPTER 5

# In Search of the Spiritual Motherland

When Kurd Lähn, an old Alt-Wandervogel and leader of the small philhellene *Bund* Südlegion, looked back on three decades of youth movement in 1933, he characterized the purpose of the youth movement as a search for *Heimat*. The *Heimat* Lähn referred to was not the geographically confined political or cultural space one would usually call homeland. The homeland of youth was a spiritual one (*eine geistliche Heimat*). To clarify this statement, Lähn linked the youth movement's search for *Heimat* to the task the oracle of Apollo at Delos set the Trojan refugees in Virgil's *Aeneid*: 'antiquam exquirite matrem' ('seek your ancient mother').[1] The Trojans initially misunderstood the oracle by taking its meaning literally; they believed that after the Greek destruction of their city, the gods urged them to seek refuge in their ancestral homeland Crete. Only after a series of misfortunes and ill ventures did it dawn that the homeland was not the land of maternal ancestry, but the spiritual motherland or mother earth: the land of divine calling and providence, which proved to be Italy.[2]

Like the Trojans seeking shelter after the Greek destruction of their city, German youth sought *Heimat* after the lost war and after the territorial and economical cataclysm of the Versailles treaty. But the youth movement had – according to Lähn – not made the same mistake as the Trojans to believe that seeking a physical land of ancestry would suffice to fulfil destiny. Instead, Lähns *Heimat* referred to an existential horizon, which German youth had constituted out of an 'inner predestination', rather than one appropriated from their ancestors.[3] In the *Heimat* of youth 'all forces accumulate from blood and soil, speech and custom', which had neither to do with 'reasoning on German essence and

Notes for this section begin on page 183

German nature', nor with the question 'who of us embodied German being best and purest'.[4] These forces simply defined the world of German youth and therefore their destiny. This 'spiritual' *Heimat* was part of a 'reality' different from the reality of modernity – a reality in which 'over man the forces of nature preside; the cosmos, the ancient mother, in whose hands all threads of destiny lie'.[5] Such a reality is primarily lived organically amidst the divinely ordered elements. The recognition of this reality implied the confirmation that life itself is subordinated to destiny. The youth movement had found organic life in the woods, the fields, near creeks, at dawn and dusk; but becoming at home in the world meant more than finding oneself amidst nature. After all, the position of man in nature is different from that of the animal. Man has skills, creativity – not to subordinate nature, but to shape life and society in harmony with divine order. To find one's home in the world therefore required an engagement with tradition, with history, in order to be able to recognize fate and become truly at home. Personally, Lähn understood this search for the continuities in tradition, custom and speech as an engagement with the spirit of Greek antiquity. He aimed to 'de-Germanize in the South only to become more German than before; to become more Hellenic, to become only German'.[6]

Lähn hinges on the spherical conception of time, because in his conception of *Heimat*, transmitted customs, language and heritage hurl together in a concrete, experienced 'now', which forms the basis of future expectations. The future was defined as a journey to the origin. By turning to Greece as one of the many cradles of German being, the German could once again become what he already was or ought to be: he could realign life with fate, with the gods, and drop the modern arrogance that the world could be subdued to human action and cognition.

In this chapter, I will analyse how the journeys to the various corners of Europe that the Bündische Jugend undertook in the 1920s and early 1930s related to the utopian expectations of the German nation. However, some preliminary remarks on the concept of utopia are necessary. When Lähn speaks about Greece as a land where the German could find what he ought to become, he obviously does not speak about Greece as a utopia in the modern definition of the concept. Since the late eighteenth century, the concept of utopia refers to a future ideal society to be realized through human action. This idea of utopia is, however, based on the linear conception of time as progressive development.[7] For Lähn, utopia was not the product of human agency; it was situated in the ancient past.

To properly conceive the utopian content in the Bündische Jugend, I will understand utopia with Paul Tillich as an existential category. In his often forgotten lectures on 'Die politische Bedeutung der Utopie im Leben der Völker' (1951), Tillich was one of the first – and surprisingly also one of the few – to broaden the concept of utopia beyond being a function of modern historical consciousness, and beyond seeing space as little more than an (often imagined) realm onto which temporal utopias are projected.[8] For Tillich, utopia is rooted in the structure of *being*, as man is continuously projecting himself in time. When utopia is an existential category, not only individuals, groups, societies and eras who think historically – like those in modernity – produce utopias, but also those who think unhistorically can have utopias. Tillich defines unhistorical thought as 'a comprehension of history which is born out of something else than history, and which consequently attributes no self-reliance, no autonomy to history. This comprehension makes history reliant on other forces and thereby dissolves it'.[9] Nonetheless, unhistorical utopian thought also gains meaning in a temporal framework. In the Stoic conception of an ancient Golden Age, the hopes for a better life are, for example, projected into a mythical past. In unhistorical thought, projecting utopian dreams into the future is only possible because these dreams were already once realized. But – and this is the crucial point – this ancient past never was the product of human action or the product of divine action: it entirely depended on cosmic principles of cyclical rebirth to which both the gods and man were subjected. Furthermore, in the attitude to life that depends on the 'backwards-oriented utopia' of unhistorical thought, space overrides time as the utopian expectation is bound to spatial metaphors, such as 'the circle' and 'Divine Ground'. The question therefore is how the spatially foreign functioned as a source of utopianism for the Bündische Jugend.

In this chapter, I will answer this question by analysing the foreign hikes of the Bündische Jugend in the 1920s and early 1930s. First, I will discuss the rising popularity of trips abroad in the interwar youth movement, after which I will study the relationship between the interpretation of different destinations and their relations to the idea of the journey back to the origin, in which 'origin' could mean various things, such as original Being, original Germanness or spiritual origin. I will analyse the idea of the 'East' as frontier and the German eastern border as the original 'heart' of Germany, of England as a successful mediation between past and future, of Greece as the 'spiritual home' of Germany, and of Scandinavia as the Germanic source of German destiny.

## The Discovery of 'the Abroad'

The journey abroad was a novelty among the activities of the youth movement in the interwar period. Before 1914, the Wandervogel had discovered hiking and had turned it into an art. But Sunday hikes were mainly confined to the vicinity of the city, and vacations meant wandering through other German regions. The criticism of modernity and bourgeois society as it was phrased in the pre-war Wandervogel was mainly derived from the binary opposition between city and countryside, in which the countryside had been the source of longing and often literally became a site of dwelling for the Wandervogel. The postwar critique of the pre-war youth movement's Romantic 'escapism' made clear that evading dialogue about, and lacking understanding of, urban modernity actually undercut the educative intentions of the movement: Romanticism merely provided a sense of security without creating a basis to overcome the problems of modernity.

As we have seen, the war significantly changed the geographical horizon, as well as the topics of discussion of those involved in the youth movement. Moreover, the youth movement's new members had grown up in a world in which there was no longer an established bourgeois value system on which to blame all kinds of social and educational problems. The opposition between city and countryside, between life-neglecting bourgeois modernity and regenerative folk culture, was replaced by a formative tension between two unknown entities: a new Germany and 'the abroad'. I say formative, for finding a way of relating (to) the two poles of this oppositional scheme – rather than providing clear-cut ideological answers – shaped the youth movement and its members from the mid-1920s onwards.

Before the war, cases of international understanding were rare. In 1909, a representative party of Alt-Wandervogel had journeyed to Britain by invitation of Robert Baden-Powell to get acquainted with his Boy Scouts and to tour many historical sites in Scotland and England.[10] Other foreign encounters had a less official character and were the initiative of local Wandervogel groups that wandered to, for example, Scandinavia or Bohemia. It was, ironically, the war that intertwined individual biographies with the abroad. These wartime travels still bore the marks of the pre-war interest in rural culture. We have seen how wartime encounters with Flemish folklore behind the trenches of the Western front were apprehended in the light of the youth movement's anti-urbanism. In the East, however, the expedition against Russia had led to the 'discovery' of basically unknown German settler communities in Livonia and Courland.[11] The interest was initially folkloristic and apolitical, but after the end of the war the youth movement became emerged in the border tensions, which were – again – felt most urgently in the East.

In 1919, the Treaty of Versailles had deprived Germany of a significant part of its territory: Alsace and much of Lorraine were annexed by France, Eupen-Malmedy by Belgium, and Northern Schleswig was ceded to Denmark after a plebiscite. Especially problematic was the situation in the East, where most of Posen and West Prussia had become part of the newly established Polish state, separating East Prussia from the German mainland by means of the Polish Corridor. The changing borders had a direct effect on the youth movement's practices. While before the war, their hikes were seen as an implementation of a different attitude to nationhood, there was little discussion over the German nation as a political entity. The apolitical stance of the youth movement was thus facilitated by the stability of the borders of the German Empire and resulted in a rejection of 'individualistic' domestic party politics, from which the youth movement strove to remain independent. With the loss of the self-evidence of the German borders, the youth movement could no longer remain apolitical. Although party politics were still rejected and democracy was feared for institutionalizing a type of politics that would not operate in favour of the common good, the breakdown of Germany offered possibilities for a cultural politics that referred to the spiritual content of Germanness beyond the confinements of the German state.[12] The cultural-political interest of the youth movement was primarily aimed at the German communities in Eastern Europe. Although voices calling attention to the problematic situation of Germans in the East had been present in the youth movement since the early days of Karl Fischer, for many the border problem was an eye-opener to the fact that there were Germans outside of the empire, and that they lived in social and economic hardship and were in danger of losing their ethnic identity due to nationalization politics of various East European states.[13]

This problem was felt hardest in the border regions. In Upper Silesia, where prior to the ordained plebiscite a number of Polish uprisings occurred, a *Freikorps* comprised exclusively of Wandervögel was formed in 1919. Called the Wandervogel Hundertschaft, the *Freikorps* lived after the Wandervogel principles of abstinence and non-smoking. Service in the Wandervogel *Freikorps* was regarded as a moral duty in service of the regeneration of the German people as a totality, rather than the defence of a bygone empire torn apart by different parties and individuals attaining personal interests and profit:

> Our nation is sick, miserably sick since the collapse – and while we remain confident in finding a new, more beautiful building rising out of the ruins of the old, this building is in fact covered with the worst rubbish and mildew: it is covered in the spirit of indifference and tiredness, selfishness and negligence of moral commitment. Only when we rise out of this disastrous reposure, only when the *will to fulfil duty for the sake of duty itself and not for the sake of salary*, only when the firm commitment to voluntary subsumption to the Volksgemeinschaft is common again – *only then will we be able to say that the present is no disgrace*.[14]

The doctrine of duty to the German people as a whole implied a neutral position to the political development of the German state. When, in August 1919, the danger of a Polish invasion in Silesia had been evaded, and the *Wandervogel Hundertschaft* was about to be deployed in Germany in inner political affairs, this *Freikorps* was voluntarily disbanded.

Due to these border conflicts, it may not surprise that the initiative for a structural and binding cultivation of foreign hiking came from the Wandervogel groups near the border. Especially the Saxon Wandervogel leader Hermann Krügler and the Silesian Hans Dehmel – commander of the Wandervogel Hundertschaft – took the lead. Both in Saxony and Silesia, their Wandervogel groups had emerged from the old declined Wandervogel; both groups were reorganized as all-male *Bünde*, called Jungenschaft (Saxony) or Jungmannschaft (Silesia), which were to carry on the spirit of the Wandervogel, but with a renewed tendency for deeds instead of words. They closed ranks with Martin Voelkel's Neupfadfinder on this matter.

In April 1922, the Neupfadfinder and an array of Wandervogel branches gathered at Wartburg Castle, where they agreed to simultaneously organize summer hikes to the border regions and further abroad. For the Neupfadfinder, the fate of the Germans in the East had provided a possibility for becoming a *Volk* and for the establishment of a new Reich. The unity of the Germans may have been a reaction to foreign pressure, but while most Germans were still struggling to find out 'what unites them in fate, blood and history, a new wave of creativity and becoming rises and carries it forward'.[15] This new wave was the youth movement, and it was believed that it was social work in the border regions that could turn the sense of unity from a position that the Germans were put into by fate, into positive virtues. Visiting the border regions and working there thus became 'an expression of a becoming, which is deeply evoked by the fate of misery, and which conveys the better and the coming'.[16]

The trips to the border region had the double function of getting acquainted with hitherto largely unknown German communities and mastering the concrete historical situatedness in which youth found itself. This was an urgent task because of the extremely troublesome position of Germany after the Versailles Treaty, after famine, political instability and hyperinflation. Because there was neither a firmly established state nor a firmly established social order, finding a home, a *Heimat*, appeared more urgent in Germany than elsewhere. The situation in which they found themselves was what they called 'destiny': it was not the result of conscious action, but a coincidental situation which youth had to master.

The present international situation was meticulously researched and discussed with members of foreign youth movements and foreign students. The position of the Germans in the East was, in particular, the subject of research: during trips to German settlements, the demographical, social, economic and political situation of German settlers was analysed and discussed.[17] International student exchange and international forum discussions were organized, all with the primary goal of understanding – understanding one another and understanding the given situation in Europe. Countries that had not been involved in the war or that had been victorious were approached with a mixture of envy and unbelief: envy, for the people living there seemed so untroubled and easy-going, as if they were masters of the universe and had no fate bestowed upon them; and unbelief, because such an attitude must have implied an ignorance of the problems of modernity. These would eventually catch them unprepared. Therefore, the youth movement's affiliation with the East was much stronger than with the West and the North, not just because here German settlers lived in need of redemption, but also because the young nation states were – like Germany – in a struggle for self-formation and could not lean back on the deeds of their forebears, or clear-cut historical narratives, to sustain an identity.

These nations had to become a *Heimat* as well, which implied harking back to the origin as a future prospect. Such attempts by other nations were respected and even venerated as long as it happened on the principles that the youth movement deemed proper: in recognition of a cosmological worldview.

In the summer of 1922 the promise of foreign hikes was fulfilled. Forty-nine members of Krügler's Saxon branch of the Wandervogel-Jungenbund (later named the Sächsische Jungenschaft) sailed down the Danube from Passau to Budapest, met with Hungarian Boy Scouts and visited German enclaves near Fünfkirchen (Pécs) that were threatened by the Magyarization politics of the Hungarian government.[18] Getting to understand this situation was the prime objective of the journey. At least, this was the task of the older Wandervogel:

> The boys are full of the venture of the hike; those seven weeks of unbound freedom, and the luring faraway land with gypsies and steppe. For the older ones, for the leaders, there are other tasks ahead: to grasp the essence of this foreign people by heart and reason, to know and acknowledge the relationships between peoples, to learn to understand the position of Germans in Hungary and their relations with the Magyars, and to review trade and economy, mores and customs.[19]

The Sächsische Jungenschaft was primarily struck by the esteem with which people in Hungary spoke of Germany. For the German settlers, Germany was the Promised Land; the Magyars spoke about Germany 'as if it was still there in its old greatness and might'.[20] These were impressions that, by then, one could not easily obtain at home in Germany; yet for them the recognition of the greatness of a bygone Germany – even if this imperial Germany was the subject of strong criticism within the youth movement – was encouraging for the project of a new Germany. Moreover, a sense of pride was gained by the fact that the very spiritual basis of their regenerative thought remained incomprehensible to the Hungarian Boy Scouts.

> The experience that there is something present in German youth which is not conveyable in words, which other nations encounter with complete incomprehension – the pride of this and the duty to nurture this spirit which has nothing to do with outer manifestations, as well as to carry this spirit forth and to show it to others – this insight is one of the most valuable lessons of this hike.[21]

The recognition of this difference by a leader of the Hungarian scouts was taken as a great compliment by the Saxon Wandervogel. They saw the recognition of Germany's greatness as an affirmation that the path of experience-fuelled spirit was the right way to go – or even that this path was Germany's fate, because it apparently touched upon the essence of German nationhood. The Hungarian scouts, however, were not entirely at ease with the restless drive of these German youths, and the Hungarian leader stated that they more feared than admired the 'uncanny zest for action and desire for freedom' of the Saxon Wandervogel.[22]

In the same summer in which the Saxons visited Hungary, the Silesians under Hans Dehmel went to Siebenbürgen and the Harz-Elbe-Gau marched in five columns over the Alps. The Berlin Alt-Wandervogel-Gau visited East Prussia and the Memel Territory; the Brandenburger Gau went to Carinthia; the Berlin E-V-Gau went to Finland and the Neupfadfinder to Hungary and Tyrol.[23] All understood the hike as a mission, which – according to Kurt Mattusch – had a twofold character. First, the discovery of German enclaves abroad urged the youth movement to include them in Germany's destiny – in the constitution of a new Germany. Second, they encountered a distorted image of Germany in foreign countries, in reaction to which they strove 'to carry the image of the coming Germany abroad', and attempted 'to gain the respect and friendship of the youth' of their neighbouring peoples.[24] The Deutsche Freischar – the *Bund* in which in 1926 and 1927 various smaller Wandervogel and Boy Scout organizations merged – phrased this task in these words:

> In the consciousness of foreigners, the image of the open-minded, self-conscious and Volks-conscious, occidentally educated, spiritually and physically truthful young German man must and will be placed next to the image of the English gentleman – replacing the beer-drinking, sauerkraut-eating, swaggering German.[25]

During the 1920s, the number of journeys abroad increased so significantly that it was said that the Bündische Jugend practically 'lived beyond the border'; not as reposure, but to find its own centre, ideally without resorting to self-confirmation and narrowness:

> One learns quite vividly where Germany is actually situated, which particular tasks it has in maintaining the equilibrium of the West, where and which exceptional currents flow from East, West, North and South through the middle.[26]

With the improvement in international relations in the second half of the 1920s, an increasing number of trips aimed explicitly at fostering international relations – primarily through engagements with foreign youth and student associations.[27] Whereas the ordinary hikes abroad could entail an entire *Bund* and could draw up to a few hundred participants, smaller investigative study trips, aimed at international understanding, were reserved for those in their late teens and early twenties, and these trips often had a scholarly character. The difference between the mainstream of the youth movement and the *völkisch*-oriented right-wing *Bünde* such as the Adler und Falke and the Geusen was not that the latter resorted per se to a self-centred nationalism. Rather, in their view, German settlements were outposts of German culture and needed safeguarding as ethnic minorities, and therefore required attention.[28] Mainstream *Bünde*, such as the Sächsische Jungenschaft (later part of the Deutsche Freischar), explained the presence of Germans abroad not as defensive 'bridgeheads, but as bridges to the different nations of South East Europe'.[29]

In the course of the 1920s, foreign hikes were increasingly organized to accomplish certain aims – be it international fraternization, the study of the landscape, culture and economy of other countries, the study and help of German communities abroad, or the performance of German folk songs and plays.[30] Nonetheless, the old 'aimless' and 'adventurous' Wandervogel tradition of hiking was continued by a small number of *Bünde*, such as the Nerother Wandervogel. However, for most *Bünde* foreign journeys combined adventure with goals such as establishing reciprocal relationships with German settlements through singing, dancing or performing *Laienspiele*. More practically, support with harvesting was offered to German settlers in the East, and cultural activities and adult education for Germans from both within and outside of the empire were offered in adult educational centres (*Volkshochschulen*), in which many pedagogically engaged members and former members of the youth movement had found employment.

Table 5.1 provides an indication of foreign hiking destinations of groups of the Deutsche Freischar in 1928 and 1929. These numbers are, however, just indicative, because approximately a quarter of the groups did not return the questionnaire. Moreover, the number of people visiting a country does not necessarily express the popularity of the destination, but can also be an effect of the size of the *Bund* that chose that country as a destination. Large groups often visited Eastern Europe, while Western Europe was visited by smaller groups. Nonetheless, the table shows the popularity of destinations in Eastern Europe

**Table 5.1** Summer hikes to the border regions and abroad by groups of the Deutsche Freischar.

| 1928 | | 1929 | |
| --- | --- | --- | --- |
| Destination | No. people | Destination | No. people |
| Czechoslovakia | 271 | Czechoslovakia | 260 |
| | | Alsace | 59 |
| Austria | 127 | Austria and (South) Tyrol | 61 |
| Denmark | 37 | Denmark and Northern Schleswig | 53 |
| East Prussia and the Baltic | 176 | East Prussia, Danzig and the Baltic | 280 |
| England | 12 | England | 29 |
| | | Estonia, Latvia and Lithuania | 253 |
| Finland | 53 | Finland | 23 |
| France | 24 | France | 12 |
| Hungary and Romania | 47 | Hungary, Romania, Bulgaria and Turkey | 138 |
| Luxembourg | 57 | Luxembourg and the Saar area | 40 |
| Spain | 3 | Spain | 16 |
| Sweden and Norway | 396 | Sweden and Norway | 99 |
| | | Switzerland | 13 |
| | | The Netherlands | 72 |
| Turkey and Greece | 41 | Upper Silesia and Poland | 189 |
| Yugoslavia | 91 | Yugoslavia | 43 |
| **Total** | **1,335** | **Total** | **1,640** |

*Source*: Ernst Buske, 'Die Grenz- und Auslandfahrten des Sommers 1928', *Deutsche Freischar* 1(3) (1928–1929), 167–68; Ernst Buske, 'Grenz- und Auslandfahrten des Sommers 1929', *Deutsche Freischar* 2(2) (1929–1930), 142–43.

and Scandinavia, and the unpopularity of France, Spain and Italy. In general, this difference can be explained in reference to the popularity of visiting German-speaking settlements in other countries – hence Alsace is considered to be a destination on its own.

## Grenzland: The Eastern Frontier

Having determined that the East was the prime destination for foreign journeys of the Bündische Jugend, the question arises what the 'utopian' content of the East was for the youth movement. With regard to the East, one image dominated the movement's imagination: that of the Teutonic Knight. This image was, as one member of the Bund Der Reichspfadfinder wrote, relevant for the Bündische Jugend in two ways: for the 'inner construction of the image of a community based on order and the craft of chivalry', and also for the 'historical memory about the expansion of the habitat of the German people and the protection of the Eastern border against the attacks of the Eastern people'.[31] By connecting the image of the Teutonic Knight to the concrete situation in which Germany found itself as a result of the Versailles treaty, this historical image could be projected into the future as Germany's destiny. The symbol that reflected this destiny was the cross of the Teutonic Order, the *Baltenkreuz* (later named *Balkenkreuz*). Many groups carried this cross on the banners under which they would venture into the East: 'the symbol of the Order brings us back to the age of the Crusades, in which every knight – enthused by the sacrality of the idea – pinned the cross to his coat as a sign of participation in the fight for Christianity'.[32]

The choice for this cross was made on the night of 3 August 1923, when nineteen *Bünde* gathered for a 'border fire' at the Fichtelgebirge in northeastern Bavaria. The fire was organized to celebrate the fact that Boy Scouts and Wandervögel had found each other in the common goal of venturing abroad. Here, in the compelling spell of unknown destiny, youth and *Volk*, centre and periphery, past and future were brought in connection. The fire represented the common destiny of the German people. Such destiny was unintelligible, not in the least because in the youth movement's worldview there was no such thing as a preconceived nation or national identity – only a perennial task of self-formation in the light of ever-changing destinies. The Fichtelgebirge represented the origin and centre around which German history and nationhood revolved:

> Here from Losburg to Epprechtstein the mountaintops reach the sky. This is the wellspring of four German streams. Here the dark lake and the black bog pines lead us back to the Ice Age. Here, bear and lynx have lived the longest. The poet of the 'Flegeljahre' was born here and Luise – the genius of Prussia – resided here with pleasure. And according to the ancient legend, in the inside of the mountain

Emperor Charles holds court with the real emperor's throne. Thus we stand truly in the heart of Germany.[33]

But this origin was not something to hark back to, it was an origin that bestowed upon youth the task of realizing itself, to individually and collectively acquaint one's historicality – in other words: to come home.

> Let the right hour and the country find a worthy and devout generation in us! This is what is demanded of us, of every individual and of us together. And one looks at the other to judge whether we are ready, as Germany's new youth, simple, strong, fair and true to life.[34]

When the Bund Der Reichspfadfinder visited Courland in 1928, it was with the clear intention of 'seeking the homeland; seeking Germany'.[35] Courland – which was a duchy ruled by German nobility until it was ceded to Russia in 1795 – had little to offer but silent testimonies of bygone German presence. Since the Russian government had promoted land ownership among the Latvian population in the mid-nineteenth century, German land ownership had diminished, and with it German language and culture. They found people with German names who could speak broken German only in infinitives; they found huge empty manors of which just a few rooms were inhabited by Latvian farmers – testimonies of German presence that could no longer be maintained. 'What seems familiar is sorrowful; what tells us about the Germans only testifies of German suffering, murder, destruction and expulsion.'[36]

Visiting what was left of German nobility did offer some consolation. Baron von Hahn, for example, was still able to live on the estate where his ancestors had lived for over six hundred years. In his art collection, which had survived the war and the revolution, the Ringpfadfinder saw 'the tasteful culture, the mental activity of the Baltic nobility of the nineteenth century in front of us in this dignified room where the treasures of Italy had found their place. Yes, we feel it – we are in the West, where Asiatic Russia had found a German stronghold'.[37] The journey back could now be conceived as the journey to the 'holy mother soil', from where the German Balts initially originated.[38]

## England: Shared Destiny

In the Bündische Jugend, ties with England were primarily maintained through connections with the English rural revivalist and youth leader Henry Rolf Gardiner.[39] Gardiner had close ties with the movement – primarily with the Deutsche Freischar and the Jungnationale Bund. During the 1920s he befriended a number of prominent German youth leaders, including the leader of the Deutsche Freischar Ernst Buske, philosopher and adult educationalist

Eugen Rosenstock-Huessy, reform pedagogue Adolf Reichwein and music pedagogue Georg Götsch.[40] Often misunderstood in the British academic climate, Gardiner felt at home in the German youth movement, with which he shared the basic tenets of their understanding of past, present and future. For Gardiner too, finding oneself was a journey through the foreign 'which will lead him to the country of his heart, to that place or region where he can ultimately take root and bear fruit like a tree, and which for him becomes symbolic of the unseen home whence he is sprung and whither he will return'.[41]

In this homecoming, the past was a source of inspiration; it could instigate emotional refreshment as on the journey unmediated, historical experiences could occur when wandering through old towns and foreign lands. Experiences such as the 'rediscovery of the past by which man is made whole' needed, however, to be connected to concrete action and self-responsibility.[42] Gardiner argued that too often the world of future-oriented action had been related to adulthood, while unconcerned experiences of different times and places was attributed to childhood. The task ahead was to connect these distinct worlds by turning experience into action – in Gardiner's words: to 'carry the wealth of our soul's tradition into the merciless open of the future and make it flower there'.[43] This would be the task of individuals, but also of nations: returning to organic life for replenishment, but in constant need of appropriating, adapting and relating to new influences, challenges and possibilities that the current historical situation demands. Out of dying cultures new ones grow, and the growth of a new England was what Gardiner envisaged. However, this could only happen when England opened its eyes to its role in European destiny, as well as to the fact that new, true polity would be religious polity. This is where a reappropriation of the sources of European culture was needed: what new polity had lost was virtue and godliness. Modernity had resorted to what the Greeks called *hubris*: the arrogance to challenge natural order for personal benefit. Therefore modernity had called the wrath of the gods upon itself. A turn to origin – to 'the community of the gods on earth, the kingdom of heaven realised in flesh and blood' – was needed to re-acknowledge natural order and man's position in it, rather than man's dominance over it.[44] But Gardiner warned: 'this does not imply any ideal of static Utopia or Paradise; far from it. It points to a world of men striving to manifest a power bestowed upon them by forces which they reverence and trust'.[45]

Surprisingly, Gardiner's lack of trust in contemporary English society was not shared by his friends in the German youth movement. For them, England was still a source of inspiration and, as the Wandervogel Albrecht von Fritsch wrote in his memoirs, of envy. England had been the 'envied Elder Brother who has got all the things the younger wants and has not got'.[46] It was not so much assets that Von Fritsch had in mind when making this remark. Wealth, colonies and the navy were often mentioned in German public discourse, but conceal the true objects of jealousy:

> the careless, easy way of Being British without falling into a convulsive patriotism, the secret of dressing well without showing off, and of wearing a dress-suit with the same matter-of-fact lack of concern as one does a dirty bush-tunic, the knowledge of how to reconcile tradition and progress, the practical sense to rule big countries and to run big businesses, the apparently slack and easy diplomatic practice which usually wins in the long run, and last but not least the weekend, the glorious symbol of a nation that wants to know what it is working for.[47]

These latter traits were certainly what defined the youth movement's fascination for England. The Briton seemed so apparently at home in the world, far more self-evident and unconcerned than the German – and certainly more unconcerned than German youth.

In 1926 Georg Götsch travelled to England at the head of his Märkische Spielgemeinde, a performance group specialized in sixteenth-century madrigals and Bach's polyphonic motets, which had grown out of the Brandenburg branch of the Alt-Wandervogel. During his journey he realized that conquering the deficiencies of German historical culture was not just a matter of overcoming bourgeois philistinism or historicism. In England he encountered a bourgeoisie for whom heritage had never been problematic or in need of reinvention. The reason for this, Götsch believed, was not a historical matter, but the result of the spatial, insular isolation of England. This isolation equated the English nation to insular communities of previous times, such as the German settlements in Eastern Europe, monasteries, and the fortresses of crusading German military orders. These were communities in which Götsch found no traces of modern mass politics, or of corrupt power and self-interested career politicians, because they bore the traits of Plato's ideal *polis*: they were based on natural order.

Contrary to Germany, the insular character of the country had made the English a nation for which order was not a divine gift, but something attainable and achievable for the community itself. Order was never seriously challenged in England because the borders of the nation were never challenged, thus the microcosmic character of the nation remained in effect over centuries. Götsch understood closed space to be a prerequisite for a proper appreciation of the heritage of bygone centuries. Because in Germany spatial order had continuously been challenged since the Reformation and the Thirty Years War, the Germans lived not with the 'spirits of the past', but with the 'unborn children of the future'.[48] Whereas to the Englishman his past and history possessed a great degree of self-evidence, the absence of a rooted order in Germany and the insecurity of its own identity turned its past into a source of distant longing. Idealism, the continuing aim of German philosophy to think the world anew as a realization of Ideas, and the philosophy that states that the world only commences as a constitution of the human mind, had led Germany astray. But as the order which Germany experienced between ad 1000 and ad 1500 was now long gone, Germany stood at the brink of exchanging its medieval delight in forms for sinking into the deep well of ideas. According to George Götsch:

> One observes her glut of ideas not finding corresponding expression in real forms, that she is exchanging power for knowledge, and the role of leadership, which she held in medieval Christendom, for the profession of a teacher; that she is withdrawing from an incalculable but full-blooded reality into the smiling realm of ideas and the beautiful consistency of theories.[49]

The magnitude of ideas that flooded Germany, and the overproduction of pamphlets and philosophies that the youth movement unsuccessfully tried to eradicate in its own ranks, should be replaced by a simple reverence of historical forms, as was the case in England: 'Germany does not lack leaders or discoverers, talents or ideas, and she need only follow the example of England's quiescence and balance to develop her own form with similar clarity and distinction'.[50] Then it would be comprehensible that the quiet releasement with which the English gentleman underwent his fate – quite similar to Ernst Wurche's releasement – was not dissociation from the troublesome world, an anti-modern flight into the private sphere, but a necessary step to radiate into the outer world with meaning, rather than ideas. Just as the old monks understood that only retirement and seclusion give the strength for extraversion, and inversion of insular historical forms gives the strength to rule the world.[51] For Götsch, England was the living proof of this statement.

## Hellas as a Spiritual Home

We have already seen how the youth movement reacted to classical *Bildung* in the Wilhelmine Empire. Yet, the youth movement's criticism of humanism was not directed at antiquity per se, but at the way in which, in the course of the nineteenth century, Hellenism had dwindled from being a creative cultural force – as it had been for the neo-humanists – to being a mere asset of the educated bourgeoisie. In the gymnasium, the Classics were treated in line with contemporary academic philology, which under the influence of positivism had reinvented itself as a positivistic *Altertumswissenschaft*. All these developments undercut the exemplary function of ancient Greece for *Bildung*. Although the idea of Greece as the subject of scientific investigation rather than as a site for cultural edification took longer to be implemented in secondary education than in the academic curriculum, it was, as we have seen, exactly the de-idealizing and investigative way in which the Classics were treated in the decades before the war that had led the youth movement to oppose the humanist tradition.[52]

Although the youth movement opposed the positivist treatment of the Classics, their own appropriation of Greek heritage did not comprise a return to the Greece of traditional German Hellenism, to the Greece of Goethe and Winckelmann, the Greece of Apollonian forms, of Winckelmann's 'Edle einfalt und stille Grösse'. In this tradition, Greece stood at an unattainable height of perfection through the intimate bond between man and nature in life and art. Modern man could only approach this situation aesthetically because he was burdened with the Christian consciousness of fall and guilt, and with the consciousness of his subjectivity, of the dichotomy between the rational self and the external world. The linear conception of time arising from these different ideas of consciousness supported the idea that only in art could the unity of man and nature could be approximated, because there could be no 'return' to a historical state of unconscious harmony.[53] However, having disposed of this Christian eschatology in favour of an immanent eschatology, parts of the youth movement developed a Hellenism different from the traditional 'Winckelmannian' German Hellenism. Their approach was more 'poetic' in the sense that Greece was not an object of aesthetic interest, but a realm in which man could be reconciled with the world and the gods, with nature and destiny. A member of the Deutsche Freischar, Karl Seidelmann, spoke about the youth movement's humanism as a 'third humanism' after the Renaissance and the Goethe Era.[54]

The term 'third humanism' was first coined in 1921 in a speech by the German philosopher Eduard Spranger – a student of Wilhelm Dilthey – to denote the humanism of the youth movement and educational reform circles.[55] Rather than being an intellectual movement, this 'third humanism' was practised and lived. In contrast to the earlier humanisms, experience prevailed over thought, and formative action prevailed over literary-philosophical ruminations: 'it is an existential humanism, a humanism of relentless, but spirited faith in reality'.[56] As a result, this humanism strives to comprehend historical formations and to be formed through this understanding – not just intellectually, but as a whole human being.

In the youth movement, the works of Friedrich Hölderlin exemplified the possibility to derive, at least poetically, truly future prospects from an encounter with ancient heritage. Between 1913 and 1916, Norbert von Hellingrath's edition of *Hölderlins Samtliche Werke* was published. It was in the youth movement that the forgotten poet quickly gained a large audience. Hölderlin's poems sang the song of a world disenchanted and uprooted by the absence of the gods, but contained the prophecy of the return of the gods. Such prophecies struck a nerve among German youth and were cited at meetings, in journals and in letters. 'Hölderlin', it was called, 'is not the dreamer of a romantic epoch – that dreamful life which shattered in confrontation with harsh reality. He was the first to cultivate a new image of Hellas in some portentous poems … and to disclose a prospect of a völkisch future'.[57] The value of Hölderlin was that he provided the possibility to see immortal gods, heroes and destiny in Greece, rather than works of art and artefacts of bygone times. Thereby ancient Greece gained actual value as a vision of an age in which life was disclosed through holiness, heroism and destiny. By shifting attention from the aesthetic and historical value of ancient Greece to its poetic value, this vision could be projected into the utopian future as a mythical time beyond history.

Joachim Boeckh noted that reading Hölderlin as a prophet of a new age was the main inspiration for the intellectual and spiritual development of his Gau Königsbühl in the Bund der Köngener from being a small circle of friends with backgrounds in Bible study groups to becoming an integral part of the Bündische Jugend.

> As far as our history is concerned, I can report that the purity of his faith, the salient fullness and compelling clarity of his announcement of a new empire, his ... image of a waning night and coming day, his heated dedication to the fatherland, and his loving thankful praise of the Swabian homeland meant a totally incredible affirmation, overhaul and safeguard for four first dawning insights.[58]

More than any other German poet, Hölderlin had captured the coming empire as a new 'aeon' in its ancient meaning: not as a historically better future of Germany or as the coming of the Empire of Christ, but as a new dawn with new gods. Thus, for the Königsbühl youths, Hölderlin permeated an understanding of history beyond the linearity of (post-)Christian thought; an understanding that necessarily turned history back to the premises of mythology. Mythology was understood in its ancient meaning as well: neither logos nor mythos was seen as related to the modern autonomic subject as the domain of knowledge corresponding to reality or to imagination. Rather, with Hölderlin, logos and mythos were again understood in reference to the immaterial world of spirit that had primacy over the spatiotemporal world of physical existence. Logos, then, as the knowledge gained by man through thought and exploration, was the addendum of myth as revelation of immaterial truth. Mythos denotes the presence of the gods and the sacred signs of the spiritual world. As Hölderlin was regarded as a poet writing from a mythical vision and wrote in a language that eludes common logic, he could count as a visionary and his works could count as prophecy for the youth movement's quest for a 'spiritual homeland'.

The unstoppable drive for the creation of new forms, which was omnipresent in the youth movement's endeavours, thus drove on pre-Socratic metaphysics. It was youth's task to constitute new concrete forms of a spiritual Germany that was apt to the demands of time. But the constitution of form was not a voluntative act, but the organic moulding of order in which one could find oneself at home, just as one could find oneself as a member of the larger body of the *Bund*. The quest for the constitution of a new Germany was therefore necessarily a return to the origin of Germanness. As a large part of Germanness was shaped by philhellenism, this quest brought the youth movement to the shores of the Aegean Sea as well.

In the autumn of 1926, a group of Potsdam Neupfadfinder hiked in four weeks from Constantinople to Patras, although parts of the journey were undertaken by train and boat.[59] They visited every site on the Greek peninsula that was significant to German cultural memory. This included Athens, Delphi, Corinth, Tiryns, Sparta and Olympia. Here they found themselves in a situation of renegotiating the premises of the neo-humanist tradition in which they had been educated. 'A journey to the South', they wrote, 'has for the German since day one been the expression of a spiritual quest. He learns to understand himself anew through the sources of his culture. Thus, the motif of the presented journey to Hellas lies in the struggle to search spiritual possessions, and its objective lies in the deeper knowledge of the fatherland.'[60] For them, 'fatherland' meant 'the power of the young generation to relate immediately to the spiritual values that determine its nature'.[61] They thus understood the fatherland as a spiritual entity in ever-continuing need of appropriation and formation rather than a given and historically legitimated socio-political constellation. Every generation that was by a quirk of fate born in the sphere of influence of these spiritual values had the duty to take up the unending quest for appropriation.

The Neupfadfinder interpreted the Greek landscape they encountered in a similar way. To them, Greek landscape was 'a spiritual landscape of mysterious power' – not a space containing objects of interest, but a setting in which spirit dwells.[62] The colours of the landscape, its vegetation, light and air, all comprise this setting. What makes landscape, they acknowledged, was not its climate or geography, but the ungraspable intrinsic connection between Greek being and the surroundings from which it sprang and in which it dwelt. They captured this idea in the formula 'nature is spirit and spirit is nature'.[63] Such musings on landscape did not, however, take away the expectation to encounter a specific image of Greece. They also found out that they could not fully dispose of naive presumptions or of an idealized image of what they were about to encounter in Greece. But, whenever settings were encountered that were at odds with their expectations – such as contemporary Piraeus with its industrial chimneys, its gasometers and its electric railway – they had to confess to having buried 'foolish ideas as if the Athenian still looked up to his acropolis in piety'.[64] Yet, despite the omnipresence of the modern world and its liberal dogma of progress, the travellers contended that still 'the pure, intense sun remains victorious over this evolution of technique'.[65]

Overcoming prejudices did not so much mean bridging an apparent verge between ancient Greece and modern Greece, but meant detaching interest in the classical from veneration. After all, it was veneration that first constituted the abyss between present and past. They sought to understand Greece in its historicity rather than in its historical uniqueness. Entering modern Athens from the railway station, with its 'covetous crowd of tourist guides and car owners', did therefore not rouse the sense of historical discontinuity that has so often been described in modern travelogues in which disharmonious modern elements distorted a purported 'authenticity' of a historical site to the dismay of the travellers.⁶⁶ The metaphysical, yet mythical, quest of the Neupfadfinder, for the 'highest and eternal image of man' – a quest in which they saw themselves accompanied by the gods of Hellas – meant that the tourist industry and the modernity of the city were not regarded as inauthentic in the modern sense, but were seen as 'the first page of a new book' that they were to encounter in Greece.⁶⁷ Modernity was as much an expression of spirit as Greek heritage was. Therefore it could not be dissonant, for 'neither can the Athenian of our century live on pious memories'.⁶⁸ The way in which the Athenian lived outwards rather than inwards, the absence of a conscious proletariat and of class differences, and the omnipresence of political discussions meant that they did not see *essential* differences between the classical and the modern Athenian. Perhaps the only noticeable difference was the lack of a sense of art in modern Athens.

The Neupfadfinder had the most profound experience of classical Greece in Corinth – the 'most African of the Greek cities' – with its dazzling white primary light. There, above the excavations, stood the remnants of the sixth-century Temple of Apollo. The seven Doric pillars appeared as a 'monument of the most noble, pure antiquity'.⁶⁹ This pure antiquity was, again, pre-classical antiquity, which still had perfection as a trait rather than as an objective. It was this antiquity that was the homeland of youth: 'the presence of the phenomenon, which aroused a resonation in the heart without mediation of knowledge, was nowhere felt this profoundly'.⁷⁰ It was here that they confessed to themselves 'in silent agreement that Hellenism is a fate, with birth, completion and death, like ours, and that there is no formula for it but the formula of life'.⁷¹

The cycle of life, interpreted as a primordial temporality in relation to modern linear history, was not only deemed relevant because it related to a worldview preceding the classical concept of man that humanism dwelled on, but also because life cycles had immediate relevance for their own position as youths in an unsheltered society. The position of youth in the life cycle was equated with the position of pre-classical Greek art in the development of Greek history. The remnants of pre-classical antiquity, such as the Temple of Apollo at Corinth and the even older Mycenian excavations at Tiryns, were seen as part of the youth of Hellenic culture, full of vigour and potency, as captured in Homer's poetry, but not yet bothered with the high image of man which developed in the later centuries when Hellenic culture found its completion. Perhaps because 'every completion already carries with it the seed of death, the early Greek art, with its uncompleted promise, appeals so much more to our young generation in need of hope than the mature art of, for example, the fifth century [BC]'.⁷²

The discovery of Greece had a twofold meaning for the youth movement. First, it was the rediscovery of one of the main sources of German nationhood. The Potsdam Neupfadfinder duly noted growing up in times of identity crisis, but were grateful for the fact that they were educated by teachers who instilled the legacy of ancient Greece as one of the formative powers of German nationhood. The journey to Greece therefore became a journey to explore Hellas as a 'spiritual home' out of personal experience. Thus the old philhellene bond between ancient Greece and modern Germany was reinvigorated in order to gain clarity on the contemporary status of German nationhood.[73] Second, the journey to Greece became a renegotiation of the historical bonds between German national self-understanding and ancient Greece. Contrary to the views of the Weimar Classicism of the late eighteenth century and the neo-humanism of the early nineteenth century, Greece served not as the prime site of idealized humanity, but – hence the interest in pre-classical antiquity – as an origin and therefore an inspiration for a nascent Germany. Yet, it was an inspiration that was never completely finished.[74]

'Are we humanists, dreamers of a bygone world and deaf to the demands of time?', the Neupfadfinder wrote:

> We certainly do not hope so! We cling to this Greece ..., but not dogmatically – we see something different, something new in front of us, constellations and facts, tasks and goals, for the achievement of which one need not have seen Greece. But we have taken the liberty to see it, to see it our way. Others may travel to America and find there what we have found: oneself.[75]

## Nordland

Many groups in the Bündische Jugend took the liberty to travel to other destinations in search of themselves. Scandinavia stood at the other end of a North–South axis on which Germany balanced in the middle. The German obsession with the North was by no means the work of the youth movement or the Lebensreform movement. The world exhibitions and the polar expeditions of the late nineteenth century had spurred interest, but it was mainly Emperor Wilhelm II who generated public attention for the North.[76] The emperor made twenty-five well-covered trips to Scandinavia, styling himself as a Germanic monarch, thus constructing historical legitimacy for the young nation. According to many, it was the emperor himself who coined the term '*Nordland*'. This concept initially referred to Norway's North only, but soon became a mythical landscape that could range from Scotland to St Petersburg, thus transcending the borders of modern states in an imagined space of common descent.[77] In the German imagery of the North, *Nordland* was an Ossianic landscape, ideal for the projection of mythical Germanic imagery. It was the land of Germanic nativity, a land where Germanic culture and folklore were still alive.

This image of the North was widespread in the youth movement, but not necessarily connected to the Germanic phraseology or the racial ideology that was popular in some Lebensreform circles. Georg Götsch remarked after a journey to Norway with his Märkische Spielgemeinde in 1925 how they found 'people with that inner tranquillity and releasement, which in earlier centuries must also have been traits of us'.⁷⁸ It hints at a common origin, but was meant as an explanation of the Norwegian's receptiveness of the German Renaissance and baroque repertoire of the Märkische Spielgemeinde. Norway was understood as an active part of Western culture. But, Götsch remarked, contrary to Germany, they found Norway less well equipped to face the challenges of modernity. Norway had not experienced the same struggles, pain and devastation as Germany had, and the country, Götsch feared, was therefore unaware of the serious problems that modernity posed. Whenever a discussion became too serious or too substantial, his educated discussion partners tended to turn the conversation to lighter subjects. He feared discussing sorrowful subjects was a luxury for a small people of two million souls, living in a vast country with no enemies. As they were in a position to evade existential questions of life, death and survival, the main problems in Norway were the 'imagined' 'public' issues of, for example, party politics.

> They fight about unreal ideas, rather than shaping real life. They want to preserve the country's waterfalls in an unspoilt state, and are even aesthetic, they select from French, English and German culture the best and most pleasant, as if Europe is a cake, and close the eyes or pray in devout sects for those who are hopelessly lost when Europe fights a war. Norway is certainly not the only country exposed to this danger of one's precious self; Sweden, Denmark, Holland, Switzerland and recently also Austria – in sum the tribes whose essence is not more remote from the unified German essence than the Bavarian or Frisian essence – are exposed as well. Germanic man does not appear to gain culture by itself, on blessed isles, far from the compulsion, the error and the sinfulness of surging historical life – then he easily falls into satiety.⁷⁹

Norway, for Götsch, was certainly not what Julia Zernack once called a 'regressive Utopia' – an imagined landscape where pure, true and loyal Germanic life still dwells.⁸⁰ He basically reversed this logic: imagined and untrue was a Norwegian public life that drew on conceptions of selfhood and identity that were not rooted existentially, that could be fitted willingly to different situations to serve self-preservation. It was a false mode of being that served nothing but the possibility to evade self-reflection to evade constituting life anew according to inner, existential needs. Here, Götsch saw a task for the German youth movement: to establish *inner* bonds with Norway through ties with Norwegian youth. Only on such a basis could Norwegian and German boundaries be truly experienced.

Götsch's not being able to engage German origin through an encounter with the Norwegian people was luckily compensated by a deep experience of Norwegian nature. Hikes through the country's mountain valleys, over its hill moors and glaciers, along its fjords and becks, in sum: the engagement with a raging nature brought the members of the Märkische Spielgemeinde closer together and made them better comprehend their Germanness:

> Being pressed from all sides, we shrank together salutary to our true size and ordered in silent hours, shook or even startled our sense of self. The mountains of

Norway are not just high like the Alps, but are wide as well, aired the lust to rush to the top, retained unrest and unsubstantial activity, proved to be the ancient treasuries of sleep, the dreams of Europe, the surging, unfinished shapes of the future. Here we understood ourselves as a people from the middle of Europe, between Norway and Italy, between the idea, vision, legend and myth of the North and the art, thingness, artistic power and easiness of the South.[81]

However, not all branches of the youth movement could accept this position of Germany as a nation mediating between the North and the South. In the *völkisch-* or German-national-oriented youth associations, such as the Adler und Falken, the Jungnationale Bund and the Schilljugend, the Lebensreform imagery of the North did play a decisive role. It must be mentioned that these movements were not dogmatically *völkisch* in ideology because they did adhere to the Bündisch principle of autonomy. It was through the personal interest and orientation of the leadership and older members of these movements that in the group culture questions of race and eugenics were discussed.[82] Yet, in this way, ideas from the Lebensreform movement or of the 'Deutsche Bewegung' did make up a significant part of the cultural orientation of these *Bünde*. Their quest for *Heimat* was less spiritual and far more practical, and therefore also less concerned with bringing about a new 'aeon' than with the socio-political, economic and racial situation of the German *Volk* as such.

Erwin Friz recalled that, for the Adler und Falken especially, ancient Iceland was the object of longing. They frantically read Arhur Bonus's *Islanderbuch* (1907–1909), a three-volume collection of extracts from the great Icelandic sagas, as well as the many translations of Icelandic and Norwegian sagas and poetry that were published in Eugen Diederichs's Thule series under redaction of the Lebensreform journal *Der Kunstwart*.[83] The image of Iceland they derived from these sources was one where on the mythic Isle of Thule in the Viking era 'freedom-loving Germanic peoples, sailors and farmers – who had fled from Norway and tyrant rulers – had found a new, barren home'.[84] Because of this escape, the sagas they read counted as the written testimony of original Germanic life as it had been preserved and conserved in relative isolation on an island where Christianity only set foot in the eleventh century.

Such imagery was enhanced by the writings of Bernhard Kummer, a national-socialist Germanist with close personal ties to the Adler und Falken. His journal *Nordische Stimmen. Zeitschrift für nordisches Wesen und Gewissen* and his dissertation *Midgards Untergang* (1927) were widely read. In his dissertation, Kummer stated that there had not been a homogenous Germanic religion after the Migration Period. The martial cult of Wotan with the Einherjer and Valkyries were, according to him, based on imported cults related to the Huns. The older Germanic faith was more rooted to the soil, more connected to the *Heimat* and more peaceful. Rather than Wotan, Thor embodied this faith, as he gathered the men to save their *Heimat* Midgard against the evil forces of nature and other demonic powers.

Attracted by such beliefs, many members of the *völkisch* wing of the Bündische Jugend were drawn to the neo-pagan faith, the development of which is best illustrated by the example of the Nordungen – a small *Bund* with approximately one hundred to two hundred members, which had developed out of Otger Gräff's short-lived *völkisch* Greifenbund.[85] The Nordungen strove to transfer the experience of the youth movement into what they called a '*neugermanische Glaubensgemeinschaft*' – a neo-pagan community of faith. It was closely connected to the Germanische Glaubensgemeinschaft and many Lebensreform groups.[86] In the years before the First World War, the *völkisch* wing of the youth movement developed ideas that saw Christianity as a Mediterranean religion alien to the German people. They believed that Germanic values such as immutable loyalty, service and heroism had been dissolved by Christian creeds such as love and humility.

Of the numerous Germanic cults that existed in the *völkisch* movement, the Nordungen was the only association which was regarded to be part of the Bündische Jugend. Apart from the generational position and the fact that many of its early members came from Wandervogel circles, a main reason for regarding the Nordungen part of the youth movement was that they neither strove to implement preconceived Germanic values on their lifestyle nor to reconstruct a neo-pagan religion. Rather they wanted to provide 'Germanic being' with a 'joyful and secure faith in light' based on the Wandervogel experience.[87]

The religious leader of the Nordungen was Hildulf Flurschütz from Leipzig, who fuelled criticism of occultism by appearing in public in the black robe of a Germanic seer.[88] One of his religious rites included drumming the Hillebille – a wooden instrument similar to the Basque txalaparta. The rhythmic beat was meant to establish a connection with Wodan's heavenly hosts – a metaphor for the experience of the dissolution of the self in the totality of nature. The turn to the Germanic gods was to a large extent driven by the same need that drove the mainstream of the youth movement to the gods of Hölderlin and George: overcoming both modern objectivism with its philosophy of progress and the Christian eschatology of sin and repentance. The Nordungen found their alternative faith, based on 'vision and direct experience, not on external dogma and commandment', in Germanic mythology.[89]

They also visited the North. Alexander Boß, a member of the Nordungen, answered the question of why the North had such a strong attraction to German youth as follows:

> Because they – consciously and unconsciously – feel that it is a homeland up North, more pure and genuine than ours today. There in the lands up North, the soul of the Nordic man can live right in his own domain, in the forest, can still converse with himself and with the universe and can feel himself united with mother nature and God. There on the blue lakes, which free the mind and open the heart,

the voice of the Father of All still speaks audibly to the Nordic soul. There, the voice grasps with mighty force the vortex into the endless, in accordance with the infinite, like the architects of the Gothic cathedrals also felt, when they chiselled the Nordic soul – their own soul – into their creations.[90]

The quest for infinity, which was a central element in the youth movement's postwar eschatology, had been specified as a trait or an attitude of life of the Nordic soul in the *völkisch* youth movement. Landscape was understood cosmologically as a concrete given part of the universe in which a people found themselves in relation to the gods. Yet, when Boß visited Sweden, he was less concerned with getting to know how the Swedes dwelt in such surroundings than with recognizing the truth of his Germanic worldview. He visited the old university library of Uppsala, where two valuable books were held: the Snorri-Edda, 'which tells of the times in which man was still rooted in his own being', and the flaunty Codex Argenteus, the fourth-century Gothic Bible translation, 'which brought the alien God to the Nordland'.[91] For him, German origin was not defined by its axial position in the middle of Europe, but was bound to the North, from which the Christian forces from the South had wrongfully tried to lead it away.

Criticism from within the youth movement of the *völkisch* engagement with the North was neither directed against the North itself, nor against an engagement with ancient Germanic culture. It was, after all, undeniable that Nordic-Germanic heritage was an essential source of German culture and thus as valuable as a source for prospects as Greece was to others. The engagement with the North became problematic when values such as 'purity' were over-idealized and attributed merely to a Germanic primordial age. Implying such beliefs implicitly meant adhering to the belief that a specific *Zeitgeist* was at work in history, which forms ages on its own accord and neglects common origin. This line of thought neglected the Nordic element of Germanic traits in Renaissance art and baroque music, in the variety of Gothic forms of the Middle Ages and in Romantic literature. In all these cultural forms 'one must acknowledge that what is homebred, truly Nordic, for not derived from thought, is culture created out of a specific attitude'.[92]

The early 1930s saw a new wave in the popular imagination of the North in the youth movement. This was mainly the work of Eberhard Köbel (nicknamed 'tusk'). Köbel – an old Wandervogel and later member of the Deutsche Freischar – established the Deutsche Jungenschaft vom 1.11.1929 (dj.1.11) in, not surprisingly, 1929. This *Bund* for teenagers intended to become a vehicle for creating a reorientation in the youth movement, as by the end of the 1920s the cultural forms and activities of the Bündische Jugend had become so self-evident for the younger generation that it was hard to associate with them emotionally, or to understand its meaning.[93] Köbel had also initiated a renewal of the style and content of the youth movement's magazines as the editor of the magazine *Briefe an die deutsche Jungenschaft*. Not only were the typography and layout of the magazines modernized, but the writing style of the travelogues as well. The emotional and philosophical ruminations which had been a central element of youth movement literature for two decades were replaced by a clear writing style, and by articles in which impressions and adventures dominated. Other innovations included the introduction of a new characteristic blouse, the introduction of the balalaika and the banjo and the *Kohte*, a conical tent based on the design of the traditional tents of the nomadic Sami people of northern Scandinavia. Köbel's fascination for Scandinavia was also triggered by the nomadic culture of the Sami, amongst whom he had lived for three months in 1927. His zeal for the North was less culturally inspired than that of other youth groups: 'Culture and taste – we have it better and more in Germany. ... And we have preserved more vikingness than all Scandinavians together'.[94] What drew him to the North were not visits to museums or monuments, but a visit to 'the border of civilization'.[95] A 1931 trip would take him even further into the wilderness: to the Russian island Novaya Zemlya.

In Köbel's dj.1.11, the glorification of military virtues such as loyalty and sacrifice reached an apex; local branches were called 'garrisons', its younger members 'budding warriors' and the virtues and traditions – including ritual suicide – of the Japanse samurai were amongst Köbel's sources of inspiration.[96] Yet, the history of Köbel and the dj.1.11 is indicative of the very troublesome relationship between the Bündische Jugend and the rising National Socialist Party. Köbel was a nationalist, who in the mid-1920s admired Hitler and even visited him in Munich in 1925. Köbel once noted that there were two ways to unify German youth: by the inner powers of youth, or by external intervenience. As the first option still remained without result, the second was left. But because the liberal state had failed as well, Hitler remained the only option. Köbel urged the Jungenschaft to join the Hitler Jugend, and he himself tried to seize a leadership position. Yet, in 1932 Köbel had joined the German Communist Party (Kommunistische Partei Deutschlands) and had actively recruited in the youth movement for political involvement on the other side of the political spectrum, leaving later commentators with the problem of whether he was an opportunist or a resistance fighter.[97]

In 1934, Köbel was arrested by the Gestapo for his communist activities and writings, which were considered to be a threat to the Hitler Jugend, only to be released because the Nazis feared he would become a martyr after two suicide attempts.[98] While Köbel escaped to England in 1934, the various *Bünde* of the Bündische Jugend had either been forbidden or *gleichgeschaltet* (brought into line). Baldur von Schirach – Hitler's *Reichsjugendführer* since 1931 – characterized the *Bünde* as the 'enemies' of National Socialism in 1933, an allegation that was invigorated by Nazi propaganda discrediting the *Bünde* for their – sometimes alleged, sometimes factual – homosexualism.[99] Yet, some *Bünde* voluntarily merged into the Hitler Jugend, while others disbanded and others continued illegally or even partook in resistance. No clear patterns are visible, just as it is hard to find any correlation between participation in the youth movement and adherence or opposition to the Nazi cause on the level of individual biographies.[100] It would however be interesting to compare the youth movement's understanding of history with the central role of direct experience and community to that of the Hitler Jugend – bearing in mind that this too would be a question of correlation and not of causation. Unfortunately, this question lies beyond the scope of this study.

## Conclusion

As a result of the changed conception of history in the youth movement, utopian expectations were increasingly grasped in spatial terms. Foreign destinations functioned as sites that could lead back to the German origin. This origin was not situated in a historically distant past, but was defined in spatial terms as something that one *is* through destiny. When German origin was situated in the Bavarian borderlands, in German colonies in Hungary and Romania, or in Greece, this meant that these were environments where destiny opened up ways to find the origin of what it meant to be German. Being at sites that could expose or bring forth what it meant to be German, a German origin that had already been could become a future prospect. This was the utopian value of the youth movement's international journeys in the 1920s and early 1930s. They attested to what art historian August Wiedmann called a contingent 'primalism' – the restoration of man's primary ties to his fellow men, to nature, to life, and to the 'Great Beyond', based 'on the belief that the deeper one cuts through the historically accumulated 'crusts' of thinking, sensing, feeling – of society, culture and religion – the closer one approaches the original core of things, the truth and the mystery of life'.[101]

Visiting the abroad thereby meant renegotiating a position vis-à-vis tradition. Germany was found to be the centre of a North–South axis and an East–West axis. Whereas the East–West axis was primarily important for an understanding of current politics, the North–South axis was historically important. Visits to the North meant renegotiating a stance towards Germanic heritage; travelling to the South meant a confrontation with humanism. However, because the past was not believed to be a domain of historical deeds that constituted the present, it was not something from which an identity could be derived. What they found on their hikes were historical forms of nations that had realized themselves in specific epochs, and that prompted them with the need to generate a new Germany in accord with European destiny.

The tragedy of the youth movement was perhaps that, despite its many achievements, such a specific form was never found. Still in 1929, Josef Köning remarked that 'the right form has not yet been found for what lies behind nature and World; they only sense the metaphysical'.[102] Those involved in the youth movement perhaps remained, as Albrecht von Fritsch called it, 'amateur philosophers'.[103] They took pride in not being understood by their Norwegian, British or Hungarian conversational partners, and considered this to be the proof that the German character was originally spiritual, and that it was their duty to find the tasks for the realization of that spirituality proper to their own time. But they did so on the basis of an understanding of history that was so remarkably consistent and so at odds with modern historical consciousness that even the words 'originally spiritual' must be read out of the context of a logic that thinks of origin as being rooted in historical time. For them, origin was rooted in eternity – ever in need of realization.

## Notes

1. Virgil, *Aeneid* III: 96.
2. For an explanation of Apollo's riddle, see: Clara Shaw Hardy, 'Antiqua Mater: Misreading Gender in "Aeneid" 3.84–191', *The Classical Journal* 92(1) (1996), 1–8.
3. Kurd Lähn, *Von der geistigen Heimat deutscher Jugend* (Plauen: Gunther Wolff, 1933), 10.
4. Ibid., 10, 11.
5. Ibid., 15.
6. Ibid., 20.
7. On the modern temporalization of Utopia, see: Lucian Hölscher, 'Utopie', in Otto Brunner, Werner Conze and Reinhart Koselleck (eds), *Geschichtliche Grundbegriffe. Historisches Lexikon zur politisch-sozialen Sprache in Deutschland. Vol. VI* (Stuttgart: Klett-Cotta, 1990), 583–671; Reinhart Koselleck, 'The Temporalization of Utopia', in Reinhart Koselleck (ed.), *The Practice of Conceptual History: Timing History, Spacing Concepts* (Stanford, CA: Stanford University Press, 2002), 84–99.
8. Paul Tillich, 'Die politische Bedeutung der Utopie im Leben der Völker', in Renate Albrecht (ed.), *Gesammelte Werke, Bd. 6* (Stuttgart: Evangelisches Verlagswerk, 1963), 157–210.
9. Ibid., 173.
10. Heinz Rocholl, *Englandfahrt 1909 und 1927. Ein Beitrag zur Geschichte der deutschen Jugendbewegung* (Potsdam: Voggenreiter, 1929), 77–86.
11. Cf. Alice Gräfin Hardenberg, *Bündische Jugend und Ausland* (Munich: Uni-Druck, 1966), 15–16.
12. Cf. Ernst Buske, 'Die außenpolitische Schulung der Bündischen Jugend', *Deutsche Freischar* 2 (1928), 111ff.
13. Cf. R. Kneip, *Jugend zwischen den Kriegen – Eine Sammlung von Aussagen und Dokumenten* (Heidenheim: Südmarkverlag Fritsch, 1967), 63ff.; Peter E. Nasarski, 'Aufbruch der Jugend im Grenz- und Ausland', in Peter E. Nasarski (ed.), *Deutsche Jugendbewegung in Europa. Versuch einer Bilanz* (Cologne: Verlag Wissenschaft und Politik, 1967), 19–24: 22.
14. Ernst Michler, Hans Burkart and Hans Dehmel, 'Freideutsche Tausendschaft für den Grenzschutz!', in Kindt, *Die Wandervogelzeit*, 940–41.
15. Erich Maschke, *Ostland* (Berlin: Der Weiße Ritter Verlag, 1922), 16.
16. Ibid., 16.
17. Cf. Hans Freiherr von Rosen, *Wolhynienfahrt 1926* (Siegen: J.G. Herder-Bibliothek Siegerland, 1982).
18. Kneip, *Wandervogel*, 93–108.
19. 'Pfingsten – Gautag – Heerschau!', *Der Jungenbund* (1923), 5–8. Cf. Kneip, *Wandervogel*, 96.

20. Cited in: Kneip, *Wandervogel*, 99.
21. Cited in: ibid., 99.
22. Cited in: ibid., 99.
23. Kurt R. Mattusch, 'Auf dem Weg zum grossen Bund', in Will Vesper (ed.), *Deutsche Jugend. 30 Jahre Geschichte einer Bewegung* (Berlin: Holle & Co., 1934), 103–20.
24. Ibid., 119.
25. 'Auslandsfahrten selbständiger Wandervogelgruppen', printed in: Hardenberg, *Bündische Jugend und Ausland*, 33–34.
26. Rocholl, *Englandfahrt 1909 und 1927*, 5.
27. Friederike Stuke, *Die Auslandsfahrten der Bündischen Jugend am Beispiel der Sächsischen Jungenschaft. Zwischen Selbsterfahrung, 'Volkstumpflege' und transnationaler Annährung (1920–1934)*. Master's thesis (Leipzig: Universität Leipzig, 2008), 37–45.
28. Hardenberg, *Bündische Jugend und Ausland*, 37.
29. Kneip, *Jugend zwischen den Kriegen*, 69.
30. Hardenberg, *Bündische Jugend und Ausland*, 26.
31. *Die Grosse Fahrt des Bundes der Reichspfadfinder nach Lettland. Sommer 1928*, (Plauen i.Br: Das Junge Volk, 1929), 15.
32. Ibid., 16.
33. *Grenzfeuer der vereinigten deutschen Jugendbünde im Fichtelgebirge am 3. u. 4. Erntings 1923*, 4–5.
34. Ibid., 5.
35. *Die Grosse Fahrt des Bundes der Reichspfadfinder nach Lettland. Sommer 1928*, 20.
36. Ibid., 20.
37. Ibid., 21.
38. Ibid., 21.
39. Historiographical interest in Gardiner has mainly focused on his positive attitude to Nazi Germany – only recently has Gardiner been valued for his work for international fraternization in the interwar period. Cf. Malcolm Chase, '"North Sea and Baltic": Historical Conceptions in the Youth Movement and the Transfer of Ideas from Germany to England in the 1920s and 1930s', in Stefan Berger, Peter Lambert and Peter Schumann (eds), *Historikerdialoge. Geschichte, Mythos und Gedächtnis im deutsch-britischen kulturellen Austausch 1750–2000* (Göttingen: Vandenhoeck & Ruprecht, 2003), 309–30; David Fowler, 'Rolf Gardiner: Pioneer of British Youth Culture, 1920–1939', in Matthew Jefferies and Michael Tyldesley (eds), *Rolf Gardiner: Folk, Nature and Culture in Interwar Britain* (Farnham, Surrey: Ashgate, 2011), 17–46.
40. Laqueur, *Young Germany*, 241.
41. Rolf Gardiner, 'Meditations on the Future of Northern Europe', in Rolf Gardiner and Heinz Rocholl (eds), *Britain and Germany: A Frank Discussion Instigated by Members of the Younger Generation* (London: Williams and Norgate, 1928), 121–32: 121.
42. Ibid., 122.
43. Ibid., 122.
44. Ibid., 131.
45. Ibid., 131.
46. Halkett (pseud. Albrecht von Fritsch), *The Dear Monster*, 189.
47. Ibid., 189.
48. Georg Götsch, 'Englandfahrt 1926', in Georg Götsch (ed.), *Musische Bildung 2: Bericht* (Wolfenbüttel: Karl Heinrich Möseler, 1953), 72–102: 94.
49. Georg Götsch, 'Germany between Russia and England', in Gardiner and Rocholl, *Britain and Germany*, 93–104: 103.
50. Ibid.
51. Götsch, 'Englandfahrt 1926', 97.
52. Wolfgang Mann, 'The Past as Future? Hellenism, the Gymnasium, and Altertumswissenschaft', in Randall Curren (ed.), *A Companion to the Philosophy of Education* (Malden, MA: Blackwell, 2003), 143–60: 152.

53. Walter Jens, 'The Classical Tradition in Germany: Grandeur and Decay', in E.J. Feuchtwanger (ed.), *Upheaval and Continuity: A Century of German History* (Letchworth: The Garden City Press, 1973), 67–82: 71.
54. Seidelmann, *Bund und Gruppe als Lebensformen deutscher Jugend*, 304.
55. Eduard Spranger, *Der gegenwärtige Stand der Geisteswissenschaften und die Schule* (Leipzig: B.G. Teubner, 1922), 10.
56. Seidelmann, *Bund und Gruppe als Lebensformen deutscher*, 305.
57. 'Aus den Blättern des Führerkreises Wandervogel/Norddeutscher Bund', *Philosophie der Jungen. Sonderheft Der Weiße Ritter* (1922), 150–51.
58. Joachim G. Boeckh, 'Schicksal Königsbühl', in Kindt, *Die deutsche Jugendbewegung 1920 bis 1933*, 228–37: 233.
59. Seidelmann, *Gruppe – soziale Grundform der Jugend*, 123–24.
60. Ernst Lehmann and Herbert Lehmann, *Hellas: Tagebuch einer Reise* (Potsdam: Voggenreiter, 1929), 7.
61. Ibid., 7.
62. Ibid., 16. Cf. Hubert Cancik, 'Jugendbewegung und klassische Antike (1901–1933)', in Bernd Seidensticker (ed.), *Urgeschichten der Moderne: die Antike im 20. Jahrhundert* (Stuttgart: Metzler, 2001), 114–35: 120.
63. Lehmann and Lehmann, *Hellas: Tagebuch einer Reise*, 47.
64. Ibid., 19.
65. Ibid., 19.
66. Ibid., 20.
67. Ibid., 13.
68. Ibid., 20.
69. Ibid., 54.
70. Ibid., 54.
71. Ibid., 54.
72. Ibid., 63.
73. Ibid., 8.
74. Mann, 'The Past as Future?'.
75. Lehmann and Lehmann, *Hellas: Tagebuch einer Reise*, 115.
76. Silke Göttsch-Elten, 'Populäre Bilder vom Norden im 19. und 20. Jahrhundert', in Annelore Engel-Braunschmidt et al. (eds), *Ultima Thule: Bilder des Nordens von der Antike bis zur Gegenwart* (Frankfurt am Main: Lang, 2001), 123–43: 140–41. Cf. Birgit Marschall, *Reisen und Regieren: die Nordlandfahrten Kaiser Wilhelms II* (Heidelberg: C. Winter, 1991).
77. Göttsch-Elten, 'Populäre Bilder vom Norden im 19. und 20. Jahrhundert', 141.
78. Georg Götsch, *Aus dem Lebens- und Gedankenkreis eines Jugendchores. Jahresbericht 1925 der Märkischen Spielgemeinde* (Wolfenbüttel: Georg Kallmeyer, 1926), 30.
79. Ibid., 32.
80. Julia Zernack, 'Anschauungen vom Norden im deutschen Kaiserreich', in Uwe Puschner, Walter Schmitz and Justus H. Ulbricht (eds), *Handbuch zur 'Völkischen Bewegung'* (Munich: Saur, 1996), 483.
81. Götsch, *Aus dem Lebens- und Gedankenkreis eines Jugendchores*, 30.
82. Erwin Friz, *Adler und Falken 1920–1935: Bündische Jugend* (Oldenburg: Erwin Friz, 1990), 43.
83. Arthur Bonus, *Islanderbuch. Sammlung altgermanischer Bauern- und Königsgeschichten I-III* (Munich: Callwey, 1907). On the Thule series, see: Julia Zernack, 'Der "Mythos vom Norden" und die Krise der Moderne. Skandinavische Literatur im Programm des Eugen Diederichs Verlages', in Meike Werner and Justus H. Ulbricht (eds), *Romantik, Revolution und Reform. Der Eugen Diederichs Verlag im Epochenkontext 1900 bis 1945* (Göttingen: Wallstein Verlag, 1999), 208–23.
84. Friz, *Adler und Falken 1920–1935*, 77.
85. Ulrich Nanko, *Die Deutsche Glaubensbewegung: eine historische und soziologische Untersuchung* (Marburg: Diagonal, 1993), 48.

86. Ibid., 46–48.
87. Cited in: Ehrenthal, *Die deutschen Jugendbünde*, 52.
88. Nanko, *Die Deutsche Glaubensbewegung*, 47.
89. Hildulf Rudolf Flurschütz, *Vom Wesen und Werden junggermanischen Glaubens* (Berlin-Lichterfelde: Germanen-Verlag, 1926), 31.
90. Alexander Boß, 'Nordlandfahrt. Gedanken und Erlebnisse aus meinem Fahrtenbuche', *Der Zwiespruch* 7(93) (1925), 382.
91. Ibid., 382.
92. Hans Rütting, 'Vom Sinn der Gemeinschaft. Eine zeitgemässe Betrachtung', *Der Zwiespruch* 8(52/53) (1926), 381–84: 382–83.
93. Werner Kindt, 'Deutsche autonome Jungenschaft (dj.1.11)', in Kindt, *Die deutsche Jugendbewegung 1920 bis 1933*, 1197–99: 1197.
94. Eberhard Köbel, 'Fahrtbericht 29 (Lappland)', in Fritz Schmidt (ed.), *Tusk. Gesammelte Schriften und Dichtungen* (Stuttgart: Verlag der Jugendbewegung, 1996), 83–123; 91.
95. Ibid.
96. Laqueur, *Young Germany*, 168. For Köbel's reception of Japan, see: Müller, '"Das Leben ist nicht mehr als Maienblüte" – Eberhard Koebels Japanrezeption', in Franziska Ehmcke, Andreas Niehaus and Chantal Weber (eds), *Reisen, Dialoge, Begegnungen. Festschrift für Franziska Ehmcke* (Berlin: Lit, 2012), 129–48.
97. Ferdinand Horst, 'Eberhard Köbel', in Bernd Ottnad (ed.), *Baden-Württembergische Biographien 1* (Stuttgart: Kohlhammer, 1994), 194–97: 196.
98. Silvia Klein and Bernhard Stelmaszyk, 'Eberhard Köbel, "tusk". Ein biographisches Porträt über die Jahre 1907–1945', in Matthias von Hellfeld and Wilfried Breyvogel (eds), *Piraten, Swings, und Junge Garde. Jugendwiderstand im Nationalsozialismus* (Bonn: Dietz, 1991), 102–37: 129.
99. Ulrich Herrmann, *Von der HJ-Führung zur weißen Rose. Hans Scholl vor dem Stuttgarter Sondergericht 1937/38* (Weinheim: Beltz Juventa, 2012), 23; Arno Klönne, 'Jugendliche Subkulturen im Dritten Reich', in Michael Andritzky (ed.), *Schock und Schöpfung – Jugendästhetik im 20. Jahrhundert* (Darmstadt: Luchterhand, 1986), 308–13: 311.
100. Stambolis, 'Einleitung', 21.
101. Wiedmann, *The German Quest for Primal Origins*, 4.
102. Joseph König, *Das Ethos der Jugendbewegung in Deutschland mit besonderer Berücksichtigung der freideutschen Jugendbewegung* (Düsseldorf: Schwann, 1929), 19.
103. Halkett (pseud. Albrecht von Fritsch), *The Dear Monster*, 97..

# Conclusion

In this study I have examined which dominant conceptions of history and time circulated in the German Youth Movement between 1900 and 1933, how they developed and how they related to historical representations and to historical experience. In this concluding chapter I will summarize and synthesize the main findings.

In the nineteenth century, modernity implied that history had become the prime referential framework for interpreting the world, and with it the primacy of reason was affirmed. A major outcome of my research is that in the interwar period the youth movement believed that overcoming modernity required something more fundamental than an image of a better future inspired by the past: it required a revision of the very premises of the modern 'worldview'. In the *lived* experience of the various joint hiking tours, dances and celebrative commemorations of the youth movement – articulated in diaries, reports and articles – the past appeared as something independent of human agency, but as the storage for different expressions of the eternal task of man to cope with destiny. The orientation towards the 'eternal' was the youth movement's answer to the 'crisis of historicism'. Making the 'eternal' spatially present in new social and cultural forms was the mission that the 'amateur philosophers' of the youth movement had bestowed upon themselves. The reference to the eternal rather than the historical is what made the postwar youth movement part of the 'Conservative Revolution'.

★

In 1935, the sociologist Hans Freyer looked back on his days in the Sera circle: 'when at the beginning of this century the youth movement arose, every one of us who was present back then had the distinct feeling that we were the carriers of a revolution, and that this new revolution was the dawn of a new era'.[1] Freyer did not refer to the common understanding of revolution as socio-political upheaval which tries to replace an outmoded social or political order with a new one. He explicitly stated that this kind of revolution cannot be comprehended in the conventional mode of historical thinking as a progressive development, because this was precisely what the youth movement revolted against: the 'conventional' conception of history. Freyer conveniently equated the object of the 'revolution' with the nineteenth century. The nineteenth century was 'bourgeois society, it was capitalism, it was the idolization of technique; it was – to paraphrase Nietzsche, who started to have effect in those days – cultural philistinism and the incapability of creative culture'.[2] But at the core of all these repudiated phenomena stood the 'spirit' of that century, which was essentially the unbridled self-evidency of progress and the tendency to understand the world as the exponent of the historical development of mankind. Rejecting the historical a priori of the *Weltanschauung* of historicism, it was clear for Freyer that the revolution did not simply strive to replace the old bourgeois worldview with a new worldview or value system. This would merely mean operating within the historicist framework, presuming the necessity of historical development and the unilinearity of the historical process. It would still confirm the historicist axiom that history only develops by qualifying the previous condition as qualitatively 'old'.

Therefore, Freyer argued, the German youth movement not only aimed at a reinterpretation of the past, but at a revision of the very premises of historical thought. The struggle was not about changing the course of history or fostering historical consciousness, but about the rise of what Freyer called a historical *self*-consciousness – an existential consciousness that does not entail an awareness of the past (like the notion historical consciousness), but an awareness of the problematic relationship between the self and the past. It is this relationship that was in need of reconfiguration. 'Not just the theoretical, but the practical relation of the present to history, the relation between life and the past recasts itself. Not only history's contents, but also its historicity is experienced differently.'[3] Only on the basis of a historical self-consciousness did the youth movement turn to the past again; neither to look for a historical affirmation for the forms of the existing social world, nor to find a *historical* legitimacy for new utopias, but as a ground for human agency in the present. 'This is neither historicism, nor just historical consciousness. It is rather living tradition, an existential embedding of contemporary life in its own origins.'[4]

Freyer called the broader intellectual movement that the German youth movement was part of, and in which these vitalist conceptions of history developed, a 'revolution from the right'.[5] It was his firm belief that this revolution did not commence with the implementation or realization of a specific philosophy of the necessary clash of historical forces, like all previous philosophies of revolution had done. Rather, it had to commence with the very literal 'embodiment' of changing times, for only when those who are free of mind 'represent historically changing times in their existential presence', can something be accomplished which no revolution before had achieved: transcending the principle of struggle because the coming age stopped defining itself in negative terms vis-à-vis the old.[6]

When defining what was to become known as the 'Conservative Revolution', Freyer started by elaborating on exactly that aspect that later critics – such as Stefan Breuer – seem to have forgotten: the fact that Weimar Germany was a laboratory for experimenting with different kinds of temporality. The 'Conservative Revolutionary' aspect of the youth movement becomes quite clear during the 1920s, when the Bündische Jugend radically renounced the alterity of the past. But to trace this conception of history back to the pre-war youth movement, as Freyer did, seems a bit overdone.

The pre-war Wandervogel still considered the past to be a historical past, in which the 'historical' had already lost the liberal undertone of progressive development in favour of ideas of organic development. But it was nonetheless a distant past. While cognition was rejected for being one of the causes of the past appearing as temporally distant due to objectification, this distance could be bridged through direct experience which was actively cultivated in hiking to heritage sites, historical commemorations and folklore. By apprehending such sites and traditions in its embeddedness in the lifeworld without cognitive mediation, the historical appeared as part of a continuous 'stream' of life, rather than as an object of consciousness. Thus, *Erlebnis* bridged the gap between present and past, and underlined the value of tradition in the present. It is therefore too easy to renounce the emphasis on experience and the cultivation of folklore within the youth movement as a mere 'escape' from modernity into the past. The idea of escape holds true when the past that one seeks has no actual value. One then closes the eyes to the problems of the present and indulges in bygone times in order to fence off the responsibilities of the present. The appropriation of the past through experience was, however, primarily intended as a moral mission. The emphasis that the youth movement put on the responsibility to fashion one's own life, as laid down in the Meißner formula, had as its primary task the self-education of personality. One could gain personality when one was able to apprehend the world in relative freedom from transmitted frameworks of interpretation. In sum, one could gain personality on the basis of being able to experience the world directly. Experience was therefore also an educational concept.

The First World War caused significant changes in this understanding of history that was a peculiar mixture of idealism and vitalism. First, the war provided the experience of a people's community. The experience of August 1914 was formative for the belief that an 'inner' sense of Germanness had arrived to replace the Wilhelmine patriotism of 'outer' manifestations. But when Germany's fate in the war turned and the initial enthusiasm made way for horror and disillusionment, the belief that form and content had finally merged faded. The war changed from being a new beginning to being the final struggle of the 'old'

Europe. Nevertheless, the war had put the bourgeois Wandervogel in contact with the working class, and the experience of the dissolution of social stratifications in the army contributed to the concept of *Volksgemeinschaft*, which transcended all social classes. Second, the war strengthened the awareness that the personal problems that were experienced with the school or with parents were social problems that demanded social answers. This ignited the idea that the youth movement had a mission to fulfil, which would result in various social projects after the war. Third, definite loss of faith in progress, as well as the existential experience of death, resulted in a longing for metaphysical certainty. A strong sense of religiosity developed in what remained up until the war an areligious youth movement. This religiosity was not, however, dogmatic, and had nothing to do with the church as an institution, but was related to experience. Experience did now relate to the communal and the eternal, which had significant consequences for the conception of history.

After the war, experience lost its lustre when related to personality, and rather than rethinking the way in which to individually apprehend the past, the premises on which one could think historically were revised. Although it is common in modernity to define one's identity in relation to the past, the postwar youth movement rather developed a meta-critique of modern historical thought, historical consciousness, and the 'historicist' worldview. The reason for the rise of this meta-critique, which Freyer called historical self-consciousness, was that during the war faith in the moral agency of man – on which the youth movement's educational programme had been built – was shattered when the initial faith in the establishment of a *Volksgemeinschaft* in August 1914 appeared to be false. Because man's moral agency is one of the main presumptions of modern historical thought, the lack of faith in this agency resulted in a lack of faith in the very system of historical thought, rather than just in the course of history.

The pantheistic religiosity that developed during the war radically renounced the differentness of the past, present and future, as all temporal and historical forms were now seen as expressions of the eternal, of God, the gods, of the All, or the cosmos. Whatever word one used to refer to irrepresentable 'eternity' was of secondary importance because it laid beyond the comprehensible. It nonetheless formed the ground or source of life. This idea of history reintroduced the concepts of fate and destiny, and gave them actual value. Furthermore, after 1918, those aspects of culture that had only temporary value, such as capitalism, formalism and individualism, were rejected as being forms without content – expressions of nothing significant but the short-term advancement of social and material gains.

With the rise of this religiosity, the youth movement's conception of time changed significantly between approximately 1917 and 1921. Before the war, the unilinearity of historical time was unequivocally accepted, but it was the positivist, intellectualist and Prussianist appropriation of a distant past which was challenged and replaced by an appropriation based on experience. During and after the war, the unilinearity of historical time was itself called into question, urging the search for a new metaphysics and a new religiosity. Although this search did not result in religious doctrines, it did form the basis for an understanding of history in which heritage was understood as a temporal actualization of universal ideas. The autonomy of the subject was abandoned, lost categories such as 'fate' regained meaning, and the past was no longer 'strange' or 'foreign'. In this conservative mind-set, the past is ever present in our habits, speech, customs, rituals and institutions. To gain insight in the past does not imply the appropriation of something alien, but the uncovering of the alien as already present.

The turn towards the eternal was expressed in what I have called an 'immanent eschatology', which was the intuitive expectation that a new age was dawning. Because of the turn towards the eternal, this new age was neither something to be established by man, for this would affirm the premises of modern historical consciousness, nor was it clear how exactly this age could come about. In the immediate postwar years, tendencies in the youth movement ranged from a revolutionary activism to a mystical fatalism; and with an absence of concrete goals, the organizational structures of the Wandervogel and the Freideutsche Jugend broke down. In the development from Wandervogel to Bündische Jugend we witnessed a development from experiencing the past as an object for individual moral development into an experience of the past as an entry into the eternal. Under the influence of a number of rogue Boy Scout associations, which reinvented their own identity in line with the Wandervogel ideology, apart from adult guidance, the concept of *Bund* developed as the notion that conveyed the voluntary subordination to an overarching totality, in which the totality and the individual mutually constituted each other. This idea of *Bund* became a model for new organizational forms of the youth movement, as well as the model for visions of political and social organization of a 'new' Germany. The imagery that accompanied these visions was often drawn from the Middle Ages.

The appropriation of the Middle Ages in the Bündische Jugend was based on images such as the knight, which did not represent a particular history, but symbolically disclosed a world that had actual value. With Hans-Ulrich Gumbrecht we could say that these images 'produced' 'presence'. When we recall that Gumbrecht uses the term 'production' in its Latin meaning of 'bringing forth' objects in space, we can understand the value of such disclosure.[7] Since the early 1910s the youth movement had already opposed the 'meaning' aspect of modern society. At various stages in the movement's history, the school, positivism, and modernity in general were criticized for reducing the world to that which could be grasped cognitively. In *Erlebnis* the world appeared in a pre-rational way, had presence, and touched upon the body without cognitive representation. But while in the Wandervogel days, the presence of the world – and also the presence of the past – was 'discovered' and *Erlebnis* was cultivated as an unburdened path away from meaning-filled society, the Bündische Jugend wanted to change the world and used 'presence effects' as a tool to make the experienced non-rational bond of community bodily palpable for an audience. Making such a bond present bore the character of a revelation instead of an interpretation, and the youth movement presented itself as the initiator of such revelations.

But 'changing' the world based on the revelation of certain truths implies that 'change' is not the result of the autonomous action of man. Rather, the youth movement conceived change as giving an eternal substance a new temporal form. This is why the Middle Ages were so relevant to the youth movement, for this was an age that sought to do the same in different times and under different circumstances. The Gothic cathedrals were not only symbols, but also reminders of the possibility to make the eternal actual in the present. The Middle Ages were thus something different from an era with which one could identify. This was an era in which a particular attitude to the world was dominant. This attitude – which comprised faith, the presence of the sacred and holy life as the embodiment of eternal ideas – was relevant in a world that appeared to be deprived of faith in the absolute, and hinged on the false certitude of subjective cognition. The case of the youth movement supports Peter Raedts' thesis that the longing for authenticity and community 'is not about anti-modernity or marginality, [but] is a story about a second type of modernity'.[8] Yet, for the nineteenth-century cases of medievalism that Raedts studied, the Middle Ages were the *historical* proof that harmonious community laid within the realm of the humanly possible and realizable. However, the rejection of historicism after the First World War and the return of religious and metaphysical thought – combined with the vitalist emphasis on life in the here and now – resulted in a different relevance of the Middle Ages. For the German youth movement, the Middle Ages were not valued for their *historical* content – as if harmony and community could be an 'effect' of a specific historical social organization – but for being an era in which there was no possibility to have individualistic or disharmonious thoughts because there was no subjectivity. In the relevance of the Middle Ages, the 'Conservative Revolutionary' character of the Bündische Jügend's conception of time becomes clear: this is neither progressive time, nor cyclical time insofar as the image of the cycle depends on Euclidean geometry.

When Gumbrecht writes that in presence cultures people do not want to transform the world like in meaning cultures, but aim at 'inscribing their bodies … into the rhythms of cosmology', we immediately recognize the round dances of Friedrich Lamberty.[9] Here, the ring that was formed was itself the symbol of the eternal, and 'swinging on the rhythm of eternity' was an experience in which the bodily movement of swinging was in harmony with the 'swinging' of the soul. The same accounts for other 'presence effects' initiated by the youth movement, such as the *Laienspiel* in which one did not play a role, but performed community.

The emphasis on presence resulted in a dominance of space over time. This became clear in the utopian function of foreign hikes in the 1920s and 1930s. Many of these hikes were framed as journeys to the origin. In the presence-oriented culture of the Bündische Jugend, utopia was a spatial utopia – not a spatial representation or projection of a better world, but the spatial disclosure of what once has been as a new prospect. Thus both Greek and Norwegian landscapes could bear the presence of the gods, and the origin of German character. And although such contemplations are basically essentialist, we have to bear in mind that this essentialism was no historical essentialism – nor were they coherent theories or interpretation, but often attempts to attribute meaning to experience. Although Gumbrecht's ideal types are based on a dichotomy between mind-centred 'meaning culture' and body-centred 'presence culture', such a dichotomy is not easily recognized in the case of the youth movement. The movement suffered from what Armin Mohler called the 'intellectual anti-intellectualism' of the Conservative Revolution: its members were continuously engaged in philosophical debates, and took pride in the intellectual heights they reached, but at the same time they envied the British for achieving a great deal with far fewer concerns.

With respect to the Conservative Revolution, I hope to have proven three points. First, that the 'Revolution' was not just an intellectual effort instigated by leading right-wing intellectuals, but that it resonated in the broader society. At least in the interwar youth movement, conservative-revolutionary ideas and phraseology were adapted because it provided a mode of speech that best conveyed a range of very concrete experiences – ranging from the presence and tactility of death in the trenches during the war to the breakdown of Wilhelmine society and the urge for social and metaphysical order – into shared meaning.

Second, the Conservative Revolution was more than a political discourse against both Wilhelmine nationalism and Weimar democracy. Anglophone literature on this topic has still not gone beyond the fixation on the failure of the Weimar Republic and the rise of Nazism;[10] the German discourse seems to have reinstated such a fixation. In Germany, the critique of the apologetic nature of Mohler's book, and his attempt to depoliticize the Conservative Revolution, has resulted in the opposite: namely, overemphasizing its political dimension as a new 'nationalism', which Breuer understands in line with John Breuilly to have the existence of a nation with specific traits of character as a prerequisite.[11] In the youth movement, political questions gained significantly more importance in the Weimar Republic, but the political discourse could never be clearly distinguished from the educational discourse. Political questions were often regarded as *educational* questions, and nationhood was not a prerequisite but something to be attained morally, spiritually and physically through (self-)education. And as education never ends, as generations come and pass, the question of the constitution of nationhood was perennial and could never attain a 'fixed' state with 'fixed' (i.e. empirically and historically traceable) traits of character. Nonetheless, German values and characteristics were often defined as eternal values and characteristics. This, however, does not mean that they are matters of fact – this would mean misunderstanding the eternal as the enduring present. Instead they were Ideas, awaiting and requiring realization. This moral or educational element was as much part of the Conservative Revolution as of its political discourse.

Third, the Conservative Revolution cannot and should not be seen as anti-modern reactionism.[12] The very concept of 'conservatism' should be read in the light of the dynamism of Weimar Germany, in which its proponents made a great effort to rid the concept of the nineteenth-century connotation of striving for the reinstatement of an *ancien régime* or of a lost state of affairs. In the youth movement, the criticism of rationalism, positivism, liberalism, historicism, capitalism and bourgeois society in general was relevant because these ideologies held normative claims to the present – justified by a firm belief in progress. On the rejection of these claims followed the rejection of the very idea of progress and the urge for a metaphysical, rather than a historical, foundation of morality. When in the 1920s the moral principles of the youth movement developed from personal self-realization to the social task of realizing the eternal in the ephemeral, history ceased to be the domain of the moral development of mankind and turned into a realm not intrinsically different from the present. Thereby, not a reaction against, but the transformation of modernity was what the Conservative Revolution aimed for. Such a transformation included a transformation of the premises of modern thought, including the premises of the linearity and progressive character of time and the distance of the past. Whether the intention of overcoming the premises of modernity is in itself modern or modernist remains a question of definition.

## Notes

1. Hans Freyer, *Das geschichtliche Selbstbewußtsein des 20. Jahrhunderts* (Leipzig: Heinrich Keller, 1935), 5.
2. Ibid., 5.
3. Ibid., 11.
4. Ibid., 24–25.
5. Cf. Hans Freyer, *Die Revolution von Rechts* (Jena: Eugen Diederichs, 1931).
6. Ibid., 15.
7. Cf. Gumbrecht, *Production of Presence*, xiii.
8. Raedts, *De ontdekking van de Middeleeuwen*, 351.
9. Gumbrecht, *Production of Presence*, 82.
10. Cf. Anton Kaes, Martin Jay and Edward Dimendberg, *The Weimar Republic Sourcebook* (Berkeley: University of California Press, 1994), 330–31; Roger Woods, *The Conservative Revolution in the Weimar Republic* (London: Macmillan, 1996), 111ff.
11. Breuer, *Anatomie der konservativen Revolution*, 182.
12. A recent example of the tendency to remain caught in reproducing a binary opposition between modernity and the 'Conservative Revolution' in scholarly analysis is found in: Martin

Travers, *Critics of Modernity: The Literature of the Conservative Revolution in Germany, 1890–1933* (New York: Peter Lang, 2001). For a critique of this opposition, see: Peter Fritzsche, 'Critics of Modernity: The Literature of the Conservative Revolution in Germany, 1890–1933 (review)', *Modernism/Modernity* 10(1) (2003), 194–95.

# Sources and Literature

## Archives

*Archiv der deutschen Jugendbewegung (AdJb), Witzenhausen*
A2   Wandervogel, Ausschuss für Schülerfahrten
A5   Wandervogel, Deutscher Bund für Jugendwandern
A11  Feldwandervogel
A19  Nerother Wandervogel
A84  Sächsische Jungenschaft
A102 Akademische Vereinigung Marburg
A104 Freideutsche Jugend

*Central Zionist Archives (CZA), Jesusalem*
A66  Blau-Weiß and Kadima Youth Movements (Germany – Israel)

## Periodicals

*Blau-Weiß-Blätter* (1913–1919; 1923–1925)
*Blau-Weiß-Blätter – Führerzeitung* (1917–1923)
*Der Anfang* (1911–1914)
*Der Adler* (1920–1926)
*Der Herold. Bundesschrift der Nerother* (1928–1932)
*Der Jude* (1916–1917)
*Der Jungenbund* (1923)
*Der Kunstwart* (1910–1925)
*Der Neue Bund* (1921–1922)
*Der Vortrupp. Halbmonatsschrift für das Deutschtum unserer Zeit* (1916)
*Der Weiße Ritter* (1919–1926)
*Der Zwiespruch* (1919–1933)
*Der Zwiespruch. Rundbrief der Feldwandervögel im Westen* (1917–1918)
*Deutsche Freischar* (1928–1932)
*Die Falke* (1930–1931)
*Die Tat* (1910–1925)
*Fahrtenblatt des Wandervogels Nordthuringgau* (1913–1916)

*Freideutsche Jugend* (1915–1926)
*Jenaer Volksblatt* (1919)
*Jerubbaal. Eine Zeitschrift der jüdischen Jugend* (1918–1919)
*Junge Menschen* (1921)
*Jung–Wandervogel* (1911–1918)
*l'Humanité* (1918)
*Mark. Eine Gauzeitung in der Deutschen Freischar* (1932)
*Ockershäuser Blätter. Zeitschrift der Akademischen Freischar Marburg* (1928–1933)
*Ostmark. Gaublatt der Posenschen Wandervögel* (1917–1918)
*Psychiatrisch–Neurologische Wochenschrift* (1924)
*Volksstimme: Tageszeitung der Sozialdemokratischen Partei im Regierungsbezirk Magdeburg* (1927)
*Volkszeitung (Berlin)* (1918)
*Wandervogel Führerzeitung* (1912–1920)
*Wandervogel (Monatsschrift für deutsches Jugendwandern)* (1910–1921)
*Wandervogel. Gaublatt für Posen* (1913–1915)
*Wandervogel. Gaublatt für Schlesien* (1912–1915)
*Westermanns Monatshefte* (1921)

## Sourcebooks

Kindt, W., *Grundschriften der deutschen Jugendbewegung, Dokumentation der Jugendbewegung I* (Düsseldorf: Diederichs, 1963).
———, *Die Wandervogelzeit. Quellenschriften zur deutschen Jugendbewegung 1896–1919* (Düsseldorf: Diederichs, 1968).
———, *Dokumentation der Jugendbewegung. Band III: Die deutsche Jugendbewegung 1920 bis 1933. Die Bündische Zeit* (Düsseldorf: Diederichs, 1974).
Kneip, R., *Jugend zwischen den Kriegen – Eine Sammlung von Aussagen und Dokumenten* (Heidenheim: Südmarkverlag Fritsch, 1967).
Reinharz, J., *Dokumente zur Geschichte des deutschen Zionismus 1882–1933* (Tübingen: Mohr Siebeck, 1981).
Schmidt, F., *Tusk. Gesammelte Schriften und Dichtungen* (Stuttgart: Verlag der Jugendbewegung, 1996).
Seidelmann, K., *Gruppe – soziale Grundform der Jugend; Teil 2. Quellen und Dokumente* (Hannover: Hermann Schroedel, 1971).
Ziemer, G., and H. Wolf, *Wandervogel und freideutsche Jugend* (Bad Godesberg: Voggenreiter, [1905] 1961).

## Other Published Primary Sources

'Aus den Blättern des Führerkreises Wandervogel/Norddeutscher Bund', *Philosophie der Jungen. Sonderheft Der Weiße Ritter* (1922), 150–51.
*Bericht über die Ostertagung der Freideutschen Jugend in Jena (11.-19.4)*, G. Steiger (ed.), *'Fall Hodler': Jena 1914–1919: Der Kampf um ein Gemälde* (Jena: Friedrich-Schiller-Universität, 1970).
*Blau-Weiss Liederbuch* (Berlin: Jüdischer Verlag, 1918).
*Des Wandervogels Liederbuch* (Berlin & Osterwieck: A.W. Zickfeldt, 1905).
*Die Grosse Fahrt des Bundes der Reichspfadfinder nach Lettland. Sommer 1928* (Plauen i.Br: Das Junge Volk, 1929).
*Die Marburger Tagung der Freideutschen Jugend* (Hamburg: A. Saal, 1914).
*Grenzfeuer der vereinigten deutschen Jugendbünde im Fichtelgebirge am 3. u. 4. Erntings 1923* (Regensburg: Heinrich Schiele, 1923).

*Unser Weg.: Stimmen aus dem Bunde der Köngener. Sammelband aus drei Jahren* (Berlin: Der Weiße Ritter, 1923).
Ahlborn, K., *Krieg, Revolution und Freideutsche Zukunft. Die Reden und Aussprachen der Jenaer Tagung 1919* (Hamburg: Freideutscher Jugendverlag Adolf Saal, 1919).
Albrecht, P., *Geschlechtsnot der Jugend* (Berlin: Verlag Junge Anarchisten Hans Strempel, 1926).
Assisi, St F. of, K.J. Friedrich and W. Geißler, *Der Sonnengesang des heiligen Franziskus von Assisi* (Hartenstein: Greifenverlag, 1920).
Becker, H., *Zwischen Wahn und Wahrheit: Autobiographie* (Berlin: Verlag der Nation, 1972).
Blüher, H., *Die deutsche Wandervogelbewegung als erotisches Phänomen; ein Beitrag zur Erkenntnis der sexuellen Inversion* (Tempelhof-Berlin: B. Weise, 1914).
———, *Die Rolle der Erotik in der männlichen Gesellschaft I: Der Typus Inversus* (Jena: Eugen Diederichs, 1919).
———, *Wandervogel 1–3. Geschichte einer Jugendbewegung* (Frankfurt am Main: Dipa-Verlag, 1976).
Bojarzin, O., and L. Tschuncky, *Vom Wandervogel und vom bunten Rock. Skizzen und Erzählungen* (Wolfenbüttel: Zwissler, 1916).
Bonus, A., *Isländerbuch. Sammlung altgermanischer Bauern- und Königsgeschichten I-III* (Munich: Callwey, 1907).
Breuer, H., *Erinnerung und Vermächtnis: ein Gedenkbüchlein um Hans Breuer* (Hartenstein: Matthes, 1932).
Carnap, R., 'Intellectual Autobiography', in P.A. Schilpp (ed.), *The Philosophy of Rudolph Carnap* (LaSalle, IL: Open Court, 1963), 3–86.
Copalle, S., *Chronik der Deutschen Jugendbewegung* (Bad Godesberg: Voggenreiter Verlag, 1954).
Dissel, K., and R. Rosenhagen, *Verhandlungen der achtundvierzigsten Versammlung deutscher Philologen und Schulmänner in Hamburg vom 3. bis 6. Oktober 1905* (Leipzig: Teubner, 1906).
Dörfler, W., and H. Weinberg, *Weihnachtsspiel aus dem baierischen Wald* (Munich: Chr. Kaiser, 1923).
Eckhel, A.H. von, *Auf der Lenzfahrt des Lebens: Tagebuch eines Wandervogels* (Breslau: Bergstadtverlag, 1922).
Ehrenthal, G., *Die deutschen Jugendbünde. Ein Handbuch ihrer Organisation und ihrer Bestrebungen* (Berlin: Zentral-Verlag, 1929).
Engelhardt, E., *Gegen Muck und Muckertum. Eine Auseinandersetzung über die höhere freie Liebe mit Muck-Lamberty und Gertrud Prellwitz* (Rudolstadt in Thüringen: Greifenverlag, 1921).
———, *Jugendbewegung gegen Anthroposophie: Eine Absage an Dr. Rudolf Steiner* (Rudolstadt: Greifen Verlag, 1922).
Fichte, J.G., *Addresses to the German Nation* (Indianapolis: Hackett Publishing Company, Inc., 2013).
Fischer, F., F. Brauns and W. Liebenow (eds), *Wandern und Schauen. Gesammelte Aufsätze von Frank Fischer* (Hartenstein: Greifenverlag, 1921).
Flex, W., 'Der Wanderer zwischen beiden Welten. Ein Kriegserlebnis', in W. Flex (ed.), *Gesammelte Werke, Band 1* (Munich: C.H. Beck, 1925), 185–266.
———, *Briefe von Walter Flex*, eds W. Eggert-Windegg and K. Flex (Munich: C.H. Beck, 1927).
Flurschütz, H.R., *Vom Wesen und Werden junggermanischen Glaubens* (Berlin-Lichterfelde: Germanen-Verlag, 1926).
Freyer, H., *Die Revolution von Rechts* (Jena: Eugen Diederichs, 1931).
———, *Das geschichtliche Selbstbewußtsein des 20. Jahrhunderts* (Leipzig: Heinrich Keller, 1935).
Fulda, F.W. (ed.), *Sonnenwende. Ein Büchlein vom Wandervogel* (Leipzig: Hofmeister, 1919).
Gardiner, R., and H. Rocholl (eds), *Britain and Germany: A Frank Discussion Instigated by Members of the Younger Generation* (London: Williams and Norgate, 1928).
Gerst, W.C. (ed.), *Gemeinschafts-Bühne und Jugendbewegung* (Frankfurt am Main: Verlag des Bühnenvolksbundes, 1924).
Goethe, J.W. von, 'Von deutscher Baukunst (1772)', in J.W. von Goethe and S. Seidel (eds), *Berliner Ausgabe Bd. 19. Kunsttheoretische Schriften und Übersetzungen. Schriften zur bildenden Kunst 1* (Berlin: Aufbau-Verlag, 1985), 29–39.
Götsch, G., *Aus dem Lebens- und Gedankenkreis eines Jugendchores. Jahresbericht 1925 der Märkischen Spielgemeinde* (Wolfenbüttel: Georg Kallmeyer, 1926).

———, *Musische Bildung 2: Bericht* (Wolfenbüttel: Karl Heinrich Möseler, 1953).
Grabowsky, A., and W. Koch (eds), *Die Freideutsche Jugendbewegung. Ursprung Und Zukunft* (Gotha: Perthes, 1921).
Gurlitt, L., *Der Deutsche und sein Vaterland. Politisch-pädagogische Betrachtungen eines Modernen* (Berlin: Verlag von Wiegandt & Grieboy, 1902).
———, *Pflege und Entwicklung der Persönlichkeit* (Leipzig: R. Voigtländer, 1905).
Haass-Berkow, G., 'Experiences in the Realm of Dramatic Art', *A Man before Others. Rudolf Steiner Remembered: A Collection of Personal Memories from the Pages of The Golden Blade and Other Sources* (Bristol: Rudolf Steiner Press, 1993), 34–45.
Halkett, G.R. (pseud. Albrecht von Fritsch), *The Dear Monster* (London: Jonathan Cape, 1939).
Hartmann, H., *Oswald Spengler und Deutschlands Jugend* (Rudolstadt: Greifenverlag, 1925).
Hauer, J.W. *Werden und Wesen der Anthroposophie. Eine Wertung und eine Kritik* (Stuttgart: Kohlhammer, 1922).
Hesse, H., *Wandern und Reisen, Dürerbund 14. Flugschrift zur ästhetischen Kultur* (Munich: Callwey, 1906).
———, *The Journey to the East* (New York: Farrar, Straus & Giroux, 1968).
Jünger, E., *Der Kampf als inneres Erlebnis* (Berlin: E.S. Mittler & Sohn, 1926).
Keller, G., 'Das Fähnlein der sieben Aufrechten', in G. Keller (ed.), *Gottfried Keller's gesammelte Werke* (Berlin: Wilhelm Hertz, 1891), 258–334.
Korth, G., *Wandervogel 1896–1906: quellenmässige Darstellung nach Karl Fischers Tagebuchaufzeichnungen von 1900 und vielen anderen dokumentarischen Belegen* (Frankfurt am Main: dipa-Verlag, 1967).
Kracke, A., *Freideutsche Jugend: zur Jahrhundertfeier auf dem Hohen Meißner 1913* (Jena: Diederichs, 1913).
Lähn, K., *Von der geistigen Heimat deutscher Jugend* (Plauen: Gunther Wolff, 1933).
Landsberg, P.L., *Die Welt des Mittelalters und wir. Ein geschichtsphilosophischer Versuch über den Sinn eines Zeitalters* (Bonn: Cohen, 1923).
Lehmann, E., and H. Lehmann, *Hellas: Tagebuch einer Reise* (Potsdam: Voggenreiter, 1929).
Maschke, E., *Ostland* (Berlin: Der Weiße Ritter Verlag, 1922).
Matthes, E., *Wandervogels Tagebuch* (Leipzig: Matthes, 1915).
Mirbt, R., *Die Bürger von Calais: Das Spiel eines Volkes* (Munich: Kaiser, 1925).
———, *Möglichkeiten und Grenzen des Laienspiels: ein Vortrag* (Munich: Kaiser, 1928).
———, *Münchener Laienspielführer: eine Wegweisung für das Laienspiel und für mancherlei andere Dinge* (Munich: Kaiser, 1931).
———, 'Laienspiel', in R. Mirbt (ed.), *Laienspiel und Laientheater: Vorträge und Aufsätze aus den Jahren 1923–1959* (Kassel: Bärenreiter, 1960), 9–18.
———, *Laienspiel und Laientheater: Vorträge und Aufsätze aus den Jahren 1923–1959* (Kassel: Bärenreiter, 1960).
Mittelstraß, G., *Freideutscher Jugendtag 1913* (Hamburg: Adolf Saal, 1919).
Moeller van den Bruck, A., *Das dritte Reich* (Berlin: Der Ring, 1923).
Natorp, P., *Deutscher Weltberuf: geschichtsphilosophische Richtlinien. Vol. 2* (Jena: Eugen Diederichs, 1918).
———, *Hoffnungen und Gefahren unserer Jugendbewegung* (Jena: Eugen Diederichs, 1920).
———, *Individuum und Gemeinschaft* (Jena: Diederichs, 1921).
Nietzsche, F., 'On the Uses and Disadvantages of History for Life', in *Untimely Meditations* (Cambridge: Cambridge University Press, 1997), 57–124.
———, 'Schopenhauer as Educator', in *Untimely Meditations* (Cambridge: Cambridge University Press, 1997), 125–94.
———, *Thus Spoke Zarathustra* (Cambridge: Cambridge University Press, 2006).
Oelbermann, R., 'Die Entstehung des Jugendburggedankes', *Werbeschrift für die Rheinische Jugendburg* (Bonn: Bund zur Errichtung der Rheinischen Jugendburg, 1921).
Rabe, H.-G., *Otto Neumann: Leben und Soldatentod eines Osnabrücker Wandervogels* (Osnabrück: Wegmann, 1980).

Ritzhaupt, A., *Die 'Neue Schar' in Thüringen* (Jena: Eugen Diederichs, 1921).
Rocholl, H., *Englandfahrt 1909 und 1927. Ein Beitrag zur Geschichte der deutschen Jugendbewegung* (Potsdam:Voggenreiter, 1929).
Rosen, H. Freiherr von, *Wolhynienfahrt 1926* (Siegen: J.G. Herder-Bibliothek Siegerland, 1982).
Schleicher, F., *Jugendbewegung gegen Bühnenvolksbund. Eine Dokumentensammlung* (Hamburg: Die Fahrenden Gesellen, 1927).
Schlünz, F., 'Intellektualismus und Historizismus', in F. Jöde (ed.), *Pädagogik deines Wesens. Gedanken der Erneuerung aus dem Wendekreis* (Hamburg: Freideutscher Jugendverlag Adolf Saar, 1919).
———, *Wandervogel wach auf!* (Hamburg: Friedeutscher Jugendverlag Adolf Saal, 1919).
Schmalenbach, H., 'Die soziologische Kategorie des Bundes', *Die Dioskuren. Jahrbuch für Geisteswissenschaften* 1 (1922), 35–105.
Scholem, G., *Walter Benjamin: The Story of a Friendship* (New York: Schocken, 1981).
———, *Von Berlin nach Jerusalem* (Frankfurt am Main: Jüdischer Verlag, 1994).
Schrank, G., and R. Schuch, *Wandervögel im Hunsrück: das Fahrtenbuch der Birkenfelder Wandervögel von 1914 bis 1933* (Nijmegen: Schank, 2001).
Schröer, K.J., *Deutsche Weihnachtspiele aus Ungern, geschildert und mitgetheilt* (Vienna: Wilhelm Braumüller, 1862).
Schurtz, H., *Altersklassen und Männerbünde* (Berlin: Georg Reimer, 1902).
Schweitzer, C. (ed.), *Das religiöse Deutschland der Gegenwart. Band I: Der allgemein-religiöse Kreis* (Berlin: Hochweg, 1928).
Siegmund-Schultze, F., *Ver sacrum: was die im Kriege gefallenen Mitarbeiter der sozialen Arbeitsgemeinschaft dem deutschen Volk zu sagen haben. Mitteilungen und Aufzeichnungen* (Berlin: Furche-Verlag, 1919).
Steiner, R., *Die Erkenntnis-Aufgabe der Jugend (GA 217a)* (Dornach: Rudolf Steiner Verlag, 1981).
Tetzner, L., and H. Pape, *Im Land der Industrie zwischen Rhein und Ruhr. Ein buntes Buch von Zeit und Menschen* (Jena: Eugen Diederichs, 1923).
Thurnwald, R. (ed.), *Die Neue Jugend* (Leipzig: C.L. Hirschfeld, 1927).
Trummler, E., *Der kranke Hölderlin, Urkunden und Dichtungen aus der Zeit seiner Umnachtung* (Munich: O.C. Recht, 1921).
Wright, M., and E. Albertz, *Anni. Letters and Writings of Annemarie Wächter* (Rifton, NY: Plough Publishing House, 2010).
Wyneken, G., 'Die Jugendburg', in K. Hiller (ed.), *Tätiger Geist. Zweites der Ziel-Jahrbücher* (Munich: Georg Müller, 1918).
——— (ed.), *Der Kampf für die Jugend: Gesammelte Aufsätze* (Jena: Eugen Diederichs, 1919).
———, *Schule und Jugendkultur* (Jena: Eugen Diederichs Verlag, 1919).
———, *Was ist "Jugendkultur"? Öffentlicher Vortrag gehalten am 30. Oktober 1913 in der Pädagogischen Abteilung der Münchner Freien Studentenschaft* (Munich: Steinicke, 1919).

# Literature

Adriaansen, R.J., 'Generaties, herinnering en historiciteit', *Tijdschrift voor Geschiedenis* 124(2) (2011), 221–37.
Ahrens, R., 'Heinz-Dietrich Wendland (1900–1992)', in B. Stambolis (ed.), *Jugendbewegt geprägt. Essays zu autobiographischen Texten von Werner Heisenberg, Robert Jungk und vielen anderen* (Göttingen: V&R unipress, 2013), 725–37.
Ankersmit, F., 'Historical Representation', *History and Theory* 27(3) (1988), 205–28.
———, *De sublieme historische ervaring* (Groningen: Historische Uitgeverij, 2007).
Applegate, C., *A Nation of Provincials: The German Idea of Heimat* (Berkeley: University of California Press, 1990).
Aufmuth, U., *Die deutsche Wandervogelbewegung unter soziologischem Aspekt* (Göttingen: Vandenhoeck & Ruprecht, 1979).

Autsch, S., *Erinnerung – Biographie – Fotografie. Formen der Ästhetisierung einer jugendbewegten Generation im 20. Jahrhundert* (Potsdam:Verlag Berlin-Brandenburg, 2000).
Baader, M.S., 'Naturreligiöse Gestimmtheit und jugendbewegte Aufbruchsgeste. Bildgedächtnis der Jugendbewegung und mentales Gepäck: Fidus' "Lichtgebet"', in B. Stambolis and R. Koerber (eds), *Erlebnisgenerationen – Erinnerungsgemeinschaften. Die Jugendbewegung und ihre Gedächtnisorte* (Schwalbach/Ts.:Wochenschau-Verlag, 2009), 153–68.
Bausinger, H., *Typisch deutsch: wie deutsch sind die Deutschen?* (Munich: C.H. Beck, 2000).
Becker, H., *German Youth: Bond or Free* (New York: Oxford University Press, 1946).
Berger, P.L., and T. Luckmann, *The Social Construction of Reality: A Treatise in the Sociology of Knowledge* (Garden City, NY: Anchor, 1967).
Berger, S., and C. Lorenz, *Nationalizing the Past: Historians as Nation Builders in Modern Europe* (New York: Palgrave Macmillan, 2010).
Berger, S., M. Donovan and K. Passmore, *Writing National Histories: Western Europe since 1800* (London: Routledge, 2002).
Biccari, G., *'Zuflucht des Geistes'? Konservativ-revolutionäre, faschistische und nationalsozialistische Theaterdiskurse in Deutschland und Italien, 1900–1944* (Tübingen: G. Narr, 2001).
Biemann, A.,'The Problem of Tradition and Reform in Jewish Renaissance and Renaissancism', *Jewish Social Studies* 8(1) (2001), 58–87.
Blackbourn, D., and G. Eley, *The Peculiarities of German History: Bourgeois Society and Politics in Nineteenth-century Germany* (Oxford: Oxford University Press, 1984).
Blochmann, E., *Herman Nohl in der pädagogischen Bewegung seiner Zeit 1879–1960* (Göttingen: 1969).
Bohnenkamp, H.,'Jugendbewegung als Kulturkritik', in W. Rüegg (ed.), *Kulturkritik und Jugendkult* (Frankfurt am Main: Suhrkamp, 1974), 24–34.
Bollnow, O.F., *Das Wesen der Stimmungen* (Würzburg: Königshausen & Neumann, 2009).
Borinski, F., and W. Milch, *Jugendbewegung: The Story of German Youth* (London: Clarke & Co., 1945).
Boterman, F., *Oswald Spengler en "Der Untergang des Abendlandes". Cultuurpessimist en Politiek Activist* (Assen:Van Gorcum, 1992).
Braun, R. *Individualismus und Gemeinschaft in der deutschen Jugendbewegung* (Erlangen: Karl Döres, 1929).
Breuer, S., *Anatomie der konservativen Revolution* (Darmstadt: Wissenschaftliche Buchgesellschaft, 1993).
———, *Die Völkischen in Deutschland: Kaiserreich und Weimarer Republik* (Darmstadt: Wissenschaftliche Buchgesellschaft, 2008).
Breuer, S., and I. Schmidt, *Die Kommenden. Eine Zeitschrift der Bündischen Jugend (1926–1933)* (Schwalbach/Ts.: Wochenschau Verlag, 2010).
Breyvogel, W., *Eine Einführung in Jugendkulturen: Veganismus und Tattoos* (Wiesbaden: VS Verlag, 2005).
Bruendel, S., *Volksgemeinschaft oder Volksstaat: die 'Ideen von 1914' und die Neuordnung Deutschlands im Ersten Weltkrieg* (Berlin: Akademie Verlag, 2003).
Brügmann, H.G., *Karl Brügmann und der freideutsche Sera-Kreis Untersuchung eines Modells von Jugendleben und Geist der Meißner-Generation vor 1914* (Frankfurt am Main: 1965).
Brunotte, U., *Zwischen Eros und Krieg. Männerbund und Ritual in der Moderne* (Berlin: Klaus Wagenbach Verlag, 2004).
Bruns, C., *Politik des Eros: der Männerbund in Wissenschaft, Politik und Jugendkultur (1880–1934)* (Cologne: Böhlau, 2008).
———, 'The Politics of Eros: The German Männerbund between Anti-Feminism and Anti-Semitism in the Early Twentieth Century', in K.M. Faull (ed.), *Masculinity, Senses, Spirit* (Lewisburg, PA: Bucknell University Press, 2011), 153–90.
Bullivant, K.,'The Conservative Revolution', in A. Phelan (ed.), *The Weimar Dilemma: Intellectuals in the Weimar Republic* (Manchester: Manchester University Press, 1985).
Burckhardt, J., *The Civilization of the Renaissance in Italy* (New York: The New American Library of World Literature, 1960).

Busse-Wilson, E., *Stufen der Jugendbewegung – Ein Abschnitt aus der ungeschriebenen Geschichte Deutschlands* (Jena: Eugen Diederichs, 1925).
Campbell, K.J., *German Mystical Writings* (New York: Continuum, 2002).
Cancik, H., 'Jugendbewegung und klassische Antike (1901–1933)', in B. Seidensticker (ed.), *Urgeschichten der Moderne: die Antike im 20. Jahrhundert* (Stuttgart: Metzler, 2001), 114–35.
Canning, K., 'The Politics of Symbols, Semantics, and Sentiments in the Weimar Republic', *Central European History* 43 (2010), 567–80.
Chase, M., '"North Sea and Baltic": Historical Conceptions in the Youth Movement and the Transfer of Ideas from Germany to England in the 1920s and 1930s', in S. Berger, P. Lambert and P. Schumann (eds), *Historikerdialoge. Geschichte, Mythos und Gedächtnis im deutsch-britischen kulturellen Austausch 1750–2000* (Göttingen: Vandenhoeck & Ruprecht, 2003), 309–30.
Collingwood, R.G., 'History as Re-enactment of Past Experience', in *The Idea of History* (Oxford: Oxford University Press, 1946), 282–302.
Cramer, K., 'Erleben, Erlebnis', in Joachim Ritter, Karlfried Gründer and Gottfried Gabriel (eds), *Historisches Wörterbuch der Philosophie. Vol. II* (Basel: Schwabe Verlag, 1972).
Dilthey, W., 'Fragmente zur Poetik (1907/8): Das Erlebnis', in G. Misch (ed.), *Gesammelte Schriften 6: Die geistige Welt. Einleitung in die Philosophie des Lebens II* (Stuttgart: B.G. Teubner, 1924), 313–17.
Dougherty, R.W., *Eros, Youth Culture and Geist: The Ideology of Gustav Wyneken and its Influence upon the German Youth Movement* (Madison: University of Wisconsin, 1978).
Dudek, P., *Fetisch Jugend: Walter Benjamin und Siegfried Bernfeld – Jugendprotest am Vorabend des Ersten Weltkrieges* (Bad Heilbrunn/Obb.: Klinkhardt, 2002).
Eckart, W., 'Intuition und Stimmung als Spielgesetz', in W. Frantzen (ed.), *Laienspiel in der Weimarer Zeit* (Münster: Landesarbeitsgemeinschaft für Spiel und Amateurtheater im Land Nordrhein-Westfalen, 1969), 41–47.
Eley, G., *Reshaping the German Right: Radical Nationalism and Political Change after Bismarck* (New Haven, CT: Yale University Press, 1980).
Eloni, Y., *Zionismus in Deutschland: von den Anfängen bis 1914* (Gerlingen: Bleicher, 1987).
Engelhardt, V., *Die deutsche Jugendbewegung als kulturhistorisches Phänomen* (Berlin: 1923).
Erll, A., *Kollektives Gedächtnis und Erinnerungskulturen* (Stuttgart: Metzler, 2005).
———, 'Cultural Memory Studies: An Introduction', in A. Erll and A. Nünning (eds), *Cultural Memory Studies: An International and Interdisciplinary Handbook* (Berlin: Walter de Gruyter, 2008), 1–15.
Ferreira, B., *Stimmung bei Heidegger: das Phänomen der Stimmung im Kontext von Heideggers Existenzialanalyse des Daseins* (Dordrecht and Boston: Kluwer Academic Publishers, 2002).
Fick, L., *Die deutsche Jugendbewegung* (Jena: Diederichs, 1940).
Fiedler, G., 'Beruf und Leben: die Wandervogel-Idee auf dem Prüfstand', in J.H. Knoll and J.H. Schoeps (eds), *Typisch deutsch: die Jugendbewegung: Beiträge zu einer Phänomengeschichte* (Opladen: Leske & Budrich, 1988), 71–100.
———, *Jugend im Krieg. Bürgerliche Jugendbewegung, Erster Weltkrieg und sozialer Wandel. 1914–1923* (Cologne: Verlag Wissenschaft und Politik, 1989).
Fischer, M., 'Zwischen Jugendbewegung, Lebensreform und Kriegsbegeisterung. Der Wandel des Erlebnisbegriffs in den Reformbewegungen des ausgehenden Kaiserreichs und der Weimarer Republik', in G. Häffner (ed.), *Religiöse Erfahrung II: Interkulturelle Perspektiven* (Stuttgart: W. Kohlhammer Verlag, 2007), 141–55.
Flasch, K., *Die geistige Mobilmachung. Die deutschen Intellektuellen und der Erste Weltkrieg – ein Versuch* (Berlin: A. Fest, 2000).
Foerster, F.W., *Jugendseele, Jugendbewegung, Jugendziel* (Erlenbach-Zurich: Rotapfel-verlag, 1923).
Föllmer, M., and R. Graf, *Die 'Krise' der Weimarer Republik: Zur Kritik eines Deutungsmusters* (Frankfurt am Main: Campus Verlag, 2005).
Fowler, D., 'Rolf Gardiner: Pioneer of British Youth Culture, 1920–1939', in M. Jefferies and M. Tyldesley (eds), *Rolf Gardiner: Folk, Nature and Culture in Interwar Britain* (Farnham, Surrey: Ashgate, 2011), 17–46.

Fritzsche, P., 'Review: Did Weimar Fail?', *The Journal of Modern History* 30(3) (1996), 629–56.

———, 'Critics of Modernity: The Literature of the Conservative Revolution in Germany, 1890–1933 (review)', *Modernism/Modernity* 10(1) (2003), 194–95.

———, *Stranded in the Present: Modern Time and the Melancholy of History* (Cambridge, MA: Harvard University Press, 2004).

Friz, E., *Adler und Falken 1920–1935: Bündische Jugend* (Oldenburg: Erwin Friz, 1990).

Frobenius, E., *Mit uns zieht die neue Zeit. Eine Geschichte der deutschen Jugendbewegung* (Berlin: Deutsche Buch-Gemeinschaft, 1927).

Fussell, P., *The Great War and Modern Memory: The Illustrated Edition* (New York: Sterling Publishing Company, 2009).

Gadamer, H.-G., 'The Problem of Historical Consciousness', in P. Rabinow and W.M. Sullivan (eds), *Interpretive Social Science: A Second Look* (Berkeley: University of California Press, 1987), 82–140.

———, *Truth and Method* (London: Continuum, 2004).

Gerber, W., *Zur Entstehungsgeschichte der deutschen Wandervogelbewegung. Ein kritischer Beitrag* (Bielefeld: Gieseking, 1957).

Geuter, U., *Homosexualität in der deutschen Jugendbewegung* (Frankfurt am Main: Suhrkamp Verlag, 1994).

Giffei, H., *Martin Luserke und das Theater* (Recklinghausen: Landesarbeitsgemeinschaft für Spiel und Amateurtheater Nordrhein-Westfalen, 1979).

Gillis, J.R., *Youth and History* (New York: Academic Press, 1974).

Göttsch-Elten, S., 'Populäre Bilder vom Norden im 19. und 20. Jahrhundert', in A. Engel-Braunschmidt et al. (eds), *Ultima Thule: Bilder des Nordens von der Antike bis zur Gegenwart* (Frankfurt am Main: Lang, 2001), 123–43.

Graf, R., *Die Zukunft der Weimarer Republik: Krisen und Zukunftsaneignungen in Deutschland 1918–1933* (Munich: Oldenbourg Wissenschaftsverlag, 2008).

———, 'Either–Or: The Narrative of "Crisis" in Weimar Germany and in Historiography', *Central European History* 43 (2010), 592–615.

Grever, M.C.R., 'Nationale identiteit en historisch besef. De risico's van een canon in de postmoderne samenleving', *Tijdschrift voor Geschiedenis* 119(2) (2006), 160–77.

———, 'Fear of Plurality: Historical Culture and Historiographical Canonization in Western Europe', in A. Epple and A. Schaser (eds), *Multiple Histories? Changing Perspectives on Modern History* (Frankfurt and New York: Campus Verlag, 2009), 45–62.

Grever, M.C.R., P.A.C. de Bruijn and C.A.M. van Boxtel, 'Negotiating Historical Distance: Or, How to Deal with the Past as a Foreign Country in Heritage Education', *Paedagogica Historica* 48(6) (2012), 873–87.

Grob, M., *Das Kleidungsverhalten jugendlicher Protestgruppen in Deutschland im 20. Jahrhundert: am Beispiel des Wandervogels und der Studentenbewegung* (Münster: Coppenrath, 1985).

Gruner, R., 'The Concept of Speculative Philosophy of History', *Metaphilosophy* 3(4) (1972), 283–300.

Gumbrecht, H.U., *Production of Presence: What Meaning Cannot Convey* (Stanford, CA: Stanford University Press, 2004).

———, 'Presence Achieved in Language (With Special Attention Given to the Presence of the Past)', *History and Theory* 45(3) (2006), 317–27.

Hackeschmidt, J., *Von Kurt Blumenfeld zu Norbert Elias: die Erfindung einer jüdischen Nation* (Hamburg: Europäische Verlagsanstalt, 1997).

Hahn, H.-W., 'Zwischen Freiheitshoffnung und Führererwartung: Ambivalenzen bürgerlicher Erinnerungskultur in Jena 1870 bis 1930', in J. John and J.H. Ulbricht (eds), *Jena. Ein nationaler Erinnerungsort?* (Cologne: Böhlau-Verlag, 2007), 73–92.

Hamann, R., *Stilkunst um 1900* (Frankfurt am Main: Fischer, 1977).

Han, B.-C., *Heideggers Herz. Zum Begriff der Stimmung bei Martin Heidegger* (Munich: Fink, 1996).

Hanke, B. *Geschichtskultur an höheren Schulen von der Wilhelminischen Ära bis zum Zweiten Weltkrieg. Das Beispiel Westfalen* (Münster: LIT Verlag, 2010).

Hardenberg, A. Gräfin, *Bündische Jugend und Ausland* (Munich: Uni-Druck, 1966).
Hardtwig, W., *Hochkultur des bürgerlichen Zeitalters* (Göttingen: Vandenhoeck & Ruprecht, 2005).
———, *Deutsche Geschichtskultur im 19. und 20. Jahrhundert* (Munich: Oldenbourg, 2013).
Hardy, C.S., 'Antiqua Mater: Misreading Gender in "Aeneid" 3.84–191', *The Classical Journal* 92(1) (1996), 1–8.
Harrison, M.H., *Modern Religious Drama in Germany and France: A Comparative Study* (Boston, MA: The Stratford Company, 1936).
Heidegger, M., *Sein und Zeit* (Tübingen: Max Niemeyer Verlag, 1967).
Helwig, W., *Die Blaue Blume des Wandervogels: Vom Aufstieg, Glanz und Sinn einer Jugendbewegung. Überarbeitete Neuausgabe* (Braunach: Deutscher Spurbuchverlag 1998).
Henne, H., 'Zur Sprache der Jugend im Wandervogel. Ein unbekanntes Kapitel deutscher Sprachgeschichte', *Zeitschrift für germanistische Linguistik* 9 (1981), 20–33.
Herf, J., *Reactionary Modernism: Technology, Culture and Politics in Weimar and the Third Reich* (Cambridge: Cambridge University Press, 1984).
Hermand, J., *Old Dreams of a New Reich: Volkish Utopias and National Socialism* (Bloomington: Indiana University Press, 1992).
Herrmann, U., *Von der HJ-Führung zur weißen Rose. Hans Scholl vor dem Stuttgarter Sondergericht 1937/38* (Weinheim: Beltz Juventa, 2012).
Hetherington, K., *Expressions of Identity: Space, Performance, Politics* (London: SAGE, 1998).
Hettling, M., 'Die Nationalisierung von Kunst. Der "Fall Hodler" 1914', in M. Hettling (ed.), *Was ist Gesellschaftsgeschichte? Positionen, Themen, Analysen (Hans-Ulrich Wehler zum 60. Geburtstag)* (Munich: C.H. Beck, 1991), 215–24.
Hinde, J.R., *Jacob Burckhardt and the Crisis of Modernity* (Montreal: McGill-Queen's University Press, 2000).
Hirsch, E., and C. Stewart, 'Introduction: Ethnographies of Historicity', *History and Anthropology* 16(3) (2005), 261–74.
Hobsbawm, E., 'Introduction: Inventing Traditions', in E. Hobsbawm and T. Ranger (eds), *The Invention of Tradition* (Cambridge: Cambridge University Press, 1983), 1–14.
Hohmann, C., *Dienstbares Begleiten und später Widerstand: der nationale Sozialist Adolf Reichwein im Nationalsozialismus* (Bad Heilbrunn: Klinkhardt, 2007).
Hölscher, L., 'Utopie', in O. Brunner, W. Conze and R. Koselleck (eds), *Geschichtliche Grundbegriffe. Historisches Lexikon zur politisch-sozialen Sprache in Deutschland. Vol. VI* (Stuttgart: Klett-Cotta, 1990), 583–671.
Horst, F., 'Eberhard Köbel', in B. Ottnad (ed.), *Baden-Württembergische Biographien 1* (Stuttgart: Kohlhammer, 1994), 194–97.
Huizinga, J., *Homo Ludens: A Study of the Play-Element in Culture* (London: Routledge & Kegan Paul, 1949).
Iggers, G.G., *Geschichtswissenschaft im 20. Jahrhundert* (Göttingen: Vandenhoeck & Ruprecht, 2007).
Ille, G., 'Steglitzer Wandervogelführer. Lebenswege und Lebensziele', in G. Ille and G. Köhler (eds), *Der Wandervogel. Es begann in Steglitz* (Berlin: Stapp Verlag, 1987), 99–127.
Ireland, C., *The Subaltern Appeal to Experience: Self-Identity, Late Modernity, and the Politics of Immediacy* (Montreal: McGill-Queen's University Press, 2005).
Jaeger, F., 'Theorietypen der Krise des Historismus', in W. Bialas and G. Raulet (eds), *Die Historismusdebatte in Der Weimarer Republik* (Frankfurt am Main: Lang, 1996), 52–70.
James, D., 'Fichte on the Vocation of the Scholar and the (Mis)use of History', *The Review of Metaphysics* 63(3) (2010), 539–66.
Jantzen, H., *Namen und Werke 1. Biographien und Beiträge zur Soziologie der Jugendbewegung* (Frankfurt am Main: Dipa-Verlag, 1972).
Jantzen, W., 'Die soziologische Herkunft der Führungsschicht der deutschen Jugendbewegung 1900–1933', in *Führungsschicht und Eliteproblem. Jahrbuch III der Ranke-Gesellschaft* (Frankfurt am Main: Moritz Diesterweg, 1957), 127–35.

Janz, R.-P., 'Die Faszination der Jugend durch Rituale und sakrale Symbole. Mit Anmerkungen zu Fidus, Hesse, Hoffmannsthal und George', in T. Koebner, R.-P. Janz and F. Trommler (eds), *Mit uns zieht die neue Zeit: der Mythos Jugend* (Frankfurt am Main: Suhrkamp, 1985), 310–37.

Jens, W., 'The Classical Tradition in Germany: Grandeur and Decay', in E.J. Feuchtwanger (ed.), *Upheaval and Continuity: A Century of German History* (Letchworth: The Garden City Press, 1973), 67–82.

Kaes, A., M. Jay and E. Dimendberg (eds), *The Weimar Republic Sourcebook* (Berkeley: University of California Press, 1994).

Kaiser, H., 'Zur Freiheit berufen', in H. Kaiser (ed.), *Begegnungen und Wirkungen: Festgabe für Rudolf Mirbt und das deutsche Laienspiel* (Kassel: Bärenreiter-Verlag, 1956), 46–48.

Kannberg, G., *Der Bühnenvolksbund: Aufbau und Krise des Christlich-Deutschen Bühnenvolksbundes 1919–1933* (Cologne: Ralf Leppin, 1997).

Karl, W., *Jugend, Gesellschaft und Politik im Zeitraum des Ersten Weltkriegs* (Munich: Stadtarchiv München, 1973).

Kaufmann, A., *Vorgeschichte und Entstehung des Laienspieles und die frühe Geschichte der Laienspielbewegung*. Dissertation (Stuttgart: Universität Stuttgart, 1991).

———, '"Der Gottesdienst der neuen Zeit": Laienspiel und neue Religiosität', *Jahrbuch des Archivs der Deutschen Jugendbewegung* 20 (2002), 111–22.

Klein, S., and B. Stelmaszyk, 'Eberhard Köbel, "tusk". Ein biographisches Porträt über die Jahre 1907–1945', in M. von Hellfeld and W. Breyvogel (eds), *Piraten, Swings, und Junge Garde. Jugendwiderstand im Nationalsozialismus* (Bonn: Dietz, 1991), 102–37.

Klönne, A., *Jugend im Dritten Reich: die Hitler-Jugend und ihre Gegner* (Cologne: PapyRossa, 2003).

———, 'Jugendliche Subkulturen im Dritten Reich', in M. Andritzky (ed.), *Schock und Schöpfung – Jugendästhetik im 20. Jahrhundert* (Darmstadt: Luchterhand, 1986), 308–13.

Kneip, R., *Jugend der Weimarer Zeit: Handbuch der Jugendverbände 1919–1938* (Frankfurt am Main: Dipa-Verlag, 1974).

———, *Jugend zwischen den Kriegen – Eine Sammlung von Aussagen und Dokumenten* (Heidenheim: Südmarkverlag Fritsch, 1967).

———, *Wandervogel – Bündische Jugend 1909–1943. Der Weg der sächsischen Jungenschaft zum großen Bund* (Frankfurt am Main: Dipa-Verlag, 1967).

Köhler, G., 'Steglitz zur Jahrhundertwende. Preußens größtes Dorf, ein zentraler Ort des Bildungsbürgertums', in G. Ille and G. Köhler (eds), *Der Wandervogel. Es begann in Steglitz* (Berlin: Stapp Verlag, 1987), 9–29.

Kohut, T.A., *A German Generation: An Experiential History of the Twentieth Century* (New Haven, CT: Yale University Press, 2012).

König, J., *Das Ethos der Jugendbewegung in Deutschland mit besonderer Berücksichtigung der freideutschen Jugendbewegung* (Düsseldorf: Schwann, 1929).

Konrad, F.-M., '"… Unsere einzige, unsere letzte Hoffnung". Die Jugendbewegung als Thema und Herausforderung der Pädagogik Paul Natorps', *Pädagogische Rundschau* 55(5) (2001), 523–42.

Korn, E., 'Das neue Lebensgefühl in der Gymnastik', in E. Korn, O. Suppert and K. Vogt (eds), *Die Jugendbewegung: Welt und Wirkung; zur 50. Wiederkehr des freideutschen Jugendtages auf dem Hohen Meißner* (Düsseldorf: Eugen Diederichs Verlag, 1963), 101–19.

Körting, A., 'Jugendkultur und Jugendburg-Idee', *Köpfchen* 3–4 (2000), 4–9.

Koselleck, R., 'Bund', in O. Brunner, W. Conze and R. Koselleck (eds), *Geschichtliche Grundbegriffe. Historisches Lexikon zur politisch-sozialen Sprache in Deutschland. Vol. I* (Stuttgart: 1972), 583–671.

———, '"Space of Experience" and "Horizon of Expectation": Two Historical Categories', in *Futures Past: On the Semantics of Historical Time* (Cambridge: MIT Press, 1985), 267–324.

———, 'The Temporalization of Utopia', in *The Practice of Conceptual History: Timing History, Spacing Concepts* (Stanford, CA: Stanford University Press, 2002), 84–99.

———, 'Time and History', in *The Practice of Conceptual History: Timing History, Spacing Concepts* (Stanford, CA: Stanford University Press, 2002), 100–114.

———, 'Transformations of Experience and Methodological Change', in *The Practice of Conceptual History* (Stanford, CA: Stanford University Press, 2002), 45–83.

———, 'On the Disposability of History', in *Futures Past: On the Semantics of Historical Time* (New York: Columbia University Press, 2004), 192–204.
Koshar, R., *Germany's Transient Pasts: Preservation and National Memory in the Twentieth Century* (Chapel Hill, NC: University of North Carolina Press, 1998).
Krolle, S., *Musisch-kulturelle Etappen der deutschen Jugendbewegung von 1919–1964: Eine Regionalstudie* (Münster: Lit, 2004).
Labrie, A., *Zuiverheid en Decadentie. Over de Grenzen van de Burgerlijke Cultuur in West-Europa, 1870–1914* (Amsterdam: Bakker, 2001).
Landsberg, E., A. Landsberg and P.L. Landsberg, *Gedächtnisschrift für Prof. Dr. Ernst Landsberg (1860–1927), Frau Anna Landsberg geb. Silverberg (1878–1938), Dr. Paul Ludwig Landsberg (1901–1944)* (Bonn: Rechts- und Staatswissenschaftlichen Fakultät der Rheinischen Friedrich Wilhelms-Universität, 1953).
Laqueur, W., *Young Germany: A History of the German Youth Movement* (New Brunswick: Transaction Publishers, 1984).
Leggewie, C., *Der Geist steht rechts: Ausflüge in die Denkfabriken der Wende* (Berlin: Rotbuch, 1987).
Linse, U., *Barfüßige Propheten. Erlöser der zwanziger Jahre* (Berlin: Siedler Verlag, 1983).
———, *Zurück, o Mensch, zur Mutter Erde: Landkommunen in Deutschland, 1890–1933* (Munich: Deutscher Taschenbuch Verlag, 1983).
Lipp, A., *Meinungslenkung im Krieg: Kriegserfahrungen deutscher Soldaten und ihre Deutung 1914–1918* (Göttingen: Vandenhoeck & Ruprecht, 2003).
Maier, H., 'Ideen von 1914 – Ideen von 1939?', *Vierteljahrshefte für Zeitgeschichte* 38(4) (1990), 525–42.
Mann, W., 'The Past as Future? Hellenism, the Gymnasium, and Altertumswissenschaft', in R. Curren (ed.), *A Companion to the Philosophy of Education* (Malden, MA: Blackwell, 2003), 143–60.
Mannheim, K., 'Historicism', in *Essays on the Sociology of Knowledge* (London: Routledge & Kegan Paul, 1952), 84–133.
———, 'The Problem of Generations', *Essays on the Sociology of Knowledge* (New York: Routledge & Kegan Paul, 1952), 276–320.
Marschall, B., *Reisen und Regieren: die Nordlandfahrten Kaiser Wilhelms II* (Heidelberg: C. Winter, 1991).
Mattusch, K.R., 'Auf dem Weg zum grossen Bund', in Will Vesper (ed.), *Deutsche Jugend. 30 Jahre Geschichte einer Bewegung* (Berlin: Holle & Co., 1934), 103–20.
Mau, H., 'Die deutsche Jugendbewegung, Rückblick und Ausblick', *Zeitschrift für Religions- und Geistesgeschichte* 2(7) (1948), 135–49.
Messer, A., *Die freideutsche jugendbewegung: Ihr Verlauf von 1913 bis 1923* (Langensalza: Hermann Beyer & Söhne, 1924).
Meyboom, I., *Erziehung zum Zionismus. Der Jüdische Wanderbund Blau-Weiß als Versuch einer praktischen Umsetzung des Programms der Jüdischen Renaissance* (Frankfurt am Main: Peter Lang, 2009).
Midelfort, H.C.E., *A History of Madness in Sixteenth-Century Germany* (Stanford, CA: Stanford University Press, 1999).
Mitgau, H., 'Der Feldwandervogel', in W. Vesper (ed.), *Deutsche Jugend. 30 Jahre Geschichte einer Bewegung* (Berlin: Holle & Co., 1934), 63–83.
Mogge, W., 'Oberdada und Wandervögel. Johannes Baader, Burg Ludwigstein und die Jugendbewegung 1922/23', *Jahrbuch des Archivs der deutsche Jugendbewegung* 18 (1999), 233–316.
———, *"Ihr Wandervögel in der Luft …": Fundstücke zur Wanderung eines romantischen Bildes und zur Selbstinszenierung einer Jugendbewegung* (Würzburg: Königshausen & Neumann, 2009).
Mogge, W., and J. Reulecke, *Hoher Meißner 1913: der Erste Freideutsche Jugendtag in Dokumenten, Deutungen und Bildern* (Cologne: Verlag Wissenschaft und Politik, 1988).
Mohler, A., *Die konservative Revolution in Deutschland 1918–1932. Ein Handbuch* (Darmstadt: Wissenschaftliche Buchgesellschaft, 1972).

Mommsen, W.J., 'Einleitung: Die deutschen kulturellen Eliten im Ersten Weltkrieg', in Wolfgang J. Mommsen (ed.), *Die Rolle der Intellektuellen, Künstler und Schriftsteller im Ersten Weltkrieg* (Munich: Oldenbourg, 1996), 1–15.

Mosse, G.L., *The Crisis of German Ideology: Intellectual Origins of the Third Reich* (New York: Grosset and Dunlap, 1964).

Müller, A., 'Drei Blätter der Erinnerung. Aus einem Kranz für die "Münchener Laienspiele"', in H. Kaiser (ed.), *Begegnungen und Wirkungen: Festgabe für Rudolf Mirbt und das deutsche Laienspiel* (Kassel: Bärenreiter-Verlag, 1956), 18–22.

———, 'Laienspiel – Spiel der Gemeinschaft', in E. Korn, O. Suppert and K. Vogt (eds), *Die Jugendbewegung: Welt und Wirkung; zur 50. Wiederkehr des freideutschen Jugendtages auf dem Hohen Meißner* (Düsseldorf: Eugen Diederichs Verlag, 1963), 67–84.

———, *Als München leuchtete: der Jugendring und der Spielkreis Mirbt, 1920–1925: Blätter zur Erinnerung an Rudolf Mirbt und an den Mirbtkreis* (Weinheim: Deutscher Theaterverlag, 1974).

Müller, J., *Die Jugendbewegung als deutsche Hauptrichtung neukonservativer Reform* (Zurich: Europa Verlag, 1971).

———, '"Das Leben ist nicht mehr als Maienblüte" – Eberhard Koebels Japanrezeption', in F. Ehmcke, A. Niehaus and C. Weber (eds), *Reisen, Dialoge, Begegnungen. Festschrift für Franziska Ehmcke* (Berlin: Lit, 2012), 129–48.

Munslow, A., 'Constructionist History', in A. Munslow (ed.), *The Routledge Companion to Historical Studies. Second Edition* (London: Routledge, 2006), 66–67.

Nanko, U., *Die Deutsche Glaubensbewegung: eine historische und soziologische Untersuchung* (Marburg: Diagonal, 1993).

Nasarski, P.E., 'Aufbruch der Jugend im Grenz- und Ausland', in P.E. Nasarski (ed.), *Deutsche Jugendbewegung in Europa. Versuch einer Bilanz* (Cologne: Verlag Wissenschaft und Politik, 1967), 19–24.

Neuhaus, A., *Das geistliche Lied in der Jugendbewegung: zur literarischen Sakralität um 1900* (Tübingen: Francke, 2005).

Neuloh, O., and W. Zilius, *Die Wandervögel. Eine empirisch-soziologische Untersuchung der frühen deutschen Jugendbewegung* (Göttingen: Vandenhoeck & Ruprecht, 1982).

Neumann, M., 'Fidus – Ikonograph der Jugend', in G. Ille and G. Köhler (eds), *Der Wandervogel. Es begann in Steglitz* (Berlin: Stapp Verlag, 1987), 256–65.

Nevin, T.R., *Ernst Jünger and Germany: Into the Abyss, 1914–1945* (Durham, NC: Duke University Press, 1996).

Niemeyer, C., '"Plündernde Soldaten". Die pädagogische Nietzsche-Rezeption im Ersten Weltkrieg', *Zeitschrift für Pädagogik* 45(2) (1999), 209–29.

———, 'Nietzsche als "Prophet der Jugendbewegung" – ein Mißverständnis?', in R. Reschke (ed.), *Zeitenwende – Wertewende: Internationaler Kongreß der Nietzsche-Gesellschaft zum 100. Todestag Friedrich Nietzsches vom 24.–27. August 2000 in Naumburg* (Berlin: 2001), 181–87.

———, 'Sozialpädagogik und Jugendbewegung', in C. Niemeyer (ed.), *Sozialpädagogik als Wissenschaft und Profession* (Weinheim: Juventa Verlag, 2003), 110–22.

———, 'Jugendbewegung und Nationalsozialismus', *Zeitschrift für Religions- und Geistesgeschichte* 57(4) (2005), 337–65.

———, 'Werner Kindt und die "Dokumentation der Jugendbewegung". Text- und quellenkritische Beobachtungen', *Historische Jugendforschung. Jahrbuch des Archivs der deutschen Jugendbewegung* 2 (2005), 230–49.

———, *Die dunklen Seiten der Jugendbewegung. Vom Wandervogel zur Hitlerjugend* (Tübingen: A. Francke Verlag, 2013).

Nipperdey, T., 'Jugend und Politik um 1900', in W. Rüegg (ed.), *Kulturkritik und Jugendkult* (Frankfurt am Main: Vittorio Klostermann, 1974).

Nora, P., 'Between Memory and History: Les Lieux De Mémoire', *Representations* 26 (1989), 7–24.

Oesterreicher, J.M., *Walls are Crumbling: Seven Jewish Philosophers Discover Christ* (New York: Devin-Adair, 1962).

Oexle, O.G., 'Das Mittelalter und das Unbehagen an der Moderne. Mittelalterbeschwörungen in der Weimarer Republik und danach', in O.G. Oexle (ed.), *Geschichtswissenschaft im Zeichen des Historismus: Studien zu Problemgeschichten der Moderne* (Göttingen: Vandenhoeck & Ruprecht, 1996), 137–62.

———, 'German Malaise of Modernity: Ernst H. Kantorowicz and his "Kaiser Friedrich der Zweite"', in R.L. Benson and J. Fried (eds), *Ernst Kantorowicz. Erträge der Doppeltagung* (Stuttgart: Steiner, 1997), 33–56.

Paetel, K.O., *Das Bild vom Menschen in der deutschen Jugendführung* (Bad Godesberg: Voggenreiter, 1954).

———, *Jugend in der Entscheidung 1913 – 1933 – 1945* (Bad Godesberg: Voggenreiter, 1963).

Peterson, B.O., *History, Fiction, and Germany: Writing the Nineteenth-century Nation* (Detroit: Wayne State University Press, 2005).

Peukert, D.J.K., *The Weimar Republic: The Crisis of Classical Modernity* (London: Penguin, 1991).

Preuß, R., 'Freideutsche Jugend und Politik. Politische Orientierungen und Manifestationen innerhalb der bürgerlichen Jugendbewegung 1913–1918/19', *Jahrbuch des Archivs der deutschen Jugendbewegung* 16 (1986), 229–40.

Pross, H.E., *Jugend Eros Politik. Die Geschichte der deutschen Jugendverbände* (Frankfurt am Main: Büchergilde Gutenberg, 1965).

Puschner, U., *Die völkische Bewegung im wilhelminischen Kaiserreich: Sprache, Rasse, Religion* (Darmstadt: Wissenschaftliche Buchgesellschaft, 2001).

———, '"One People, One Reich, One God". The Völkische Weltanschauung and Movement', *Bulletin (German Historical Institute)* 24(1) (2002), 5–28.

Raabe, F., *Die bündische Jugend: ein Beitrag zur Geschichte der Weimarer Republik* (Bonn: Studienbüro für Jugendfragen, 1961).

Raedts, P., *De ontdekking van de Middeleeuwen. Geschiedenis van een illusie* (Amsterdam: Wereldbibliotheek, 2011).

Ras, M.E.P. de, *Body, Femininity and Nationalism: Girls in the German Youth Movement 1900–1933* (New York: Routledge, 2008).

Reichhold, K., 'Laienspiel – Kleine Schule der Menschenliebe', in H. Kaiser (ed.), *Begegnungen und Wirkungen: Festgabe für Rudolf Mirbt und das deutsche Laienspiel* (Kassel: Bärenreiter-Verlag, 1956), 132–34.

Reis, A., *Die Jugendbewegung als religiöses Phänomen* (Frankfurt am Main: Johann-Wolfgang-Goethe-Universität, 1994).

Reulecke, J., 'Männerbund versus Familie. Bürgerliche Jugendbewegung und Familie in Deutschland im ersten Drittel des 20. Jahrhunderts', in Th. Koebner (ed.), *Mit uns zieht die Zeit: der Mythos Jugend* (Frankfurt am Main: Suhrkamp, 1985), 199–223.

———, 'Hat die Jugendbewegung den Nationalsozialismus vorbereitet? Zum Umgang mit einer falschen Frage', in W.R. Krabbe (ed.), *Politische Jugend in der Weimarer Republik* (Bochum: Universitätsverlag Dr. N. Brockmeyer, 1993), 222–43.

Rohmann, G., 'The Invention of Dancing Mania Frankish Christianity, Platonic Cosmology and Bodily Expressions in Sacred Space', *The Medieval History Journal* 12(1) (2009), 13–45.

Runia, E., 'Presence', *History and Theory* 45(1) (2006), 1–29.

Rüsen, J., 'Was ist Geschichtskultur? Überlegungen zu einer neuen Art, über Geschichte nachzudenken', in J. Rüsen (ed.), *Historische Orientierung: über die Arbeit des Geschichtsbewußtseins, sich in der Zeit zurechtzufinden* (Cologne: Böhlau, 1994), 3–26.

———, 'Introduction: Historical Thinking as Intercultural Discourse', in J. Rüsen (ed.), *Western Historical Thinking: An Intercultural Debate* (New York: Berghahn Books, 2002), 1–11.

———, 'Historical Consciousness: Narrative Structure, Moral Function, and Ontogenetic Development', in P. Seixas (ed.), *Theorizing Historical Consciousness* (Toronto: University of Toronto Press, 2004), 63–85.

Sachße, C., 'Friedrich Siegmund-Schultze, die "Soziale Arbeitsgemeinschaft" und die bürgerliche Sozialreform in Deutschland', in H.-E. Tenorth et al. (eds), *Friedrich Siegmund-Schultze*

*(1885–1969): ein Leben für Kirche, Wissenschaft und soziale Arbeit* (Stuttgart: Kohlhammer, 2007), 35–49.
Sauer, W., 'Die deutsche Jugendbewegung – Schwierigkeiten einer Ortsbestimmung', in W. Sauer (ed.), *Rückblicke und Ausblicke die deutsche Jugendbewegung im Urteil nach 1945* (Heidenheim: Südmarkverl. Fritsch, 1978), 9–41.
Scharff, E., 'Neues Pathos: "Das Wesentliche"', in W. Frantzen (ed.), *Laienspiel in der Weimarer Zeit* (Münster: Landesarbeitsgemeinschaft für Spiel und Amateurtheater im Land Nordrhein-Westfalen, 1969), 67–68.
Schatzker, Ch., 'Martin Buber's Influence on the Jewish Youth Movement in Germany', *Leo Baeck Institute Yearbook* 23 (1968), 151–72.
Schenk, D., *Die Freideutsche Jugend, 1913–1919/20: Eine Jugendbewegung in Krieg, Revolution und Krise* (Münster: LIT-Verlag, 1991).
Schierer, H., *Das Zeitschriftenwesen der Jugendbewegung: ein Beitrag zur Geschichte der Jugendzeitschrift* (Berlin: Lorentz, 1938).
Schlemmer, H., *Der Geist der Deutschen Jugendbewegung* (Munich: Rösl & Cie., 1923).
Schneider, H., *Die Waldeck: Lieder – Fahrten – Abenteuer; die Geschichte der Burg Waldeck von 1911 bis heute* (Potsdam: Verlag für Berlin-Brandenburg, 2005).
Schneider, T.S., et al., *Die Autoren und Bücher der deutschsprachigen Literatur zum 1. Weltkrieg 1914–1939* (Osnabrück: Universitätsverlag Osnabrück, 2008).
Schoeps, H.-J., *Die letzten dreissig Jahre. Rückblicke* (Stuttgart: Klett, 1956).
———, *Zeitgeist im Wandel* (Stuttgart: Klett, 1967).
Scholder, K., *Die Kirchen und das Dritte Reich I: Vorgeschichte und Zeit der Illusionen, 1918–1934* (Frankfurt am Main: Propyläen, 1977).
Schönemann, B., 'Geschichtskultur als Forschungskonzept der Geschichtsdidaktik', *Zeitschrift für Geschichtsdidaktik* 1(200) (2002), 78–86.
Schröder, P., *Die Leitbegriffe der deutschen Jugendbewegung in der Weimarer Republik: Eine ideengeschichtliche Studie* (Berlin: Lit, 1996).
Schütz, O., 'Friedrich Nietzsche als Prophet der deutschen Jugendbewegung', *Neue Jahrbücher für Wissenschaft und Jugendbildung* 5 (1929), 64–80.
Seidelmann, K., *Bund und Gruppe als Lebensformen deutscher Jugend: Versuch einer Erscheinungskunde des deutschen Jugendlebens in der ersten Hälfte des XX. Jahrhunderts* (Munich: Wiking Verlag, 1955).
———, *Die Pfadfinder in der deutschen Jugendgeschichte* (Hannover: Schroedel, 1977).
Siefert, H., *Untersuchungen zur Entstehung und Frühgeschichte der Bündischen Jugend* (Erlangen: Friedrich-Alexander-Universität, 1964).
Sontheimer, K., *Antidemokratisches Denken in der Weimarer Republik* (Munich: Deutscher Taschenbuch-Verlag, 1978).
Speiser, H., *Hans Breuer, Wirken und Wirkungen: eine Monographie* (Witzenhausen: Stiftung Jugendburg Ludwigstein, 1977).
Spengler, Oswald, *The Decline of the West: Form and Actuality* (London: George Allen & Unwin Ltd., 1926).
Spranger, E., *Der gegenwärtige Stand der Geisteswissenschaften und die Schule* (Leipzig: B.G. Teubner, 1922).
———, *Psychologie des Jugendalters* (Heidelberg: Quelle & Meyer, 1929).
———, 'Fünf Jugendgenerationen 1900–1949', in E. Spranger (ed.), *Pädagosische Perspektiven. Beiträge zu Erziehungsfragen der Gegenwart* (Heidelberg: Quelle & Meyer, 1955), 25–57.
Stachura, P.D., *The German Youth Movement 1900–1945: An Interpretative and Documentary History* (London: Macmillan, 1981).
Stambolis, B., 'Einleitung', in B. Stambolis (ed.), *Jugendbewegt geprägt. Essays zu autobiographischen Texten von Werner Heisenberg, Robert Jungk und vielen anderen* (Göttingen: V&R unipress, 2013), 13–42.
———, 'Wallfahrtsstätten der Religion, der Nation und der Jugend. Zur Bedeutung heiliger Orte in der Jugendbewegung', *Jahrbuch des Archivs der deutschen Jugendbewegung* 20 (2002), 148–58.

Stark, G.D., *Entrepreneurs of Ideology: Neoconservative Publishers in Germany, 1890–1933* (Chapel Hill, NC: University of North Carolina Press, 1981).
Steiger, G., *'Fall Hodler': Jena 1914–1919: Der Kampf um ein Gemälde* (Jena: Friedrich-Schiller-Universität, 1970).
———, 'Feierstunde anläßlich der 50. Wiederkehr der Enthüllung des Gemäldes von Ferdinand Hodler "Aufbruch der Jenaer Studenten 1813"', *Sozialistische Universität* 12(8) (1969), 6.
Stern, F.R., *The Politics of Cultural Despair: A Study in the Rise of the Germanic Ideology* (Berkeley: University of California Press, 1961).
Strassner, E., 'Zur Sprache der Wandervogel 1890 bis 1923', *Neuphilologische Mitteilungen* 108(2) (2007), 399–422.
Strauss, L., 'The Living Issues of German Postwar Philosophy', in H. Meier (ed.), *Leo Strauss and the Theologico-Political Problem* (Cambridge: Cambridge University Press, 2006), 115–40.
Stuke, F., *Die Auslandfahrten der Bündischen Jugend am Beispiel der Sächsischen Jungenschaft. Zwischen Selbsterfahrung, 'Volkstumpflege' und transnationaler Annährung (1920–1934)*. Master's thesis (Leipzig: Universität Leipzig, 2008).
Susser, B., 'Ideological Multivalence: Martin Buber and the German Volkish Tradition', *Political Theory* 5(1) (1977), 75–96.
Thamer, H.U., 'Das Meißner-Fest der Freideutschen Jugend 1913 als Erinnerungsort der deutschen Jugendbewegung', *Jahrbuch des Archivs der deutschen Jugendbewegung* NF5 (2008), 169–90.
———, 'Der Meißner-Tag: Probleme einer jugendbündischen Erinnerungskultur', in B. Brachmann et al. (eds), *Die Kunst des Vernetzens. Festschrift für Wolfgang Hempel* (Berlin: Verlag für Berlin-Brandenburg, 2006), 399–409.
Thomas, N., *'Der Aufstand gegen die sekundäre Welt': Botho Strauss und die 'Konservative Revolution'* (Würzburg: Königshausen & Neumann, 2004).
Thomas, R.H., *Nietzsche in German Politics and Society, 1890–1918* (Manchester: Manchester University Press, 1983).
Thys, W., and H. Nohl, *Ein Landsturmmann im Himmel. Flandern und der Erste Weltkrieg in den Briefen von Herman Nohl an seine Frau* (Leipzig: Leipziger Universitätsverlag, 2005).
Tielke, M., 'Peter Hermann Zylmann', in M. Tielke (ed.), *Biographisches Lexikon für Ostfriesland III* (Aurich: Ostfriesische Landschaft, 2001), 446–54.
Tillich, P., 'Die politische Bedeutung der Utopie im Leben der Völker', in R. Albrecht (ed.), *Gesammelte Werke, Bd. 6* (Stuttgart: Evangelisches Verlagswerk, 1963), 157–210.
Tönnies, F., *Community and Society* (New York: Courier Dover Publications, [1887] 2002).
Travers, M., *Critics of Modernity: The Literature of the Conservative Revolution in Germany, 1890–1933* (New York: Peter Lang, 2001).
Troeltsch, E., *Gesammelte Schriften 3: Der Historismus und seine Probleme* (Tübingen: J.C.B. Mohr, 1922).
Ulbricht, J.H., 'Ein "Weißer Ritter" im Kampf um das Buch. Die Verlagsunternehmen von Franz Ludwig Habbel und der Bund Deutscher Neupfadfinder', in W. Schmitz and H. Schneidler (eds), *Expressionismus in Regensburg. Texte und Studien* (Regensburg: Mittelbayerische Druck.- und Verlag-Gesellschaft, 1991), 149–74.
———, 'Nietzsche als "Prophet der Jugendbewegung"? Befunde und Überlegungen zu einem Rezeptionsproblem', in U. Herrmann (ed.), *'Mit uns zieht die neue Zeit …' Der Wandervogel in der deutschen Jugendbewegung* (Weinheim: Juventa, 2006), 80–114.
Utley, P.L., 'Radical Youth: Generational Conflict in the Anfang Movement, 1912 – January 1914', *History of Education Quarterly* 19(2) (1979), 207–28.
Verhey, J., *The Spirit of 1914: Militarism, Myth, and Mobilization in Germany* (Cambridge, MA: Cambridge University Press, 2000).
Victor, W., 'Freideutsch. Zur 25. Wiederkehr des Jugendtages auf dem Hohen Meißner', *Das Wort* 3(10) (1938), 95–102.
Viehöfer, E., 'Der Verleger als Organisator: Eugen Diederichs und die bürgerlichen Reformbewegungen der Jahrhundertwende', in R. Wittmann and M. Kleiss (eds), *Archiv*

*für Geschichte des Buchwesens. 30* (Frankfurt am Main: Buchhändler-Vereinigung, 1988), 1–148.

Waller, J., *The Dancing Plague: The Strange, True Story of an Extraordinary Illness* (Naperville, IL: Sourcebooks, 2009).

Wangelin, H.,'Der Wandervogel und das Völkische', *Jahrbuch des Archivs der deutschen Jugendbewegung* (1970), 43–77.

———, *Der Wandervogel in Tagebüchern Frank Fischers und anderen Selbstzeugnissen* (Tübingen: Selbstverlag, 1982).

Wäsche, C., *Vom Singen im Volke: Richard Poppe (1884–1960) und die Ideale des Finkensteiner Bundes* (Weikersheim: Margraf, 2007).

Weber, M., *Max Weber: A Biography* (New Brunswick: Transaction Publishers, 2009).

Weberman, D., 'Phenomenology', in A. Tucker (ed.), *A Companion to the Philosophy of History and Historiography* (Malden, MA: Wiley-Blackwell, 2009), 508–17.

Wehler, H.-U., *Das Deutsche Kaiserreich* (Göttingen: Vandenhoeck & Ruprecht, 1973).

———, *Deutsche Gesellschaftsgeschichte. Vom Beginn des Ersten Weltkriegs bis zur Gründung der beiden deutschen Staaten, 1914–1949. Vol. IV, VII. Teil* (Munich: Beck, 2003).

Weißler, S., *Fokus Wandervogel: der Wandervogel in seinen Beziehungen zu den Reformbewegungen vor dem Ersten Weltkrieg* (Marburg: Jonas Verlag, 2001).

Wellbery, D.E., 'Stimmung', in K. Barck (ed.), *Ästhetische Grundbegriffe. Historisches Wörterbuch in sieben Bänden. Band 5* (Stuttgart: Metzler, 2003), 703–33.

Werner, M., 'Jugendbewegung als Reform der studentisch-akademischen Jugendkultur. Selbsterziehung – Selbstbildung – die neue Geselligkeit: Die Jenenser Freistudentenschaft und der Serakreis', in U. Herrmann (ed.), *"Mit uns zieht die neue Zeit" – der Wandervogel in der deutschen Jugendbewegung* (Weinheim: Juventa, 2006), 171–203.

White, H., *Metahistory: The Historical Imagination in Nineteenth-Century Europe* (Baltimore, MD: Johns Hopkins University Press, 1973).

Wiedmann, A.K., *The German Quest for Primal Origins in Art, Culture, and Politics 1900–1933: die "Flucht in Urzustände"* (Lewiston, NY: E. Mellen Press, 1995).

Wietschorke, J., 'Der Weltkrieg als »soziale Arbeitsgemeinschaft«. Eine Innenansicht bildungsbürgerlicher Kriegsdeutungen 1914–1918', *Geschichte und Gesellschaft* 34(2) (2008), 225–51.

Will, C., *Das deutsche Jugendwandern* (Hilchenbach: Reichsverband für Deutsche Jugendherbergen, 1932).

Williams, J.A., *Turning to Nature in Germany: Hiking, Nudism, and Conservation, 1900–1940* (Stanford, CA: Stanford University Press, 2007).

Winnecken, A., *Ein Fall von Antisemitismus: zur Geschichte und Pathogenese der deutschen Jugendbewegung vor dem Ersten Weltkrieg* (Cologne: Verlag Wissenschaft und Politik, 1991).

Woods, R., *The Conservative Revolution in the Weimar Republic* (London: Macmillan, 1996).

Zernack, J. 'Anschauungen vom Norden im deutschen Kaiserreich', in U. Puschner, W. Schmitz and J.H. Ulbricht (eds), *Handbuch zur 'Völkischen Bewegung'* (Munich: Saur, 1996).

———, 'Der "Mythos vom Norden" und die Krise der Moderne. Skandinavische Literatur im Programm des Eugen Diederichs Verlages', in M. Werner and J.H. Ulbricht (eds), *Romantik, Revolution und Reform. Der Eugen Diederichs Verlag im Epochenkontext 1900 bis 1945* (Göttingen: Wallstein Verlag, 1999), 208–23.

Ziemann, B., 'Weimar was Weimar: Politics, Culture and the Emplotment of the German Republic', *German History* 28(4) (2010), 542–71.

Zwierlein, E., *Die Idee einer philosophischen Anthropologie bei Paul Ludwig Landsberg: zur Frage nach dem Wesen des Menschen zwischen Selbstauffassung und Selbstgestaltung* (Würzburg: Königshausen & Neumann, 1989).

# Index

activism, 104, 108, 191
Adler und Falken, 127, 129, 165, 178
adult
   education, 166, 168
   interference, 3, 9
   involvement, 10, 122, 135
   morality, 38
   supervision, 31, 90, 127, 191
aeon, 173, 178
agency
   and cosmic thought, 105, 113
   and meaning cultures, 123
   and progress, 113, 187–190
   and utopianism, 20, 159, 188
Ahlborn, Knud, 94
Akademische Vereinigung Jena, 78
Akademische Vereinigung Marburg, 46–47
Alps, 165, 178
Alsace, 70, 161, 166–167
Alt-Wandervogel, 35–37, 39–42, 46, 56, 67, 77, 127, 133, 142, 158, 161, 165, 170
Ammon, Otto, 34
anachronism, 70, 101
*ancien régime*, 13, 17, 194
Ankersmit, Frank, 6
anthroposophy, 104, 112, 139–140
antiquity
   Greek, 159, 171, 175–176
   late, 136
   order of, 136
Antwerp, 76–77, 80
Aquinas, Thomas, 136
Artamanen, 127
artisans, 32, 148–149
Athens, 174–175

attunement, 20, 57, 67, 100, 120, 125, 140, 144. *See also Stimmung*
August 1914, 74–76, 91, 99, 112–113, 189–190
Austria, 34–35, 68, 129, 177
authenticity, 50, 174, 192
Avenarius, Ferdinand, 34, 46, 48, 106
AWV-Mädchenbund, 127

Bach, Johann Sebastian, 170
Baden-Powell, Robert, 134, 161
*Baedecker*, 38–39, 60
Balser, Karl, 45
baroque music, 177, 180
Bartels, Adolf, 34
*Bauhütte*, 120, 147–149
Bavaria, 31, 167, 177, 182
Benjamin, Walter, 42, 73
Berlin, 30–32, 39–40, 42, 47, 70–73, 91, 134, 165
bestowing virtue, 94
Bibelkreis, 126
Bible, 71–72, 173, 180
*Bildung*, 33–34, 50, 171
Bismarck, Otto von, 33, 106
Bismarckjugend, 146
Blau-Weiß, 57, 68–74, 83
Blüher, Hans
   and elitism, 142
   on *Männerbund*, 131–133
   on Platonic eros, 100
   on Wandervogel history, 9–10, 72
Boeckh, Joachim, 173
Bohemia, 34, 161
Bohemian Forest, 2, 31, 35, 40

Bohnenkamp, Hans, 82
Bojarzin, Otto, 41
Bondy, Max, 131
Boß, Alexander, 179–180
bourgeoisie
  emancipation of, 10
  English, 170–171
  nationalism of, 28, 33
Boy Scouts
  British, 134, 161, 164–165, 167, 191
  and the Bündische Jugend, 9, 20, 127–128, 165, 191
  Hungarian, 164
Brandenburg, 37
Bratislava, 139
Breuer, Hans
  cultural criticism, 41–42, 50
  and folk music, 32
  and the Heidelberger Pachantey, 40, 41
Breuer, Stefan, 14–15, 189–190
Bruck, Arthur Moeller van den, 13–14, 128–129
Brügmann, Karl, 80
Brussels, 76
Buber, Martin, 69, 71, 73
Budapest, 164
Buddhism, 104
Bühnenvolksbund, 146
Bulgaria, 166
*Bund*, 126–130, 191
Bund der Köngener, 126, 173
Bund der Reichspfadfinder, 167–168
Bündische Jugend
  and the Conservative Revolution, 13, 193–194
  eschatology, 120, 126–130, 149–150, 159–160, 189–193
  hikes abroad, 158–183
  knighthood, 132–134
  and Nazism, 11–12
  performance groups, 146
  rise of, 9, 20, 126
Burckhardt, Jacob, 69, 136
Burschenschaften, 106, 121
Buschhüter, Karl, 148
Buske, Ernst, 166, 168

Calais, 145
capitalism
  critique of, 82, 147, 188, 190, 194
  negative, 104
Carinthia, 165
Carnap, Rudolf, 78

Chamberlain, Houston Stewart, 14, 34
chiliasm, 120, 126, 128. *See also* millennialism
choreomania, 122, 126, 151
Christ, Franz, 89, 113
Christdeutsche Jugend, 146
Christengemeinschaft, 108
Christianity, 89, 94, 102–103, 128, 167, 178–179
Christmas play, 138–139. *See also* mystery play
Cicero, Marcus Tullius, 33
Classicism, 82, 176
Clauren, Heinrich, 106
Coburg, 140
Cologne, 143
commemoration
  of the Battle of the Nations, 29–30, 44–49, 67
  of fallen Wandervögel, 149
  in Wilhelmine Germany, 27–28, 33
communism, 14, 104–105, 181
community
  criticism of, 73–74
  and education, 48, 49
  experience of, 5, 56–57, 61–62, 69, 75, 90, 93, 98, 105, 123–150, 182, 189
  and history, 66, 102, 169–170, 192–193
  and the individual, 111–112
Conservative Revolution, 3, 13–17, 137, 150, 187, 189, 193–194
Constantinople, 31, 173
Copalle, Siegfried, 31, 34–37
Corinth, 174–175
cosmology, 7, 123, 137, 193
cosmos, 5, 98, 105, 123, 135–136, 159, 190
countryside
  city versus, 63, 79, 160–161
  German, 2, 69–74, 80, 138
  hikes in, 41, 91
Courland, 94, 161, 168
Cramer, Konrad, 59–60, 82–83
Crete, 158
crisis
  Badeni, 34
  of classical modernity, 15–16
  economic, 19, 83
  of experience, 99–103
  of historicism, 79, 90, 99, 103, 110, 187
cyclical conception of time, 135, 150, 160, 192
Czechoslovakia, 166

Dahlem, 31
Damaschke, Adolf, 34

Damme, 80–81
dance macabre, 139. *See also Totentanz*
Danzig, 166
*Dasein*, 65, 67, 78, 82
Dehmel, Hans, 162, 164
Delos, 158
Delphi, 174
Denmark, 161, 166, 177
*Der Anfang*, 42–43, 48, 63, 104
Descartes, René, 7
destiny
   European, 169
   finding, 158–159, 163, 172–173, 182
   German, 29, 74, 104, 112, 160, 167
   Heidegger on, 66
   and memory, 109–110
Deutsche Akademische Freischar, 46, 78, 131
Deutsche Bund abstinenter Studenten, 40
Deutsche Freischar, 9, 18, 165–166, 168, 172, 180
Deutsche Jungenschaft vom 1.11.1929, 180–181
Diederichs, Eugen, 78, 107, 151, 178
Dilthey, Wilhelm, 58–60, 78, 172
Döring, Gertrud, 80
Dürer, Albrecht, 64, 134
Dürerbund, 34

Eckart, Walter, 144
Eckhart, Meister, 92–93, 97, 112, 130
education
   adult, 166
   critique of, 33–34, 42–44, 68
   historical, 27, 43, 49–50, 58–59, 63–64, 91–92, 99–100
   self-, 47–50, 121, 140, 189
Engelhardt, Viktor, 18–19
England, 81, 161, 166, 168–171, 181
Englishman, 170
Enlightenment, 1, 10–11, 13, 16, 58, 99
Epprechtstein, 167
Epting, Karl, 129
Erfurt, 122–124
*Erlebnis*
   and community, 144
   criticism of, 73–74, 99–103
   and hiking, 38
   and history, 58–63, 68–72, 82–83, 93–94, 102, 112, 189, 193
   and representation, 19, 65
   versus cognition, 5–6, 57
Eros, 100, 126, 131–132

eschatology
   *Bund* and, 129–130
   experience and, 90, 112
   and history, 130, 143
   immanent, 119–120, 149–151, 172, 180, 191
   rise of, 20
experience. *See under Erlebnis*
expressionism, 106, 138, 143

fatalism, 103–105, 108, 111, 191
Feldwandervogel, 76–83, 93, 98, 127
Fichte, Johann Gottlieb, 47–50, 67, 72, 75, 103, 120
Fichtelgebirge, 31, 167
Fidus (Hugo Höppener), 66
Finkensteiner Bund, 144
Finland, 165–166
Fischer, Karl, 10, 31–39, 39–41, 63–65, 162
Flanders, 74, 76–83
Flurschütz, Hildulf, 179
folk
   culture, 36, 49, 53, 57–58, 76–77, 80, 85, 100, 169
   dances, 38, 54, 71, 128–133, 146, 193
   songs, 7, 10, 18, 38–39, 44, 49, 53, 76, 91, 146, 173
Foucault, Michel, 7
Frankfurt, 39, 114
Freideutsche Jugend
   dissolution of, 114, 123, 126–127, 191
   on education, 47–49
   establishment of, 9, 19, 30
   and the First World War, 75, 78, 94
   and historicism, 44–46, 99–104
   and Romanticism, 100
Freideutsche Jugendtag, 44, 66
Freideutsche Kreis, 11–12
Freie Schulgemeinde Wickersdorf, 43, 46, 139, 148
Freikorps, 104–106, 132, 162
Freyer, Hans, 16, 188–190
Friese, Gerhard, 100
Fritsch, Albrecht von, 122–123, 169
Fritzsche, Peter, 15
Friz, Erwin, 178

Gadamer, Hans-Georg, 3, 58
Gardiner, Rolf, 168–169
*Gelassenheit*, 97, 111. *See also* releasement
*Gemeinschaft*, 5, 61–62, 73, 128. *See also* community
George, Stefan, 14, 128, 136, 142

Gerlach, Dankwart, 147
Germania, Abstinentenbund an deutschen Schulen, 40, 46
Germanische Glaubensgemeinschaft, 179
Geusen, 165
Ghent, 78
Glaser, Karl, 74
Glatzel, Frank, 92, 104
Godhead, 97–98, 111
gods
  Germanic, 179–180, 193
  Greek, 111, 158–160, 173, 175, 193
  reattaching to, 109, 134, 135, 169, 172
  twilight of the, 1
Goethe, Johann Wolfgang von, 30, 64–65, 102, 109, 114, 172
gothicism, 50, 71, 111, 125, 130–131, 140, 147, 151, 180, 192
Götsch, Georg, 1–3, 169–171, 176–177
Göttingen, 56, 114, 151
Gräff, Otger, 92, 179
Gräser, Gusto, 122
Greece, 82, 159–160, 166, 171–176, 180, 182
Greifenbund, 92, 179
Grimm brothers, 41, 145
Grosche, Robert, 143
guilds, 64, 93, 129, 131, 147
Gumbrecht, Hans Ulrich, 7–8, 123, 191–193
Gurlitt, Ludwig, 33–35

Haass-Berkow, Gottfried, 139–141, 145
Habbel, Franz Ludwig, 130
Haberkorn, Rudolf, 90–94, 96–99, 101–102, 111–114
Haeckel, Ernst, 106
Halle, 90
Hamann, Richard, 108
Hamburg, 39, 46
Hanstein Castle, 56–57, 60–61
Harz Mountains, 31, 65, 164
Hausmann, Manfred, 56–57, 60–61
Hedicke, Walter, 80
Hegelianism, 8, 43–44
Heidegger, Martin, 8, 65–67
Heidelberg, 40–41
Heidelberger Pachantey, 40–41
Heidenreich, Alfred, 61
Heilmann, Max, 60
*Heimat*
  exploring, 65, 74
  image of, 76, 80, 81
  search for, 158–183
Hellas, 171–176. *See also* Greece

Herf, Jeffrey, 16–17
heritage
  English, 170
  experience of, 63–64, 159
  exploring, 20, 50, 189
  Greek, 171, 175
  Jewish, 57, 69–70, 92
  Nordic, 180–182
Herzl, Theodor, 69
Hesse, Hermann, 38–39, 46, 122, 147
hikes, 177
hiking
  abroad, 160–167
  in Germany, 2, 9, 18–20, 31, 36–37, 61, 63–64, 68–69, 73–74
historical culture
  of Nazi Germany, 3
  of Wilhelmine Germany, 19, 27–30, 32, 42–43, 46, 49, 58, 62, 67, 69
historicism
  crisis of, 79, 90, 99, 103, 110, 187
  critique of, 99–103, 114, 131, 192
  overcoming, 137, 143, 170, 188
Hitler, Adolf, 11, 138, 181–182
Hodler, Ferdinand, 105–108, 114
Hoffmann, Hermann, 30–31, 40
Hofmannsthal, Hugo von, 14, 143
Hohe Meißner, 29–30, 46–48, 66–67, 108, 113, 189
Hölderlin, Friedrich, 104, 109, 111, 172–173, 179
Holland, 177
homeland, 59, 71, 158, 168, 173, 175, 179. *See also Heimat*
Homer, 175
Höppener, Hugo, 66
Huizinga, Johan, 141
Hungary, 34, 68, 164–166, 182
Hunsrück, 148
Husserl, Edmund, 59, 135

Iceland, 178
Idealism, German, 45, 47–49, 50, 58, 132, 136
imagination, 110, 132–133, 167, 173, 180
infinity, 58, 110–111, 120, 180
Israel, 68, 72–73
Italy, 158, 167–168, 178

Jena, 36, 46, 78, 101, 104–107, 111, 151
Jerusalem, 121
Jewishness, 57, 68–70, 73–74
journeymen, 32, 40–41

*Jugendburg*, 148. *See also* youth castle
*Jugendkultur*, 43–44
Jugendring, 142
Jung-Stahlhelm, 146
Jung-Wandervogel, 30, 42, 45–46, 60
Jungdeutsche Bund, 127
Jünger, Ernst, 13, 16, 132
Jungmannschaft, 135, 162
Jungnationale Bund, 119, 127, 168, 178

Kantianism, 5, 130, 137
Keller, Gottfried, 38, 97
knighthood, 35, 65, 120, 130, 132–134, 167, 191
Köbel, Eberhard, 180–181
Köning, Josef, 182
Koselleck, Reinhart, 4–5, 58, 113, 126
Kotzde, Wilhelm, 129
Kronacher Bund, 127, 146–147
Krügler, Hermann, 162, 164
Kühnemann, Eugen, 47
Kummer, Bernhard, 178
Kutzleb, Hjalmar, 60

Lagarde, Paul de, 34, 102
Lähn, Kurd, 158–159
*Laienspiel*, 120, 137–139, 141–147, 150, 166, 192
Lamberty, Friedrich (Muck), 121, 125, 145, 151, 192
Landsberg, Paul Ludwig, 135–137
*Landsknecht*, 132–133
Landvolkbewegung, 13
Langbehn, Julius, 34, 102
Lao Tzu, 108, 111
Laqueur, Walter, 10–11, 34, 76
*Lebensreform*, 40, 46, 66, 79, 176, 178–179
Leipzig, 27, 29–30, 39, 44–45, 179
Lemke, Bruno, 46
Lenz, Eduard, 108–109, 111
liberalism, 11, 13, 15, 28, 40, 45, 75, 194
lieux de mémoire, 30
Lißner, Hans, 40–42
Lithuania, 98
Livonia, 161
logos, 112, 132, 173
Lorraine, 27, 95, 161
Ludwigstein Castle, 147–148
Luserke, Martin, 139
Luther, Martin, 33, 64, 121, 125, 140

Maccabees, 71–72
Magdeburg, 146

Magyars, 164
Mainz, 65
Mainz Cathedral, 64
Mann, Thomas, 14
Männerbund, 35, 130–133
Mannheim, Karl, 99
Marburg, 41, 46–48, 144
Märkische Spielgemeinde, 170, 176–177
Mattusch, Kurt, 165
meaning cultures, 6–8, 123, 192–193
Mebes, Hellmut, 65
Menschheit, 93, 108. *See also* humanity
metaphysics, 2, 7, 13, 90, 131–132, 137, 173, 191
Meyen, Wolfgang, 31–32, 40
Middle Ages, 10, 20, 32, 64, 100, 114, 130–131, 135–137, 139, 147–148, 180, 191–192
millennialism, 122. *See also* chiliasm
Mirbt, Rudolf, 138–139, 141–146
Mohler, Armin, 13–14, 17, 150, 193
Müller, Alwin, 144
Munich, 41, 137–138, 142, 181
mystery play, 2, 139, 143, 145
mysticism, 104–105, 110, 112, 120, 126, 129, 133, 137, 149
myth, 12, 131, 135, 173, 178

Napoleon, 27–28, 109, 111
Narten, Enno, 80–81, 147–148
nationalism, 11, 14, 28–30, 33–35, 45, 47, 50, 69–70, 92, 106, 112, 165, 193
Natorp, Paul, 47–48, 63, 74, 111
Nazism, 3, 11–12, 15–16, 149, 181–182, 193
Nerother Wandervogel, 19, 133–134, 148–149, 166
Neue Schar, 120–126, 150–151
Neumann, Otto, 76, 81
Neupfadfinder, 127–128, 130, 134–135, 163, 165, 173–176
Niebergall, Friedrich, 130
Niemeyer, Christian, 12, 49
Nietzsche, Friedrich
on historicism, 43, 49–50, 79, 91–92, 94, 96, 99, 101–103, 110, 114, 150
and vitalism, 13, 43, 73, 188
Nohl, Herman, 78–81
nominalism, 136
Nonne, Johann Heinrich Christian, 67
*Nordland*, 176, 180
Norway, 166, 176–178
nostalgia, 39, 133
Novaya Zemlya, 181

Oelbermann, Robert, 133
Oppenheim, Hans, 70
Osnabrück, 76, 81

Paetel, Karl Otto, 126
paganism, 128
pantheism, 58, 98, 110, 120, 124, 149, 190
Passau, 164
passivism, 104, 111
Patras, 173
patriotism, 29–30, 33, 44–45, 63, 170, 190
Pécs, 164
personality
  education for, 33–34, 49–50, 61, 93, 111, 189
  leading, 95–96
  and performance, 142–144
Peukert, Detlev, 15–16
philhellenism, 158, 171–176
philistinism, 42–43, 170, 188
Plato, 78, 100, 109, 131–132, 170
Platter, Thomas, 32, 64
Plüschow, Gunther, 95
Poppe, Richard, 141, 144
Posen, 90–92, 95, 161
presence cultures, 6–8, 123, 192–193
Proust, Marcel, 80
Prussia, 27–28, 33, 95, 105–106, 161, 165–167
Prussianism, 28–29, 32, 190

Quickborn, 142–143

rationalism, 5, 8, 13, 33, 131, 136, 194
redemption, 93, 112, 121, 134–135, 143, 151, 163
Reformation, 125, 138, 170
Regenstein Castle, 65
Reichhold, Karl, 142
Reichsstand, Gefolgschaft deutscher Wandervögel, 129
Reichwein, Adolf, 169
releasement, 94, 97, 111, 138, 171, 176
religiosity, 20, 83, 90, 96, 98, 103, 112–114, 119, 149, 190–191
religious Bolshevism, 104–105
Renaissance, 69, 136, 172, 177, 180
renovation, 103, 105, 148
Rhein, 151
Rheinische Jugendburg, 148. *See also* Waldeck Castle
Rhineland, 19, 148–149
Riehl, Heinrich, 38, 40

Ringpfadfinder, 127, 168
Ritzhaupt, Adam, 123, 125, 151
Romania, 182
Romanticism, 2, 9–11, 20, 32, 39–42, 71–72, 100–101, 130, 161
Rosenblüth, Felix, 72
Rosenstock-Huessy, Eugen, 169
Russia, 97–98, 161, 168, 181

Sachs, Hans, 32, 40, 138, 145
Sächsische Jungenschaft, 162, 164–165, 180–181
Sami, 181
Saxonia, 162
Scandinavia, 160–161, 167, 176, 181
Schilljugend, 178
Schirach, Baldur von, 181
Schlünz, Friedrich, 99–101
Schmalenbach, Herman, 128
Schmidt, Ina, 129
Schmitt, Carl, 16
Schoeps Hans-Joachim, 18
scholasticism, 7, 136–137
Scholem, Gerhard (Gershom), 73–74
Schönfelder, Otto, 77–79
Schopenhauer, Arthur, 96, 136
Schröder, Peter, 128
Schröer, Karl Julius, 139
Schultze-Naumburg, Paul, 34
Schurtz, Heinrich, 131
Schütz, Heinrich, 145
Seidelmann, Karl, 172
Sera-circle, 46, 78, 107, 187
Settlement Committee (*Ansiedlungskommission*), 35
Shakespeare, William, 139, 144
Siebenbürgen, 164
Silesia, 19, 162, 166
Snell, Victor, 106
socialism, 11, 14, 99, 103, 125, 181
Soest, 140
Sohnrey, Heinrich, 34
solstice feast, 35, 66–67, 72, 83, 103
Sombart, Werner, 16
*Sonderweg*, 10–11, 15
Soziale Arbeitsgemeinschaft Berlin-Ost, 91
Spain, 166–167
Sparta, 174
Spengler, Oswald, 13, 16, 101–103
Spranger, Eduard, 172
St Petersburg, 176
St Quentin, 147
Stahlhelm, 129, 146

Steglitz, 30–36, 40
Steglitzer e.V., 35–42. *See also* Wandervogel, Eingetragener Verein zu Steglitz
Steiner, Rudolf, 112, 139
*Stimmung*, 20, 57, 67, 100–101, 120. *See also* attunement
Strasbourg, 64–65
Strauss, Leo, 101
Stroh, Else, 110
Stuttgart, 70, 114
Südlegion, 158
Swabia, 142
Sweden, 166, 177, 180
Switzerland, 70

Tagore, Rabindranath, 104, 112
Taoism, 104
Tetzner, Lisa, 121, 151
theosophy, 105, 108
Thiede, Bruno, 31
Thuringia, 120–122, 140
Tillich, Paul, 93, 110, 119, 151, 159–160
time
   conception of, 15
   as flow, 65, 68
   fulfilled, 120
   historical, 8, 16, 65, 90, 101, 119, 183, 190–191
   mythical, 2, 173
   spherical, 150–151, 159, 192–193
   unilinear, 1–3, 7, 17, 102, 113, 123, 150, 190–191
Tönnies, Ferdinand, 128
*Totentanz*, 139–140, 144. *See also* dance macabre
Traub, Gottfried, 46–47
Treaty of Versailles, 129, 158, 161, 163, 167
Treitschke, Heinrich von, 28
Troeltsch, Ernst, 99
Trummler, Erich, 109, 111
Tübingen, 41
Tyrol, 165–166

Uppsala, 180
utopia, 159–160, 169, 177, 193

Vetter, Ferdinand, 40
Virgil, 158
vitalism, 2, 43, 78, 91, 108, 188–189, 192

Voelkel, Martin, 134–135
Voelkel, Martin, 163
*Volk*, 63, 70, 75, 114, 128, 141, 145–146, 163, 167, 178
*Volksgemeinschaft*, 20, 76, 105, 121, 138, 144, 162, 190
Vorwerk, Friedrich, 104–105

Wächter, Annemarie, 110
Wagner, Richard, 106
Waldeck Castle, 148–149
Wandervogel-Ausschuß für Schülerfahrten e. V., 9, 31
Wandervogel, Deutscher Bund für Jugendwanderungen, 39–42, 59
Wandervogel, Eingetragener Verein zu Steglitz, 35–42
Wandervogel e.V., Bund für deutsches Jugendwandern, 42, 46, 75, 101, 104, 126–127, 133, 140, 142
Wandervogel Hundertschaft, 162
Wandervogel-Jungenbund, 127, 164
Wandervogel-Mädchenbund, 127
Wandervogel, Wehrbund deutscher Jugend, 133
Wartburg Castle, 30, 121, 163
Weigel, Theodor, 147
Wendland, Heinz-Dietrich, 119–120, 126
Wiedmann, August, 5, 182
Wiemer, Rudolf, 124
Wilhelmshaven, 80–81
Winckelmann, Johann Joachim, 172
worldview, 2, 4, 15, 20, 37, 82, 92, 96, 98–99, 102–103, 105, 108, 112, 114, 135–137, 151, 164, 167, 175, 180, 187–188, 190
Wurche, Ernst, 90, 94–98, 112–113, 171
Wyneken, Gustav, 42–44, 46, 48–49, 63, 104, 136, 139, 148

youth castle, 148–149. *See also Jugendburg*
youth culture, 43, 148. *See also Jugendkultur*
Ypres, 75

Zarathustra, 94–97, 150
Zernack, Julia, 177
Zionism, 68–73
Zurich, 70
Zylmann, Peter, 77

www.ingramcontent.com/pod-product-compliance
Lightning Source LLC
Chambersburg PA
CBHW072152100526
44589CB00015B/2202